BRIDGES AND BORDERS

DIVERSITY IN AMERICA

Copyright © 1994, Time Inc.

TIME Magazine
Managing Editor: James R. Gaines
President: Lisa Valk Long
Publisher: John E. Haire
Consumer Marketing Director: Kenneth Godshall
TIME Education Program Director: Lisa Quiroz

BRIDGES AND BORDERS: Diversity in America
Editor: Kelly Knauer
Research Director: Leah Gordon
Photo Research: Kathy Nelson
Editorial Advisors: Sophronia Scott Gregory, Jack E. White
Project Director (Warner Books): Tricia DeFelice
Art Director: Giorgetta Bell McRee
Production Director: Brian Healy

For information on the TIME Education Program,
please call 1-800-882-0852.

Printed in the United States of America.
ISBN: 0-446-67131-2
LC: 94-60791

BRIDGES AND BORDERS

DIVERSITY IN AMERICA

READINGS FROM

TIME MAGAZINE

1923-1994

BY THE EDITORS OF TIME

Published for TIME by

Warner Books

A Time Warner Company

Contents

Foreword

THE IDEA OF PUBLISHING THIS ANTHOLOGY was suggested by the positive response from TIME Education Program teachers to the fall 1993 special issue on Diversity in America. The book is intended as a resource for teachers in a wide range of disciplines. It offers stories from TIME that span most of our century in a variety of forms: profiles of important figures, essays by such writers as Toni Morrison and Barbara Ehrenreich, news stories covering major historical events, feature stories on demographic trends like "the changing face of America."

Since the book is designed to be a collection of source materials for research, writing and teaching, it presents the stories as they were first published in the pages of TIME — even though some of the language and attitudes of the magazine's early days may make today's readers wince. The articles have not been changed to meet current notions of political correctness, but some of them have been edited slightly for space. Again because of space limitations, the book deliberately restricts its definition of diversity. Though TIME has devoted many stories to such issues as women's liberation and individual sexual identity, we have excluded those subjects in order to concentrate on issues of race, culture, and religion.

Likewise, since the book treats the specific span of American history covered by the publication of TIME, it offers only a single story on the great immigration movements of the 19th and early 20th centuries. This volume is not a comprehensive history of American immigration and diversity; it is an anthology that captures key moments in the drama of diversity in America just as they were first reported by TIME. ■

Journalism and the Multi-*Everything* Society

BY JACK E. WHITE

THIS COLLECTION of TIME Magazine articles on American diversity tells the astonishing story of the social upheaval that brought our nation face to face with its original sin. In 1923, when TIME was founded, the gap between America's democratic ideals and its shameful treatment of minorities was appallingly wide. Today, in large part because of the men and women who are chronicled in this book, our nation is fast becoming the most pluralistic, polyglot, heterogeneous, multiracial, multinational, multiethnic, multicultural, multireligious, multi-*everything* society that the world has ever seen. In the New America that will emerge only 60 years or so from now, everyone, from the descendants of European colonialists and African slaves to the most recent arrivals from Ecuador or Sri Lanka or Laos, will belong to a minority group for the simple reason that there will no longer be a majority group.

This extraordinary experiment has already transformed every aspect of our national life, from what we learn in school to the languages in which ballots are printed to the foods we eat and the music we listen to. As the articles in this book illustrate, it has also forever altered the way that journalists practice their profession, especially at TIME. The tumultuous events of the past seven decades have forced reporters to re-examine the comfortable assumptions that shaped the way they once wrote about an America that was never as simple as their stories suggested. The resulting revolution in journalism was no less radical than the social upheaval that inspired it. To coin a word (an old TIME tradition), it amounted to a journalistic re-*visioning* of America: a new way of looking at our complicated and fractious country and explaining it to itself.

One measure of how far we have come toward a new America is the striking evolution of our national mythology of diversity. As recently as the 1960s, social scientists, politicians and journalists usually described the U.S. as a "melting pot" in which immigrants from every corner of the globe were transmuted into "Americans" by a mysterious alchemical process that began at Ellis Island. Never mind that the process of becoming an "American" was much more complicated than the melting pot image suggested— or that many people who were not white were never melted. That was not nearly so important as the fact that most Americans believed in the melting pot myth and acted on it. They might be Irish-American or Italian-American or any other kind of hyphenated American, but they tended to accentuate the word that followed the hyphen: "American." By so doing, they collectively stressed the intangible but no less real set of values that seemed both to unite Americans and set them apart from people everywhere else.

Today the emphasis is on the word in front of the hyphen. The melting pot image has become hopelessly outdated—except to say that the melting pot is boiling over. It has been replaced by a new set of images that evoke our differences: a mosaic, or a salad, or a quilt composed of people of disparate cultural and racial backgrounds, each vying to preserve its own unique identity and grab its fair share of the pie—and more, if it can get it. Once again, the new clichés oversimplify reality. As social critic Albert Murray points out, Americans, no matter where their ancestors hail from, resemble each other far more than they do anyone else. But that is less important than the fact that a growing number of Americans seem to accept the new myths as truth and act on them. The tenuous national consensus has been strained as never before.

The U.S. today is unquestionably a more open and equitable society than it was seven decades ago, but it is also considerably more divided. It is likely to become even more so during the 21st century. By the year 2056, as TIME noted in a 1990 cover story that is included in this anthology, Americans who trace their roots back to Europe will for the first time constitute less than half of our population. "As the numbers of minorities increase," observed TIME's William A. Henry III, "their demands for a share of the national bounty are bound to intensify, while whites are certain to feel ever more embattled." For journalists, politicians, social scientists and average citizens, answering the question, Who is an American, will never again be as simple as it was in the 1920s, when race relations seemed, quite literally, to be all black and white.

That is the context in which these articles should be read, keeping in mind that the journalists who created them were products of their time. Until the late 1960s TIME, like most major publications, was written and edited by a staff composed almost exclusively of white males largely drawn from the privileged ranks of Ivy League universities (white women were, for the most part, confined to subordinate editorial roles). Moreover, unlike the majority of publications, which made a fetish of so-called objectivity, TIME in its early days proudly reflected the point of view of its cofounder, Henry Luce. The Yale–educated son of a

Presbyterian missionary, Luce shared the world view of the white Anglo-Saxon Protestant power structure that dominated the country's affairs. He was a racial paternalist who believed passionately in fair treatment for minority groups but did not see them as equals.

Thus, TIME, from its early days, was a fierce foe of bigotry and a strong supporter of civil rights. But, paradoxically, even when the magazine wrote sympathetically about blacks, Indians and other minorities, it often lapsed into stereotypes and offensive name calling. For example, a 1927 article about school segregation in Gary, Indiana, described 24 Negro students as "dusky newcomers." Nearly a decade later TIME reported, without any hint that its readers might find the term insulting, that 32 "blackamoor delegates and alternates" had attended the 1936 Democratic convention. And when the magazine applauded the feats of sprinter Jesse Owens, who won four gold medals at the 1936 Olympics in Berlin, it could not resist noting that the champion had marched to the victory stand to have "a laurel wreath stuck on his kinky head." The use of racial epithets reached a peculiar nadir in a 1938 story decrying a wave of racially motivated lynchings in the South. It referred to a lucky man who had narrowly escaped from a mob as "Negro Jones" so forcefully you would have thought "Negro" was his first name! (It actually was Lee.)

Other minorities got equally short shrift in the pages of TIME. Like blacks, Jews were labeled: actress Sarah Bernhardt was "Jewess Bernhardt." Stories about American Indians were liberally salted with descriptions of "braves and squaws" and "war-painted savages." Hispanic Americans and Asian Americans were all but ignored by TIME, unless they were unfortunate enough to be attacked by a racist mob. Thus the magazine devoted space to the notorious "Zoot Suit War" of 1943 in which roving bands of servicemen randomly assaulted scores of Mexican-American youths in the streets of Los Angeles. But the magazine never mentioned the founding in 1929 of the League of United Latin American Citizens, a civil rights organization that many Hispanics consider their equivalent of the National Association for the Advancement of Colored People.

Yet all those years TIME continued to recognize and support the battle against bigotry. It reported approvingly on the civil rights movement and named Martin Luther King Jr. its Man of the Year for 1963. The mismatch between the content of its coverage and its characterizations of minorities began to change during the 1960s as the civil rights and anti-Vietnam War movements picked up steam and spawned a host of similar campaigns aimed at recognition by other ethnic groups and women. The turning point was the racial rioting that swept across the nation during the middle of the decade. Journalists found themselves unable to explain why these outbursts of black rage were occurring just as the nation was making progress toward its long-sought goal of racial justice. Indeed, the Kerner Commission, a committee appointed by President Lyndon Johnson to explore the causes of the violence, blamed the frustrations that underlay the disturbances in part on the news media's insensitivity and ignorance about the plight of minorities. "[The news media] have not communicated to the majority of their audience—which is white—a sense of the degradation, misery and hopelessness of living in the ghetto," the commission declared. "If the media are to report with understanding, wisdom and sympathy on the problems of the cities and the problems of the black man—for the two are increasingly intertwined—they must employ, promote and listen to Negro journalists." It soon became clear that the same concerns applied to other minorities.

Along with the other media, TIME responded, adding growing numbers of African-American, Hispanic-American and Asian-American journalists to its staff. Though their numbers are still small, these minority writers, reporters, researchers and editors have had an enormous impact on the way TIME does its work. The past 20 years have seen a dramatic expansion in the amount of space the magazine devotes to the coverage of minorities, along with a new sophistication and depth. Among the articles in this anthology are TIME cover stories on the astonishing success of Asian Americans, the dazzling explosion of Hispanic-American culture, the ambivalent plight of today's brightest African-American students. There are also many shorter pieces on complicated issues such as bilingual education, immigration policy and political correctness, which all arise from the more fundamental question of how our nation can accommodate such a wide variety of people fairly without destroying the intangible commodity that makes us all Americans.

These issues are likely to grow even more complex with the dawn of a new century, forcing journalists once again to reinvent, to re-*vision*, their craft. At TIME, we look forward to the challenge.

JACK E. WHITE *is a Senior Correspondent for* TIME, *based in the New York Bureau. He has written, reported and edited for* TIME *since 1972 in a variety of positions, including Editor of the Nation section.* ■

Prelude: The Great Migration

THE MOST SALIENT fact about American history is this: the ancestors of everyone who lives in the U.S. originally came from somewhere else. That includes even the Inuits and other Native Americans, whose forebears first crossed from Siberia to Alaska on a land bridge that now lies beneath the icy Bering Sea. From its colonial beginnings, the history of America has largely been the story of how immigrants from the Old World conquered the New. As the historian Carl Wittke noted, eight nationalities were represented on Columbus' first voyage to a continent that eventually received its name from a German mapmaker (Martin Walseemüller) working in a French college, who honored an Italian explorer (Amerigo Vespucci) sailing under the flag of Portugal.

The tide of humanity that has washed over the American continent during the last three or four decades of the 20th century has had profound consequences, to be sure. But in relative terms, it is no match for the waves that came ashore during the 19th. Between Napoleon's defeat at Waterloo in 1815 and the assassination of Austrian Archduke Franz Ferdinand at Sarajevo in 1914, more than 30 million Europeans left their homelands—some involuntarily—to settle in the U.S. It was by far the greatest mass movement in human history. The influx continues, in ever greater variety. For people in search of better lives, America remains the ultimate lure.

America's immigration story actually starts in the darkness of prehistory. Archaeologists estimate that Paleo-Indians began their great trek from Asia around 30,000 B.C., in pursuit of shaggy, straighthorned bison (now extinct) and other edible fauna. They gradually moved south and east from Alaska as the glaciers of the Ice Age melted. By 19,000 B.C., the Indians—a short, hardy people who suffered from arthritis and poor teeth, among other infirmities—had built primitive homes in cliffs along Cross Creek, a few miles from present-day Pittsburgh, Pennsylvania. One tribal nation, the Cahokia federation, had the sophisticated skills to build a thriving trade center of 40,000 people, across the river from what is now St. Louis, Missouri, between A.D. 1000 and 1250.

When the first Europeans arrived, the Indian population of North America north of Mexico was about 1 million. According to Ronald Takaki's *A Different Mirror: A History of Multicultural America*, some Indian sages had forecast the coming of white-skinned aliens. On his deathbed, a chief of New England's Wampanoag tribe said that strange white people would come to crowd out the Indians. As a sign, a great white whale would rise out of the witch pond. The night he died, the whale rose, just as he had predicted. Similar prophecies can be found in the lore of Virginia's Powhatans and the Ojibwa of Minnesota.

Until recently, American history texts were resolutely Anglocentric, beginning the immigration story with the first successful English settlements—at Jamestown, Virginia, in 1607 and Plymouth Rock, Massachusetts, in 1620. The British, in fact, were latecomers. In 1565 a convicted Spanish smuggler named Pedro Menéndez de Avilés, leading a ragtag army of perhaps 1,500 that included blacksmiths and brewers as well as foot soldiers, built the first permanent European settlement on American soil at St. Augustine, Florida. (The ruins of Menéndez's first fort were discovered only last summer.) Thirty-three years later, Juan de Oñate established a colonial capital at San Gabriel in what is now New Mexico.

The Spanish, typically more interested in the pursuit of gold than in settlement, easily subjugated the Indians, enslaving those who did not die of imported diseases like smallpox. The 500,000 or so Indian inhabitants of Eastern North America at the time of the first English settlements were not so easily conquered. These resilient and warlike nations—principally the Algonquin and Iroquois in the north, the Muskoghean and Choctaw in the south—were happy to trade with the white man and adopt his weapons, but not his Christian faith or his mores. And they would fight to the death to defend their lands from encroachment.

Many of the first immigrants from the British Isles were unwilling voyagers. Long before Australia became the fatal shore for millions of convicts, North America was London's principal penal colony. Others came to the New World as indentured servants, bound into service to pay the cost of their passage for specified terms—usually three to seven years—before being set free. During the 17th century, for example, 75% of Virginia's colonists arrived as servants, some of whom had been kidnapped by unscrupulous "recruiters."

And then there were the slaves. In 1619 the Virginia settler John Rolfe made a diary note of a dark moment in American history. "About the last of August," he wrote, "came in a dutch man of warre that sold us twenty Negars." In Virginia alone, the slave population grew from about 2,000 in 1670 to 150,000 on the eve of the American Revolution. Most of the slaves sailed from West Africa, chained together in dank, fetid holds for transatlantic journeys that often lasted three months or more. The conditions were unspeakable, the mortality rate horrifying: on some ships more than half the slaves died during the passage.

Initially, blacks worked alongside whites in the tobacco fields of Virginia and the Carolinas, but by 1650 field hands were invariably men and women of color. One reason: because of what science now knows is the sickle-cell trait,

blacks were often less susceptible than whites to the depredations of malaria. More important, a terrible distinction had been made, first informally but then in legislation: white servants were considered persons despite their temporary state of servitude; blacks were mere property that could be bought and sold.

IN SHARP CONTRAST to Mother England, the 13 American colonies were heterogeneous in character. By the mid-18th century, Welsh and Germans had settled in Pennsylvania and the Carolinas, which also had a substantial population of Scotch-Irish. South Carolina and the major towns of New England were home to thousands of French Huguenots. There were Swedes and Finns in Delaware, Sephardic Jews from Holland and Portugal in Rhode Island and Dutch in New York. Visiting New Amsterdam in 1643, the French Jesuit missionary Isaac Jogues was amazed to discover that in this town of 8,000 people, 18 languages were spoken. In his famous *Letters from an American Farmer*, J. Hector St. John Crévecoeur wrote in 1782, "Here individuals of all nations are melted into a new race of men, whose labors and posterity will one day cause great changes in the world."

But did these myriad groups really melt? A unique characteristic of the U.S. immigration experience, historian Daniel Boorstin has noted, is the way in which so many ethnic communities were able to preserve their separate identities. Instead of "*E pluribus unum*" (From many, one), Boorstin suggests, the American motto should have been "*E pluribus plura*." New York offers an early case history. The Dutch lost political control of the Hudson River within 40 years of New Amsterdam's founding in 1624, but their cultural influence proved longer lasting. As late as 1890, some inhabitants of villages near Albany still spoke a form of Dutch at home.

Early immigrants found their way to the New World for a variety of reasons. The Huguenots and German

Mennonites were escaping religious persecution. The Irish had been deprived of their farmlands. As Crévecoeur observed, the primary motive for most newcomers was economic: "*Ubi panis ibi patria* [Where there is bread there is country] is a motto of all emigrants." A primitive form of advertising helped the cause. William Penn wrote pamphlets extolling the attractions of what was called "Quackerthal" in German, which were circulated widely in the Netherlands and the Rhineland. "Newlanders appeared in Old World villages as living specimens of New World prosperity, dressed in flashy clothes, wearing heavy watches, their pockets jingling with coins."

Brochures promoting the New World's glories understandably did not emphasize the difficulty of getting there. An 18th century journey from, say, Amsterdam to Philadelphia or Boston could last anywhere from five weeks to six months. The tiny ships, whose height between decks seldom exceeded 5 ft., braved pirates as well as North Atlantic storms. Conditions below decks were hardly better than on slave ships. Fatal outbreaks of scurvy, dysentery and smallpox were common. And yet the tide of emigration could not be halted. Between 1700 and 1776, 450,000 Europeans crossed the ocean to find a new life.

Most 18th century immigrants were peasant farmers—the poor, huddled masses of Emma Lazarus' famous poem. Some, though, elevated the quality of life in the colonies. The Huguenots and their descendants—Paul Revere among them—maintained a tradition of craftsmanship and provided the colonies with many of their physicians. Royalist political refugees from the French Revolution turned up as dancing masters in the salons of Philadelphia.

In the early years of the new American republic, however, immigration was modest. Apart from slaves, only about 4,000 foreigners entered the U.S. annually between 1800 and 1810. One reason for the laggard pace was Britain's Passenger

Act of 1803, which raised the cost of transatlantic tickets and served to discourage a brain drain of talented workers who might carry with them England's industrial secrets.

The U.S. government did not begin to record immigration data until 1820. A decade later, the population was around 13 million, of whom only 500,000 were foreign-born. But by then the century's great tide of immigration had begun, primarily from Ireland, Germany and Scandinavia. Profoundly influencing this exodus were the so-called America letters—glowing accounts of life in the New World by recent voyagers that became as popular in Europe as best-selling novels. In Ole Rynning's *America Book* (1838), the U.S. is described as a classless society with high wages, low prices, good land and a nonrepressive government.

Ads by shipping firms and land-speculation companies also beckoned peasants from the Old World to the New. Midwestern states, beginning with Michigan in 1848, set up their own immigration agencies and offered special inducements to newcomers, like voting rights after only six months' residency. In the Dakotas a poetasting huckster promised women that the territories were prime land for husband hunting: "There is no goose so gray, but, soon or late,/Will find some honest gander for a mate."

In one key respect, emigrating to America was different from moving from one country to another in Europe. The newcomers would face hostility and prejudice from native-born Americans. But in the eyes of the law, once they became citizens they were fully equal to those whose ancestors had sailed aboard the *Mayflower*. In the words of Marcus Hansen, the pioneering historian of U.S. immigration, "The immigrant was to enjoy no special privileges to encourage his coming; he was also to suffer no special restrictions." With that goal in mind, Congress in 1818 rejected requests from Irish societies in Eastern cities to set aside certain frontier lands for colonies of indigent Hibernians. America was not to become "a patchwork nation of foreign settlements."

RELATIVELY FEW EMIGRANTS found the paradise promised by the ads and the letters home. The early arrivals were, by and large, poor, ill-schooled and young (two-thirds were between 15 and 39 years old). In Europe's principal ports of exodus—Liverpool and Cork, Bremen and Rotterdam—they were beset by thieves and hucksters, cheated by ship's captains (there was no set fee for tickets to America) and, until the age of steam, often even ignorant of where they would eventually land. If they survived the journey—and as many as one-third died aboard ship or within a year of landing in the New World—fresh hazards awaited them in America. Among them were streetwise recent immigrants who would rob them of their few remaining shillings or kronen.

No European nation lost proportionately more of its sons and daughters to the U.S. than Ireland: in all, some 4,250,000 from 1820 to 1920. Native–born Americans sniffed at these Gaels—made desperate by the potato famine that devastated their homeland in the 1840s—as filthy, bad-tempered and given to drink. The haunting, taunting employment sign No Irish Need Apply became a bitter American cliché. And yet

Irish lasses made the clothmaking factories of New England hum. Irish lads built the Erie Canal, paved the highways and laid tracks for the railroads. In the South the Irish were sometimes considered more expendable than slaves and were hired, at pitifully low wages, for the dirtiest and most dangerous jobs, like clearing snake-infested swamps.

But the Irish had a gift for mutual self-help and taking care of their own. Out of this instinct, manifest in America's dozens of "little Dublins," emerged institutions, like New York City's notorious Tammany Hall, that would transform the quality and character of urban politics in America. Some 210,000 Irish fought during the Civil War, 170,000 of them on the Union side.

As Irish migration began to recede, a second great wave—of Germans (or perhaps more properly, German speakers)—began. As Oscar Handlin pointed out in his classic study *The Uprooted*, most 19th century European immigrants thought of themselves not as ex-citizens of a national state (which, in the case of Poland, for instance, did not even exist) but as speakers of a common tongue, or residents of a particular village or province. The Germans were lured by the vision of unlimited economic opportunity and greater freedom than Central Europe offered in the post-Napoleonic era.

If the Irish brought a new spirit to American politics, the Germans brought culture in varied forms, from singing groups to vineyards to poetry societies. More pioneering than the Irish, they helped develop America's hinterland, from Ohio to Texas. (In 1900, 1 out of 3 Texans was German in origin.) The town of Hermann, Missouri, still known for its wines, was typical: when laid out in 1837, streets were named for Schiller, Gutenberg, and Mozart.

"The Scandinavian immigrant to the United States," wrote historian Wittke, "has been the Viking of the Western prairie country." In the mid-19th century, American newspapers carried accounts of immigrant Swedes disembarking en masse from cargo ships and marching—often with their country's flag carried aloft—to railway depots where trains would take them upriver to Buffalo, along the Erie Canal and thence to the prairie country of the upper Mississippi valley. Today about 400 place names in Minnesota are of Scandinavian origin.

AFTER 1880, IMMIGRATION CHANGED once again. Most of the newcomers were from Eastern and Southern Europe: Russian Jews, Poles, Italians and Greeks. They too left the Old World to escape poverty and, in the case of the Jews, persecution. Like their predecessors, they were mostly peasants, but they faced a different and unhappy prospect. The great era of frontier settlement was coming to an end. After being processed at Ellis Island in Upper New York Bay and other immigration centers, millions of these rural folk found themselves confined to the mean streets of urban ghettos like Manhattan's festering Lower East Side, working at menial jobs and crammed into narrow railroad flats that lacked both heat and privacy.

The nativist sentiment that foreigners are somehow inferior to the American-born may be the nation's oldest and most persistent bias. (Curiously, it was not until 1850 that the U.S. Census took note of where Americans were born.) Apart from slaves, Asians (principally the Chinese) suffered most from this prejudice. Seeking fortune and escape from the turmoil of the Opium Wars, Chinese first began arriving in California during the 1840s. Initially, they were welcomed. During the 1860s, 24,000 Chinese were working in the state's gold fields, many of them as prospectors. As the ore gave out, former miners were hired to build the Central Pacific Railroad; others dug the irrigation canals that poured fertility—and prosperity—into the Salinas and San Joaquin valleys.

The Chinese were rewarded for their labor with low wages, typically a third less than what white workers could earn. Even so, hostility forced them from many jobs as times got tough. Excluded from the mines and farms, many set up shop as laundrymen, a trade that did not exist in their homeland. They were ineligible for citizenship under a 1790 federal law that limited that privilege to whites. In 1882 Chinese workers were barred from entering the U.S. by an act of Congress that was extended indefinitely in 1902 and was not rescinded until 1943.

After the Chinese were excluded, Japanese became the principal concern of nativists who feared America's contamination by a "Yellow Peril." The shameful nadir of this bias followed the attack on Pearl Harbor in December 1941. Under pressure from security-conscious Army officials, the Federal Government exiled more than 100,000 Japanese and Japanese Americans from their homes on the West Coast to internment camps in Arizona, Arkansas, California, Colorado, Idaho, Utah and Wyoming. Despite this humiliation, 30,000 Japanese Americans served in uniform, and the all-Nisei 442nd Regimental Combat Team and the 100th Battalion became the most decorated units in U.S. military history.

American immigration is like a book with no ending. Despite a resurgence of nativism, newcomers continue to seek entry, with the same sense of hope that fired their 19th century predecessors. Illegal Irish seek jobs, escaping an 18% unemployment rate in their homeland. Jews from the former Soviet Union want relief from an ugly surge of anti-Semitism at home. Perhaps 80% of the newcomers in recent years have come from Asia and Latin America, adding to the country's unparalleled cultural and racial diversity. (New York City alone has more than 170 distinct ethnic communities.) "Of every hue and caste am I," wrote Walt Whitman in *Song of Myself*. True enough when he composed that line in 1881. Truer still today. ∎

After the Great Migration: Sometimes the Door Slammed Shut

FOR MOST OF ITS HISTORY, the U.S. has been wide open to immigrants—those from Europe, that is. Countless 19th century voyagers from the Old World pursued the uniquely egalitarian shelter of a New World so different from Europe's rigidly structured nation-states. Barriers to immigration did not square with the American ideal of opportunity for all.

Not that each newcomer was welcomed by a fledgling society entirely free from fear and bias. In 1798 Congress raised the residency requirement for citizenship from 5 to 14 years, largely to exclude political refugees from Europe who might foment revolution. Later some states imposed taxes on alien ship passengers they feared might become public charges.

Such nativist sentiments only grew after the Civil War. The once vast frontier seemed less vast, and economic recessions raised fears that cheap foreign laborers might take American jobs. There was also the openly racist argument that some newcomers, Asians especially, could not be "assimilated." In 1882 Congress passed the Chinese Exclusion Act, imposing a head tax and excluding whole categories of people—convicts and the mentally ill, for example. For the first time there were real limits on European immigration. Twelve years later, a group calling itself the Immigration Restriction League adopted the pseudo science of eugenics as the basis for its contention that breeding from "inferior stock" would fatally weaken America.

After World War I, there were fears that millions of displaced Europeans, newly influenced by Bolshevism, would infect America with alien ideology. As a result, a series of racism-tinted national-origins laws passed during the 1920s established an annual immigration quota of 150,000 that favored established groups like the Germans and Irish. Some nationalities, notably the Japanese, were excluded entirely. The national-origins system was preserved in the 1952 McCarran-Walter Act, though that notorious law did establish tiny quotas—100 or so a year—for such previously barred groups as Indians and Filipinos.

Underlying these laws was the belief that preserving America's ethnic mix as it existed in 1920 was politically and culturally desirable. After World War II, the quotas were relaxed only to allow in politically favored groups, such as the 38,000 Hungarians who fled the 1956 Soviet crackdown. Inspired by Lyndon Johnson's Civil Rights Act, Congress in 1965 at last ended the national-origins system and opened America's doors to the Third World.

The 1980 Refugee Act radically expanded the definition of those eligible for political asylum. But because it has been poorly enforced and easily abused, it helped bring on today's growing demand for new limits on aliens. Still, for the first time in its history, the U.S. has an immigration policy that, for better or worse, is truly democratic. ∎

The United States was still absorbing newcomers from the last great wave of European immigration, and many Americans regarded Jews and Catholics with suspicion. The Ku Klux Klan flourished, proclaiming white supremacy and opposing such novelties as the celebration of Columbus Day. The 1924 immigration law excluded Japanese and favored northern and western over southern and eastern Europeans. Jim Crow laws and the threat of lynching kept the South firmly segregated. In 1925 racial demonstrators filled the streets of Washington, as Klan members paraded in a show of strength.

THE 1920s

Ellis Island Revisited

57 years later, a German immigrant remembers her journey to America

SOPHIE WOLF, 83, is a small, solid woman with curly white hair. She speaks softly but forcefully in faintly accented English. One day not long ago Sophie visited Ellis Island. The cold weather reminded her of the raw foggy day 57 years ago when she saw Ellis for the first time.

She was Sophie Steurer then, 25 years old, one of eleven children born to a German hatter and his wife. They had lived comfortably in Ebingen, about 40 miles south of Stuttgart. But the inflation and unemployment that ravaged Germany in the 1920s changed all that. By 1923 a loaf of bread cost up to 3 million marks. Sophie could find work only half a day a week—sewing men's shirts. Her friends sought jobs in The Netherlands and Spain. "But for me," Sophie recalls, "America was the thing." She was fortunate in having a sponsor: an uncle who ran a bakery in Madison, Ind. He paid for her steerage-class ticket and sent $25, the amount needed to prove to the U.S. that she would not become a public charge.

With only one suitcase, filled with clothing and favorite photographs, she set sail from Bremen on the steamship *München*. "I had seen the Rhine, but this was the biggest puddle of water." The ship reached New York on Dec. 11, 1923. The spectacle of the Statue of Liberty and the New York skyline lavishly lit up at night seemed to be a sign of America's astounding wealth. "At home, lights were out after 9," says Sophie. Her overwhelming sensation was fear: "If you didn't pass the tests, they would send you back."

For a place once so feared, Ellis Island has a surprisingly welcoming air today, though most of its 35 buildings have badly deteriorated from decades of neglect and vandalism. It would take an estimated $150 million to save them all. "It sure looked better then," admits Sophie. The low-slung main building of warm red brick with limestone trim has large paned windows to let in air and light. Trees and lawns sweep to the gently lapping waters of the harbor. But at the time, immigrants like Sophie did not notice such things. They simply felt lost, especially in the great registry hall, where 5,000 immigrants a day were processed. A constant babble of incomprehensible tongues rose like flocks of starlings to the ceiling. Sophie did not speak English, but managed to comply with directions: "I just followed the pointing."

"It was so impersonal," she says. "Bring the cattle in and ship them out." There was a rapid legal examination. In two minutes, inspectors aided by interpreters fired 29 questions

A family of Italian immigrants at Ellis Island, circa 1905

at a newcomer. Among them: "Are you an anarchist?" And the trick question: "Do you have a job?" A few proud would-be citizens could truthfully answer "Yes." But a yes answer raised suspicion that the newcomer was a strikebreaker—or had been conned into a slave-labor agreement.

The medical examination began before immigrants were even aware of it. Doctors stationed in the hall simply observed the newcomers as they walked by. In six seconds, physicians checked off 15 diseases. They placed chalk marks on the lapels of those who needed closer scrutiny: H for heart, L for limp, X for mental defect. With still evident embarrassment, Sophie recalls a distressing moment when a nurse "put her hand under my skirt. She was checking for I don't know what, but she did it to everyone." Then a doctor dipped a buttonhook into an antiseptic solution and used it to flip back the eyelid. The reason: to check for trachoma, a blinding disease that would leave the immigrant an unwanted public charge. Trachoma was the most common medical reason for sending immigrants back to their native countries. (In fact, out of 12 million or so people who came to Ellis, most during the peak years of 1900-24, only 250,000 were turned away.)

Sophie may have been the unwitting object of another American worry: that young single women would become prostitutes. So great was that concern that if a woman claimed she was engaged, immigration officials actually hunted up her fiance and saw to it that they were married before relinquishing control over the newcomer. Authorities wired Sophie's uncle in Madison before letting her visit relatives in New York. The first days in Manhattan were overwhelming. Sophie had never seen subways, trolley cars, coal stoves, pineapples and mobs of people "so friendly you did not have to be afraid to talk even if you didn't speak English. In Europe we'd have made fun if you couldn't speak right. I thought, that's America." She looked askance at only one thing: "What got you as a European was the filth." She remembers a shiny red apple she wanted to buy. It cost only a penny. But she didn't want to break her uncle's $25.

On her way west, during a stopover in Cincinnati, she used pin money from relatives to buy her first machine-made piece of clothing, a short-sleeved dress in French blue. After three years, selling the bread, macaroons and cake in her uncle's bakery in Indiana, she saved enough for a trip east to visit her aunts. One night, dancing to the music of a German band in Manhattan's Yorkville section, she met Fritz Wolf, a baker from Baden who had also graduated from Ellis in 1923. They married, settled in Queens and had two sons, who now live in Los Angeles. One is in the refrigeration and air-conditioning business. The other served in the U.S. Army for 20 years. Sophie became a U.S. citizen in 1937. She has since voted in every election, federal, state and local.

She is proud of her sons and troubled about the new wave of Cuban, Mexican and Vietnamese immigrants. "We should not let anyone in," she says firmly. "When we came, the rules were you could not be a burden to the state. There were no schools where you could learn the language." Then she sighs, and adds: "But you've got to give people a chance. You can't send them back." As for herself, at 83, she is busy organizing outings for senior citizens and looking forward. Says Sophie: "You give up and you're dead, and I am not yet." ∎

National Origins

"Science" and race quotas: The mathematics of exclusion

A SURGEON, about to make a transfusion, scientifically matches a donor's blood to his patient's to such purpose that no shock results. In like manner Congress has ordained that Immigration shall be scientifically matched to the U. S. racial bloodstream.

It is far simpler, however, to match up the blood of individuals than the many mixed bloods of a populous nation. In attempting to execute the orders of Congress, a large corps of census experts, statisticians and genealogists have wrestled for four years with the problem of tracing back for 140 years the ancestry of 120,000 people. The chief results so far have been expert disagreements and rancorous race disputes.

QUOTAS. In 1921 the quota system was first applied to restrict European immigration into the U. S. A slot method of admission was set up, its size crudely fixed at 3% of the number of foreign-born U. S. residents enumerated in the Census of 1910. This slot seemed still too large. In 1924 it was closed to 2% of the foreign-born population of the 1890 census.

NATIONAL ORIGINS. This was not a scientific way to filter aliens into the U. S. if the original native stock of the country was to be preserved. The 1924 law therefore carried a provision for the establishment of quotas based on National Origins.

Scientists were to determine the racial composition of the present day U. S., starting from the first U. S. census (1790, pop. 3,900,000), analyzing the growth of population to date with reference to national ancestries and thus, in effect, fixing the proportion each foreign country contributed to U. S. "native stock" and the development of that stock since. To the U. S. were then to be admitted 150,000 immigrants annually, in direct proportion to the contributions their native countries have made to the whole U. S. population, past and present, Negroes excluded. This new policy was to go into effect by Presidential proclamation July 1, 1927.

POSTPONEMENT. The British burned most early U. S. census details in the sack of Washington in 1814. Native stock, clear in the early days, was blurred by intermarriage with alien newcomers. Historical data is scant or unreliable. Racial names have become meaningless through social changes. So the 20th Century scientists bogged down in confusion and Congress in 1927, postponed the effective date of National Origins to July 1, 1928; later to July 1, 1929, where it now remains.

HOOVER. Herbert Hoover, as Secretary of Commerce, with the Secretaries of State and Labor, constituted a special commission to report the scientists' findings. This report said: "Although this is the best information we have been able to secure, we wish to...state that in our opinion the statistical and historical information available raises grave doubts as to the whole value of these computations."

As a Presidential candidate Herbert Hoover again said: "The basis now in effect [2% quota] carries out the essential principle of the law and I favor repeal of that part of the law calling for a new [National Origins] basis of quotas."

CHANGES INVOLVED. Last week President Coolidge sent to Congress the final "scientific" figures, showing what would happen under National Origins. No great numerical difference would mark the change. At present the 2% quota system admits about 164,000 immigrants per year. Under National Origins about 153,000 aliens—150,000 as set in the law, plus the 100 minimum allowance to all countries— would come in. There would, however, be a marked change in the composition of U. S. immigration.

For example, the 2% quota system now admits 51,227 Germans each year. Just prior to the census of 1890, there was a heavy tide of German immigration, far above Germany's average in earlier and subsequent periods. Under National Origins, the German quota would be cut down to 25,957.

On the other hand, the majority of U. S. people are of British ancestry. British immigration had dwindled when the 1890 census was taken. The British quota on that basis allows only 34,007 newcomers. Under the National Origins system Great Britain's quota would be 65,721.

National Origins would reduce Irish immigration from 28,500 to 17,500; Norwegian, from 6,400 to 2,300; Swedish, from 9,500 to 3,300. It would increase Italian immigration from 3,800 to 5,800, Dutch from 1,600 to 3,153, Spanish from 131 to 252. ■

Imperial Diet

Excluded and angry, the Japanese promise revenge

BOTH HOUSES met for the first time since the formation of the Kato Government. Premier Takaaki Kato, in an address, expressed regret at the enactment of the U.S. Immigration Bill, promised that he would seek a new solution.

Much interest was evinced at the able speech made by Foreign Minister Baron Shidehara (onetime Ambassador to Washington). After declaring that his foreign policy would be to promote and to protect Japanese interests "with due respect to those of other nations," and after affirming Japan's duty to be the maintenance of peace in the Far East and on the Pacific, he dwelt upon three points: exclusion, relations with Russia, relations with China. Excerpts:

U.S. EXCLUSION. "The genesis of the Immigration Act lies in the marked increase of immmigration, especially from Southern and Eastern Europe.

"It is generally believed it would be a matter of practical difficulty to merge these foreign elements in a homogeneous country of original Americans…

"The new Act intended rigorous restrictions of immigration in general. There was no reason for embodying in this Act a provision designed specifically to exclude Japanese immigrants. Three points engage our attention:

"First, exclusionists say the Japanese are unassimilable with American life, and the introduction of such alien elements would prove a source of danger to the United States. This formed the essential plea for the exclusion of the Japanese. It was not on account of inferiority of the Japanese race that the exclusion clause was adopted.

"Secondly, it has always been consistently maintained by the United States that control of immigration is one of the essential attributes of the inherent sovereign rights of each nation. The importance placed on this point by the United States is due to special conditions in that country….

"Thirdly, it should be appreciated that the President and the Secretary of State of the United States have, from the outset, shown opposition to the exclusion clause. Public opinion in the United States, reflected in a great section of the American press, appears sympathetically disposed toward Japan's position.

"Our protest against the exclusion clause is based on the conviction that discriminatory treatment, as laid down in that clause, is contrary to the dictates of justice and fairness, and is imposed upon us in disregard of the ordinary rules of international comity. Legislation is now an accomplished fact in the United States, but we can by no means concede the question closed.

"Until just contentions shall have been given satisfaction, we shall maintain our protest and shall use our best possible endeavors to seek an amicable adjustment of the question and ensure forever the traditional friendship between the two nations."

GENERAL. "We shall not confine our attention to questions relating to the United States, Russia and China. Our efforts will be directed to maintain and to strengthen friendly relations with all nations having important territorial, economic interests in the Far East and on the whole Pacific, and generally to do our whole part in securing to the world the blessings of peace and stability."

At the conclusion of the speeches, the House of Peers passed a resolution expressing its approval of the Government's policy in regard to the U.S. Immigration Act.

The House of Representatives condemned the offending law by declaring that it blotted 70 years of friendship between the two countries, passed the following resolutions:

Resolved, that the House of Representatives expresses profound sentiment opposed to this discriminatory enactment; and be it further

Resolved, that the House requests the Imperial Government promptly to take all proper measures which the situation requires.

PROTEST. As a protest against the U.S. Immigration Act, the Japanese people staged a national demonstration.

In Tokyo, masses assembled to give ear to anti-American ardor. One of the largest meetings was held at the sacred Meiji shrine (religious symbol of modern Japan erected in memory of the present era which began in 1867, when the terrible Shoguns who had for years been *de facto* sovereigns of Japan were ousted). "Hate" societies plastered the city with placards which read:

"Japanese must never forget July 1, when America inflicted an intolerable insult on Japan. Always remember that date. Prepare for such steps as are demanded by the Honor of the Fatherland when the occasion comes. Every Japanese must remember the following rules:

"1) Alter your mode of living so as to impress the date lastingly upon your mind.

"2) Hate everything American, but remain kind to American individuals.

"3) Deny yourself all luxury.

"4) Never forget national Honor for private gain.

"5) Never enter a church supported or guided by Americans or United States missionaries."

NATIONAL INSULT. The day was that upon which the U.S. Immigration Act went into force. In the U.S. Embassy Compound in Tokyo, the Stars and Stripes flew proudly from a tall mast. A Japanese, watched by an unsuspecting Tokyo "bobbie," hauled the flag down, cut it from the halyards with a razor, crumpled it up, fled. The "bobbie" suddenly came to, realized the gravity of the man's action, made off after him—but in vain; his quarry escaped him.

Jefferson Caffery, U.S. Charge d'Affaires, called upon Foreign Minister Baron Shidehara (onetime Ambassador to the U.S.) and asked him to make immediate investigation. Twice did the Foreign Minister call upon Mr. Caffery in order to express his concern over the incident and to offer the "most sincere regrets" of his Government. "Surely," said he, "no one in the U.S. would believe the Japanese people capable of sympathizing with an outrage of this kind." He also said that the police would do their utmost to apprehend the culprit—which they later succeeded in doing.

The U.S. State Department in Washington, inclining toward the Latin maxim: *Ira furor brevis est*, discounted from the first the significance of the incident, feeling certain that it was but the act of an irresponsible. ∎

President's Visit

Calvin Coolidge becomes the first President to set foot on a reservation

TO HIS HAUGHTY redskin brothers, to the haughty strong Sioux nation, with his wife and son beside him, with big medicine in his pocket, came the pale Wamblee-Tokaha, (Leading Eagle) New White Chief and High Protector—otherwise Calvin Coolidge, 29th U. S. President, but first President ever to visit any Amerindians on one of the reservations set aside for them by their Caucasian conquerors.

He came and was received in peace and friendship.

Wrapping Mrs. Coolidge in a horseblanket on the grandstand of the Pine Ridge fairgrounds, the President first beheld a Sioux pageant—including war-painted savages, bareback riding and children dressed as beets, carrots,

New white chief and high protector

cabbages. He received presents from the Misses Nancy Redcloud, Rosa Redhair, Jessie Marrowbone, Mary Little Iron, Jennie Blue Horse, Emma No Horse and several chiefs.

Massed 7,500 strong in a semicircle in front of the platform, the Sioux listened to their Council's memorial, of which the burden was that the Sioux are too proud to ask for anything not rightly theirs but must insist that the Government restore to them certain lands taken away after supposedly permanent treaty settlements.

The President did not reply directly to this demand but launched upon a short history of the Indian Problem, which began when white and red men first saw each other some four and one quarter centuries ago; which ceased to be violent with the battle of Wounded Knee, S. Dak., (near Pine Ridge) in 1890; which entered a new phase in 1924 when President Coolidge signed the Indian Citizenship Act, declaring all native-born Indians citizens of the U.S.

TRIBES TO CITIZENS. The policy of disorganizing the more than 200 tribes and bands of Amerindians in the U.S. and treating their members individually, like any other racial group of U.S. citizens, was begun by Congress in 1871. The Government then formally refused to acknowledge or recognize any independent nation or tribe within U.S. boundaries. That put an end to treaties, but it was not retroactive. Land that had been acknowledged, in various of the 370 prior treaties made between the U.S. and the Indians, as belonging to tribes of Indians, was allotted to individual Indians in those tribes under an act of 1897. Some 206,000 Indians received private property by these allotments.

With so many new charges on its hands, the Government, through its Indian Bureau (established in 1824) had to set about a program of social work—building schools, hospitals, etc. The discovery of oil on Indian-owned properties kept Federal agencies busy.

The final step of declaring all U.S. Indians citizens by birth did not come until nearly two-thirds of all Indians in the U.S. had obtained the franchise through naturalization.

LET LIVE. It is doubtful that more than one-half of President Coolidge's swarthy audience at Pine Ridge understood all that he said. Perhaps there were a few who bridled momentarily at the simple words: "...Many Indians are still in a primitive state." The President noted that a great portion of Indians, "mostly the older ones, still cling to the old ways, stoically refusing to go further along the modern road. They wish to live and die according to the old traditional ways of the Indians, and they should be permitted to do so."

BONNET. The close of the president's speech was most effective. He recalled how, as the final rite at the burial of the Unknown Soldier in Arlington, Va., some old Indian warriors surrounded the tomb while one of them, acting for his entire race, took off and laid upon the bier his eagle-feathered war-bonnet. ∎

Jim Crow Jr.

Racism goes to school in Indiana

YOUTH IS BRAVE, but youth is cruel. Last week, two dozen young Negroes of Gary, Ind., were mortified by 1,357 young whites of Gary, Ind., probably more painfully than any adult Negro ever lynched by rabid adult whites.

The thing began when the pupils of Emerson High School returned to their classes and found the 24 Negroes enrolled in their midst. Emerson High School is in the "nice" residential section of Gary. It has never before had more than four or five Negro pupils. But during the summer, Gary's school districts were re-defined. Because they lived where they did, the 24 Negroes were entitled by law to attend Emerson High School.

Law or no law, the Emerson pupils whispered, gestured, glowered at the dusky newcomers. They told their parents, who protested to Superintendent William A. Wirt and Principal A. E. Spaulding, who said nothing could be done. "Segregation is impossible because of economic reasons," said Mr. Wirt as tactfully as possible.

Winfield Eschelman of the Emerson senior class, glib talker, good swimmer, got together with Jack Keener, sleek cheerleader, and Sam Chase, smart debater, and some of the athletically "big men" of Emerson, to talk things over. Result: on Monday morning, instead of attending classes, some 800 Emersonians in floppy trousers, sporty sweaters, trim skirts and fetching blouses, went shouting and laughing through Gary's business section. Police disbanded them for "obstructing traffic" but many of them later stood around outside Emerson High School, hissing, gibing, cat calling at non-striking students when school let out. Policemen saw to it that the 24 Negroes went home unmolested.

Next day the "nice" residential part of Gary was littered and scrawled with placards and signs: "WE WON'T GO BACK UNTIL EMERSON IS WHITE…NO NIGGERS FOR EMERSON…EMERSON IS A WHITE MAN'S SCHOOL," etc., etc.

The strikers' ranks swelled to 900 that day. Then, emboldened by their elders' actions or kept at home by nervous parents, Emerson's seventh and eight grades walked out, making a total of 1,357 strikers. Police broke up attempted Negro mass meetings. The school authorities threatened the strikers in vain.

Led by talkative Winfield Eschelman, the strikers formulated their demands at a mass meeting which the school officials attended: 1) Let all Negroes be segregated in corners of Emerson classrooms and in the school cafeteria. 2) Let no disciplinary reprisals be made upon the strikers when they should return. 3) Let the strikers not have to "make up" school work missed during the strike. 4) Let the Emerson Negroes be transferred to other schools as soon as possible. 5) Let an all-Negro high school be built in Gary as soon as possible.

The school authorities were helpless. President Ralph Snyder of the Board of Safety, representing Mayor Floyd E. Williams, arbitrated the situation and the strikers won all their demands. Magnanimous, Winfield Eschelman and friends permitted three Negro seniors to finish out the year at Emerson because they had been there all along, but the rest were transferred temporarily to an all-Negro junior high school elsewhere in town. The strikers returned to classes.

The issue then shifted to the City Council, a special sitting of which was called to hurry through a $15,000 temporary all-Negro high school. The galleries were packed with "race people" who came to hear their viewpoint at last expressed without hindrance, by three Negro Councilmen. The Council has 15 members, and in the absence of three white members, the three Negroes were sufficient to block the passage of the $15,000 temporary appropriation, which required a two-thirds council vote.

Negro Alderman A. B. Whitlock did not insinuate that Ku Klux Klannism lay behind the Emerson strike. Instead, he firmly said: "This [appropriation] is a useless expenditure of the taxpayers' money. We have plenty of room now for all the schoolchildren of Gary. This money [$15,000] wouldn't equip a shack, and the site you propose is in a wilderness. There are no streets, no sewers, no facilities there at all."

White Alderman Merritt Martindale, senior Councilman, interrupted Mr. Whitlock. "Now, Bill." he said, "I hope you're not going to take a wrong view of us whites. The difference is there and it does no good to try to hide it."

"My people are taxpayers," protested Colored Alderman William Burrus. "They have a right to as good an education as anyone. You are setting an awful example by yielding to these striking students…These young people are taking the law into their own hands." The whites promised that a $60,000 permanent high school would be built for Negroes as soon as possible. A Negro replied: "Even if you offered us a million-dollar school we wouldn't take it. We're fighting for the principle of the thing."

Numbers won. When the three absent white members were obtained for another council meeting, the two-thirds vote went through. Gary is to have $15,000 temporary quarters for the Emerson High Negroes. More suitable, permanent all-Negro quarters will probably be furnished in time.

Pondering this outcome, students of U. S. race problems reflected that 95% of all U. S. Negroes are descended from slave stock, some of which has been in the U. S. even longer than genuine *Mayflower* stock. They also reflected that, whereas U. S. Negroes form 14% of Gary's population, U. S. whites form 36%, foreign born whites form 50%. Thus a large majority of Winfield Eschelman & friends were—if representative of Gary's population—descended 14% from Slavs, 10% from Poles, 4% from Hungarians, 3% from Austrians, 3% from Croats, 3% from Italians, 2% from Germans, 1% from Greeks, 1% from Mexicans, 8% from miscellaneous white races, 1% from races of other colors. ■

Southern Senators Vexed

Outrage over "Hoover Chocolates"—but the census Bureau is integrated

"THE BIGGEST PAIR of shoes that ever walked out of Mississippi" belonged, according to Senator Pat Harrison of that State, to John Sharp Williams, onetime (1911-23) U. S. Senator, who now dozes in gardenia-scented retirement on his plantation near Yazoo City, Miss. To fill the Williams shoes, Mississippi sent to Washington Hubert Durett Stephens, a man who was considered brilliant as a youth because he started practicing law at the tender age of 20, but who has yet to distinguish himself either as a shoe-filler or as a Senator.

Last week, almost in spite of himself, Senator Stephens found himself in the public eye. He did not get up in the Senate, where his voice is seldom heard, but in the press, to which he released a correspondence he had been having with Secretary of Commerce Hoover.

Secretary Hoover had ordered the U. S. Census Bureau to discontinue its custom of segregating Negro clerks from white clerks. Senator Stephens called this an "unfortunate action." Senator Stephens referred to "personal political advantage." He said it was a grave injustice to both races and that certain white men and women would have a Negro for their superior officer.

"Foolish untruths," replied Secretary Hoover, "I have received no complaint from either group."

Senator Stephens replied: "A good position has often been lost for a smaller offense than protesting the action of a superior." He reported an instance he had heard about Negroes who had been assigned to desks among white men and women. The Negroes, he said, were "all grins, and congratulated … on the recognition that had been given them."

He further charged that white and Negro women were obliged to use the same washroom. Senator Stephens said his protest was "in the interest of decency and the welfare of Government. Whenever there has been a step toward social equality between the races, dire results have followed."

The matter might never have come to public notice and the Stephens-Hoover exchange might not have been published but for two colleagues of Senator Stephens whose faith and skill in oratory are great.

Senator Coleman Blease of South Carolina, who "loves all the citizens of America," made a speech quoting an anonymous woman in the Census Bureau as having written: "We call these colored Census Bureau employes 'Hoover Chocolates' and all wish we could make him eat them."

And Senator James Thomas ("Tom-Tom") Heflin, who mortally hates and fears the Roman Pope, made a speech, saying:

"Such a thing is a shocking outrage upon these fine American girls, and a shame on any Administration....

"Senators, Mr. Hoover cannot play with this question in this fashion.... And you have no business, Mr. Hoover, to undertake to interfere with the handiwork of the Almighty....

"Just as the eagle is the King of all fowls, just as the lion is the King of all beasts, and just as the whale is the King of all the fishes of the seas, the white race is the crowning glory of the four races of black, yellow, red and white!..."

But the Census Bureau's Negroes remained unsegregated, except of their own volition. Southerners continued to be vexed. ∎

White Primaries

In Texas, old attitudes and new ways to disenfranchise Negroes

TWO FEDERAL JUDGES IN TEXAS—Judge Joseph C. Hutcheson at Houston, Judge Duval West at San Antonio—last week handed down decisions that may bear critically on the November election. Each decided that the Democratic Party, being in no sense a governmental agency but only a social-political organization, is entirely within its rights in determining for itself what shall be the qualification for citizens who cast votes in primary elections held under its auspices.

The suits were brought, of course, by Negroes who asked that the Democrats be enjoined from barring out Negroes. The decisions made it clear that the Democrats had discovered the simplest method yet of disfranchising Negroes. Certificates from Democratic primaries in the South are virtually the same as election certificates, so ubiquitously preponderant is the party. Where any rising tide of black Republican votes may occur, white concern for the all-white ticket is calculated to insure the Democrats against the dangers of sloth, carelessness, disaffection among themselves.

The new Texas method of disfranchising Negroes by simple race discrimination in the party membership supersedes early, cruder methods. Texas used to bar Negroes from the polls by a State law. But Negroes had this law declared unconstitutional. Other methods have been:

1) Literacy tests—requiring voters to prove that they could read and write. Education of the Negroes spoiled this.

2) Property requirements—the Negroes' post-slavery discovery of industry and thrift spoiled this.

3) The "Grandfather clause"—admitting to suffrage any man who voted in 1867 or before, or was one son or grandson of such a man.

The practical effect, if not the technical process, of denying Negroes a share in the government is, of course, a violation of the 14th and 15th Amendments to the U. S. Constitution. It has become trite to point out the inconsistency of such nullification by citizens who prate about the sanctity of the 18th Amendment. Last week's dark plaintiffs in Texas will not have time before November to carry their cases to the U. S. Supreme Court. But predictions were made that when the appeals are heard, the South's constitutional dilemma will grow more acute than it has been for a generation. ∎

Apology to Jews

Henry Ford recants his anti-Semitism

HENRY FORD, having permitted his weekly magazine, the *Dearborn Independent*, generally to vituperate Jews since 1920 and so stir up an anti-Semitism strange to the U.S., last week recanted everything that that weekly had printed against Jews. His confession of error:

"To my great regret I have learned that Jews generally, and particularly those of this country, not only resent these publications [the *Dearborn Independent* and the pamphlets entitled "The International Jew,"] as promoting anti-Semitism, but regard me as their enemy. Trusted friends...have assured me that the character of the charges and insinuations made against the Jews...justifies the righteous indignation entertained by Jews everywhere toward me because of the mental anguish occasioned by the unprovoked reflections made upon them.

"This has led me to direct my personal attention to this subject, in order to ascertain the exact nature of these articles. As a result of this survey I confess that I am deeply mortified that this journal, which is intended to be constructive and not destructive has been made the medium for resurrection of exploded fictions, for giving currency to the so-called protocols of the 'Wise Men of Zion,' which have been demonstrated, as I learn, to be gross forgeries, and for contending that the Jews have been engaged in a conspiracy to control the capital and the industries of the world, besides laying at their door many offenses against decency, public order and good morals.

"Had I appreciated even the general nature, to say nothing of the details, of these utterances I would have forbidden their circulation without a moment's hesitation, because I am fully aware of the virtues of the Jewish people as a whole, of what they and their ancestors have done for civilization and for mankind toward the development of commerce and industry, of their sobriety and diligence, their benevolence and their unselfish interest in the public welfare....

"Those who know me can bear witness that it is not in my nature to inflict insult upon and to occasion pain to anybody and that it has been my effort to free myself from prejudice. Because of that I frankly confess that I have been greatly shocked as a result of my study and examination of the files of the *Dearborn Independent* and the pamphlets entitled 'The International Jew.'

"I deem it to be my duty as an honorable man to make amends for the wrong done to the Jews as fellowmen and brothers, by asking their forgiveness for the harm I have unin-

tentionally committed, by retracting so far as lies within my power the offensive charges laid at their door by these publications, and by giving them the unqualified assurance that henceforth they may look to me for friendship and good will."

THE CONFESSORS. Henry Ford's confessors in this matter were Arthur Brisbane, William Randolph Hearst's editor, and Louis Marshall of Manhattan, potent constitutional lawyer and president of the American Jewish Committee.

To Lawyer Marshall, Mr. Ford had sent two of his agents (Earl J. Davis of Detroit, onetime [1924-25] Assistant Attorney General of the U.S., and one Joseph Palma of Manhattan). They asked Lawyer Marshall how Mr. Ford could most efficaciously erase the Jewish animosity that he had created against himself. Mr. Marshall, speaking for all U. S. Jews, asked for a clearly defined, written recantation of the *Dearborn Independent* and "International Jew" articles.

Mr. Ford's answer to this was last week's statement, a copy of which he sent to Arthur Brisbane with the instructions: "Here's a statement that I have made. Write around it in any way you like." Editor Brisbane with a newspaper "scoop" in his hands, forebore using it exclusively; shared it with all press associations and Manhattan newspapers.

"DEARBORN INDEPENDENT." William J. Cameron, editor of the Dearborn Independent, last week professed to find Mr. Ford's statement unexpected. The current issue of that weekly mentioned no change in policy. Said Editor Cameron: "It is all news to me, and I cannot believe it is true. This is the first time I have heard of any such intention on the part of Mr. Ford, and I most certainly will get in touch with him and find out what is behind it."

MOTIVES. Despite Henry Ford's plain words, some newspapers imputed base motives to him. The New York *World* published: "Looking for material motives, some ascribe political ambitions to the automobile king.

"Mr. Ford's action is taken by political observers at Washington to be the first step in a move toward entering the 1928 campaign for the Presidency. The fact that he chose the Hearst newspapers as the initial vehicle for putting his change of heart before the country is interpreted as indicating William Randolph Hearst will push his candidacy.

"Others believe he is alarmed by the Ford Motor Co.'s striking loss of business in the last few years, although this has been due largely to competition of other manufacturers."

The Chicago *Tribune*, more circumspect, quoted

an anonymous "Jewish financier and industrialist";

"'I think that Ford has at last realized that he has been making a boob of himself. He knows Jews won't buy his cars. Even if they did not they are only 3,000,000 out of 118,000,000. But this is a funny country, the majority are inclined to take up for the under dog, and it is very likely that Ford's attacks on Jews did hurt his business with the vast number of Gentiles associated with Jews one way or another.

"'Ford has been operating his plants as little as two or three days a week lately—a most expensive way to operate— and since he is under every compulsion to sell his new car, he cannot afford to indulge in any hobbies which create enemies and sales resistance.'"

CHEERS. Upon the appearance of the recantation comments—both cheers and jeers broke forth at once. Some potent Jews, including Nathan Straus and Otto Hermann Kahn, resolutely refused to talk. Some cheers:

"We are glad he is getting sensible."—Samuel Phillipson, Chicago merchant.

"Henry Ford shows himself to be a man of real character."—Judge Harry M. Fisher of Chicago.

"His apology comes late, and we hope it is sincere and that he will not again be led into harming a people as he has done to the Jews."—Manager S. H. Simon of B. Manischewitz Matzoth Co., Chicago.

"Ford has shown himself after all a man of some reason."—Max Shulman, Chicago Zionist.

"I am glad Mr. Ford is alive and will reap the joy of righting the almost unforgivable wrong he visited upon the Jewish people."—Rabbi Isaac Landman, editor of the American Hebrew.

JEERS. "We respectfully suggest that the last sweet dose of love and kisses be ladled out to Mr. Ford's new-found friends by leaving the name Ford off the new car. Let it be called instead, let us say, the Solomon Six, or the Abraham Straight-8"—New York Daily News.

"Mr. Ford's statement is very greatly belated. It would have been much more to his credit had it been written five years ago." Julius Rosenwald of Sears, Roebuck & Co.

"While it is better late than never to confess having done an injury, it is impossible to overlook the fact that in Mr. Ford's case it is decidedly late."—New York Times. ■

Whispers

Roman Catholic Presidential candidate Al Smith and his "foreign sovereign"

WHAT IS A "whispering campaign"? Is it a pack of slanders deliberately and covertly set afoot by one's political opponents in an organized way? Is it a mixture of fact, exaggeration and gossip on unprintable subjects which one's political opponents know is being passed around and over which they secretly gloat? Is it a parcel of prejudice circulated by the ignorant and the fanatical, which one's opponents would be powerless to arrest however fairminded they might be?

Whatever it is, an anti-Al Smith "whispering campaign" has been suspected, proclaimed, viewed-with-alarm, pointed-with-shame, loudly flayed by the Democrats. Last week the Democratic outcry reached a new pitch and counter-action was planned against the three outstanding Whispers. The first:

ROMAN CATHOLICISM. Meeting at Columbus, Ohio, the National Lutheran Editors' Association, a body representing two million readers of Lutheran literature, brought out of the whispering gallery and into the amplifiers the old-time subject of Nominee Smith's Roman Catholicism. While not presuming to campaign openly for Hoover, the Lutheran editors voted to tell their readers that the Roman Catholic Church requires of its members allegiance to a "foreign sovereign...who has worldwide political interests of his own which may severely clash with the best interests of our country."

The day after the Lutherans published their resolution, Nominee Smith, in a New Year's message to U.S. Jewry, published these balanced phrases: "The separation of Church and State is a fundamental American principle. The pursuit of virtue sanctioned by religion is at the basis of any civilized State...."

Democrats yet more practical called attention to anti-Catholic propaganda of the lowest type and insinuated that the G. O. P. was responsible, if not for starting it, then for not stopping it. New York City's glib and artful Mayor Walker last week suggested that the Republican-run Post Office Department was deliberately lax about letting "scurrilous slanderous" matter from "fanatical bigots" pass through the mails.

The arch-Democratic New York World reprinted bits from a widely-distributed pamphlet which said:
Born
On the 28th day of June, 1928,
at Houston, Tex.,
The Papal Party of the United States
Its Candidate
Sir Knight Alfred E. Smith, K.C., F.F.M. ■

Issues of race and ethnicity drove events around the world, as Hitler rose to power in Germany preaching Aryan supremacy. Far from advocating equal rights, African Americans struggled simply to survive the Depression—and injustice. Even when the nation was horrified by events like the blow-torch lynchings in Duck Hill, Mississippi, the N.A.A.C.P. and its supporters could not overcome a Southern filibuster and pass an anti-lynching law. Still, when a young black athlete from Ohio, Jesse Owens, upstaged Hitler's Aryan athletes at the Berlin Olympics, Americans of every color cheered.

The "Scottsboro Boys"

A series of questionable trials puts Southern justice on the defense

Scottsboro Case

JUNE 22, 1931

CRASH, CRASH! went two windows in the U. S. consulate at Dresden. *Plump* fell a bottle on the consulate's floor. While young German Communists hooted and whistled outside, an American clerk picked up the bottle, found a note: "We protest the execution of eight young Negro workers in Alabama. Down with American murder and imperialism! For the brotherhood of black and white young proletarians! An end to the bloody lynching of our Negro coworkers!"

Thus last week did the case of eight blackamoors, condemned to death for rape, take on its first international aspect. Beginning with the same violent methods at U. S. embassies and consulates, Reds made the Sacco-Vanzetti case a world issue.

Two months ago the population of Scottsboro, Ala., temporarily increased five-fold. Some 10,000 visitors swarmed to town to be on hand for the trial of nine itinerant Negroes who had been charged with assaulting two white girls. The girls, clad in overalls and accompanied by seven white men,

The Scottsboro Boys pose for the camera under heavy guard

had been "bumming" their way in a freight car from Chattanooga, Tenn., to Huntsville, Ala., when the Negroes, aged from 14 to 21, boarded the train, pitched out five of the young women's companions, knocked the other two unconscious. Then, the girls said, they were raped. Their assailants were surrounded, overcome by a posse when the train reached Paint Rock, Ala. Within two weeks and two days of the arrest, three juries returned a verdict of guilty against eight of the Negroes. They were sentenced to death in the electric chair on July 10. A mistrial was ordered for the youngest. Throughout the trials, 1,000 National Guardsmen were held in readiness to suppress race disorders.

Startled by the celerity of Alabama justice, the International Labor Defense protested "the legal lynching of Negro workers on framed charges." Liberal and racial organizations began to bestir themselves for an appeal in behalf of the condemned. Although ready with praise for the State's having made "every honest effort to give the accused a fair trial," these groups claimed: 1) that a fair trial was impossible under the circumstances; 2) that physicians were unable to find conclusive evidence of rape on the girls; 3) that the girls were bad, anyway.

While the new defense was being prepared for the Negroes, a split occurred within the ranks of their supporters. The Chattanooga Interdenominational Ministers' Alliance of Negro Divines denounced the International Labor Defense, accused it of interesting itself in the case "mainly for the purpose of drawing Negroes of the South into the Communist organization."

First public figure to enter the altercation was Author Theodore Dreiser, who protested the Scottsboro affair to Governor Miller of Alabama.

Meanwhile the condemned men have made small outcry. Jailed at Gadsden, Ala., one complained: "We just don't like that death sentence." ■

In Tallapoosa

BLACK MIXED WITH RED last week to make a bloody brew for Tallapoosa County, Ala. At a rural church in the woods outside Camp Hill several hundred Negroes met furtively by night. Ostensibly they came together to form a share-croppers' union against what they were told was the oppression of white landowners. One Ralph Gray was posted outside as a picket. Inside, the management of the meeting was taken over by a black Communist from Chattanooga. He represented, he said, the "Society for the Advancement of Colored People." He told his auditors to demand social equality and white intermarriage. If they did not get what they demanded, they were to take it anyway.

To inflame his hearers more the speaker directed their attention to the death sentence passed on eight young blackamoors at Scottsboro for raping two white girls in a freight train. He denounced these sentences as "legal lynching," demanded that the black boys be retried by a black jury. Into such a frenzy of excitement and protest did he whip his audience that they were openly threatening the life of Governor Benjamin Meek Miller unless he released the condemned men.

At the height of the meeting Sheriff Kyle Young and his deputies arrived at the church to disperse the assembly as a menace to the white man's peace. Words passed between the sheriff and Picket Gray. A round of shots was fired in the dark. Sheriff Young and a deputy fell wounded. So did Picket Gray. From the church came a volley of fire. Deputies on the outside volleyed back. The Negroes inside the church went scampering away to cover through the night. Four of them were left behind wounded. The deputies burned the church to the ground. Later a posse sought Gray in his cabin. When they were met with a fusillade, they broke in, shot Gray dead. Next day 200 white men scoured the county with bloodhounds, rounded up 60 thoroughly terrified Negroes who had been at the meeting, jailed 32 on charges of attempted murder and assault, criminal conspiracy, and carrying concealed weapons. The four wounded fugitives had vanished. Camp Hill's police chief cryptically remarked: "They went out to chop stove wood and haven't returned yet."

By the end of the week most of Tallapoosa's Negro population had moved to neighboring counties. Still uncaught was the Red black from Chattanooga who had incited the outbreak.

Tallapoosa's racial clash produced reverberations outside Alabama. In New York the National Association for the Advancement of Colored People which has been conducting a legal defense of the Scottsboro convicts denied that it was connected in any way with the Camp Hill affair. It charged that Communist agitators were deliberately "muddling the matter" and warned that their tactics to win Negroes to Communism were "the best means in the world" for getting the Scottsboro boys hanged or mobbed. The International Labor Defense, a Red organization which has been exploiting the Scottsboro case for political purposes, said the Camp Hill meeting was instigated for economic reasons and that white landowners had ordered it broken up to suppress the idea of a share-croppers' union.

Meanwhile, bewildered by all the outcry their case was creating, the eight blackamoors of Scottsboro sat in death cells at Kilby prison waiting for the Supreme Court of Alabama to review their convictions next winter. ■

"Get It Done Quick"

IN APRIL 1931, Herbert Hoover was just back from his first and last visit as President to the Virgin Islands ("a poorhouse" to him). Same month eight young Negroes were sentenced to death at Scottsboro, Ala. for raping two white female hoboes in a Southern Ry. freight gondola.

In November 1932, the North was being treated to an orgy of self-righteousness by a semi-autobiographical film called *I Am a Fugitive from a Chain Gang*. Same month, the U. S. Supreme Court set aside the Scottsboro verdicts on the ground that the defendants had not been provided with adequate counsel.

In April 1933, the U. S. S. *Akron* was lost off the New Jersey coast. Same month, this time in Decatur, Ala., bullet-headed Haywood Patterson, leader of the "Scottsboro Boys," was found guilty of rape by a jury that fixed the death penalty. Scrupulous Judge James E. Horton set aside the verdict as unwarranted by the evidence, thereby signed his own political death warrant.

In December 1933, millions of citizens were sampling Repeal liquor for the first time. Same month, for the third time, at Decatur Negro Patterson heard himself condemned to death by a jury of twelve white men.

BRIDGES AND BORDERS   27

In April 1935, Congress appropriated four billion dollars for work relief, and the word "boondoggling" rushed headlong into the U. S. vocabulary. Same month, the U. S. Supreme Court again overruled the Alabama courts on the Scottsboro case, finding that since Negroes had been "systematically excluded" from the jury rolls, the defendants had been deprived of their rights under the 14th Amendment of the Constitution. Governor Bibb Graves firmly declared: "Alabama is going to observe the supreme law of America!"

By last week, when the Scottsboro affair was ending its fifth year and beginning its fourth trial scene, the accused Negroes had long since ceased to be a handful of friendless vagrants. Instead they had become black symbols of economic bitterness, race prejudice, sectional hatred and political conflict. To the Communist Party of the U. S., which had rushed to the Negroes' side with cash & counsel, the Scottsboro Boys were martyrs to Southern injustice and intolerance. To Southerners, the defendants were a gang of "bad niggers" whose crime was being brazenly exploited by malicious Reds, Jews and Yankees. Responsible Southern sentiment indicated, however, that a fair trial might finally be guaranteed if the defense would abandon its obvious air of partisanship. Apparently in response to this feeling, shortly before the trial the Reds involved in the defense had retreated rather clumsily behind a committee of intersectional liberals. To do the actual pleading, an Alabama lawyer had been hired. But Samuel Leibowitz of New York City, who had been through the second and third trials, remained as No. 1 counsel for the defense. Similarly, the State's representatives in court were oldtimers too, the judge and prosecutor being the same who had caused Trial No. 3 to be characterized by the U. S. Supreme Court as a fine exhibition of Jim Crow justice.

Since he had helped convict Haywood Patterson in 1933 when he was State's Attorney General, Thomas Edmund Knight Jr. had risen to be Lieutenant Governor of Alabama. The defense soon pointed out that the State constitution forbade a man's holding two public jobs for pay. While Thomas Knight "laughed off" this objection, Judge William Callahan breezily overruled a plea that Knight be barred as special prosecutor at Trial No. 4 at Decatur.

In the ten months since he had last laid a fishy eye on Defendant Patterson and his Yankee counsel, Judge Callahan had not changed much. At the earlier trial he had had to be reminded at the last minute to instruct the jury what to do in case it happened to find Patterson innocent. In much the same spirit he now viewed the first Negroes who had shown up in the Morgan County courthouse since Reconstruction times in the role of possible trial jurors. As Bibb Graves had promised, Alabama was "going to observe the supreme law of America."

A Negro had actually been a member of the grand jury which swiftly reindicted Patterson. However, it was one thing to allow a Negro to participate briefly in such a routine ceremony, and quite another to permit one to serve in the body that actually decided Patterson's fate. Every Negro in Alabama knew this. Therefore, the twelve black veniremen in Decatur last week were thoroughly uncomfortable.

Judge Callahan was in no mood to put them at their ease. He had a few chairs placed outside the jury box for the Negroes to sit on. When one stage-struck blackamoor vacantly wandered into the jury box, his honor leaned over his bench, barked: "Here boy! Sit over there!" One of the Negroes lost no time explaining that his boss had recently shot himself while hunting, urgently needed him back home to run things. Two others guessed they were past the legal age limit of 65 for jurymen. One by one, the dusky dozen who would no more have dreamed of sitting on a jury with the "white captains" than they would of walking up and slapping the devil in the face, escaped from the courthouse by their own devices or were eliminated by the prosecution.

It took just seven hours for Prosecutor Knight to restate his case. It did not differ from the one his father, as a State Supreme Court Justice, had previously upheld in vain. Hard-faced Victoria Price who, it was charged, had slept with hoboes in a Chattanooga "jungle" the night before the alleged crime, told for the eighth time in public how Patterson and the other Negroes had chased off her white "boy friends" and raped her in the freight car—a tale long since repudiated by Ruby Bates, the other alleged victim of the attack. When the State rested it was after 5 P.M. The courtroom was fetid. The defense had no witnesses on hand except Defendant Patterson, whom it did not want to call at that time. Nevertheless, Judge Callahan peremptorily ordered that the trial continue, that Patterson take the stand.

In the course of the trial he ruled out testimony relating to Victoria Price's poor past, objected to defense procedure which the State had let pass as satisfactory, was vague about noting defense exceptions and, when the defense tried to illustrate physical details about the freight train, complained: "It won't help anyone to see anything. It will just delay things."

In summation, the State asked for the death penalty, otherwise "we might have to buckle six-shooters about our waists." "Don't go out and quibble over the evidence," roared the young county prosecutor who was helping Prosecutor Knight. "Say to yourselves: 'We're tired of this job' and put it behind you. Get it done quick and protect the fair womanhood of this great State." The defense was for the protection of womanhood, too, but also asked for "the protection of the innocent."

The jury got it done fairly quickly. Within eight hours it was back with the regular verdict of guilty but decided that Defendant Patterson be spared the electric chair, to spend the next 75 years in prison. "I'd rather die," scowled Patterson.

Since a live man is better off than a dead one, and since Haywood Patterson will probably be safer behind bars for the next few years anyhow, the defense could count the verdict something of a triumph. In fairly good spirits Counsel Leibowitz was proceeding with the case of another Scottsboro boy when the prosecution suddenly challenged written medical testimony made at the second trial by a physician now too ill to go to court and substantiate it orally. Thereupon Judge Callahan indefinitely postponed all further trials, ordered the prisoners back to jail in Birmingham.

Going down Lacon Mountain 20 miles out of Decatur, the five cars carrying prisoners and officers came suddenly to a halt. Later there was no agreement as to how and why the affray started. But, in sum, Negro Ozie Powell leaned forward and sliced a deputy sheriff in the neck with a knife. The sheriff then shot off a portion of Ozie Powell's forehead. The deputy was rushed off to a physician who closed the wound with twelve sutures. Ozie Powell, still conscious and still chained between two of his fellow prisoners, was driven 70 miles on to Birmingham where a surgeon extracted a slug sunk one inch in his brain.

Nearest thing to an official comment from the law's side was the dark observation of the sheriff of Morgan County: "Somebody smarter than those Negroes... figured it all out."

To this Counsel Leibowitz taunted: "Does the sheriff claim that three Negroes shackled together in the rear seat of a rapidly moving automobile...with two men in that automobile armed to the teeth, this car preceded in front by an automobile carrying two other armed officers of the law and followed by still another car with armed guards and with state highway patrolmen as an escort, did attempt to escape by using a penknife?" ∎

∎ RACES

Battle over Lynching

A blow-torch lynching shocks the nation, but a Southern filibuster sinks an anti-lynching law

Lynch & Anti-Lynch   APRIL 26, 1937

IN WASHINGTON, before a gallery crowded with Negroes, the U.S. House of Representatives was beginning to debate a drastic anti-lynching bill introduced by Congressman Gavagan from New York's black Harlem. In Jackson, Miss., before delegates to a farm conference, Governor Hugh Lawson White was boasting that Mississippi had not had a lynching in 15 months. In Winona, Miss., in a jampacked courtroom in Montgomery County's white brick courthouse, Roosevelt Townes and Bootjack McDaniels, 26-year-old Negroes, were pleading not guilty to a charge of murdering a crossroads country grocer during a robbery last December at nearby Duck Hill. One day last week these simultaneous events were the prolog of a bloody melodrama, peculiarly Southern.

As the debate at Washington droned on, furnishing a strange far-off accompaniment, Negroes Townes and McDaniels were led handcuffed from the courtroom. If their minds registered anything as the sheriff and two deputies escorted them down the back stairs to return them to jail, it was relief. The Court had assigned counsel to defend them, set a date for trial by jury. Everything was according to law. But when they stepped out of a side door of the courthouse, they found themselves face to face with what so often handles cases like theirs in the South. An angry mob surged forward, took them from the custody of their guardians without a struggle, threw them into a school bus.

Followed by 40 automobiles, the bus sped down the highway toward Duck Hill. Two miles from the scene of last December's murder, 500 country folk, including women and children, waited expectantly in a patch of pinewood. When the motorcade from Winona arrived, the mob closed in to watch as the terrified Negroes were dragged from the bus. People in the back rows could hear heavy chains clink as the two blackamoors were made fast to trees.

Bootjack McDaniels, a lanky Negro with powerful shoulders, was asked to confess first. He gibbered that he was innocent. A mobster stepped forward with a plumber's blow torch, lighted it. Another ripped McDaniels' shirt off. Again he refused to confess. Then the blue-white flame of the torch stabbed into his black chest. He screamed with agony. The torch was withdrawn. He reiterated his innocence. Again the torch was turned on him and the smell of burned flesh floated through the woods. Again he screamed, and when it was withdrawn this time he was ready to confess. He was with Townes, he sobbed, when Townes poked a shotgun through the grocery window, fired into the grocer's back. When his confession was delivered in sufficient detail, the lynchers fell back and a volley of bullets crashed into Bootjack McDaniels, 1937's lynching victim No. 2.

Despite what he had just witnessed, Negro Townes was not yet ready to repeat the confession which county officers had said he signed with his X after he was arrested last fortnight. But the blow torch soon burned the story out of him. As he hung limp in his chains, some of the mob went off to get another Negro he named as an accomplice. Back they came with one Shorty Dorroh. After he satisfied them that he had had nothing to do with the murder, they horsewhipped him, ordered him to get out of the State. Then they piled brush high about sobbing Negro Townes, drenched it with gasoline, touched him off—1937's lynching victim No. 3.

Back in Winona, the judge who had heard the Negroes' pleas of not guilty promised a Grand Jury investigation, but the sheriff and his men said they had not recognized any of the mobsters who seized their prisoners. Said Deputy Sheriff Hugh Curtis: "It was all done very quickly, quietly and orderly."

In Washington the House debate rose to a furious crescendo after Michigan's Michener read a press report of what had just happened at Duck Hill. Negroes in the gallery, who had cheered and applauded intermittently throughout the day when one of their champions made a good point on the floor, were shocked into silence. Two days later, with all but 17 Southern Representatives out of 123 voting against it, the Gavagan anti-lynching bill, which would make mobsters and law officers who yield up their prisoners liable to stiff Federal prosecution, was passed by the House.

Few proposals have caused more excited debate in the halls of Congress than Federal anti-lynching bills. At least one is offered every session. This session there were 59. The first anti-lynching bill, introduced in the house in 1902, was inspired not by lynchings of Southern Negroes but by the large number of lynchings in the 1880s and 1890s in which white aliens were the victims. These crimes caused the Government no end of embarrassment, resulted in payments of $475,500 in indemnities to foreign governments. When the South continued to lynch Negroes after alien lynchings ceased, the National Association for the Advancement of Colored People was organized to do something about it and anti-lynching legislation became a permanent sectional issue. The first bill to get through the House did so in 1922. Southern Senators killed it with a 21-day filibuster. In 1935 the Southern bloc in the Senate filibustered six days to smother a similar bill.

Few Washington observers would concede last week's bill an outside chance in the Senate. Many doubted that it would ever get out of committee. The fact that the Administration needs the support of Southern Senators to get the President's Court Plan passed, caused considerable speculation when the anti-lynching bill got through the House. A filibuster, which seemed almost certain, could jam up the legislative mill and thus delay or prevent passage of the Court legislation. Administration leaders feared that Southern Senators who oppose the Court Plan might welcome a filibuster on this other issue of such powerful interest to the folks back home as a disguise for their opposition to the White House. ∎

Black's White

TO NEGRO LEE JONES, a 31-year-old mill-hand of Greensboro, Ala., last week's doings in the U. S. Senate were good news. Negro Jones had been arrested, charged with jumping on the running board of a car to kidnap Mrs. Robert Knox Greene, wife of a white planter. When Mrs. Greene's friends began to gather he did not need to be told what familiar, ugly thought they had in mind. At the crucial moment when Sheriff Calvin Hollis was trying to calm the crowd, up stepped Planter Robert Knox Greene himself. How Planter Greene, a cousin of Alabama's Representative Sam Hobbs, persuaded the mob to disperse he was soon explaining to the Associated Press. "I told them I was the aggrieved person," said he, with some self-satisfaction, "and I ought to have the final say. I also reminded them our Southern Senators were fighting an anti-lynching bill in Washington and violence might hamper them...."

"SKUNK MEAT." Had it not been for Planter Greene's timely intervention, Millhand Jones might have been the first person to be lynched in the U. S. in 1938. There were eight lynchings in 1937, 13 in 1936. There have been some 5,000 in the U. S. since complete records began in 1882. There have been lynchings in every State in the Union save four—Massachusetts, Rhode Island, New Hampshire, and Vermont. But if the practice has been general, the opposition to laws intended to suppress it has centred in the South. For two generations Southern Representatives and Senators have greeted every lynching bill that came up for debate with a reaction as sharp and unfailing as would be produced by a polecat. Snorted Georgia's Richard Russell last week of the latest and one of the most threatening Federal attempts to prosecute and punish lynchers: "Skunk meat."

Week previous to this pronouncement Kentuckian Alben Barkley had settled down to the bitterest of the many unpleasant tasks that he has had since he succeeded the late Joseph Taylor Robinson as Majority Leader of the Senate. Leader Barkley was paying for a serious mistake. Last August in the closing days of Congress, when every minute of the Senate's time was plotted out, he fell asleep at the switch. Senator King who was supposed to rise at a certain moment to present the District of Columbia Airport Bill, missed his cue and before Senator Barkley woke New York's Senator Wagner had the floor. Senator Wagner brought up the Wagner-Van Nuys Anti-Lynching Bill. Although Alben Barkley has cast a good Southern vote against anti-lynching bills in the past, he was caught in a legislative trap. To prevent a new filibuster from wrecking the closing hours of the session, he promised Senator Wagner if he would withdraw it for the time, that it would be considered, second only to the Farm Bill, next session.

When the special session opened last November with no Farm Bill in sight, Alben Barkley, like a Confederate general trapped into acting as a front for a group of carpetbaggers, unhappily unloosed the Wagner-Van Nuys Bill and its inevitable filibuster. It was temporarily laid aside when the Farm Bill appeared, but nothing is more important to a legislative leader than to keep his promises to the letter. So no sooner was the President's message out of the way last fortnight than Alben Barkley, still smarting from the abuses of the last filibuster, fulfilled his pledge, produced the Anti-Lynching Bill for what he hoped would be the last TIME.

Last spring under the spur of the two blow-torch lynchings at Duck Hill, Miss., the Gavagan Bill, a similar anti-lynching measure, passed the House. Passage by the Senate therefore meant that the bill would become law barring the unlikely event of a Presidential veto. So as predicted, Texas' Tom Connally promptly organized a filibuster. Not as predicted, that filibuster last week rounded out ten days and had gathered so much momentum that Tom Connally jubi-

lantly announced he would keep it going if necessary until Christmas.

FILIBUSTER. The actual contents of the Wagner-Van Nuys Bill, as simple as they were familiar, would scarcely keep the U. S. Senate busy for that period. Like its predecessors, it provided for Federal prosecution, and a $5,000 fine or up to five years' imprisonment, or both, for sheriffs & peace officers who did not afford criminals and suspected criminals reasonable protection from mobs (any gatherings of more than three persons). Its other principal provision, the payment of an indemnity up to $10,000 to the family of a victim of mob violence by the country whose officials are responsible, is already in the statue books of twelve States.

But filibusters rarely have to talk about bills. As Tom Connally's loyal little band—Georgia's Russell, North Carolina's Bailey, South Carolina's James Byrnes, Tennessee's Kenneth McKellar, Louisiana's Ellender, and Pat Harrison—began their operations they had one stroke of luck. Illinois' porky, cautious William Dieterich had persuaded the Judiciary Committee to tack on an amendment exempting counties (i. e., Illinois' Cook) from liabilities arising from gang murders and labor violence. This gave Kenneth McKellar an opportunity to bait Illinois' Ham Lewis into a voluble debate on Chicago jurisprudence. North Carolina's Robert Reynolds helped out by discussing Europe, the Orient, the British Isles, South America, Africa, the Malay States.

"Whenever the Republican Party, the Democratic Party or the New Deal Party or any other party," rumbled North Carolina's Josiah Bailey, "caters to the Negro vote, it is going to elect to office common fellows of the baser sort." But when Kenneth McKellar began scornfully quoting from the bill in an effort to establish its unconstitutionality, Senator Wagner pointed out that the passage in question was a quotation from the Fourteenth Amendment. "Yes," stammered Senator McKellar, "it is."

Jimmy Byrnes dropped the first real bomb. Pointing straight at a small man seated quietly in the gallery, his voice tense with passion, the wiry South Carolinian cried: "The South may just as well know...that it has been deserted by the Democrats of the North....One Negro....has ordered this bill to pass and if a majority can pass it, it will pass....If Walter White," and Jimmy Byrnes was fairly shouting his angry tribute, "should consent to have this bill laid aside, its advocates would desert it as quickly as football players unscramble when the whistle of the referee is heard."

PALEFACE. The Negro who did not acknowledge this extraordinary attention was Secretary Walter Francis White of the National Association for the Advancement of Colored People. Not the least reason for Southern hatred of anti-lynching bills is that for the past decade they have been inextricably associated with Walter White, and that the gradual growth of the anti-lynching movement had by last week made spunky, dapper, 44-year-old Negro White the most potent leader of his race in the U. S.

Son of a fair-skinned Georgia postman and his fair-skinned wife, Walter White is blond and palefaced. He himself does not know how much Negro blood runs in his veins; Harvard's far-ranging Anthropologist Earnest Alfred Hooton computes it at 1/64. But despite a skin that last week fooled fellow guests at Washington's Hay-Adams House, Walter White has always regarded himself as a Negro. He remembers that his father's house was almost burned down during an Atlanta race riot in his childhood. He recalls too that his father died in agony when the surgeons of the white ward of an Atlanta hospital, to which he had been mistakenly taken for an emergency operation, balked upon learning his race and insisted on shipping him in the rain to the Negro ward across the street.

Ironically, Walter White's pale skin got him into the Negro movement. In 1918 the National Association for the Advancement of Colored People wanted an investigator who looked white enough to circulate among crowds at lynchings, and young White, recently graduated from the Negro Atlanta University, was well qualified for the job. Founded nine years before as the result of a disastrous race riot in Abraham Lincoln's home town of Springfield, Ill. the N.A.A.C.P. was then a smallish but idealistic organization with a masthead of big names, among them liberal Editor Oswald Garrison Villard and famed Boston Lawyer Moorfield Storey.

The Association published *The Crisis*, later to reach its peak of influence under the editorship of Atlanta University's scholarly W. E. Burghardt Du Bois. It circulated a news service to the Negro press, which now numbers over 200 papers and magazines. It lobbied for Negro legislation, and, when a post-War wave of lynchings carried off ten returned Negro soldiers in 1919 (two of them burned alive), it began to spend an increasing amount of its energy promoting State and then Federal anti-lynching laws.

Palefaced Negro White did his job well. He talked to members of mobs that executed some 40 lynchings. Occasionally he had to evade such triumphant questions as "Well, how would you like to have your daughter marry a nigger?" Once, while investigating a race riot, in Arkansas, he narrowly escaped a mob who had heard he was a Negro investigator, breathlessly boarded a train only to have the conductor say: "You're leaving too soon—they're looking for a yellow nigger." He helped the N.A.A.C.P. publish the first case history of lynching, covering 3,224 cases between 1889 and 1918. And as assistant to N.A.A.C.P. Secretary James Weldon Johnson, he sat in the Senate gallery and heard the Dyer Bill talked to death in 1922.

In *Rope & Faggot*, which he wrote in France on a Guggenheim Fellowship in 1927-28, Author White maintained that the long tradition of U. S. vigilantism has finally narrowed down to the Southern Negro, not to protect Southern woman-hood as was usually claimed (he found

rape charged in less than one lynching in five), but to shackle and harry a growing economic competitor. *Rope & Faggot* also maintained that lynch law dated back to Colonial days when a Quaker named Charles Lynch sat as magistrate in an extra-legal court at what is now Lynchburg, Va., to try horse thieves, to the 1830s when a St. Louis judge, aptly named Lawless, advised a jury that mob murder was "beyond the reach of law." The N.A.A.C.P. record still is that after 99.4% of U. S. lynchings, sheriffs had reported with melancholy unanimity: no arrests, no indictments, no convictions.

LOBBYING. When James Weldon Johnson retired to teach literature at Fisk University in 1930, Walter White succeeded to his $5,000 job and a Federal anti-lynching law officially became Item No. 1 on the N.A.A.C.P. schedule. The White argument, ceaselessly drummed into Negroes and white legislators alike, was that while talk is long, the rope is short—that in the 13 years between the Dyer filibuster and the filibuster that wrecked the Wagner-Costigan bill, mobs had lynched with practical impunity more than 290 U. S. Negroes.

In 1935, Walter White was able to get the ear of Franklin Roosevelt. Secretary Marvin McIntyre refused him an appointment with the President, but the President's Negro Valet Irvin H. McDuffie who sometimes leaves notes on his employer's pillow and tactfully gets unofficial callers in through the White House kitchen, was able to arrange a private meeting. What effect Walter White's address to the President may have had was not sure.

PAPER VICTORY. As Walter White sat peering curiously down at the Senate from his gallery seat, he had already won a paper victory. He claimed, and neutral observers were disposed to accept his estimate, 73 votes for his bill in the turbulent chamber below. But these were promissory notes, useless until a final roll call forced collection. And just as there were Representatives willing to bring the Administration's Wages-&-Hours Bill out of an obstructive rules committee but unwilling to vote for it when they got the chance, so too there were Senators last week willing to vote for an anti-lynching bill but unwilling to take the forcible measures necessary to bring it to a vote.

On paper the 73 supporters of the Anti-Lynching Bill controlled nine more votes than the two-thirds required to invoke cloture and end the filibuster, but the filibuster nevertheless went on. Alert Walter White made increasingly anxious trips downstairs to confer with Senators in the reception room. One of his departures from the gallery was noted by Jimmy Byrnes with sotto voce sarcasm: "Barkley can't do anything without talking to that nigger first."

The odds in favor of the White-Wagner-Van Nuys Anti-Lynching Bill decreased steadily last week, for time works with a filibuster. One serious blow was the refusal of Republican Leader Charles McNary, a master of minority strategy, to vote for night sessions or cloture so long as he could hamstring the Barkley leadership by refusing to do so. Another blow was the warning by oldtime Liberal George Norris that a prolonged, bitter filibuster in the face of important legislation might be too high a price even for an anti-lynching bill. Said he: "Perhaps this is not the time to open wounds that may not heal." A reporter asked Tom Connally whether he still thought he and his friends could talk until Christmas. The old Texan snorted: "Why not?" ■

New Deal for Indians

The Reorganization Act promises more power to the reservations

Red Constitution

Watched by Flathead chiefs and John Collier, Harold Ickes signs the new Flathead constitution

BRAVE IN CEREMONIAL BEADS, buckskin, war bonnets and ermine tails, six elder statesmen of Montana's Flathead Indian tribe ranged themselves one day last week behind the polished Washington desk of Secretary of the Interior Harold Le Clair Ickes. It was a great & grave occasion—the signing of the first tribal constitution under the Indian Reorganization Act of 1934. Secretary Ickes and Commissioner of Indian Affairs John Collier were as solemn as the Indians. Just as cameras were about to record the event for posterity a horrified Ickes press-agent spied, clinging to one Indian's ancestral costume, what seemed to be a thoroughly anachronistic price tag. In a flurry of embarrassment the chieftain's tag was ripped off while Secretary Ickes, covering up, seized a pen and hurriedly squiggled his signature to the constitution.

When aggressive, intense, little John Collier became Indian Commissioner in 1933, that longtime crusader for Indian justice resolved that the nation's red men (now numbering about 350,000, less than half of them full-blooded) should also have a New Deal. Since 1887 corrupt Indian agents and greedy civilians had tricked, swindled and robbed U. S. Indians of approximately one billion dollars in cash and all but the worst 47,000,000 of their 138,000,000 acres of land, largely reducing them to dependent pauperism. Since attempts to individualize and westernize Indians had obviously failed, Commissioner Collier proposed to revive the tribes' old life and culture, help them become self-supporting, largely self-governing, thoroughly Indian communities. Result was the Reorganization Act, passed last year with President Roosevelt's support over the fierce opposition of ranchers and lumbermen who stood to lose valuable properties leased from Indians and who succeeded in barring Oklahoma Indians from the Act's provisions.

Besides securing to Indians the use of their present tribal lands, the Act provides for extending their holdings. It gives every reservation the right by majority vote to secure a constitution for its government, a Federal charter for a corporation to run its business affairs. It provides a $10,000,000 revolving fund for loans to tribal organizations, up to $250,000 per year for their expenses.

Though Crusader Collier is about as popular with Indians as any white Government official could be, he has had to hold many a powwow to persuade braves & squaws that his plan is good. Justly do Indians point out that every previous Government move to help Indians has all but cost the Indians their scalps. Spirited young Indians who have strayed off the reservation to college resent any suggestion of new Government paternalism, hotly demand the right to become normal, unsegregated U. S. citizens. But Indians on any reservation may take or leave the Act's provisions as the majority chooses. Up to last week 176 reservations had voted to accept, only 76 to reject. First to draw up and approve a constitution were the Flatheads.

To the editor of the Washington Post, which had reported the "price tag" incident at the signing ceremony, went last week a solemn letter of reproach. "These costumes," it read in part, "are hereditary. That worn by Chief Charlo was inherited by him from his grandfather, Chief Little Claw, who as chief of all the Flatheads signed the Treaty of 1855. The ermine tails on this costume signified the rank of Chief Little Claw. Those worn by Subchief Bear Track were left to him according to the Indian custom of giving things away at time of death....The plain undecorated war shirt worn by another of the delegation he also inherited and it was actually worn on war parties before the Flatheads settled on the reservation.

"On Sept. 27 to 29 there was held a jubilee in honor of Father Taelman of St. Ignatius, Mont. To this jubilee we sent relics and ancient costumes....The tag which we were seen pulling off the costume was merely the exhibit tag. Our dignity has been offended and we have been incensed by these statements in your paper....

JOS. R. B. BLODGETT, president, Flathead Tribal Council

CHIEF MARTIN CHARLO (his mark)

ROY E. COUNVILLE, secretary, Flathead Tribal Council

CHIEF KOOSTATA (his mark)

DAVID COUTUNE, delegate, Flathead Tribal Council

CHIEF VICTOR VANDERBERG or BEAR TRACK (his mark)" ∎

Peace Pipe

ONE DAY LAST WEEK several thousand Floridians and visitors from the North repaired to a park on the shores of Lake Worth, between Palm Beach and West Palm Beach. There they ranged themselves in specially-built boxes and bleachers around a huge central platform. On the platform bespectacled Secretary of the Interior Harold Le Clair Ickes squatted on his haunches in a circle of squatting Seminole Indians. Seminole squaws and papooses in bright beads and dresses were bunched around the platform. Loudspeakers allowed the spectators to overhear the powwow by which Secretary Ickes proposed to advance the Administration's policy of extending its New Deal to Indians. Simultaneously the 100-year war between the Seminoles and the U. S., begun by the raw deal of that first modern Democrat, President Andrew Jackson, was to be brought to a peaceful conclusion.

Spread over fertile northern Florida, the Seminoles of the early 19th Century were a proud, virile tribe of 5,000 souls, rich in cattle and Negro slaves bought from the

British. In 1818, while Florida still belonged to Spain, General Jackson led his troops against them in the First Seminole War. Three years later, U. S. purchase of Florida sent a flood of white squatters over the Seminoles' lands. The Federal Government helped shunt the Indians south to swamps and sand dunes. Whites stole their cattle and Negroes, kept up a continuous outcry to have them driven out altogether. In 1832 the Government persuaded some of the Seminole chiefs to sign a treaty promising mass emigration to Arkansas within three years.

Proudest, craftiest and most daring of Seminole leaders was a brilliant-eyed, strikingly handsome young buck named Osceola. In 1835 the Government Indian Agent, General Wiley Thompson, summoned Seminole chiefs to sign a treaty of immediate emigration. Osceola advanced to the table, contemptuously drove his sheath knife through the paper. General Thompson threw him in chains. Osceola was shortly set free, slew General Thompson. President Jackson promptly launched the Second Seminole War. Quartering the tribe's women and children back in the swamps, Osceola led 1,600 braves in a guerrilla warfare which completely baffled the far larger forces of Federal troops and militia.

In September 1837, having captured a Seminole chief, Major General Thomas S. Jesup persuaded Osceola to meet one of his officers under a flag of truce, treat for peace. Trustingly Osceola advanced with several chiefs and 198 tribespeople. All threw down their guns. When the parley was well started, General Jesup's soldiers leaped from the bushes, captured the Indians without a struggle. Osceola was imprisoned in Charleston, S. C.'s Fort Moultrie where he died after three months, officially of "a quinsy." General Jesup spent the rest of his life trying to justify his black treachery.

The Second Seminole War continued actively for seven years, cost the Government 1,500 men and $40,000,000, drove most of the tribe to a miserable existence in Indian Territory. A stubborn few could not be dislodged from Florida's swamps. Their descendants, some of whom intermarried with Negroes, now number nearly 600. Routed by whites from every desirable acre, they are now scattered deep in the Everglades and Big Cypress Swamp. They live in evil-smelling thatched shacks perched on stilts, fish in the Everglades' black sluggish waters, hunt deer and wild turkey, make a little cash as vegetable pickers, hunting guides, sideshow attractions in amusement parks. Their chief recreation consists of listening to phonograph records, drinking a mixture of moonshine and Sloan's liniment. A Seminole marriage is complete when the bride's family has provided a shirt for the groom; the groom's family, a bed; and the groom has moved into the bride's house. To divorce his wife a Seminole husband simply moves out. Florida "crackers," delighted at having a few humans on whom they can look down, amuse themselves by shooting the Seminoles' hogs.

Because they still consider themselves at war with the U. S., few Seminoles have learned to speak English. Last week an interpreter translated for Secretary Ickes their terms of peace: 200,000 acres and $15 per month apiece.

Said Charlie Cypress: "Formerly I had many grounds to hunt upon."

Said Sam Tommie: "There is no game left for me."

Said Billie Stuart: "It seems I am in a pen."

Said Secretary Ickes: "The Seminoles are a proud and independent people. I do not know whether it will be possible to give them all they ask, but in cooperation with the State of Florida the Administration in Washington will do all in its power to give them the land and the game they require to live the lives of their forefathers." ■

■ RELIGION   OCTOBER 30, 1939

"Wait Till Hitler Comes Over Here"

Fr. Coughlin rouses the rabble

IN NEW YORK CITY, every week, some 30,000 people attend meetings which Jews do well to avoid. At the meetings, held by groups with names like "Christian Front" and "Christian Mobilizers," the streets of upper Manhattan and

The Bronx resound with cries of "Buy Christian," "Down with the Jews," "Wait till Hitler comes over here." Only the left-wing press has paid much attention to these gatherings, although in recent months they have resulted in more than

250 arrests and some 85 actual and suspended sentences. (Example last week: Patrick Kiernan, 38, reliefer; three months in the workhouse for an anti-Semitic speech—"disorderly conduct"—on a Bronx street corner.)

Leadership of the "Christian" groups, if not their rank & file, is largely Irish Catholic. Among numerous Catholic priests who have been disturbed by the participation of Catholics in these groups is Rev. Paul B. Ward, Paulist father, editor of *Wisdom* (monthly Paulist organ). Few weeks ago the October *Wisdom* appeared with a brief story about how a leader of the Christian Mobilizers had gone south to a Ku Klux Klan meeting. Forthwith, Father Ward's office was ransacked. He was warned, anonymously, that his life was in danger. He was informed, by telephone, that his church would be picketed. Father Ward called the police.

Ideological pontiff of the Christian Front, much as he today denies it, is the rabble-rousing baritone of Royal Oak, Mich., Rev. Charles Edward Coughlin. A successful phenomenon of Depression (during which he espoused inflation), a flop in Recovery (in 1936 he backed William Lemke to beat Franklin Roosevelt for President), Radiorator Coughlin began his comeback in Depression II. One Sunday in November last year, he shook his grey-flecked locks and launched into an explanation of why Hitler was renewing his persecutions of the Jews. Naziism, explained Father Coughlin, was a "defense mechanism" against Communism; and Communism was inspired by Jews.

Jews, left-wingers and some Catholics denounced Father Coughlin and his assertions, but his radio audience began to mount. During the winter, a Gallup poll indicated that he had 4,500,000 steady listeners, 15,000,000 occasional ones. At a Nazi Bund rally in Manhattan, Father Coughlin's name drew as many cheers as Hitler's. By summertime, Coughlinites in the East were organized and articulate enough to plan a parade into the "Jewish-Communist" enemy's territory, Manhattan's Union Square. Father Coughlin called them off. There were indications that he knew he had a bull by the tail. The word "Jew" appeared less often in his broadcasts, although it continued to sprinkle the pages of *Social Justice*, of which Father Coughlin pointed out he was only an "editorial counsel."

This week Father Coughlin celebrates his 48th birthday, in a new and spectacular way. For him will be held "Birthday Balls," like those for President Roosevelt. In Brooklyn, a Coughlin stronghold, an "American Citizens Committee" will hold a party whose proceeds (tickets 50¢, box seats $1) will go to Father Coughlin, who will address the party by wire.

From Father Coughlin's critics the cry continues: Why doesn't the Catholic Church crack down on him? The answer is obvious. The Church's ranking leaders undeniably distrust and disapprove of the radio priest, but doing something about him might leave them with a schism on their hands. But what the Church will not do, the U.S. radio industry has attempted. The new National Association of Broadcasters code, if enforced by the 51 stations constituting Father Coughlin's pickup chain, would effectively bar him from the air as a lone-ranging controversialist. One station (WIRE of Indianapolis) has already barred Father Coughlin, but the showdown on all 51 may not come for some months. And before then there may be a new choosing-up of sides. Said the liberal, anti-Coughlin *Christian Century* last week: "We regard this as the worst possible way of dealing with his brand of demagoguery." ∎

Olympic Games

Jesse Owens crashes Adolf Hitler's party

AT THE FIRST MODERN REVIVAL of the Olympic Games in 1896, a little crew of casually assembled athletes foundered through a helter-skelter track meet at Athens. In the four decades since, the modern Olympic Games have become what their founder, Baron Pierre de Coubertin, hoped that they might one day be and what the ancient Olympic Games actually were: World's No. 1 sports event.

Last week in Berlin, daily crowds of 110,000 packed the gigantic new Olympic stadium. Below them cavorted the finest athletes in the world. In the press stand sat 1,500 reporters, hundreds more than customarily report League of Nations doings at Geneva. Whether or not the Olympic Games actually serve their purpose of promoting international understanding remains dubious. That they afford harmless amusement to participants & spectators, a valuable chance for ballyhoo to the nation which holds them, no one is better aware than Realmleader Adolf Hitler, who attended every session except one last week, inspired his loyal Nazi followers to win the unheard of total of five track & field events.

By last week, the track & field events were finished. No. 1 hero of the world's No. 1 sports event was a Cleveland Negro named Jesse Owens. No. 1 heroine, with the possible exception of Mrs. Eleanor Holm Jarrett, because she was not allowed to compete, was a Fulton, Mo., filly named Helen Stephens. The Olympic Games had produced eight deaths, innumerable misunderstandings, enough revenue to repay all running expenses and part of what it would otherwise have cost Germany for barracks for 4,000 soldiers, the best sports arena in the world. Events:

HERO OWENS. In 1924 Finn Paavo Nurmi won three Olympic races. Last week at Berlin, Cleveland's coffee-colored Jesse Owens bettered this achievement. On the first day of competition he broke the world's record for 100 metres in a trial heat (10.2 sec.). On the second day, he won the final in world-record time (10.3). On the third, he won the broad jump with a new Olympic record (26 ft., 5 21/64 in.). On the fourth, he won the 200-metre dash with a new world's record (20.7 sec.) for a track with a turn. Finally, selected for the U. S. 400-metre relay team, he helped it equal the world's record in a trial heat, break it winning the final in 39.8 sec.

In 1933 Owens won both sprints and the broad jump in record time in the U. S. interscholastic championships. In 1935, as an Ohio State sophomore, he broke three world's records and equalled a fourth in a single afternoon. Last week, when his deeds made it apparent that he could continue this routine at least until Olympic competition becomes extra-terrestrial, Negro Owens became the most celebrated single contestant the Olympic Games have had since famed U. S. Indian Jim Thorpe, who was disqualified for professionalism after winning the pentathlon and decathlon in 1912.

At the Owens cabana in the Olympic Village, awed rivals crowded to feel the Owens muscles, get the Owens autograph. In Cleveland Governor Martin L. Davey decreed a Jesse Owens Day. Over the radio, Mrs. Henry Cleveland Owens described her son: "Jesse was always a face boy....When a problem came up, he always faced it." Said Face Boy Owens, before his fourth trip to the Victory Stand to have a laurel wreath stuck on his kinky head, be awarded a minute potted oak tree and the Olympic first prize of a diploma and a silver-gilt medal: "That's a grand feeling standing up there.... I never felt like that before....."

U. S. NEGROES. Before the Games started, U. S. track & field entrants appeared to have a good chance in eleven of the 23 men's events, but no one actually expected them to win that many. Last week, when the track & field events ended, the U. S. had actually won twelve firsts, bettering the record of eleven made by their team in 1932. The individual winners, other than Owens: Archie Williams (400-metre run); John Woodruff (800-metre run); Forrest Towns (110-metre hurdles); Glenn Hardin (400-metre hurdles); Kenneth Carpenter (discuss throw); Cornelius Johnson (high jump); Earle Meadows (pole vault); Glenn Morris (decathlon). Owens, Williams, Woodruff and Johnson are Negroes. So are Ralph Metcalfe, Mack Robinson and David Albritton, who finished second in the 100-metre, 200-metre and high jump, respectively.

Original German theory to explain Negro sport supremacy, prematurely evolved before the Schmeling-Louis prizefight, was that Negroes are not really people. Last week, Realmleader Adolf Hitler conspicuously neglected to invite Negro winners up to shake hands with him in his box, and Nazi newspapers invented an even more facile excuse for Germany's feeble showing of only three winners—Hans Woellke (shot put), Gerhard Stoeck (javelin throw), Karl Hein (hammer throw)—in the men's track & field events by describing the Negroes who between them won half the U. S. total as "a black auxiliary force." Said *Der Angriff*, run by Propaganda Minister Paul Joseph Goebbels: "Actually, the Yankees, heretofore invincible, have been the great disappointment of the games....Without these members of the black race—these auxiliary helpers—a German would have won the broad jump....The fighting power of European athletes, especially the Germans, has increased beyond all comparison..." ■

America went to war—with a segregated army. On edge and fearful of "the yellow peril," FDR's administration abandoned the Constitution and interned hundreds of thousands of patriotic Japanese Americans. Despite the prejudice they endured in America, minority groups fought for their country with distinction: black, Native American and Nisei troops earned the respect of their countrymen and a renewed chance to demand equal rights. President Harry Truman ordered the integration of the army in 1948, but it was through another integration— of the national pastime—that Americans first glimpsed a new age of more equal opportunity for all.

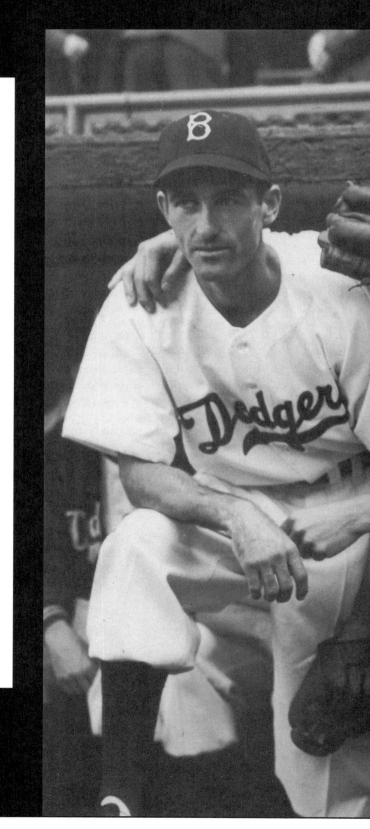

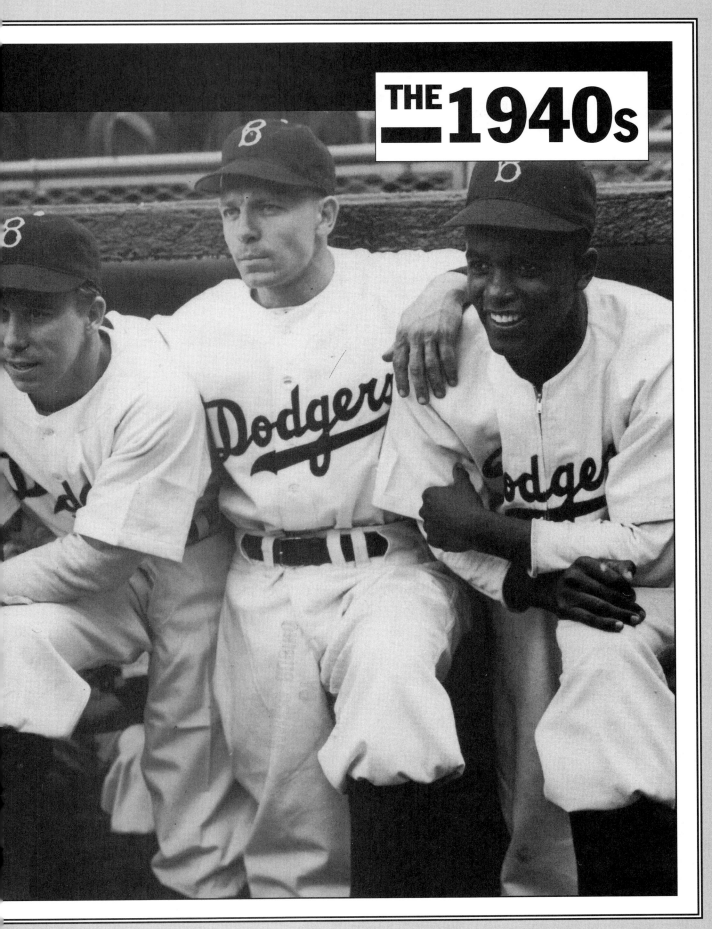

White Man's War?

A segregated army fights for freedom

The Problem

FROM MEMPHIS' BEALE STREET to Harlem's Lenox Avenue, the U.S. Negro press last week suddenly took fire. It blazed up over the Army's No. 1 social problem: what to do with Negro officers and Negro enlisted men. A War Department statement, issued fortnight ago after Franklin D. Roosevelt had talked over The Problem at the White House with Negro leaders, fanned the flames. The policy: that Negroes will get the same kind of military training as whites, but they will get it in separate Negro outfits.

Even Harlem's pro-Roosevelt *Amsterdam News* joined in the outraged hubbub. Jim Crow Army Hit, ran its page 1 banner over a story denouncing the Army's policy. Charge White House Trickery, yammered the Republican Pittsburgh *Courier*. Roosevelt Charged With Trickery in Announcing Jim Crow Army Policy, shrilled the Kansas City *Call*. Along with the War Department's statement many a paper printed the demands made on President Roosevelt fortnight ago by his White House visitors: Secretary Walter White of the National Association for the Advancement of Colored People; President A. Philip Randolph of the Sleeping Car Porters' union; T. Arnold Hill, an assistant in the N. Y. A. Division for Negro Affairs. For the Army's solution of The Problem had brusquely rejected the pivotal demand in the Negroes' seven-part memo to the President, that "existing units of the Army and units to be established should be required to accept and select officers and enlisted personnel without regard to race."

If U. S. Negroes really expected to see the U. S. Army agree to put black and white in the same outfits on an equality basis, they reckoned on a thumping overturn of precedent. Only four Negroes have ever graduated from West Point (none from Annapolis) and today the Army has only two regular Negro line officers: Colonel Benjamin Oliver Davis, commanding officer of Harlem's 369th Coast Artillery (National Guard), and his West Pointer son, Lieut. B. O. Davis Jr., military instructor at Tuskegee Institute. Before 1940's emergency the Army had only four Negro regiments of regulars (two cavalry, two infantry); all are officered by white men. Since July 1, 17 other Negro outfits have been formed (including a regiment of engineers, one of field artillery, twelve truck companies), and some may be officered by men from the 353 Negro reserve officers now on Army lists.

In World War 1, only 10% of the 404,000 Negroes drafted and enlisted for the Army saw service in overseas combat outfits. Except for a few separate regiments (like the 369th, 370th, 371st and 372nd), their record was undistinguished. Some Army men today think Negroes are as good fighting men as whites, but also think they will never be able to prove it until they go into action led by Negro officers, show once & for all that they do not need white leadership.

But to Negro leaders proof of that point was less important last week than establishing the equality of the races in the U. S.'s new Army. So concerned were they with the Jim Crow issue that they subordinated another point, somewhat less than frank, in the War Department's statement. "Negroes," intoned the Army, "are being given aviation training as pilots, mechanics and technical specialists."

Last week the only air training for Negroes was being given by the Civil Aeronautics Authority. CAA has given primary flight training to 100 black college students, qualified 91 for civil licenses, a record as good as the performance of its white students. CAA will take Negroes without racial restrictions among the 45,000 to be trained this year. Meanwhile, belatedly making good on its statement of policy, the War Department last week announced that it would establish Negro Air Corps units as soon as trained personnel could be found, and intimated that the flying officer personnel would come from CAA graduates, mechanics from N. Y. A. school courses. But it will be a long time before an Air Corps outfit is commanded by a Negro, for today there is no trained Negro military pilot in the U. S., not a single Negro commissioned in the Air Corps Reserve.

The U. S. Navy, which enlists Negroes only for mess service, other menial jobs, is less bedeviled than the Army by The Problem. As long as voluntary enlistments continue, the Navy will take no drafted men, will be able to pick & choose. But the 11,000,000 U. S. Negroes are politically potent. If they turn the heat on the Navy, The Problem may then become seagoing, too. ■

Blunder and Precedent

LAST WEEK the War Department, in trying to rectify a political blunder, broke a precedent as old as the Army. The blunder was the Administration's announcement, last month, that Negro soldiers would continue to be segregated from white troops in the expanded U. S. Army. The announcement put every big black community in the country on its ear, set newspapers and mass meetings crying "Jim Crow." Last week the Army did what it could to make amends: upped its only Negro colonel of Regulars to the rank of brigadier general.

Able, tea-colored Benjamin Oliver Davis, whose son, Captain B. O. Davis Jr., is the only other black line officer in the regular service, was the first man of his race to reach general officer rank in the U. S. Army. Leaving his old command, Harlem's 369th Coast Artillery, General Davis will automatically break the Army's segregation rule: his new assignment is command of a new brigade to be composed of the 9th and 10th (colored) Cavalry. All the officers under his command are white men. The Army can still replace them with Negro reserve officers, but that would violate its statement of policy of last month, which also said that Negro regular Army outfits would continue to be commanded by white officers. The Army's easiest way out may be to wait until General Davis reaches retirement age (64) next July. By then the election will be over. ∎

Whose War?

IN PHILADELPHIA, Negro Harry Carpenter was held for treason when he told a Negro Army sergeant: "This is a white man's war, and it's no damn good."

Negroes have fought ably in every U.S. war since the Revolution. In the Civil War, the Union had 170,000 black soldiers under arms. But when the first Negro leader, Frederick Bailey Douglass, asked why they were paid less than white soldiers, President Lincoln temporized. Negroes should be glad they could serve at all, said Mr. Lincoln. They had more to fight for than any white man.

Since World War I, the Negro's status as a U.S. fighting man has gone backward. Of the 1,078,331 Negroes registered for the draft in World War I, more than 34% were drafted (less than 27% of the white men registered were taken). Some 380,000 Negroes served as soldiers—10% of the whole Army. The 292,000 Negro troops the Army expects to have at the end of 1942 will come to 8% of the U.S. armed forces in World War II.

Some of the best U.S. soldiers in 1917-18 were black troops. The famed 15th Infantry (now the 369th Coast Artillery) from Harlem stayed longer under fire (191 days) than any other regiment, yielded no prisoners, gave up no ground, suffered casualties of 40%. Negro veterans still grin delightedly when they recall the "Battle of Henry Johnson," in which a pint-size onetime Red Cap from Albany, N.Y. killed, wounded and routed a party of 25 Germans single-handed.

BARRED GATES. In spite of the shortage of skilled labor, black citizens are unwelcome in many war industries. As the war boom got going last year, President Asa Philip Randolph of the Brotherhood of Sleeping Car Porters planned to forestall discrimination in defense plants by a protest march of 50,000 Negroes on Washington. When he got wind of the plan, Franklin Roosevelt sent for Porter Randolph. After their conference, the President issued an executive order forbidding color discrimination in defense industries. Negroes thought the President had passed a miracle second only to Lincoln's Emancipation Proclamation. The President followed up his order by setting up a Committee on Fair Employment Practice.

FEPC has held innumerable meetings, has sent field agents scooting about, has as yet got few results.

• Of an estimated 3,900,000 unemployed, 800,000 are Negroes (20%), although Negroes constitute only 10% of the total population.

• Last year the Federal Security Administration found jobs for 79,617 unemployed workers. Only 853 were Negroes.

• In Belleville, N.J., 600 girl members of the Chemical & Oil Workers Union threatened to quit if Isolantite, Inc. hired Negro girls. (A.F. of L.'s Frank Fenton retorted by threatening to remove the union's charter.)

• In the constitutions of 24 national and international unions (of which ten are affiliated with A.F. of L.) membership is barred to Negroes. But all C.I.O. unions accept Negroes.

• In Detroit's boom center, Ford lifted a challenge to other defense plants, a hope to Negroes, by admitting

Negroes to its apprentice school, distributing defense jobs proportionately.

U.S. Negroes last week, like all U.S. citizens, were deeply impressed by Japan's successes in Asia. They noted that Japs are not white men. But U.S. Negroes did no cheering for Japan. As individuals, U.S. Negroes were bitterly, resignedly or indifferently conscious that the realities of U.S. life still barred them from full equality of citizenship. Nevertheless, most of them would still prefer to be potential citizens of a fighting democracy than the slaves of a conquering dictatorship.

The 13,500,000 Negroes of the U.S. remained semi-citizens who wanted to be allowed to do their share of working or fighting to keep the U.S. free. ∎

13 Paratroopers

THEIR FACES were daubed with red, black, green and white war paint, their heads shorn except for a scalp lock. They squatted and waited before an incongruous background: a flying field in the smiling English hills.

There were 13 men in this unique parachute unit—twelve Apaches, Mohaves, Navahos, Creeks, Blackfeet, Hopis, and one youngster from Brooklyn who had become a tribesman by the ancient ceremonial of cutting a finger and mingling his blood with that of an Apache.

Beyond the standard paratrooper's armament, they carried the most bizarre equipment ever seen in modern Europe, including nylon garrotes made from stolen glider towropes (deemed more efficient for quiet strangulation than piano wire) and knives almost as thin as hatpins, for penetration of an enemy head just below the ear.

One brave demonstrated the razor sharpness of his machete by clipping tough field grass with lazy swings. Another, carrying steel knuckles crested with sharp spikes, gave the points a final affectionate polishing with emery cloth as he waited for the take-off for France.

Though the official maximum weight for a 24-ft. chute is 280 lbs., some of the Indians in full accoutrement weighed well over 350. No one was willing to make them lighten up.

For a week before invasion they had been encamped near a Ninth Air Force Station, and their presence was perceptible from afar: they had taken an oath at Christmas time not to bathe until D-day. They cooked their own meals over campfires, slept on the ground without blanket or tent.

Familiarized with jujitsu and dirty-fighting tactics devised by thugs of all nations, they feared no man on earth except the few white officers who could lick them in hand-to-hand combat (barring knives, garrotes and guns). Among these were their own jumpmaster, a handsome golden-haired lieutenant who used to sell insurance, and their colonel, a 1938 West Pointer.

When their C-47 troop carrier took off on D-day, a grimy mechanic waved and grinned. "Them poor goddam krauts," said he.

The Indians' D-day assignment was tough enough to match their blood lust—dropping on the peninsula behind Cherbourg and blowing up approach roads to airfields where later paratroopers would land. Word trickled back to their base last week that at least some of them were still alive—and therefore, of course, still fighting. ∎

The Enemy Within?

The war comes home for Japanese Americans

Moving Day for Mr. Nisei

APRIL 6, 1942

PASADENA'S ROSE BOWL looked like a second-hand auto park. In the chill dawn, 140 battered cars and sagging trucks huddled, piled high with furniture, bundles, gardening tools. At 6:30 A.M. they chuffed and spluttered, wheeled into line, and started rolling. Led by a goggled policeman on a motorcycle, a jeep and three command cars full of newsmen, they headed for the dark, towering mountains to the east.

Thus, last week, the first compulsory migration in U.S. history set out for Manzanar, in California's desolate Owens Valley. In the cavalcade were some 300 Japanese aliens and Nisei—U.S. citizens of Japanese blood. They were part of the first mass evacuation from the forbidden strip of West Coast land which Lieut. General John Lesesne DeWitt has made a military zone.

At the old Santa Fe station in downtown Los Angeles

The Nisei took clothes, furniture, garden tools, left liberty behind

another group of 500 aliens and Nisei (all men, as were the Japs who went by motor) boarded a special 13-car Southern Pacific train for Manzanar. A few impassive-faced Japanese women stood on the platform, handed up pop bottles through the open windows, waved good-by with composure. One was a white girl, clutching the hand of a small, wide-eyed, yellow-skinned boy.

DESERT CITY. At the Army "reception center," nine miles beyond Lone Pine, the Japs piled out. They were greeted by 88 Japanese men and girls who went ahead to put the camp in order. In the unfinished, tar-papered dormitories where they will live until the war ends, they made their beds on mattress ticking filled with straw, dined on rice and meat, prunes and coffee, dished out by Japanese cooks.

At Manzanar, General DeWitt may settle as many as 50,000 of the Coast's 112,353 Jap aliens and Nisei. Another 20,000 will be placed on the Colorado River Indian Reservation at Parker, Ariz.

The first emigrants to Manzanar were Japanese plumbers, carpenters, mechanics who will help build the desert city. Wives and children will follow later. Some projects with which the Army may keep its guests busy: laying broad-gauge track on the railway down the valley; driving a highway across the Sierras (nearest all-weather crossing is 400 miles away); farming. They will earn from $50 to $94 a month, with $15 deducted for living expenses. All they forfeit is their freedom. They cannot leave the camp without permission.

"GOD BLESS AMERICA." The Army hoped that most Japs and Nisei would go quietly, of their own accord. Japanese spokesmen said that was wishful thinking: some 90% of the Coast's Japs are destitute, or will be in a few weeks.

Most aliens, far from thinking the Army's haste unseemly, wished last week that General DeWitt would move them faster, before they starve. In San Francisco's Little Tokyo, store fronts were plastered with huge signs, proclaiming: "Evacuation Sale." In one window, under the sign, hung a red-white-&-blue poster: "God Bless America, the Land We Love." Under that, another sign: "Twenty Percent Off."

What kind of people were these Japs and Nisei?

• Seijiro Suchiya, born in Japan, came to Los Angeles 22 years ago with his wife and his infant son to join the fishing fleet at Terminal Island. When FBI men raided the Island two months ago, Seijiro had three grown sons, lived in a clean, comfortable house—from which he could see the U.S. fleet at anchor off San Pedro.

Seijiro's family did not know what had become of Seijiro last week. With eleven other Japanese families, they were packed into the classrooms of a Japanese-language school in Los Angeles. Said Seijiro's oldest son, 23-year-old Takeshi Suchiya, a pre-med at Compton District Junior College when the FBI rounded up his family: "When we stop to think it over, most of us understand the necessity for evacuation. But the immediate reaction is, we have got some rights as Americans....I know my parents are loyal, yet they have been picked up. Anyhow, the whole thing's a mess and we'll just have to take it...."

• Genzo Horino, son of a well-to-do Japanese landowner, set out for the U.S. at 18 with his father's blessing and 5,000 yen, rented ten acres and an old farmhouse near Torrance, Calif., for 27 years grew berries and tomatoes. Genzo retired three years ago, moved into a big, rambling home in Hollywood. There he sat last week, in U.S. clothes but wearing a black skull cap, peacefully smoking a pipe. Two of Genzo's six sons are in the Army. But Son Isamu Horino, 26, is a tough, wiry Nisei boy with a shock of unkempt hair and a stubborn jaw. He never did like the way white citizens treated him. (But he went to school in Japan for a while, did not like the way yellow men treated him either.) Rebel Isamu decided a few years ago to make a lot of money just to prove he was "as damn good as a white."

Said Isamu: "I decided if I was going to be a bastard, I'd be a first-class bastard....I figured I could beat a big bunch of white gardeners out of their business. I did. I acted just like a white man, but I did it better, and my gardens are the best in town." Isamu paid more than $1,000 in income taxes this year; owned four trucks, a half-dozen power-mowers; had three full-time assistants—two Japs and a Mexican; hired white college boys for part-time work. Said Isamu Horino: "Why should we support anything in this country with a whole heart? I don't mean any of us give a damn about Japan. We hope they get licked. But ... nobody ever let us become a real part of this country....If they want to take away all we've got and dump us out in the desert, we've got no choice. But we don't like it....And we're expected to buy bonds, too. Not me!" ∎

Uprooted Japs

Sirs:

Can there be any greater atrocity in the annals of American history than the uprooting of the Japanese families from their homes on the Pacific coast? If these people were allowed to go about their business as honorable, law-abiding Americans, no doubt the majority would behave as such. Treat them as enemy aliens and you may expect anything.

Why not transport all the native-born Italians and Germans and their American-born children to concentration camps in the Midwest? There are probably more saboteurs to the square yard among these groups than there are among the Japanese.

JOHN L. ULMER, D.O.
Toledo, Ohio

Sirs:

The very interesting account of "Moving Day for Mr. Nisei," stated in part: "Thus, last week, the first compulsory migration in U.S. history set out for Manzanar, in California's desolate Owens Valley." Apparently Mr. Nisei was not the first....

The Cherokee were driven by the U.S. Army along the "Trail of Tears" from their mountain hunting paradise to the desolation of Indian territory. History repeats itself.

LYNN H. SKEAN
Ary, Ky.

■

Go for Broke

JUNE 22, 1945

DOWN CONSTITUTION AVENUE this week marched one of the smartest, toughest fighting units the U.S. had ever sent to the battlefield. The USAF-Japanese-units and Regimental Combat Team—all Nisei except for a sprinkling of officers—was home from the wars. On the rain-soaked Ellipse adjoining the White House, the wiry little soldiers, their crisp khaki crumpling to a soggy brown, stood rigidly at attention while President Truman fixed the Presidential Unit Citation banner to the regimental colors.

For the 442nd Regimental Combat Team, the war had been doubly hard. Its men had not only fought the Germans at their defensive best up the spine of Italy and in the Vosges; they had also fought prejudice at home.

Yet the Niseis' record was unexcelled. In 240 combat days, the original 3,000 men and 6,000 replacements collected eight unit citations, one Medal of Honor, 3,600 Purple Hearts and a thousand other decorations. They lived up to their motto, "Go for Broke": no less than 650 of the Purple Hearts had to be sent to next of kin (many of them in relocation centers) because the soldiers were dead. The 442nd also set an unbeatable mark for soldierly behavior; no man in the outfit had ever deserted.

As the regiment's vanguard, 500 strong, was shipped back to the U.S., the men had no idea what sort of welcome they would get. Fellow-soldiers knew they had proved themselves the hardest way of all, but would the folks at home know—or care?

New York gave part of the answer with harbor sirens and a reception committee of skimpily dressed wiggle dancers. Harry Truman and thousands of other civilians gave another part of the answer in Washington this week. As the fighting Nisei headed for their homes, they would get the answer to the rest of Combat Correspondent Terry Shimabukuro's question: "Will we, as Japanese-Americans, come home to something we can call our own?"

■

105 Chinese

Japan asks: Does the U.S. treat Chinese as allies—or "Yellow Peril"?

AMERICA IS CHINA'S ALLY. Americans say they love and admire the Chinese. But can you go to America, can you become citizens? No. Americans don't want you. They just want you to do their fighting. Their Exclusion Act names you and says you are unfit for American citizenship. If Generalissimo Chiang really has influence in America, why has he not had this stigma erased from American law? There will be no such discrimination against you in the Greater East Asia Co-Prosperity Sphere.

Thus last week, by radio, in leaflets and posters, Jap propagandists were hammering at Chinese morale. And they had the U.S. Congress on a tough spot. Before the House Immigration Committee were three bills to modify or repeal Chinese exclusion. If the Committee failed to vote out one of the bills, Chinese feelings would be deeply hurt. If the bill were reported out and passed, the A.F.of L., American Legion and Veterans of Foreign Wars would be very angry with Congress. And if the bill were reported out and rejected, matters would be still worse: it would be a slap in the face of China, whose morale is already suffering from six years of war.

BLANKET BAN. The Immigration Act of 1924 banned all Oriental immigration. What particularly humiliates the Chinese is that, among all Orientals, including Japs, they alone are specifically singled out by name in U.S. law as undesirable citizens. The Chinese Exclusion Act of 1882 was the result of a California labor surplus (thousands of coolies helped build the U.S. railroads). But the Act, long obsolete, is still on the books.

One of the bills before Congress would weasel. It simply repeals specific mentions of the Chinese, leaving them still barred by the general ban. The two others would permit Chinese to enter and become citizens of the U.S. under the quota system. The latter bills immediately raised the specter—mainly in the Hearst press—of a horde of cheap Chinese labor swarming into the U.S. The fact: China's quota would permit the immigration of precisely 105 Chinese a year.

THE "YELLOW PERIL." Standpat "Yellow Peril" opponents of Oriental immigration have been unable to build up 105 Chinese into a menace. Their spokesman, Representative A. Leonard Allen of Louisiana, argues that repeal of the Chinese ban would immediately generate pressure for the admission of all other Orientals (except, of course, Japs). Representative Allen goes further to argue that tens of thousands of Chinese from Hong Kong might come in under the British quota. One reply was a new bill providing that 75% of the quota must be residents of China proper.

A famed Catholic prelate, Bishop Paul Yu-pin, told the Committee: "Should thousands of tanks and airplanes from America to China not be forth-coming immediately, the Chinese people and soldiers perhaps will understand that Allied strategy of global warfare dictates otherwise for the time. But should your honorable committee look unfavorably upon these bills before you today, then I assure you that my country and my people will not be able to understand. It will be a great blow to our morale in China and do irreparable harm to the Allied cause."

But Rear Admiral Harry E. Yarnell, onetime (1936-1939) Commander in Chief of the Asiatic Fleet, made the strongest argument yet for repeal of the obsolete law. He said its repeal would do the Allied cause as much good as the Soviet dissolution of the Third International. ■

Zoot-Suit War

Mexican-American youngsters are targets in L.A.—and where are the police?

Hunting for *Pachucos*: The city gave tacit approval to the mob

FOR TWO NIGHTS the mobs of soldiers and sailors had found poor hunting. In long caravans of cabs and private cars they had toured the Mexican sections, armed with sticks and weighted ropes, crashing into movie houses, looking for zoot-suited *pachucos*, the little Mexican-American youths. But they had found only a few dozen, and not all of them even wore zoot suits. They had broken the jaw of a 12-year-old boy. Said the boy, in the hospital:

"So our guys wear tight bottoms on their pants and those bums wear wide bottoms. Who the hell they fighting, Japs or us?"

One Panzer division of the cab-and-car attack had rolled down a Mexican district side street, past the rows of mean, ramshackle frame houses. But they had only found a few victims to beat. One of them was a 17-year-old Russian boy, Pete Nogikoss, talking on a street corner to two Mexicans. The Mexicans fled. Pete stood still. The sailors beat him to the ground.

Scores of Mexican youths had been stripped of their pants (some of them on the stages of movie houses), beaten and then arrested by the Los Angeles police for "vagrancy" and "rioting." (The police practice was to accompany the caravans in police cars, watch the beatings and then jail the victims. Their orders apparently were to let the Shore Patrol and the Military Police handle the rioting sailors. The service police were futile.)

But now the rioting seemed to be diminishing. The zoot-suiters lay low, the sailors and soldiers had seemingly wreaked sufficient revenge for the several occasions when zoot-hoodlums had attacked and robbed them.

HEARST MOVES IN. But then the press took up the story. The Hearst newspapers, the Los Angeles *Examiner* and the *Herald & Express*, and Harry Chandler's Los Angeles *Times* began to blaze. Late-afternoon editions printed black-faced leads about a purported anonymous call to headquarters: "We're meeting 500 strong tonight and we're going to kill every cop we see." The *Herald & Express* bannered: Zooters Threaten L.A. Police.

THE MOB MOVES IN. That night all Los Angeles stayed downtown to see the fun. When darkness came to the fog-chilled streets, the sidewalks and streets were jammed with expectant servicemen and civilians. Shore patrol cars, Military Police and police and sheriffs' cars patrolled in force.

Scores of cars loaded with soldiers and sailors poured into the area. Soon after dark a mob formed, surged down Broadway, crashed into the Orpheum Theater, went down the aisles shouting for *pachucos* to stand up. In the balcony the mob found 17-year-old Enrico Herrera, sitting with his girl. He and others were dragged downstairs to the street; the citizenry pushed back to give them room while he was beaten and stripped naked. The crowd howled. When the sailors had finished, the police dutifully edged up, took Herrera to the hospital.

The mob went happily down Broadway, repeating in every theater, the Rialto, the Tower, Loew's. Others stopped streetcars, pulled off zooters, Mexicans or just dark-complexioned males. On went the mob, ripping pants, beating the young civilians, into the Arcade, the Roxy, the Cameo, the Broadway, the Central and the New Million Dollar theaters. The mood of officialdom (the Shore Patrol, the Military Police, the city police, the sheriff's office) seemed complaisant.

HOODLUMISM. The mob split all over Los Angeles, to Watts, Belvedere, Boyle Heights, El Monte, Baldwin Park, Montebello, San Gabriel—anywhere that Mexicans lived.

Hearst's *Examiner* kept pounding: "Police Must Clean Up L.A. Hoodlumism." The first paragraph of an editorial said: "Riotous disturbances of the past week in Los Angeles by zoot-suit hoodlums have inflicted a deep and humiliating wound on the reputation of this city."

California's zoot-suit war was a shameful example of what happens to wartime emotions without wartime discipline.

Some of Los Angeles' young Mexicans, organized into zoot-suit "gangs" that were the equivalent of boys' gangs almost anywhere, had got out of hand: they had robbed and used their knives on some lone sailors on dark side streets. But probably the trouble could have been ended right there. One who thought so was Eduardo Quevedo, a plump, cigar-chewing, shock-headed amateur sociologist, president of the Coordinating Council for Latin Americans, member of the Citizens' Committee on Latin American youth.

Eight months ago, Goodman Quevedo went to work to stop youthful hoodlumism, started a kind of grown-up Boys Club for the zooters. He knew that they represented a basic American problem: the second generation. Their fathers and mothers were still Mexicans at heart. They themselves were Americans—resented and looked down on by other Americans. Jobless, misunderstood in their own homes and unwelcome outside them, they had fallen into the companionship of misery. They dressed alike, in the most exaggerated and outlandish costume they could afford: knee-length coats, peg-top trousers, yard-long watch chains, "ducktail" haircuts.

If the *pachucos* had asked for trouble, they got more than was coming to them last week. The military authorities were notably lax (all shore and camp leave could easily have been canceled), the Los Angeles police apparently looked the other way. The press, with the exception of the *Daily News* and Hollywood *Citizen-News*, helped whip up the mob spirit. And Los Angeles, apparently unaware that it was spawning the ugliest brand of mob action since the coolie race riots of the 1870s, gave its tacit approval. ■

Winter of Death?

A proud people face starvation

Hunger Stalks the "Hogan"   NOVEMBER 3, 1947

AS THE CHILL OF AUTUMN DESCENDED on their piñon-dotted desert lands last week, the Navajo Indians prepared their hearts for punishment at the hands of their old enemy, the United States of America. When winter came—the 84th winter since Kit Carson had defeated them in honorable war—it seemed almost certain that many of them were to die.

It was a difficult thing for the Navajos to understand. The U.S. had had its chance to kill them after their surrender in 1864. Blue-clad, tobacco-chewing U.S. cavalrymen had rounded them up, marched them like cattle 300 miles from Arizona Territory to New Mexico's Fort Sumner, kept them prisoners for four years. But when the Navajos agreed to peace "from this day forward," they had been freed and helped to start a new life.

They were given 3,500,000 arid, mesa-studded acres in Arizona and New Mexico; a reservation which was gradually expanded until it was almost three times the size of Massachusetts. The tribe grew from 8,000 to 56,000 people. They had been encouraged to build a rude economy on sheep-raising; as the years passed, they accumulated flocks totaling over a million animals. There was mutton to eat and wool to weave, and silver jewelry for the wrists of their women.

But in 1933 the Government discovered that its encouragement of sheep-raising was a grave mistake. The Navajo country was so disastrously overgrazed that the land was washing away with every rain and blowing away with every wind. The U.S. ordered the Indians to begin doing away with their flocks.

SOLDIER'S PAY. At first, the enormous change in the Navajos' way of life did not work insuperable hardship. During the prewar years, many a tribesman worked on CCC projects. After Pearl Harbor, more than 12,000 got wartime jobs off the reservation, and 3,600 young men went into the armed services and sent their pay back home.

But when the war ended the jobs ended; with living costs mounting, all but a handful trickled back to the reser-

vation. The Government, which had all but destroyed the Navajos' means of livelihood, did nothing to help them find new ways of making a living.

Insulated from the 20th Century by the desert and by neglect, they still live, for the most part, as they did in the 1860s. Their women wear flowing skirts copied from those worn by wives of frontier cavalry officers. Their shelter is still the "hogan," a windowless, one-room log structure with a hole in the dirt-covered roof to let out smoke. They still live far from streams because unfriendly spirits inhabit them; most must haul their water from one to 15 miles.

They are among the most destitute and underprivileged of U.S. minorities. They have no vote. About two-thirds know no English (there are schools for only 7,000 of their 24,000 children). The Navajos' tuberculosis rate is 14 times that of the U.S. as a whole, but there are only 182 hospital beds for their t.b. patients. There are too few doctors, only two dentists, only two field nurses on the reservation.

BREAD & COFFEE. But last week these deprivations seemed like minor matters. Great numbers of the Navajos are facing starvation. Only 161 of their 11,117 families own as many as 200 sheep—the number needed to maintain a mere subsistence level of living. Without big irrigation projects (which could make the reservation capable of supporting 35,000 people at most), their desolate lands are almost useless for agriculture.

Last week, the Office of Indian Affairs was doing its feeble best to bring in some food. It promised to ship two carloads of potatoes a month. But from 25,000 to 30,000 Navajos were lingering in the state between malnutrition and starvation. The whole tribe's diet averaged only 1,200 calories (the U.S. average: 3,450) and many have nothing to eat but bread and coffee. Assistant Secretary of the Interior William E. Warne visited the reservation and last week announced a ten-year, $80 million plan for solving the Navajo problem.

But all this meant nothing if Congress did not vote the

money. And the Navajos had little faith in high-sounding plans. The Government had welshed on its promises before. Last year, a group of old men had gone to Congress and asked: "What is to be done with the Navajo people?" Congress had replied by doing nothing.

And even if Congress were to change its heart, there was no likelihood that it could do so before the regular session in January. By January, if the winter was hard, there would be snowdrifts on the reservation and many of the children and old men would be dead. ■

Reprieve

DECEMBER 22, 1947

SHOCKED AT THE DISCOVERY that the Navajo Indians face starvation and even death this winter, the nation suddenly began sending them relief. The American Red Cross appropriated $100,000 for "immediate stopgap aid," rushed disaster relief workers to the barren Navajo country.

A Navajo Trail Relief Caravan Association gathered up food and clothing in California, started seven truckloads on the way to the reservation. Utah citizens helped too. Congress, conscience-stricken after neglectful years, voted a $2,000,000 relief fund for the Navajo and Hopi tribes. ■

■ RACES

Farewell to the Jim Crow Army

A. Philip Randolph—and Harry Truman—integrate the military

Face the Music

APRIL 12, 1948

IN THE BITTER ideological war between Communism and democracy, too many Americans forget what the Communists never let others forget—that democracy in the U.S. is far from perfect. Last week those Americans got a jolting reminder from beefy, deep-voiced A. Philip Randolph, president of the sleeping car porters' union.

Testifying before the Senate Armed Services Committee, Randolph declared bluntly: if a draft like that of World War II was enacted, it would result in "mass civil

disobedience" on the part of U.S. Negroes. Said he: "Negroes have reached the limit of their endurance when it comes to going into another Jim Crow Army to fight another war for democracy—a democracy they have never gotten." Grant Reynolds, chairman of the Committee against Jim Crow in Military Service and Training, soberly agreed.

Randolph demanded abolition of all racial discrimination in the armed services and under U.M.T. He minced no words: "To the rank-&-file Negro in World War II, Hitler's racism posed a sufficient threat for him to submit to the Jim Crow Army abuses. But this factor…is not present in the power struggle between Stalin and the U.S.… Since we cannot obtain an adequate congressional forum for our grievances, we have no other recourse…."

The Senators were shocked. Oregon's Wayne Morse asked whether Randolph realized that such civil disobedience would probably be prosecuted as treason. He did, and added: "We would be willing to absorb the violence, absorb the terrorism, face the music, and take whatever comes." ■

First Step

IT WAS NEARLY A YEAR since President Truman had ordered an end to discrimination in the Armed Forces, but with few exceptions, the Negro in uniform still had to eat Jim Crow and live in a second-class world. Prodded again by the White House, Secretary of Defense Louis Johnson ordered the Army, Navy & Air Force to tell what they had done to carry out the Commander in Chief's order. Last week the answers were in.

The Army & Navy, Johnson decided, had pussyfooted; he ordered the admirals and generals to give him "additional clarifying information" about their programs. The Air Force came off better. As a first step, the Air Force said that within ten days it would begin disbanding its all Negro 332 Fighter Wing at Lockbourne Air Force Base in Ohio. By the end of the year its 2,000 men would be sprinkled through the Air Force; other Negro units in the

Air Force, but not all of them, would be broken up in the same way.

The Navy insisted that it had already "integrated" its 17,500 Negroes, but it was a strange sort of integration: 10,500 of them were steward's mates in mess halls, and only five were officers. In the Marine Corps there are about 1,500 Negroes, none of them officers. The Army has given its 71,189 Negroes better assignments, more chances for promotion (there are 1,267 Negro Army officers), but all along the line Negroes and whites have been generally segregated.

Whether the Air Force really meant to end discrimination remained to be seen. "There won't be an end to segregation in the services," remarked one Negro officer, "until they call a roll some day and you can look and see black & white, black & white. It's a long way off." ■

"The Most Dangerous Negro"

WITH A RICH BARITONE VOICE that seemed destined to command, an imperturbability under fire, a refusal to bend with the times or the fashions, A. Philip Randolph overcame opposition simply by being himself. The first national labor leader among American blacks, he forged the Pullman porters into a powerful union and pushed two Presidents into conceding crucial rights by threatening a march on Washington and resistance to the draft. Relatively inactive for many years before his death at 90

last week in Manhattan, Randolph seemed remote and perhaps irrelevant to younger civil rights leader, but there are scarcely any nonviolent tactics in the whole arsenal of protest that he did not employ.

Asa Philip's father, James, a minister in the African Methodist Episcopal Church in Crescent City, Fla., liked to recall the great days of Reconstruction, when blacks served in Congress. The boy was fired with a determination to recover that glory, and he learned early that there was no

BRIDGES AND BORDERS   51 more potent weapon than the human voice. "I always liked to talk," he admitted. "Dad spoke beautifully and clearly. A word like 'responsibility' trembled with meaning the way he pronounced it." Though Randolph's youthful ambition to become an actor was thwarted by his parents, he memorized several of Shakespeare's tragedies and loved to recite them with rolling cadences.

After graduating from high school in Jacksonville, Randolph went north to the promised land of Harlem, which fell considerably short of expectations. He took odd jobs, attended night school at New York City College, and started reading Karl Marx aloud with the same enthusiasm that he showed for Shakespeare. Feeling that he now had an economic explanation for racial injustice, he joined others on the traditional soapbox to orate, as he put it, on "everything from the French Revolution and the history of slavery, to the rise of the working class. It was one of the great intellectual forums of America." He also started a radical magazine, *The Messenger*, which questioned why Negroes should fight in World War I when they were denied freedom at home. The Woodrow Wilson Administration, which moved to segregate the civil service, labeled Randolph the "most dangerous Negro in America." He was arrested in the same summer as Socialist Leader Eugene Debs, and spent two days in jail.

Stubbornly independent, Randolph was not swept up in the ideological currents of his time, resisting both Communism and the black nationalism of Jamaican Organizer Marcus Garvey. He kept his own counsel, shunning Harlem's high society and enjoying the company of his wife Lucille, a former beauty parlor operator whose sprightliness contrasted with his own solemnity.

Then, in 1925, he was approached by five Pullman porters who asked him to help organize their fledgling union. Randolph, whose earlier attempts to organize workingmen had largely failed, at first said no. He was not even a member of that fraternity that shined the shoes and cleaned the cuspidors of traveling America. But he soon saw his mission. The outraged Pullman Co. tried to crush the movement; even Negro preachers and newspapers fulminated against the union. But for ten trying years, Randolph exhorted porters across the country. Finally, Pullman capitulated in 1937 and signed its first contract with the Brotherhood of Sleeping Car Porters. Randolph was confirmed in the affectionate title of "Chief."

Now a recognized black leader, Randolph began to take stands on national issues. On the eve of World War II, he was stung by the fact that defense industries were deliberately excluding blacks from employment. After numerous conferences led nowhere, he threatened a mass march on Washington. He was hastily summoned to the White House, where President Roosevelt tried to outtalk him. "He kept cutting in, monopolizing the conversation," complained Randolph, who was not used to such treatment. Randolph refused to budge until an exasperated F.D.R.

A. Philip Randolph in 1937: the "Chief" battled both FDR and Truman

finally signed an Executive order banning discrimination in defense industries and Government employment.

During the buildup of the cold war in 1948, Randolph once again seized the opportunity to press for change. In an encounter with President Harry Truman that was just as contentious as the one with Roosevelt, Randolph insisted on eliminating segregation in the armed forces; otherwise, he warned that blacks would never bear arms again for their country. "I wish you hadn't made that statement," retorted Truman. "I didn't like it at all." But he, too, eventually capitulated and issued an Executive order banning discrimination in the military "as rapidly as possible."

In later years, as the civil rights scene changed, as the Brotherhood of Sleeping Car Porters declined along with the nation's railways, Randolph's reputation was eclipsed by that of Martin Luther King Jr. and other black leaders. But he was still an insistent voice for moderation in the background. "Don't get emotional," cautioned the man who was always able to exert pressure without getting personally involved. Though he had often been critical of the AFL-CIO for its treatment of black members, he remained totally loyal to trade unionism as a salvation for social wrongs. "We never separated the liberation of the white workingman from the liberation of the black workingman," he emphasized. Whenever a cause needed a symbol of integrity, Randolph was sure to be called—and sure to be there. ∎

In Egypt Land

A great artist fights discrimination—with a song

Go tell it on the mountain,
Over the hills and everywheah;
Go tell it on the mountain,
That Jesus Christ is aborn.

AT SALZBURG, backdropped by magical mountains, where Austria's great musical festivals were held before the war, and where he first heard Marian Anderson sing, Arturo Toscanini cried: "Yours is a voice such as one hears once in a hundred years."

Toscanini was hailing a great artist, but that voice was more than a magnificent personal talent. It was the religious voice of a whole religious people—probably the most God-obsessed (and man-despised) people since the ancient Hebrews.

White Americans had withheld from Negro Americans practically everything but God. In return the Negroes had enriched American culture with an incomparable religious poetry and music, and its only truly great religious art—the spiritual.

This religious and esthetic achievement of Negro Americans has found profound expression in Marian Anderson. She is not only the world's greatest contralto and one of the very great voices of all time, she is also a dedicated character, devoutly simple, calm, religious. Manifest in the tranquil architecture of her face is her constant submission to the "Spirit, that dost prefer before all temples the upright heart and pure."

UP FROM PHILADELPHIA. Thanks to the ostracism into which they are born, Negro Americans live very deeply to themselves. They look out upon, and shrewdly observe, the life around them, are rarely observed by it. They are not evasive about their lives; many are simply incapable of discussing them.

The known facts about Marian Anderson's personal life are few. She was born (in Philadelphia) some 40 years ago (she will not tell her age). Her mother had been a schoolteacher in Virginia. Her father was a coal & ice dealer. There were two younger sisters.

When she was twelve, her father died. To keep the home together, Mrs. Anderson went to work. Miss Anderson says that the happiest moment of her life came the day that she was able to tell her mother to stop working. Later she bought her mother a two-story brick house on Philadelphia's South Martin Street. She bought the house next door for one of her sisters.

Miss Anderson's childhood seems to have been as untroubled as is possible to Negro Americans. In part, this was due to the circumstances of her birth, family, and natural gift. In part, it was due to the calm with which she surmounts all unpleasantness. If there were shadows, she never mentions them. Perhaps the most characteristic fact about her childhood is that Marian disliked bright colors and gay dresses as much as her sisters loved them.

MARIAN ANDERSON
The Big Wheel moved by faith.
(Religion)

Shortly after her father's death, Marian Anderson was "converted." Her mother is a Methodist. But Marian was converted in her father's Union Baptist Church, largely because the late Rev. Wesley G. Parks was deeply interested in music, loved his choirs and encouraged any outstanding singer in them. At 13, Marian was singing in the church's adult choir. She took home the scores, and sang all the parts (soprano, alto, tenor, bass) over & over to her family until she had learned them. Since work is also a religion to her, Miss Anderson considers this one of the most important experiences of her life. She could then sing high C like a soprano.

At 15, she took her first formal music lesson. At 16, she gave her first important concert, at a Negro school in Atlanta. From then on, her life almost ceases to be personal. It is an individual achievement, but, as with every Negro, it is inseparable from the general achievement of her people. It was the congregation of the Union Baptist Church that gave Miss Anderson her start. Then a group of interested music lovers gave a concert at her church, collected about $500 to pay for training her voice under the late Philadelphia singing teacher, Giuseppe Boghetti.

In 1924, she won the New York Stadium contest (prize: the right to appear with the New York Symphony Orchestra). In 1930, she decided that she must study in Germany. When she had perfected her lieder, songs by Schubert, Brahms, Wolf, she gave her first concert on the Continent. It cost her $500 (the Germans explained that it was customary for Americans to pay for their own concerts). She never paid again.

Applause followed her through Norway and Sweden. In Finland, Composer Jean Sibelius offered her coffee, but after hearing her sing, cried: "Champagne!" In Paris, her first house was "papered." From her second concert, enthusiasts were turned away in droves. She swept through South America.

THE TROUBLE I'VE SEEN. In the U.S. the ovation continued. Only one notably ugly incident marred her triumph. In Washington, the management of Constitution Hall, owned by the Daughters of the American Revolution, announced that it would be unable to lease the hall on the date which Sol Hurok, Miss Anderson's manager, had asked for. The refusal resulted in Eleanor Roosevelt's resignation from the D.A.R. and an enormous ground swell of sympathy for Miss Anderson and her people. Miss Anderson, who has carefully kept herself and her art from being used for political purposes, said nothing.

But Washington heard her. She sang, first in the open air in front of the Lincoln Memorial. Later the D.A.R. leased her Constitution Hall, and she sang to a brilliant white and Negro audience. She had insisted only that there should be no segregation in the seating. Nobody knows the trouble that an incident like this one causes to a spirit like Marian Anderson's. No doubt such things are in her mind when she says, with typical understatement: "Religion, the treasure of religion helps one, I think, to face the difficulties one sometimes meets."

For this greatly gifted American, pouring out the riches of her art to houses that are sold out weeks in advance, could not for a long time travel about her country like her fellow citizens. She has given concerts in the South, where her voice is greatly admired (and where she avoids Jim Crow by traveling in drawing rooms on night trains). Even in the North, she could not until fairly recently stay at most good hotels. In the South, she must still stay with friends. In New York City, she used to leave frantically applauding audiences to sleep at the Harlem Y.W.C.A. Then Manhattan's Hotel Algonquin, longtime rendezvous of U.S. literati, received her. Now most other Northern hotels have also opened their doors.

Usually, Miss Anderson travels with six pieces of luggage, one of which contains her electric iron (she presses her own gowns before a concert), and cooking utensils (she likes to prepare snacks for herself and she has had some unpleasant experiences with hotel dining rooms).

AGRARIAN PROBLEMS. In 1943 Miss Anderson married Orpheus Fisher, an architect who works in Danbury, Conn. Now they live, not far from Danbury, on a beautiful, 105-acre farm, "Marianna." Inside, the handsome, white frame, hillside house has been remodeled by Architect Fisher. He also designed the big, good-looking studio in which Miss Anderson practices.

When not on tour or practicing, Miss Anderson dabbles in farming. She sells grade-A vegetables to the local market, regrets that Marianna, like many farms run by hired help, costs more than it brings in. And there are other problems in the agrarian life. This year, Miss Anderson was much puzzled when the big (but unbred) daughter of her registered Guernsey cow did not give milk. "Heifers have to be freshened before you can milk them," she explains with some astonishment. "Did you know that?"

The question measures the very real distance she has traveled from the peasant roots of her people. But, as she has traveled, she has taken to new heights the best that Negro Americans are. For the Deep River of her life and theirs runs in the same religious channel. In her life, as in the spiritual, the Big Wheel moves by faith. With a naturalness impossible to most people, she says: "I do a good deal of praying."

GIFT FROM GOD. For to her, her voice is directly a gift from God, her singing a religious experience. This is true of all her singing (she is preeminently a singer of classical music). It is especially true of her singing of Negro spirituals. She does not sing many, and only those which she feels are suited to her voice or which, like *Crucifixion*, her favorite, move her deeply.

There are lovers of spirituals who do not care for the highly arranged versions that Miss Anderson sings, or the finished artistry with which she sings them. But if something has been lost in freshness and authenticity, much has been gained by the assimilation of these great religious songs to the body of great music. For they are the soul of the Negro people, and she has taken that soul as far as art can take it.

As the thousands who have heard her can testify, Miss Anderson's singing of spirituals is unforgettable. She stands simply, but with impressive presence, beside the piano. She closes her eyes (she always sings with her eyes closed). Her voice pours out, soft, vast, enveloping:

They crucified my Lord,
An' He never said a mumblin' word;
They crucified my Lord,
An' He never said a mumblin' word.
Not a word, not a word, not a word.

Audiences who have heard Miss Anderson sing *Crucifixion* have sometimes been too awed to applaud. They have sensed that they are participants in an act of creation—the moment at which religion informs art, and makes it greater than itself.

BIRTH OF THE SOUL. The theme of the greatest music is always the birth of the soul. Words can describe, painting can suggest, but music alone enables the listener to participate, beyond conscious thought, in this act. The spirituals are perhaps the greatest single burst of such inspiration, communicated, not through deafness, but through the darkness of minds which knew nothing of formal music and very little of the language they were singing.

Professional musicians and musicologists are still locked in hot debate about the musical origins of the spirituals and the manner of their creation. One simple fact is clear—they were created in direct answer to the Psalmist's question: How shall we sing the Lord's song in a strange land? For the land in which the slaves found themselves was strange beyond the fact that it was foreign. It was a nocturnal land of vast, shadowy pine woods, vast fields of cotton whose endless rows converged sometimes on a solitary cabin, vast swamps reptilian and furtive—a land alive with all the elements of lonely beauty, except compassion. In this deep night of land and man, the singers saw visions; grief, like a tuning fork, gave the tone, and the Sorrow Songs were uttered.

Perhaps, in little unpainted churches or in turpentine clearings, the preacher, who soon became the pastor and social leader of his wretched people, gave the lead:

Way over yonder in the harvest fiel'—
The flock caught the vision too:
Way up in the middle of the air,
The angel shovin' at the chariot wheel,
Way up in the middle of the air.
O, yes, Ezekiel saw the wheel,
Way up in the middle of the air.

Ezekiel saw the wheel,
Up in the middle of the air
The Big Wheel moved by faith,
The Little Wheel moved by the grace of God,
A wheel in a wheel,
Up in the middle of the air.

SOUGHING WIND. It was a theological image splendid beyond any ever conceived on this continent. For a great wind of the spirit soughed through the night of slavery and, as in Ezekiel's vision, on the field of dead hope the dry bones stirred with life.

They kept stirring as, through the dismal years, the great hymnal testimonies moaned forth. Sometimes they were lyric visions of deliverance:

Swing low, sweet chariot,
Comin' for to carry me home;
I look'd over Jordan,
And what did I see,
Comin' for to carry me home,
A band of angels comin' after me,
Comin' for to carry me home.

Sometimes they were statements of bottomless sorrow:

Nobody knows de trouble I've seen,
Nobody knows but Jesus.
Sometimes they were rumbling adjurations:
Go down, Moses,
Way down in Egypt land,
Tell ol' Pharaoh
To let my people go.

Sometimes they were simple longings:

Deep River, my home is over Jordan,
Deep River, Lord,
I want to cross over into camp ground.

Sometimes they were unsurpassed paeans of death:

Ezekiel weep, Ezekiel moan,
Flesh come acreepin' off ol' Ezekiel's bones,
Church, I know you goin' to miss me when I'm gone.
When I'm gone, gone, gone.
When I'm gone to come no more,
Church, I know you goin' to miss me when I'm gone.

The Magnificat of their music has sometimes obscured the poetry of the spirituals. There are few religious poems of any people that can equal this one:

I know moon-rise, I know star-rise,
I lay dis body down.

I walk in de moonlight, I walk in de starlight,
To lay dis body, heah, down....
I lie in de grave an' stretch out my arms,
I lay dis body, heah, down.
I go to judgment in de evenin' of de day,
When I lay dis body down.

The problem of the white American and the Negro American has rarely been more simply evoked than in those last lines. The problem could be explained (and must in part be solved) in political, social and economic terms. But it is deeper than that, and so must its eventual solution be.

Well might all Americans, at Christmas, 1946, ponder upon the fact that it is, like all the great problems of mankind, at bottom a religious problem, and that the religious solution must be made before any other solutions could be effective. It will, in fact, never be solved exclusively in human terms.

Of the possible meaning of Negro Americans to all white Christians, Historian Arnold J. Toynbee wrote (in his monumental work-in-progress, A Study of History): "The Negro appears to be answering our tremendous challenge with a religious response which may prove in the event, when it can be seen in retrospect, to bear comparison with the ancient Oriental's response to the challenge from his Roman masters.... Opening a simple and impressionable mind to the Gospels, he has divined the true nature of Jesus' mission. He has understood that this was a prophet who came into the world not to confirm the mighty in their seat but to exalt the meek and the humble.... The Syrian slave-immigrants who once brought Christianity into Roman Italy performed the miracle of establishing a new religion which was alive in the place of an old religion which was already dead. It is possible that the Negro slave-immigrants who have found Christianity in America may perform the greater miracle of raising the dead to life. With their child-like intuition and their genius for giving spontaneous esthetic expression to emotional religious experience, they may perhaps be capable of rekindling the cold grey ashes of Christianity which have been transmitted to them by us, until in their hearts the divine fire glows again. It is thus, perhaps, if at all, that Christianity may conceivably become the living faith of a dying civilization for the second time. If this miracle were indeed to be performed by an American Negro Church, that would be the most dynamic response to the challenge of social penalization that had yet been made by Man."

Go tell it on the mountain,
Over the hills and everywheah;
Go tell it on the mountain,
That Jesus Christ is aborn. ■

Rookie of the Year

Jackie Robinson breaks baseball's color barrier

IT WAS ONLY A MONTH since Speedster Enos Slaughter of the St. Louis Cardinals, galloping into first base, had spiked First Baseman Jackie Robinson. Jackie, the first avowed Negro in the history of big-league baseball, looked at his ripped stocking and bleeding leg. It might have been an accident, but Jackie didn't think so. Neither did a lot of others who saw the play. Jackie set his teeth, and said nothing. He didn't dare to.

Last week the Brooklyn Dodgers faced the Cards again, and this time the pennant—and the Dodgers' none-too-healthy 4-1/2-game lead—was at stake. The Cards, somewhat housebroken descendants of the rough-&-tumble Gashouse Gang, were fighting back, late and hard. In the second inning, Jackie Robinson was spiked again—this time by trigger-tempered Catcher Joe Garagiola.

Next inning, at the plate, there was a face-to-face exchange of hot words between Robinson and Garagiola—the kind of rough passage that fans appreciatively call a "rhubarb." Umpire "Beans" Reardon hastily stepped between the two and broke it up. That was the end of it: no fisticuffs on the field, no rioting in the stands. But it was a sign, and an important one, that Jackie had established himself as a big leaguer. He had earned what comes free to every other player: the right to squawk.

That change of attitude showed, as nothing else could, the progress of Jackie Roosevelt Robinson in the toughest

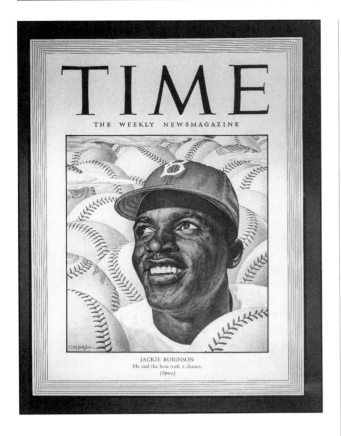

TIME
THE WEEKLY NEWSMAGAZINE

JACKIE ROBINSON
He and the boss took a chance.
(Sport)

first season any ballplayer has ever faced. He had made good as a major leaguer, and proved himself as a man. Last week *The Sporting News*, baseball's trade paper, crowned him the rookie of the year. *The Sporting News* explained, carefully and a little grandiloquently, that it had made the choice solely on the basis of "stark baseball values." Wrote Editor J. G. Taylor Spink:

"Robinson was rated and examined solely as a freshman player in the big leagues—on the basis of his hitting, his running, his defensive play, his team value. The sociological experiment that Robinson represented, the trailblazing he did, the barriers he broke down did not enter into the decision."

The "sociological experiment" may not have been foremost in Taylor Spink's mind, but it was never out of Jackie's. He, his teammates and the National League had broken baseball's 60-year color line. Only two years had passed since Rogers Hornsby declared, and baseball know-it-alls everywhere had nodded in assent: "Ballplayers on the road live close together...it won't work."

WOBBLING RABBIT. The man who had made it work is a well-muscled, pigeon-toed, 28-year-old rookie from Pasadena, Calif., who, along with Glenn Davis and Babe Didrikson Zaharias, is one of the great all-round athletes of his day.

He looks awkward, but isn't. He stops and starts as though turned off & on with a toggle switch. He seems to

hit a baseball on the dead run. Once in motion, he wobbles along, elbows flying, hips swaying, shoulders rocking—creating the illusion that he will fly to pieces with every stride. But once he gains momentum, his shoulders come to order and his feet skim along like flying fish. He is not only jackrabbit fast, but about one thought and two steps ahead of every base-runner in the business. He beats out bunts, stretches singles into doubles. Once Jackie made second on a base-on-balls; he saw that the catcher had lost the ball, so he just kept on going.

He has stolen 26 bases this season, more than any other National Leaguer. He dances and prances off base, keeping the enemy's infield upset and off balance and worrying the pitcher. The boys call it "showboat baseball." He is not, in his first year, the greatest baserunner since Ty Cobb, but he is mighty good. Cobb made a practice of coming in with spikes aimed at anyone brave enough to get in his way. It wouldn't have been politic for Jackie to do it that way very often. Robinson's base running, which resembles more the trickiness of "Pepper" Martin is a combination of surprise, timing and speed. Says Jackie: "Daring...that's half my game."

TURNSTILE SOCIOLOGY. Jackie's daring on the baselines has been matched by shrewd Branch Rickey's daring on the color line. Rickey gave Robinson his chance. As boss of the Brooklyn Dodgers, Rickey is a mixture of Phineas T. Barnum and Billy Sunday, who is prone to talk piously of the larger and higher implications of what he is doing. There were large implications of course, in signing Jackie Robinson, but the influence on the box office was a lot easier to figure. Jackie Robinson has pulled about $150,000 in extra admissions this season.

Wherever the Dodgers have played Negroes have turned out in force to see their hero. In Chicago, where Negro fans sported Jackie Robinson buttons, Jackie's fans came early and brought their lunch. In Jim Crowish St. Louis, where Negroes must sit in the right-field pavilion, the Robinson rooting section was more noticeable. Their adulation embarrassed Robbie; it made it harder for him to act like just another ballplayer. Rickey had promised to treat Jackie "just like any other rookie," and he certainly did on the payroll. Though he may have to pay Jackie more next season, so far Rickey has paid the crowd-pulling rookie-of-the-year only $5,000. Under league rules that is the least that the poorest rookie can be paid.

This week, as the Dodgers raced toward the finish seven games ahead, it was at least arguable that Jackie Robinson had furnished the margin of victory. The Dodgers are certainly not a one-man ball club. They have a bull-necked powerhouse of a catcher named Bruce Edwards, 24, whose special talents are steadiness and hustle. In Pee Wee Reese and Eddie Stanky, both short of height but long on skill, they have the best keystone combination in the league. The Dodgers also have a special affection for 34-year-old relief pitcher Hugh Casey, who has come onto the hill to save game after game, and is held in higher esteem by his team mates than strong-arm Ralph Branca, the Dodgers' only 20-game winner. And of course there is Dixie Walker, the "Peepul's Cherce," who at 36 still hits when it will do the most good—with men on base. In a locker-room gab-fest a few weeks ago, the Dodgers agreed among themselves that Jackie Robinson was the team's third most valuable player—behind Edwards and Reese.

NO DRINK, NO SMOKE. Branch Rickey, the smartest man in baseball, had looked hard and waited long to find a Negro who would be his race's best foot forward, as well as a stout prop for a winning ball team. Rickey and his men scouted Robinson until they knew everything about him but what he dreamed at night. Jackie scored well on all counts. He did not smoke (his mother had asthma and cigaret fumes bothered her); he drank a quart of milk a day and didn't touch liquor; he rarely swore; he had a service record (as Army lieutenant in the 27th Cavalry) and two years of college (at U.C.L.A.). He had intelligence, patience and willingness. He was aware of the handicaps his race encounters, but he showed it not by truculence or bitterness, and not by servility, but by a reserve that no white man really ever penetrated. Most important of all Robinson's qualifications, he was a natural athlete. Says Rickey: "That's what I was betting on."

PEPPER STREET GANGMAN. It ran in the family. His older brother, Mack, was second in the 200-meter run at the Berlin Olympics in 1936. Jackie was a broad-jumper who once set a Southern California junior college record of 25 ft. 6-1/2 in.

The Robinson family—four boys and a girl—grew up on Pepper Street in the poor section of well-to-do Pasadena. They never knew their father (mother still doesn't talk about him). To support the kids, mother Robinson took in washing & ironing. Jackie, the youngest, was a charter member of the Pepper Street Gang, half a dozen Negroes and three or four American-Japanese who liked to break street lamps and watch the changing colors of the shattered bulbs. "It was awful pretty," recalls Jackie.

He played softball on the corner lot with the gang, occasionally earned pocket money by sneaking onto neighboring golf courses to retrieve lost balls. He could outrun the gang—and the cops—every time. But a stern talk from Ma Robinson put him out of business. She was, and is, a fervent Methodist who can be volubly graphic on the subject of hell.

MAN IN MOTION. But Jackie could take care of himself. At U.C.L.A. he was one of the slickest halfbacks who ever put on cleats. His ball-carrying average: a remarkable twelve yards a try. Jackie was used mostly as the man-in-motion on offense, because of his skill at faking and feinting. He won All-America honorable mention.

Jackie has never tried boxing, but Branch Rickey is convinced that Jackie would be sensational at it—or at any other sport he tried. In basketball, Jackie was the leading scorer of the Pacific Coast Conference for two years. He did not play tennis much, but the first time he played in the Negro National Tournament, he got to the semifinals. Baseball was the game he had played longest and liked least.

Two years ago, after 31 months in the Army, Jackie signed up as a shortstop for the barnstorming Kansas City Monarchs. It was a Negro club featuring old and reliable Pitcher "Satchel" Paige, who would have been a big leaguer once, had the big leagues been willing to admit Negroes sooner. The grubby life with the Monarchs was a shock to college-bred Jackie. The Monarchs traveled around in an old bus, often for two or three days at a time (the league stretches from Kansas City to Newark) without a bath, a bed, or a hot meal, and then crawled out long enough to play a game. The smart ones got aboard the bus early, rolled up their uniforms for a pillow, and slept in the aisle. "After two months of it, I was for quitting," says Jackie. "No future." He didn't know it, but all the time Branch Rickey was getting reports of Jackie's playing, and of his .340 batting average.

When Rickey hired Jackie away from the Monarchs there were loud and angry outcries, and not all of them were in a Southern accent. Some of the ugliest comments were spoken in ripe, raucous Brooklynese. Even some owners in the low-paying Negro leagues protested against "raiding" their men. There had been Negroes in big-league ball before, but they had been careful to identify themselves as Indians or "Cubans." Rickey, ignoring the uproar, treated Jackie "white," giving him a year's seasoning in the minors. The four other Negroes who followed Robinson to the big leagues this season (and were generally failures) had no such break.

Jackie faced hostility, suspicion, curiosity and every newspaper camera within miles when he reported to the International League's Montreal club for training.

Jackie spoke to his teammates only when spoken to, and his replies were brief and polite. He had long ago made it a rule to "let them make the first move." Soon after the season opened, the Montreal players were with him. It took longer to win over some of the fans, and the other players in the League.

BLACK CAT, GOOD LUCK. He was booed in Baltimore. In Syracuse one day, the rival team let out a black cat from their dugout as Jackie walked up to bat. Jackie got mad and hit a triple with the bases loaded. By the time the season ended, his doctor told him that he was on the verge of a nervous breakdown, but nobody would have guessed it by looking at his record. Second Baseman Robinson led the International League in batting (with a .349 average) and in fielding (with a .985 average). Montreal won the pennant, and the fans, after one game, chaired Jackie and carried him around the field. Jackie Robinson was ready for the Dodgers.

DO'S & DON'TS. Montreal had been won over, but that cut no ice in Flatbush. Branch Rickey, who knows his fellow citizens, set out to soften them up. He organized a group of Brooklyn's leading Negro citizens, including one judge, into a formal "how-to-handle-Robinson committee." In every other city in the National League, Rickey set up similar committees. The Brooklyn committee drew up a list of do's and don'ts a yard long; Jackie's deportment in public & private was to be supervised as thoroughly as Princess Elizabeth's.

He could not, like other ballplayers, endorse breakfast foods (or any other product, for that matter) at the usual $1,000 per endorsement. He could sign his name to no magazine or newspaper articles. When he got what he considered a bad decision from the umpire, he was not to object. When another player insulted him, he was to grin and bear it. He had to leave the ballpark after games by a secret exit. It was as important to avoid adulation as it was to avoid brickbats; there were to be no Jackie Robinson Days at Ebbets Field. He was not to accept any social invitations, from whites or blacks, and he was to stay away from night spots.

Jackie Robinson had already learned, by a lifetime practice, the lesson another Robinson—soft-shoe dancing Bojangles—once said down while acting as the unofficial Mayor of Harlem. Bojangles' formula "Do the best you can with what you've got…and get along with the white folks." Jackie had no desire to be a martyr for his race; he was just a young fellow anxious to make a living as a ballplayer. Though he barely knew Joe Louis, he sought him out for advice. He got an earful which boiled down to three words: "Don't get cocky."

So that Jackie would have company when the Dodgers were on the road, Rickey persuaded a Negro newsman, Wendell Smith, to travel with the club. In two cities, Jackie said, he had hotel trouble; he was not welcome at the Chase, where the Brooklyn club stays in St. Louis, or at Philadelphia's Benjamin Franklin. ("They fooled me," said Jackie. "I thought it would be St. Louis and Cincinnati.")

THE OTHER CHEEK. It is impossible to measure how much better, or how much worse, Jackie's first season might have been had his handicaps been fewer. It was not just that he was playing an unfamiliar position, or that at 28 he was pretty old for a rookie. He also had to turn the other cheek to abuses and insults. First he had to overcome the attitude of his fellow Dodgers, which ranged from mere wait-&-see stand-offishness to Southern-bred hostility.

And the rough stuff from rival teams began early and has never stopped. The first time the Dodgers played St. Louis, the Cards grumbled about playing on the same field with a Negro. They changed their minds—under pressure. Philadelphia was worse, because there the opposition had the open support of Phillies Manager Ben Chapman. He bawled insults at Robinson from the dugout. Chapman's second-division Phillies, notoriously the cruelest bench-jockeys in baseball, chimed in. Says Rookie Robbie: "I'd get mad. But I'd never let them know it." The Phillies management finally called down Chapman. He had his picture taken with Robinson to prove to everyone that the ugly reports weren't true.

It was Robinson's own Dodger mates who first came round. One or two of his fellow Dodgers began to say "Hello" to him in the locker room. Jackie wrote to his high-school baseball coach: "It isn't too tough on me. I have played with white boys all my life. But they hadn't played with a Negro before, and it sure was rough on some of them." Soon he was invited to play cards on trips, but though he didn't like the deuces-wild type of poker the boys played, he joined in a few games of hearts.

As Branch Rickey had foreseen, if Jackie played good baseball, the rest took care of itself. Some of the southerners on the squad shared the attitude of an Atlanta newsman who, when asked what he thought of Jackie Robinson, replied "He's good, damn him." But they were ready to back any player, black or white, who might help bring them the bonus (about $6,000 for winners, $4,000 for losers) that each gets for playing in a World Series.

After Slaughter did his spiking job a month ago, a group of Brooklyn players came to Jackie and said: "If they give you the works, give it back to them—and the team will be behind you 100%." That was the day Jack Roosevelt Robinson won his long, patient battle. ∎

Beneath its placid surface, the post-war decade strained with what TIME called "the tension of change." The Supreme Court rose to Thurgood Marshall's challenge and ruled that America's schools must be integrated. In the Montgomery bus boycott, blacks discovered two great engines of change: the power of unified protest and the inspirational leadership of Martin Luther King Jr. A new wave of immigrants from Cuba and Puerto Rico had America dancing the mambo. Hawaii joined the Union, its rich mix of Asian, Filipino, and Polynesian influences firmly opening America's door to the Pacific.

"To All on Equal Terms"

The Supreme Court rules against school segregation

IT WAS 12:52 P.M., May 17, 1954. At the long mahogany bench sat the nine Justices of the U. S. Supreme Court. From the red velour hangings behind the bench to the great doors at the back of the room, every seat was filled. Earl Warren, Chief Justice of the U.S., picked up a printed document from his desk and began to read in a firm, clear voice.

There was an awesome quiet in the high-ceilinged, marble-columned courtroom. The eight Associate Justices gave Warren rapt attention. In the press section, reporters strained forward to catch every word. Departing from custom, the court had not given newsmen advance copies of the opinion. Shortly after the Chief Justice began reading, the first bulletin clacked out over the Associated Press wires: "Chief Justice Warren today began reading the Supreme Court's decision in the public school segregation cases. The court's ruling could not be determined immediately." At 1:12 the A.P. sent a second message to editors all over the world, who had been awaiting the momentous decision. Warren was attacking segregation in schools, but "the Chief Justice had not read far enough in the court's opinion for newsmen to say that segregation was being struck down as unconstitutional."

When Warren finished reading at 1:20 the ruling was crystal clear: the U.S. Supreme Court held that racial segregation in the public schools violates the Constitution. The decision was unanimous.

TIMELY REASSERTION. In its 164 years the court had erected many a landmark of U.S. history: *Marbury* v. *Madison*, the Bank of the United States case, Dred Scott, the Slaughterhouse cases, the "Sick Chicken case" that killed the NRA, 1952's steel seizure. None of them, except the Dred Scott case (reversed by the Civil War) was more important than the school segregation issue. None of them directly and intimately affected so many American families. The lives and values of some 12 million schoolchildren in 21 states will be altered, and with them eventually the whole social pattern of the South. The international effect may be scarcely less important. In many countries, where U.S. prestige and leadership have been damaged by the fact of U.S. segregation, it will come as a timely reassertion of the basic American principle that "all men are created equal."

The school segregation issue came before the court in cases from South Carolina, Virginia, Delaware, Kansas and the District of Columbia. In making its ruling, the court issued one opinion covering all of the state cases, a separate one to deal with the special legal aspects in the District of Columbia. A sharp note crept into Chief Justice Warren's voice as he read one section of the District of Columbia opinion: "In view of our decision that the Constitution prohibits the states from maintaining racially segregated public schools, it would be unthinkable that the same Constitution would impose a lesser duty on the Federal Government."

In his first important opinions since he became Chief Justice last October, Earl Warren was clear and concise. The court was not surprised that the history of the 14th Amendment to the Constitution ("Nor shall any state deny to any person the equal protection of the laws...") did not clearly show an intention to prohibit segregation in the schools. In 1868, there was little public education for white children, and less for Negroes. To decide the present case, the court had to consider "public education in the light of its full development."

"Today education is perhaps the most important function of state and local governments...It is the very foundation of good citzenship. Today it is a principal instrument in awakening the child to cultural values, in preparing him for later professional training, and in helping him to adjust normally to his environment. In these days it is doubtful that any child may reasonably be expected to succeed in life if he is denied the opportunity of an education. Such an opportunity, where the state has undertaken to provide it, is a right which must be made available to all on equal terms."

FOR HEARTS & MINDS. For many years the South, aware that it might be brought under Supreme Court scrutiny, has justified its segregation policy as giving "equal but separate" facilities to white and Negro children. This phrase was used by the court in an 1896 case involving Jim Crow transport. This week's opinion flatly rejected "equal but separate" as a guiding principle in education.

Even if physical facilities are equal, said the court, there are intangible factors which prevent "separate" from being "equal." "To separate [Negro children] from others of similar age and qualifications solely because of their race generates a feeling of inferiority as to their status in the community that may affect their hearts and minds in a way unlikely ever to be undone...We conclude that in the field of public education the doctrine of 'separate but equal' has no place. Separate educational facilities are inherently unequal."

Because of the complex problems involved, the

Supreme Court deferred decision on the method of implementing the new policy. It asked all sides to present arguments next fall on 1) when schools should be ordered to abolish segregation and 2) who (a special master or the district courts) should set and enforce the terms under which it will be abolished.

For a scholarly New York Negro lawyer named Thurgood Marshall, the court's decision was the victory of a lifetime. Marshall, a graduate of Jim Crow schools, handled the state cases for the National Association for the Advancement of Colored People. Said he: "The most gratifying thing, in addition to the fact it was in favor of our side, is the unanimous decision and the language used. Once and for all, it's decided, completely decided."

WISDOM & TIRADES. As the news spread through the South, the reaction was varied. In border states, *e.g.*, Kansas and Oklahoma, officials calmly said that they expected segregation to be ended with little trouble. In Texas, Governor Allan Shivers said that his state will comply, but that it might "take years" to work out the details. From Virginia's Governor Thomas Stanley came a quiet, wise reaction. He carefully read the full opinion, then told reporters: "I shall call together...representatives of both state and local governments to consider the matter and work toward a plan which will be acceptable to our citizens and in keeping with the edict of the court. Views of leaders of both races will be invited..."

In South Carolina, old (75), adamant Governor James F.

Byrnes was "shocked" but calm. The fanfare with which South Carolina changed its constitution to permit it to abandon its public schools had been interpreted as a warning to the Supreme Court. Now that the court has disregarded the warning, it remains to be seen whether South Carolina will actually carry out the threat.

The loudest roars came from Georgia, which also has a law under which it could abolish the public-school system. U.S. Senator Richard Russell, contending that the question of segregation should be decided by the legislative rather than the judicial branch of the Government, had his own label for the court's action: "A flagrant abuse of judicial power." Out of Georgia's statehouse came a tirade from Governor Herman Talmadge: "The United States Supreme Court...has blatantly ignored all law and precedent...and lowered itself to the level of common politics...The people of Georgia believe in, adhere to, and will fight for their right under the U.S. and Georgia constitutions to manage their own affairs...[We will] map a program to insure continued and permanent segregation of the races."

By legal maneuvers (*e.g.*, test cases in court, redistricting), Herman Talmadge and others could continue segregation for some time. But they have little chance of making it permanent. The Supreme Court's decision was another vital chapter in one of the greatest success stories the world has ever known: the American Negro's 90-year rise from slavery. The Herman Talmadges are not going to write the last chapter of that story. ■

The Tension of Change

Thurgood Marshall and the Constitution

One midnight in the bitter year 1932, two journalists— one white, one Negro—walked south along Philadelphia's Broad Street in a sleety drizzle. They were talking of the Negro problem, the white man with a vehement impatience for justice, his companion more calmly and out of a deeper feeling for the scope and depth of the subject. Before parting, they stood a while under the marquee of the old Broad Street Station. Across the square under the arcade of city hall, dozens of men, wrapped in newspapers, slept. Panhandlers and a few night-shift apple-sellers stood on corners. A bus from upstate unloaded job-seekers; a bus for

upstate loaded job-seekers. Soggy streetwalkers drifted to and fro in a depressed market. The Negro concluded the conversation: "After all, the very most we can hope for is complete political, economic and social equality with the white man." Then, gazing at the Hogarthian scene, he added, not derisively but with compassion: "And look at the white man."

• • •

IN THE BRIGHT, lush September of 1955, in a day of confidence—as in a time of despair—the central problems of U.S. whites and Negroes again blended into one: how to

SEPTEMBER 19, 1955

TIME

THE WEEKLY NEWSMAGAZINE

THURGOOD
MARSHALL

$6.00 A YEAR

VOL. LXVI NO. 12

shape law, government, customs, practices, schools, factories. unions and farms in ways more consistent with man's nature and man's hopes. How, within the enduring framework of U.S. society, to let one change call forth another in some reasonably harmonious order.

One of the most important changes on the U.S. scene in September 1955, as the nation's children trooped back to school, was the astounding progress of racial desegregation. In Kansas City, Mo. and Oklahoma City, in Oak Ridge, and Charleston. W. Va., white and Negro children for the first time sat together in classrooms. This simple fact, part of a vast and complex social revolution, resulted from a legal victory: the U.S. Supreme Court's decisions of May 17, 1954 and May 31, 1955, holding segregated schools contrary to the 14th Amendment.

FOR CONSCIENCE & REPUTE. The name indelibly stamped on this victory is that of Thurgood Marshall, 47, counsel for the National Association for the Advancement of Colored People. He is at his sincerest and loudest (and that is very sincere and quite loud) in declaring that he is only one of the millions, white and Negro, whose courage, sweat, skill, imagination and common sense made the victory possible. Like all great victories, the school-desegregation decision opened up terrifying vistas of future obstacles and perils for all Americans. Most centrally and immediate-

ly, Marshall must deal with the future course of desegregation and the intertwined issues of the social revolution of which he is a leading figure. He cannot set the course, not even for the N.A.A.C.P. But what he decides to do about a thousand practical legal questions will interact powerfully with the decisions and attitudes of other men of similar and quite different and opposite views. The resultant of these forces will determine the pace, the style and the success of an effort to remove from U.S. life a paralyzing sting in its conscience and the ugliest blot upon its good name in the world.

Failure to achieve an orderly solution of the Negro problem would be—and this Thurgood Marshall feels deeply—much more than defeat for the Negro. It would be a failure at the very core of the American genius—its capacity for constructing forms strong and shrewd enough to withstand the tensions of change. From the nation's start, its three chief resources have been its fabulous mines of law, politics and social (including economic) organization. The abundance of material things—the bales of cotton, bushels of corn, ingots of steel—is a byproduct of these three primary riches, not the take from a geographic roulette wheel or the hoard of materialist greed.

Today's drive of the U.S. Negro toward equality is as strong as any social tide in Asia or Africa or Europe. At the centers of those other drives for change stand agitators, conspirators, men of violence. The strength and flexibility of the U.S. Constitution make possible the fact that the man at the vortex of the Negro issue in the U.S. is a constitutional lawyer.

THE SORE ARM. His is a highly technical calling. The Constitution itself is a complex work of statecraft, put together by some of the most sophisticated political scientists who ever lived. Along with the document there is the constitutional residue of 168 years of intense legal, political and social history—a coral-like cathedral of precedent, compromise, balance and bold interpretation. It takes scholars to move in this maze—and Thurgood Marshall is a sound, conscientious, imaginative legal scholar, although by no means the best of his day.

Technical skill is not all a U.S. constitutional lawyer needs. The job is to apply the Constitution to life, which will not sit still. For example, in the mid-20th century it became a fact of life that millions of U.S. Negroes could not feel themselves clothed in the minimum dignity of men as long as they suffered under certain legal disabilities. And millions of Southern whites, with an intensity perhaps equal to that of the Negroes, resist the change the Negroes feel they must have. A constitutional lawyer involved in this conflict must understand men as well as the legal technicalities through which their raw emotions may, without violence, be composed into a more or less successful image of justice.

Thurgood Marshall's feeling of love and awe for the Constitution is exceeded only by his love and awe toward his clients: the Negroes, and especially the Negroes of the

South and the border states, who, facing threats of firing, or beating or even death, continue to sign the legal petitions and complaints that must be the starting point of Marshall's cases from the slum and the cotton field to the high and technical levels of the Supreme Court.

Of these local N.A.A.C.P. leaders in the South, Marshall says: "There isn't a threat known to men that they do not receive. They're never out from under pressure. I don't think I could take it for a week. The possibility of violent death for them and their families is something they've learned to live with like a man learns to sleep with a sore arm."

THE BIG STRETCH. Marshall must stretch all the way from an understanding of this simple horror to the labyrinthine subtleties and the well-yoked ambiguities that form the mind of Mr. Justice Felix Frankfurter. He must stretch from his hatred of inequality to a recognition that much of the opposition to Negro equality is just as honestly felt as his own convictions. ("Some of my best friends are Dixiecrats—but they're honest Dixiecrats.") He must stretch all the way from an idealist's demand for nothing less than justice ("On the racial issue, you can't be a little bit wrong any more than you can be a little bit pregnant or a little bit dead") to a practical lawyer's acceptance of what he can get when he knows he can get no more.

So stretched, his tense personality reflects the tensions of his job and his time and his nation. And somehow, also, his personality reflects the symmetry of the Constitution he serves and expounds. "Thurgood," says a psychologist friend, "is a delicate balance of turmoils."

He is a big (6 ft. 2 in., 210 lbs.), quick-footed man, with a voice that can be soft or raucous, manners that can be rude or gentle or courtly, and an emotional pattern that swings him like a pendulum from the serious to the absurd. His dignity can slide easily into arrogance and his humility into self-abasement, but not for long. Humor—his own humor—brings him back toward center. Marshall will listen so avidly to his colleagues' scholarship that he has been called a brain-picker, but he trades jokes with no man. Around him, the ceaseless flow of anecdotes is all outward. Buffoonery relaxes his tense spiritual muscles. Buffoonery and work. After the long, argumentative conferences, after the horseplay and the backslapping, when he goes home to his lonely Harlem apartment, he becomes Thurgood Marshall the scholar, reading, noting, thinking, remembering—late into the night almost every night.

He walks into a cheap Harlem bar and is greeted by friendly smiles, not because of what he has done for his race (the barflies probably don't know who he is), but because they know him as a man who tells funny stories about cotton hands and baseball games and "that little ol' boy down in Texas." He walks into the Supreme Court and is greeted by respectful nods, not because he is a crusader, but because the Justices of the U.S. Supreme Court know they can speak to Thurgood Marshall as lawyer to lawyer, technician to technician.

OUT OF THE CONGO. Thurgood Marshall says: "American Negroes have no ties with Africa. Their history begins right here." Nevertheless, like a Virginia gentleman recalling the ancestral manor in Gloucestershire, Marshall begins his family history in the old country with a great-grandfather on his mother's side. "Way back before the Civil War, this rich man from Maryland went to the Congo on a hunting expedition or something. The whole time he was there, this little black boy trailed him around. So when they got ready to come back to this country, they just picked him up and brought him along. The years passed and he grew up, and, boy, he grew up into one mean one. One day his owner came to him and said: 'You're so evil I got to get rid of you. But I haven't the heart to sell you or give you to another man. So I'll tell you what I'll do: if you'll get out of the town and county and state, I'll give you your freedom.' Well, my great-grandfather never said a word, just looked at him. And he walked off the place, settled down a couple miles away, raised his family and lived there till the day he died. And nobody ever laid a hand on him."

This most un-African parable of independence is succeeded in Marshall's repertory of family stories by his paternal grandfather, "a rough and tough sailorman. He never knew what his first name was so he took two—Thoroughgood and Thornygood. He drew two sailor's pensions till the day he died—one in each name. I was named Thoroughgood after him, but by the time I was in the second grade, I got tired of spelling all that and shortened it."

His maternal grandfather, Isaiah O. B. (for Olive Branch, he said) Williams, also went to sea, came home with money and a taste for opera and Shakespeare. He opened a grocery on Baltimore's Denmeade Street, and sired six children. Isaiah bought a house next to a white man who turned surly and mean. One day the neighbor repented because the party fence between their property needed fixing; he suggested that they do the job together. "After all," said the white man, "we belong to the same church and are going to the same heaven." But Isaiah, remembering the slights he had received, turned down the olive branch. "I'd rather go to hell," he snapped.

The chip-on-the-shoulder tradition was shared by Thurgood's father, Will, a dining-car worker on the B. & O. and later steward of Baltimore clubs, including the Gibson Island club, a yachtsman's paradise with jellyfish for serpents. Will, light-skinned and blue-eyed, used to tell Thurgood and his brother Aubrey, "If anyone calls you nigger, you not only got my permission to fight him—you got my orders to fight him." Once, Thurgood followed orders. Delivery boy for a hat store, he was trying to board a trolley with a stack of hats so high he "couldn't see over or around them. I was climbing aboard when a white man yanked me backwards. 'Nigguh,' he said, 'don't you push in front of no white lady again.' I hadn't seen any white lady, so I tore into him. The hats scattered all over the street, and we both got arrested."

Thurgood's mother, Norma Arica, has been for 28 years a Baltimore schoolteacher and numbers six other schoolteachers among her own and her husband's close relatives. As a teacher, she was among the aristocrats of Negro Baltimore, and her feeling about white-Negro relationships is balanced and moderated by her sense of service and leadership among her own people.

UP FROM THE BASEMENT. In all-Negro Douglas High School, one of Marshall's uncles gave him an A in algebra, but in grammar school he was repeatedly punished for breaking rules. Day after day, the principal sentenced Marshall to the basement, and allowed him to leave only when he had learned a section of the U.S. Constitution. "Before I left that school," he says, "I knew the whole thing by heart." He does not contend that the seeds of his career sprouted in the basement, but such discipline did reinforce a respect for authority, which he retains in uneasy balance with the strongly rebellious elements in his makeup.

He went off to Lincoln University, near Chester, Pa., an institution then with an all-Negro student body and an all-white faculty. The important event of his undergraduate years occurred at the Cherry Street Memorial Church in Philadelphia: "We went in there because we learned that's where all the cute chicks went." The one he met was Buster Burey. "First we decided to get married five years after I graduated, then three, then one, and we finally did just before I started my last semester." (Buster died of lung cancer last February. They had no children.)

Marshall decided to try law school. The University of Maryland was barred to him, so he commuted to Howard University in Washington. Within a week Marshall knew that "this was it. This was what I wanted to do for as long as I lived." Only a fair college student, he had to meet very tough standards at Howard. "I got through simply by overwhelming the job. I was at it 20 hours a day, seven days a week."

ON TO THE N.A.A.C.P. Out of Howard, he hopefully hung out a shingle in Baltimore (his mother took the rug off her living-room floor to put in his office). Nothing happened. It was 1933, and hardly anybody was worth suing. Marshall's practice lost him $1,000 the first year.

The next year he did better, building up a well-to-do clientele and a reputation, but he was increasingly involved in low-fee, hard-work cases on civil rights. In a Maryland court, he won separate-but-equal status for a client, Donald Murray, at the University of Maryland School of Law, a right about which he felt strongly. To the N.A.A.C.P. leaders, this victory tagged him as a really effective attorney in the N.A.A.C.P.'s kind of case.

In 1936 he went to work for the N.A.A.C.P. "temporarily" under his old law-school mentor, Charles Houston, but by 1938 admitted it was a permanent, double-time job. His salary then was $2,600 a year. (Present salary: $15,000.)

The N.A.A.C.P. was winning graduate-school cases in the courts, but the defendant states complied merely by setting separate "schools" for one or two students. "It was

beginning to look as though every time we won a lawsuit we were working our way deeper into the separate-but-equal hole. The fact was we just weren't ready to tackle segregation as an evil per se. We didn't know enough."

Before World War II Marshall had succeeded Houston as chief counsel of N.A.A.C.P. He won some key victories: against a union which had closed-shop contracts but discriminated against Negroes; against discrimination in the U.S. Air Corps, a long step toward the present desegregation of the armed forces; against the Democratic Party of Texas, which claimed that it was a private organization and could make its own rules barring Negroes from voting in primary elections.

THE RIVER PILOTS. Toward the end of the war, N.A.A.C.P. leaders began to face the failure concealed in the success of its separate-but-equal victories. In 1945 a group of 100 N.A.A.C.P. leaders, mostly lawyers, met in Manhattan, Marshall recalls: "Like somebody at the meeting said, while it was true a lot of us might die without ever seeing the goal realized, we were going to have to change directions if our children weren't going to die as black bastards too. So we decided to make segregation itself our target."

"Segregation itself" had long been a target of Negro spokesmen. But Thurgood Marshall is not primarily a Negro spokesman; he is a constitutional lawyer. The problem facing him and his colleagues was how to attack segregation itself on legal grounds. The weight of the precedents ran against them. Where would they find evidence to turn the balance?

The answer was peculiarly contemporary and peculiarly American. Just as U.S. military staffs swim—and sometimes drown—in rivers of expert reports, just as U.S. business turns more and more to specialized organizers of facts, so Marshall & Co. mobilized a small army of psychologists, psychiatrists, sociologists and anthropologists to prove what every Negro among them believed to be obvious: that segregated education could not be "equal."

The night before a Supreme Court school-segregation argument, Marshall & Co. went through an interesting exercise at Howard University. Dean Houston years before had started moot courts, with lawyers on the bench and students in the courtroom all trying to anticipate hard questions that the Supreme Court Justices might ask. A student threw the N.A.A.C.P. men into a nose dive by asking how they would get around an old Supreme Court decision upholding a Louisiana law which said nobody could be a Mississippi River pilot whose father hadn't been. Marshall & Co. worked far into the night on that one. Next day, it turned out to be one of the first questions Justice Frankfurter asked. Marshall took evasive action and Frankfurter, the record indicates, was diverted if not satisfied.

"I WAS SO HAPPY." In the Supreme Court arguments, Marshall was facing the man who for 30 years had been the most prestigious U.S. constitutional lawyer: John W. Davis. For weeks Marshall had been overworked, nervous, irritable. In court he was, as always, calm, polite, quick to grasp the inferences of a question, never loud, never oratorical. At one point he managed to get into a few potent sentences his analysis of the South's attitude:

"I got the feeling on hearing the discussion yesterday," he said, "that when you put a white child in a school with a whole lot of colored children, the child would fall apart or something. Everybody knows that is not true. Those same kids in Virginia and South Carolina—and I have seen them do it—they play in the streets together, they play on their farms together, they go down the road together, they separate to go to school, they come out of school and play ball together. They have to be separated in school...Why, of all the multitudinous groups of people in this country, [do] you have to single out the Negroes and give them this separate treatment? It can't be because of slavery in the past, because there are very few groups in this country that haven't had slavery some place back in the history of their groups. It can't be color, because there are Negroes as white as the drifted snow, with blue eyes, and they are just as segregated as the colored men. The only thing it can be is an inherent determination that the people who were formerly in slavery, regardless of anything else, shall be kept as near that stage as is possible. And now is the time, we submit, that this court should make it clear that that is not what our Constitution stands for."

This, and Marshall's social-scientist approach, paid off. In his opinion for the whole court, Chief Justice Earl Warren in sentence after sentence reflected the conviction that under present conditions of U.S. life, education could not be separate and equal. When he heard the decision read, says Thurgood Marshall: "I was so happy, I was numb."

UNCHANGING INSTRUMENT. He has a profound respect for the federal judiciary. He has tried case after case before Southern federal judges, whose convictions on the subject of segregation he knows to be diametrically opposed to his own. "And they believe what they believe just as hard as I believe what I believe." In all those cases, before all those judges, Marshall remembers only one judge who was, in his opinion, unfair and discourteous.

Marshall knows that he and the Southern federal judges he respects are checked by the same steely framework of the Anglo-American legal tradition and, especially, the U.S. Constitution. He says: "The difference between the Constitution and the law is something a lot of people don't seem to appreciate. The law can fluctuate because of the changing whims of the people and their legislators. But the whole purpose of the Constitution is to serve as an instrument which cannot be changed overnight, which does not change when mores and customs change."

Southerners charge that Marshall was instrumental in "changing the Constitution" in the Supreme Court's desegregation decision. But from his point of view—and from the court's—he merely produced new evidence to show that the old rule of separate-but-equal (*Plessy* v. *Ferguson*, 1896) did not really give the equality before the law which the 14th Amendment guarantees.

HARD TO PROCRASTINATE. Achieving desegregation, county by county, school district by school district, throws upon Marshall a tremendous load of responsibility and decision. The present picture from state to state varies over a wide range. Oklahoma is, from the N.A.A.C.P.'s standpoint, surprisingly good, North Carolina surprisingly bad. In some areas, Marshall may not want, for tactical reasons, to bring suit now—but when local N.A.A.C.P. people urge him, he finds it bitterly hard to procrastinate, lest those men and women who sign the petitions feel that the N.A.A.C.P. has let them down. In other areas, he might want to proceed more vigorously, but clients, because of fear, do not come forward. Marshall does not blame them.

Generally speaking, segregation is ending in areas where Negro population is less than 10%. Where it ranges between 10% and 25%, the fight may not be too hard. Where it approaches or exceeds 50%, the end can hardly be imagined. Yet Marshall will not accept a theoretical solution that the only chance for desegregation in Mississippi and other parts of the Deep South is a mass migration of Negroes that will drastically change population percentages. Perhaps he remembers his ancestor from the Congo, who would not leave the state even for his manumission.

Last week, after vacation, Thurgood Marshall was back in Manhattan, dealing briskly with scores of tactical decisions in the desegregation fight. Across the land, he guided and coordinated the work of scores of lawyers in one of the biggest legal operations in U.S. history. He seemed fresh and rested, though the vacation, his first in eight years, had been a mockery.

Work caught up with him at Miami, and at the end of the job his nerve ends were raw. He was in a mood of acute awareness of how far he and his cause had come, and at the same time, he felt a strong sense of how hard and long was the road ahead. He did not want merely to win, but to win in the way that would cause least pain to Negro and white and reflect the most credit on the U.S. Constitution.

Stretched on the rack of one of the tensest and most exciting careers in the U.S. today, Thurgood Marshall in Miami said: "I'm gonna take a two-day vacation to rest from my vacation. I'm going to Havana. Never been there; hear they treat a man fine." The ghost of an anticipatory smile flitted over his face; then the pained look came back. "Don't know why I'm going to Havana," he said slowly. "Trouble is when I get there, you know who I'm gonna find there, too? "Me." ∎

Attack on the Conscience

When Rosa Parks refused to move, Martin Luther King moved the nation

ACROSS THE SOUTH—in Atlanta. Mobile, Birmingham. Tallahassee, Miami, New Orleans—Negro leaders look toward Montgomery, Ala., the cradle of the Confederacy, for advice and counsel on how to gain the desegregation that the U.S. Supreme Court has guaranteed them. The man whose word they seek is not a judge, or a lawyer, or a political strategist or a flaming orator. He is a scholarly, 28-year-old Negro Baptist minister, the Rev. Martin Luther King Jr., who in little more than a year has risen from nowhere to become one of the nation's remarkable leaders of men.

In Montgomery, Negroes are riding side by side with whites on integrated buses for the first time in history. They won this right by court order. But their presence is accepted, however reluctantly, by the majority of Montgomery's white citizens because of Martin King and the way he conducted a year-long boycott of the transit system. In terms of concrete victories, this makes King a poor second to the brigade of lawyers who won the big case before the Supreme Court in 1954, and who are now fighting their way from court to court, writ to writ, seeking to build the legal framework for desegregation. But King's leadership extends beyond any single battle: homes and churches were bombed and racial passions rose close to mass violence in Montgomery's year of the boycott, but King reached beyond lawbooks and writs, beyond violence and threats, to win his people—and challenge all people—with a spiritual force that aspired even to ending prejudice in man's mind.

TORTURED SOULS. "Christian love can bring brotherhood on earth. There is an element of God in every man," said he, after his own home was bombed. "No matter how low one sinks into racial bigotry, he can be redeemed...Non-violence is our testing point. The strong man is the man who can stand up for his rights and not hit back." With such an approach he outflanked the Southern legislators who planted statutory hedgerows against integration for as far as the eye could see. He struck where an attack was least expected, and where it hurt most: at the South's Christian conscience.

Most of all, Baptist King's impact has been felt by the influential white clergy, which could—if it would—help lead the South through a peaceful and orderly transitional period toward the integration that is inevitable. Explains Baptist Minister Will Campbell, onetime chaplain at the University of Mississippi, now a Southern official of the National Council of Churches: "I know of very few white Southern ministers who aren't troubled and don't have admiration for King. They've become tortured souls." Says Baptist Minister William Finlator of Raleigh, N.C.: "King has been working on the guilty conscience of the South. If he can bring us to contrition, that is our hope."

JUDICIAL RECOGNITION. Sturdy (5 ft. 7 in., 164 lbs.), soft-voiced Martin Luther King describes himself as "an ambivert—half introvert and half extrovert." He can draw within himself for long, single-minded concentration on his people's problems, and then exert the force of personality and conviction that makes him a public leader. No radical, he avoids the excesses of radicalism, *e.g.*, he recognized economic reprisal as a weapon that could get out of hand, kept the Montgomery boycott focused on the immediate goal of bus integration, restrained his followers from declaring sanctions against any white merchant or tradesman who offended them. King is an expert organizer, to the extent that during the bus boycott the hastily assembled Negro car pool under his direction achieved even judicial recognition as a full-fledged transit system. Personally humble, articulate, and of high educational attainment, Martin Luther King Jr. is, in fact, what many a Negro—and, were it not for his color, many a white—would like to be.

Even King's name is meaningful: he was baptized Michael Luther King, son of the Rev. Michael Luther King Sr., then and now pastor of Atlanta's big (4,000 members) Ebenezer Baptist Church. He was six when King Sr. decided to take on, for himself and his son, the full name of the Protestant reformer. Says young King: "Both father and I have fought all our lives for reform, and perhaps we've earned our right to the name."

Perched on a bluff overlooking Atlanta's business district, the two-story yellow brick King home was a happy one, where Christianity was a way of life. Each day began and ended with family prayer. Martin was required to learn Scriptural verse for recitation at evening meals. He went to Sunday school, morning and evening services. He was taught to hold Old Testament respect for the law, but it was the New Testament's gentleness that came to have everyday application in his life.

"NEVER A SPECTATOR." From his earliest memory Martin King has had a strong aversion to violence in all its forms. The school bully walloped him; Martin did not fight back. His younger brother flailed away at him; Martin stood and took it. A white woman in a store slapped him, crying,

"You're the nigger who stepped on my foot." Martin said nothing. Cowardice? If so, it would come as a surprise to Montgomery, where Martin Luther King has unflinchingly faced the possibility of violent death for months.

The shabby, overcrowded Negro schools in Atlanta were no match for the keen, probing ("I like to get in over my head, then bother people with questions") mind of Martin King; he leapfrogged through high school in two years, was ready at 15 for Atlanta's Morehouse College, one of the South's Negro colleges. At Morehouse, King worked with the city's Intercollegiate Council, an integrated group, and learned a valuable lesson. "I was ready to resent all the white race," he says. "As I got to see more of white people, my resentment was softened, and a spirit of cooperation took its place. But I never felt like a spectator in the racial problem. I wanted to be involved in the very heart of it."

As a kid, in the classic tradition of kids, Martin wanted to be a fireman. Then, hoping to treat man's physical ills, he planned to become a doctor. Becoming more deeply engrossed in the problems of his race, he turned his hopes to the law because "I could see the part I could play in breaking down the legal barriers to Negroes." At Morehouse, he came to final resolution. "I had been brought up in the church and knew about religion," says King, "but I wondered whether it could serve as a vehicle to modern thinking. I wondered whether religion, with its emotionalism in Negro churches, could be intellectually respectable as well as emotionally satisfying." He decided it could—and that he would become a minister.

TECHNIQUES OF EXECUTION. King's Morehouse record (major in sociology) won him scholarship offers from three seminaries. But Martin Luther King Sr., a man of considerable parts, held that scholarships should go only to boys who could otherwise not afford to continue their education. King Sr. therefore reached into his own pocket to send his son to Pennsylvania's Crozer Theological Seminary.

For the first time in his life Martin King found himself in an integrated school; he was one of six Negroes among nearly 100 students at Crozer. Fearful that he might fail to meet white standards, King worked ceaselessly. Aside from his general theological studies, he pored over the words and works of the great social philosophers: Plato, Aristotle, Rousseau, Locke, Hegel (whose progress-through-pain theories are still prominent in King's thinking). Above all, he read and reread everything he could find about India's Gandhi. "Even now," says King, "in reading Gandhi's words again, I am given inspiration. The spirit of passive resistance came to me from the Bible and the teachings of Jesus. The techniques of execution came from Gandhi."

BY GUESS & BY GOD. King's Crozer career was extraordinary. He graduated first in his class, was named the seminary's outstanding student, was president of the student body (the first Negro so honored), and earned a chance to go on to Boston University for his Ph.D.

In Boston he met Coretta Scott, a pretty and talented

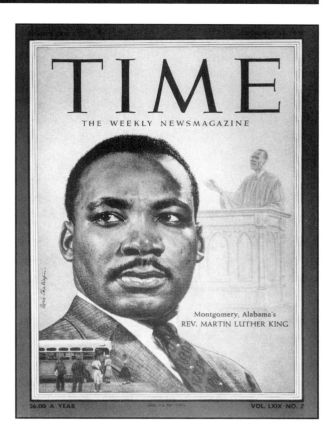

soprano who was studying at the New England Conservatory of Music. Their early dates were less than completely successful. "The fact that he was a minister made me shy away," recalls Coretta. "I had an awful stereotype in my mind." The suitor broke the stereotype: in June 1953, Coretta and King were married on the front lawn of her home in Marion, Ala. Just 15 months later they arrived in Montgomery to take up full-time pastoral duties at the Dexter Avenue Baptist Church, and to assume the role for which, as if by guess and by God, he had been preparing all his life.

ACHING FEET. Snuggled against a hairpin bend in the meandering Alabama River, Montgomery was a city where 80,000 whites pretty generally believed there was no problem with 50,000 Negroes. Working mostly as farm hands or domestic servants for $15 or $20 a week, Montgomery's Negroes had neither geographic nor political unity. There was no concentration of Negroes in one area; instead, they were split up in neighborhood pockets scattered the length and the breadth of the city. Served by a lackadaisical Negro weekly paper, they had no ready means of communication. More than that, says Martin King, the "vital liaison between Negroes and whites was totally lacking. There was not even a ministerial alliance to bring white and colored clergymen together. This is important. If there had been some communication between the races, we might have got some help from the responsible whites, and our protest might not have been necessary."

Frustrated at every turn, the Negroes had long since fallen to quarreling among themselves in bitter factionalism. "If," says King, "you had asked me the day before our protest began whether any action could or would have been taken by the Negroes, I'd have said no. Then, all of a sudden, unity developed."

It came about through the aching feet of a Negro woman. In the early evening of Thursday, Dec. I. 1955, a Montgomery City Lines bus rolled through Court Square and headed for its next stop in front of the Empire Theater. Aboard were 24 Negroes, seated from the rear toward the front, and twelve whites, seated from front to back. At the Empire Theater stop, six whites boarded the bus. The driver, as usual, walked back and asked the foremost Negroes to get up and stand so the whites could sit. Three Negroes obeyed—but Mrs. Rosa Parks, a seamstress who had once been a local secretary for the National Association for the Advancement of Colored People, did the unexpected. She refused.

"I don't really know why I wouldn't move," says Rosa Parks. "There was no plot or plan at all. I was just tired from shopping. My feet hurt." Rosa Parks was arrested and in the due course of time fined $10 and costs for violating a state law requiring bus passengers to follow drivers' seating assignments.

WHAT THEY WERE UP TO. Other Negroes had suffered worse indignities, but hers was the one that the South would long remember. The Montgomery City Lines Inc. had long been a special irritant to the Negroes, who made up 70% of its patronage. At best, they had to pay their fares in front, get off and board again in the rear; sometimes after they had dropped their money in the fare box and were going around to the rear, the bus drivers drove off. At worst, the Negroes were cursed, slapped and kicked by the white drivers. By the time of the Parks case, they had had all they could take without some sort of reply.

Overnight the word flashed throughout the various Negro neighborhoods: support Rosa Parks; don't ride the buses Monday. Within 48 hours mimeographed leaflets (authorship unknown) were out, calling for a one-day bus boycott. A white woman saw one of the leaflets and called the Montgomery *Advertiser*, demanding that it print the story "to show what the niggers are up to." The *Advertiser* did—and publicized the boycott plan among Negroes in a way that they themselves never could have achieved. The results were astonishing: on Monday Montgomery Negroes walked, rode mules, drove horse-drawn buggies, traveled to work in private cars. The strike was 90% effective.

HOW THEY DID IT. On the day of the strike, some two dozen Negro ministers decided to push for continuance of the bus boycott. The original demands were mild: 1) Negroes would still be seated from the rear and whites from the front, but on a first-come-first-served basis; 2) Negroes

Rosa Parks, on right: "I was just tired from shopping. My feet hurt."

would get courteous treatment; 3) Negro drivers would be employed for routes through predominantly Negro areas. To direct their protest, the Negro ministers decided to form the Montgomery Improvement Association. And for president they elected the Rev. Martin Luther King Jr., a relative newcomer whose ability was evident and whose newness placed him above the old feuds. That night, at a hastily called mass meeting, more than 5,000 Negroes approved the ministers' decisions.

Slowly the boycott took permanent shape. More than 200 volunteers offered the use of their cars; nearly 100 pickup stations were established. Church and mass-meeting collections kept the Montgomery Improvement Association alive at first; then donations began to flood in from across the U.S. and from as far away as Tokyo. By the end of last year the M.I.A. had spent an estimated $225,000. At every turn King out-generaled Montgomery's white officials. Example: the officials went to court to have the M.I.A.'s assets frozen, but King had the funds scattered around in out-of-reach banks that included half a dozen in the North.

GET TOUGH. Montgomery's whites reacted complacently. The city commission went through the barest motions of offering compromises, *e.g.*, the Negroes were promised that the bus drivers would show them "partial courtesy." Mayor

W. A. ("Tacky") Gayle appointed a committee to negotiate with the Negroes—and named as a member the head of the local White Citizens' Council.

The Negroes stood firm, and white complacency turned to fury. Rumors were spread that boycott leaders had used mass-meeting funds to buy themselves Cadillacs. Older Negro preachers were taunted for having yielded their seniority to a young whippersnapper. To lure the Negroes back onto the buses, the Montgomery city commission called in three hand-picked Negro ministers (who had been on the edges of the boycott) and persuaded them to agree to settlement terms that had little if any practical meaning. The commission's plan was to announce the settlement in Sunday's papers, but Saturday night word of the plan reached King (who was tipped off by a long-distance call from a Minneapolis reporter who had seen the story on the Associated Press wire). King and his top M.I.A. associates spent most of the night going from tavern to tavern warning Negroes that there had been no real settlement.

When the false armistice failed. Mayor Tacky Gayle ordered a get-tough policy. Gayle and his city commissioners made a great show of joining the White Citizens' Council. (Said Police Commissioner Clyde Sellers: "I wouldn't trade my Southern birthright for 100 Negro votes.") Police harassment followed: King was arrested for speeding; Negro car-pool drivers were hauled into court for trivial violations.

Worst of all, the whites' lunatic fringe began to take over. A letter addressed simply to "Nigger Preacher" was promptly delivered to Martin King. Up to 25 profanity-laced telephone calls a day came to the King home. Sometimes there was only the hawk of a throat and the splash of spittle against the ear piece. Montgomery was building toward the one thing that Martin King wanted most to avoid: a violent blowup.

"One night," says King, "after many threatening and annoying phone calls, I went into the kitchen and tried to forget it all. I found myself praying out loud, and I laid my life bare. I remember saying, 'I'm here, taking a stand, and I've come to the point where I can't face it alone.' " From somewhere came the answer: stand for truth, stand for righteousness; God is at your side. Says Martin King: "I have not known fear since."

His mettle was soon tested. At 9:15 one night a year ago, King was speaking at a mass meeting; Coretta King was talking to a friend in the living room of the parsonage at 309 South Jackson Street. Coretta heard a thud on the porch and thought it was a brick, nothing particularly frightening around the King home during that period. She and the friend moved to a back room to continue their conversation—and a dynamite bomb went off filling the vacant living room with a hail of broken glass.

"BE PEACEFUL." Mayor Gayle and Police Commissioner Sellers rushed out with the cops to answer the alarm and found themselves up against a Negro crowd in the ugliest sort of mood. King's nonviolent teachings had sunk deep (since the boycott began, Montgomery's crimes of violence by Negroes have decreased by an estimated 20%), but at this moment the impulse to answer white violence with Negro violence seemed irresistible. A growl of fury came from the Negro crowd; there was a forward surge that left no doubt in the mind of anyone present that Mayor Gayle and his aides were in danger. A white man rushed inside the parsonage and begged Martin King, who had been hastily summoned from his mass meeting, to stop his followers. King did.

"Please be peaceful," he said from the shattered front porch. "We believe in law and order. We are not advocating violence. We want to love our enemies. I want you to love our enemies. Be good to them. Love them and let them know you love them. I did not start this boycott. I was asked by you to serve as your spokesman. I want it to be known the length and breadth of the land that if I am stopped, this movement will not stop. If I am stopped, our work will not stop, for what we are doing is right. What we are doing is just—and God is with us."

Montgomery's Negroes walked back through the night to their homes. "I'll be honest with you," says a policeman who was there. "I was terrified. I owe my life to that nigger preacher, and so do all the other white people who were there."

VOICE FROM WASHINGTON. After the bombing, Montgomery Negroes put up floodlights around King's home and refused to let him drive or walk alone. The Kings moved most of their furniture into back rooms, leaving the living room virtually bare. King briefly considered arming himself, but decided against it ("As the leader of a nonviolent movement, I'd look pretty bad carrying a gun"). Coretta King took their infant daughter to Atlanta, but soon returned. "When I'm away from this," she says, "I get depressed. I feel completely helpless."

The boycott continued, bringing the bus company to its economic knees. King and 89 other boycott leaders were indicted on charges of violating a 1921 anti-boycott law that came straight from Alabama's legal boneyard (King's $500 fine is still under appeal). Then Montgomery's officials made a stab that very nearly paid off. They went to court for an injunction against the M.I.A. on the ground that it had set up an illegal transit system.

The move was one that King had long feared; he had, in fact, tried to forestall it by having the name of a different Negro church printed on the side of each of the 20 new station wagons that the M.I.A. had bought for the car pool. One day last November as King and his M.I.A. colleagues were in court fighting a losing battle against the injunction, there was a stir among the white lawyers. They had seen a news dispatch: the U.S. Supreme Court had declared bus segregation illegal in Montgomery. Cried a fervent Negro: "God Almighty has spoken from Washington, D.C.!"

The next night King addressed an emotion-packed

church meeting ("Look at the way they greet that guy," said a white newsman. "They think he's a Messiah"), admonished his followers to take their victory humbly. "I would be terribly disappointed," said King, "if any of you go back to the buses bragging, 'We, the Negroes, won a victory over the white people.'"

A LONG WAY TO GO. At first, integrated buses on night runs were sporadically peppered with shotgun blasts. Then things seemed to quiet down. It was a false quiet. One night last month the stillness was shattered by a series of dynamite blasts. A bomb exploded outside the home of the Rev. Ralph Abernathy, Negro pastor of the First Baptist Church, who has subordinated his own admitted ambitions for leadership to become King's strong, trusted right hand. Another bomb ripped into the home of a special object of white venom: the Rev. Robert Graetz, white pastor of the all-Negro Trinity-Lutheran Church, who has stood stoutly for integration. ("If I had a nickel for every time I've been called a nigger-loving s.o.b.," says Graetz, "I'd be independently wealthy.") Negro churches were also bombed, and later an unexploded bomb was found on King's front porch. By now the great majority of Montgomery's law-abiding citizens realized that almost any solution was better than that offered by the terrorist minority. With every new outbreak of violence, inevitably followed by a reassuring word of nonviolence from King, white opinion grew stronger for accepting bus integration in an orderly way. The bus fight was to all practical effect, over.

"We have come a long, long way," says King, "but we still have a long, long way to go." The process will take time, since King is willing to move cautiously rather than excite new passions, especially over school integration. "If you truly love and respect an opponent," he says, "you respect his fears too."

Late at night Martin Luther King Jr. talks quietly of the broad principles on which his effort is based. "Our use of passive resistance in Montgomery," he says, "is not based on resistance to get rights for ourselves, but to achieve friendship with the men who are denying us our rights, and change them through friendship and a bond of Christian understanding before God." Impossible? Maybe.

But so, only 14 months before, was the notion that whites and Negroes might be riding peaceably together on integrated buses in Montgomery, Ala. ■

MARCH 2, 1981

The Morning Bus to Durham

On the bus: "colored" seats, white seats, and no man's land

IN CAROLINA: GROWING UP BLACK IN THE '40S

Mary Mebane is lecturer in composition at the University of Wisconsin in Milwaukee. This passage is excerpted from her autobiography, Mary *(Viking; $12.95). A lifelong teacher of literature who was born in Durham County, N.C., in 1933, Mebane in her book recounts with insight, compassion and anger what it was like growing up female and black in the South before the civil rights revolution began.*

I GOT ON THE BUS and sat on one of the long seats at the back that faced each other. There were three such long seats—one on each side of the bus and a third at the very back that faced the front. I liked to sit on a long seat facing the side because then I didn't have to look at the expressions on the faces of the whites when they put their tokens in and looked at the blacks sitting in the back of the bus.

By custom the seats behind the exit door had become "colored" seats, and no matter how many whites were standing, any black sitting behind the exit door knew he or she wouldn't have to move. The disputed area was opposite the exit door. This was no man's land. White people sat there and black people sat there. If the back section was full, the next black passenger who got on sat in the no man's land seat; but if the white section filled up, a white person would take the seat. The white people, though, could sit anywhere, even in the colored section.

The seating didn't really bother me that day until the white section up front was almost full and the black section was full. Now, if the driver took on more passengers than got off, it meant that some of the newcomers would have to stand. And if they were white the driver was going to have to ask a black passenger in no man's land to move so that a white passenger could sit down.

A black man in a blue windbreaker and a gray porkpie hat was sitting in no man's land, and my stomach tightened. I had never been on a bus on which a black person was asked to give a seat to a white person when there was no other seat empty. Usually, the black person automatically got up and moved to an empty seat farther back. But this morning the only empty seat was beside a black person sitting in no man's land.

The bus stopped at Little Five Points, and one black got off. A young white man was getting on. I tensed. Would the driver ask the black man to get up and move to the lone empty seat farther back? The white man had a businessman's air about him: suit, tie, polished shoes. He saw the empty seat in the colored section, hesitated, then went to it and sat down. I relaxed a little when the bus pulled off without the driver saying anything.

At the next stop another white man got on. The whole colored section tensed. The only seat was beside the black man in no man's land. Would he stand the few stops to Main Street, or would the driver make the black man move? I looked at the other men and women, who studiously avoided my eyes. There was one woman whom I had noticed before, and I had been ashamed of her. She was a stringy little black woman. She looked as if she were a hard drinker. Flat black face with tight features, dressed in a tight boy's sweater pulled down over a nondescript skirt.

The white man who had just gotten on the bus walked to the seat in no man's land and stood there. He just stood there. He would not sit down next to the black. Two adult males, living in the most highly industrialized, most technologically advanced nation in the world, a nation that had devastated two other industrial giants in World War II, faced each other in mutual rage and hostility. The white one wanted to sit down, but he was going to exert his authority and force the black one to get up first—so that they would not have to sit side by side. I watched the driver's face in the rearview mirror.

"Say there, buddy, how about moving back?" the driver said, meanwhile driving his bus just as fast as he could. The whole bus froze—whites at the front, blacks at the rear.

They didn't want to believe what was happening was really happening. The seated black man said nothing. The standing white man said nothing.

"Say, buddy, did you hear me? What about moving on back?" The driver was scared to death. I could tell that.

"These is the niggers' seats!" the little lady in the strange outfit started screaming. "The Government gave us these seats!" I was startled at her tone and her statement—no man's land seats were not regarded as back of the bus. "The President said that these are the niggers' seats!" I expected her to start fighting at any moment. Evidently the bus driver did, too, because he was driving faster and faster. "I'm going to take you down to the station, buddy," he said.

The white man with the briefcase and the polished brown shoes who had taken a seat in the colored section looked as though he might die of embarrassment at any moment. By that time we had come to the stop before Main Street, and the black male passenger rose to get off.

"You're not getting off, buddy. I'm going to take you downtown," the driver called. He kept driving as he talked and seemed to be trying to get downtown as fast as he could.

"These are the niggers' seats! The Government plainly said these are the niggers' seats!" screamed the little woman in rage. I was embarrassed at the word nigger but I was proud of the lady. I was proud of the man who wouldn't get up.

The bus seemed to be going a hundred miles an hour, and everybody was anxious to get off. The black man stood at the exit door; the driver drove right past the A.& P. stop. I was terrified. I was sure the bus was going to the police station to put the black man in jail. The woman had her hands on her hips and she never stopped yelling. The bus driver kept driving as fast as he could.

Then, apparently, the driver decided to forget the whole thing. The next stop was Main Street, and when he got there, in what seemed to be a flash of lightning, he flung both doors open wide. He and his black antagonist looked at each other in the rearview mirror; in a second the windbreaker and the porkpie hat were gone. The little woman was standing preaching to the whole bus about the Government's gift of these seats to the blacks; the white man with the brown shoes practically fell out of the door in his hurry. I followed the hurrying footsteps. The people who devised this system thought that it was going to last forever. ■

The Meaning of Little Rock

Federal force integrates Arkansas schools

" SOME PEOPLE say it's like a dream—it can't be happening here," mused Presbyterian Minister Dunbar H. Ogden Jr., president of the Greater Little Rock Ministerial Association, as he contemplated the fate that had befallen his city. "But I haven't felt like that. This is real."

It was grimly real: a segregationist mob had ruled Little Rock for an ugly moment in U.S. history. Now the face of the law was that of a young U.S. Army paratrooper in battle gear outside Central High School. Little Rock was a name known wherever men could read newspapers and listen to radios, a symbol to be distorted in Moscow, misinterpreted in New Delhi, painfully explained in London. A great issue had been joined between law and anarchy—and as always, it was the innocents, the moderates, who suffered most.

It was small wonder that many of the ordinary citizens of Little Rock thought of their situation as a dream—a nightmare—in which they had played no part. But Presbyterian Ogden pointed up the meaning for ordinary citizens and would-be extremists alike. "This had to happen someplace in the South," said he. "It was inevitable that there was going to be a plan, worked out, approved and accepted, for gradual integration. It was inevitable that somewhere a governor, under pressure of extreme segregationists, was going to stop integration by calling out the National Guard.

"This may be looked back upon by future historians as the turning point—for good—of race relations in this country. If the Supreme Court's interpretation of the Constitution can be made good in Little Rock, then it can be made good in Arkansas. If it can be made good in Arkansas, then eventually it can be made good throughout the South."

"QUICK, HARD & DECISIVE." The President of the U.S. looked once more at the reports arriving in his vacation office near Newport. The weeks of patient working toward peaceful solution were over; a mob, stirred by the governor of Arkansas, still stood in the way of nine Negro youngsters who, by court order, were entitled to join 2,000 whites at Little Rock Central High School. Two aides and a secretary watched silently as President Eisenhower, his decision made, picked up a pen and signed a historic document: it ordered Secretary of Defense Charles Wilson to use the armed forces of the U.S. to uphold the law of the land in Little Rock.

The Pentagon was ready: informed that the President's order was on the way. Wilson rapped out his own instruc-tions. The ground and air forces of the Arkansas National Guard were placed in federal service, safely out of the hands of Governor Orval Faubus, who had used them to defy the U.S. Government. Army Chief of Staff Maxwell Taylor called Fort Campbell, Ky. and assigned the 327th Battle Group of his old outfit, the Screaming Eagles of the 101st Airborne Division, to bring law to Little Rock. Tough, battle-tried Major General Edwin Walker was placed in command of all troops in the Arkansas district. Air Force Secretary James Douglas soon had eight C-130 and 38 C-123 transport planes on the way from Tennessee to Fort Campbell.

That night, just eight hours after President Eisenhower signed his orders, the first trucks of the 101st Airborne drove up to Central High. It was one of the nation's most painful moments, and the first use of U.S. troops in a Southern racial crisis since Reconstruction days. Explained the President in a radio-TV speech to the nation: "The very basis of our individual rights and freedoms rests upon the certainty that the President and the executive branch of Government will support and insure the carrying out of the decisions of the federal courts, even, when necessary, with all the means at the President's command. Unless the President did so, anarchy would result."

LIFE OF THE PARTY. The President did not mention Orval Faubus by name, but it was Faubus, more than any other, who had confronted the U.S. with a choice between law and anarchy. During the previous three weeks, egged on by racists around him, he had stirred Little Rock into emotional turmoil. Ambitious for a third term, eager to win political support from Arkansas segregationists, he had thwarted a federal court integration order by calling out his National Guard to "prevent violence" in a city where none existed. What the National Guard was really being used for was to bar the nine Negro children from Central High. Making each new step more drastic than his last, Faubus made inflammatory statement after inflammatory state-ment. He called off the National Guard in response to an injunction issued against him by U.S. District Judge Ronald Davies, spurning Judge Davies' alternative offer: to change the National Guard's orders so that the militia would uphold—rather than defy—law and order.

Orval Faubus had thus staked his political future on his claim that there would be violence in Little Rock. Almost single-handed he had created the reality of violence from its

Honor Guard: There was dead silence as the Negro students left school

myth. After withdrawing his National Guard, he had taken off for the Southern Governors' Conference at Sea Island, Ga., stopping on the way to see the Georgia-Texas football game at Atlanta. ("He's really lapping up the glory," said one of his fellow governors. "There were 33,000 people at the game, and every time they cheered a play, Faubus stood up and bowed.") The next night Faubus cavorted in the Silver Room of Sea Island's Cloister Hotel, signing autographs, sipping bourbon and Seven-Up, and dancing. Orval Faubus was the life of the party. The night wore on—and the dawn approached when he would get violence in Little Rock.

"THERE'S A NIGGER." Monday morning in Little Rock came bright and crisp. At 6 A.M., on the day that Judge Davies had ordered integration to begin at Central High School, about 70 cops stood idly swinging billy clubs behind sawhorse barricades. These were the men that Mayor Woodrow Wilson Mann, former insurance agent turned well-meaning—but sometimes ineffectual—public servant, had said could preserve the peace in Little Rock. (Police Chief Marvin Potts apparently was not so sure: he judiciously stayed in his office.) But right at the beginning the Little Rock cops made their first and greatest mistake: they let a crowd begin to gather. It was small at first, and quiet. Asked one man in grey working clothes of another: "What're you doing here?" Came the reply: "Just came by to see what's doing."

While the cops watched with kindly detachment, the crowd grew. Some roughnecks began drifting in. The police

uneasily tried to make friends. "Do you think I like this?" asked one. "I'm just trying to do my job." An old man turned his dry, grass-fire eyes on Central High School, worked his bare gums in pleasure over the time "we burned a nigger in '27." A fat ex-schoolteacher named Arthur Bickle looked around at the crowd's hooligans, chortled his satisfaction: "They've separated the men from the boys."

Perhaps most important of all, James ("Jimmy the Flash") Karam, head of the Arkansas State Athletic Commission, was on the scene from the beginning. Karam, once a third-string halfback at Auburn (he is fond of recalling his days as an "All-American"), turned professional strikebreaker (he bossed a goon-staffed outfit called Veterans Industrial Association Inc.), then became a Little Rock haberdasher and a near, dear friend to Governor Orval Faubus. Last week, while his wife was with Orval and Alta Faubus at Sea Island, Jimmy Karam moved purposefully around the crowd outside Central High School, whispering here, nodding curtly there, ducking into a gasoline station to make telephone calls.

"IF YOU WANT TO BE CHICKEN." Assistant Police Chief Eugene Smith, in charge at the high school, watched the crowd sharply, began to feel a sense of purpose and organization, noted that "half the troublemakers were from out of town." A girl in a yellow skirt talked to a schoolboy, his books in one hand, a gallon jug with two lively brown mice in the other. "If you want to be chicken," said the girl, "go on in." The boy smiled shamefacedly—and went to school. The

Central High School class bell rang at 8:45—and at almost that instant a shriek went up: "Here come the niggers!"

Four Negro newsmen had foolishly approached the crowd from the rear. It was the tinder's spark. Some 20 rednecks turned on the Negroes, began chasing them back down the block. Other whites streamed behind. A one-armed man, his dimpled stump below his shirtsleeve, swung wildly at one Negro. Another Negro (a onetime U.S. marine) decided not to run, ambled with terrifying dignity through a gauntlet of blows, kicks and curses. A cop stood on a car bumper to get a better view. Other cops moved toward the fighting. Faubus Henchman James Karam cried angrily, "The nigger started it!" A huge man came up behind Karam and said: "Get five or six boys, and get them over there where the nigger kids came in last time." State Athletic Commissioner Karam led five bullyboys to the other end of the school.

The Negro children had already entered Central High School. While the mob's attention was distracted by the Negro newsmen, the nine students stepped from two cars and walked slowly, calmly into the school. But the mob had nonetheless won the first day's battle of Central High School: it had discovered that it could act violently without suffering at the hands of the cops. From that moment on, the result was inevitable. The mob grew from 300 to 500 to 900; it had tasted blood and liked it. It churned madly around and, in the absence of Negroes to maul, turned on Northern newsmen, beating three LIFE staffers. At noon Little Rock's Mayor Woodrow Wilson Mann ordered the Negro children withdrawn from the school.

Far away at sunny Sea Island, having kept in telephone touch, Orval Faubus proclaimed his triumph: "The trouble in Little Rock vindicates my good judgment." But the grin was soon wiped off his face by the dramatic rush of events in Washington and Newport.

"I WILL HAVE TO SIGN IT." President Eisenhower had resisted all public and private cries for drastic action, had worked determinedly to keep Little Rock's trouble where it belonged: in the courtroom instead of the street. But his personal conference with Orval Faubus in Newport heightened his growing suspicion that he might have to move, however reluctantly, into the Little Rock situation. "If I do," he told an associate, "you can bet one thing. It will be quick, hard and decisive." Preparing against the day, Attorney General Herbert Brownell drafted a proclamation ordering compliance with the court's decision and opening the way for the eventual use of U.S. troops in Little Rock.

On the Monday morning that integration began at Central High School, President Eisenhower flew to Washington for a speaking engagement before the International Monetary Fund, then held a brief, tense conference with Brownell. Barely back in Rhode Island that afternoon, Ike heard from Brownell over the maximum-security telephone in his personal quarters. The news was all bad. A mob ruled at Central High. School Superintendent Virgil Blossom (voted the city's Man of the Year in 1955, now vilified for backing a gradual integration plan) had excitedly called the Justice Department: "Mayor Mann wants to know who to call to get federal help."

To Dwight Eisenhower, the issue was not integration v. segregation; it was the integrity of the U.S. Government and its judicial decisions. Orval Faubus had left him no choice. Said he to Brownell: "I want you to send up that proclamation. It looks like I will have to sign it, but I want to read it again." That evening, on the porch of his living quarters, President Eisenhower signed the proclamation demanding all persons obstructing justice in Little Rock "to cease and desist wherefrom and to disperse forthwith."

Only one hope remained for avoiding the use of U.S. troops in Little Rock: obedience next morning to the proclamation. The President, walking to his office just before 8 A.M., noticed that "there's a cold wind blowing up." There was indeed: the reports from Brownell began flooding in. The mob had not dispersed. Shoving and shouting outside Central High School, it refrained from violence only because the Negro children did not appear. A telegram came from Little Rock's Mayor Mann: the situation was beyond the control of local authorities. Then President Eisenhower signed the order that sent the Screaming Eagles to Little Rock.

"HELLO DEFIANCE." Only a handful of people stood outside Central High School that night as the troops hove in sight. The paratroopers spilled out of their trucks, formed smartly on the school grounds. Field telephone lines were strung from the trunks of the high school's lordly oaks. Jeeps moved around to the rear of the school, parked in a line along practice-football charging machines. Pup tents blossomed in back of the school's tennis courts. Colonel William A. Kuhn, smart and salty, swung a swagger stick as he examined a map of the school grounds.

By 5 A.M. Wednesday, combat-ready paratroopers lined the two blocks of Park Avenue in front of the school, stood with fixed bayonets on corners a block away in each direction. Radio patrol jeeps sped back and forth.

A crowd began gathering a block east of the school, where "Roadblock Alpha" had been thrown up at an intersection. Major James Meyers, a thin, hard man with the glint of a hawk in his eyes, ordered up a sound truck. "Please return to your homes." said he, "or it will be necessary for us to disperse you."

Nobody moved. "Nigger lover," muttered a man. A voice came from the shadows: "Russian!" A man in a brown suit was full of bravado: "They're just bluffing. If you don't want to move, you don't have to." Meyers snapped out an order: a dozen paratroopers moved into line, rifles at the on-guard position (butts on hip, bayonets forward). Brown Suit held his ground for a moment against the advancing soldiers, then scurried away with the rest of the crowd.

ONE LAST WORD. When the class bell finally rang, the Negro students had not yet arrived. District Commander

Walker, out of rugged Hill County, Texas (where it is said of the best people: "They kill their own snakes"), called the white pupils into the auditorium, explained his mission: "You have nothing to fear from my soldiers, and no one will interfere with your coming, going, or your peaceful pursuit of your studies...One last word about my soldiers. They are here because they have been ordered to be here. They are seasoned, well-trained soldiers, many of them combat veterans. Being soldiers, they are as determined as I to carry out their orders."

A few minutes later a crisp, careful military movement put the nine Negro children safely into Central High School. A jeep rolled through the barricade at 16th Street and Park Avenue, followed by an Army station wagon and another jeep. The Negroes piled out of the station wagon. Three platoons came on the double across the school grounds, deployed in strategic positions. Another platoon lined up on either side of the Negroes, escorted them inside the building. There was dead silence around Central High School.

THE LIVING END. But not for long—trouble was developing at Roadblock Alpha, the day's hot spot. The crowd was growing again. Major Meyers ordered it to move on. Nothing happened—and Meyers was fed up. He rasped harshly over his loudspeaker: "Let's clear this area right now. This is the living end! I'll tell you, we're not going to do it on a slow walk this time."

The crowd scrambled back onto the front lawn and porch of a private home, screaming protests that the soldiers had no right to bother them there. The paratroopers came on, moved up the porch steps, began pushing people off. A Missouri Pacific switchman named C. E. Blake, for days one of the most vocal of the agitators around Central High ("I advocate violence"), grabbed for a rifle, pulled a paratrooper to the ground with him. Another trooper reversed his rifle, smashed its butt against Blake's head. Blake, blood streaming from a shallow scalp wound, scuttled away, shouting to newsmen and photographers as he went: "Who knows the name of that lowlife s.o.b. who hit me?" A top sergeant ordered his men: "Keep those bayonets high—right at the base of the neck."

The cold toughness of the Screaming Eagles abruptly put an end to violence at Roadblock Alpha—or anywhere else around Central High. The Negro children reported that they were well treated inside the school. (Arkansas N.A.A.C.P. Leader Daisy Bates had carefully coached her charges to be prepared for insults, to be dignified when vilified, and above all to reveal no bitterness when questioned by newsmen.) During the noon hour a white boy and girl, both school leaders, saw a Negro boy eating alone. They asked: "Would you like to come over to our table?" The boy smiled gratefully: "Gosh, I'd love to." And another Negro pupil recalled: "The white kids broke the ice. They talked to us." Clearly, many of the white children of Central High School were proving themselves better citizens than their elders.

MONUMENT TO DEMAGOGUERY. Orval Faubus, mean-while, had flown back from Sea Island. Arriving in Little Rock, Faubus joked feebly: "I feel like MacArthur. I've been relieved of my job." But Orval Faubus had no intention of fading away. He holed up in his executive mansion and began working on a national television speech.

It was a monument to demagoguery. "Evidence of the naked force of the Federal Government is here apparent in these unsheathed bayonets in the backs of schoolgirls," cried Faubus, holding up a photograph—but not long enough to show that the girls were merely walking, giggling, past a line of troopers. In the Faubus account, bloodied Agitator Blake was suddenly transformed into a "guest in a home." The Army had gone on an orgy of "wholesale arrests." Actual number: eight, with four fined for loitering, and four released at the police station. Teen-age girls had "been taken by the FBI and held incommunicado for hours of questioning while their frantic parents knew nothing of their whereabouts." (Said FBI Director John Edgar Hoover: Faubus was "disseminating falsehoods.")

Then, overwhelmed by the injustice of it all, Orval Faubus recalled that as a World War II officer in the 35th Infantry Division he had "helped rescue" the 101st Airborne from Bastogne (by the time the 35th arrived on the scene, it was the Germans who needed rescuing from the Screaming Eagles). Cried Orval Faubus: "Today we find the members of the famed division, which I helped rescue, in Little Rock. Ark., bludgeoning innocent bystanders, with bayonets in the backs of schoolgirls, and the warm, red blood of patriotic American citizens staining the cold, naked, unsheathed knives. In the name of God, whom we all revere, in the name of liberty we hold so dear, which we all cherish, what is happening in America?"

PLACING THE BLAME. What was happening in America was that Orval Faubus had failed in his attempt to overturn the law of the land with force. In the strongest official language he had used since entering the White House, President Eisenhower placed the blame for Little Rock's ordeal where it belonged: on Orval Faubus. Replying to a message of protest from Georgia's Senator Richard Russell (whom Ike had gone out of his way to placate during the fight on civil rights legislation in the 85th Congress), the President said:

"Few times in my life have I felt as saddened as when the obligations of my office required me to order the use of a force within a state to carry out the decisions of a federal court. My conviction is that had the police powers of the State of Arkansas been used not to frustrate the orders of the court but to support them, the ensuing violence and open disrespect for the law and for the federal judiciary would never have occurred...

"As a matter of fact, had the integration of Central High School been permitted to take place without the intervention of the National Guard, there is little doubt that the process would have gone along quite as smoothly and quietly as it has in other Arkansas communities." ∎

The Promise and the Pride

America's forgotten natives fight for their honor

Promise

ON A WARM SPRING DAY as twelve Navaho chiefs looked on, Lieut. General William Tecumseh Sherman dipped a pen and solemnly squiggled his name on the document before him. With that act in 1868, the U.S. formally promised that in return to the Navahos for keeping the peace, the Government would provide the tribe with a reservation (now extending into Arizona, Utah and New Mexico), schools, and at least one teacher for every 30 children. The promise has been badly kept. As recently as 1951, Mrs. Annie Wauneka, daughter of the last great Navaho chieftain, Chee Dodge, said sadly: "We will forever be like monkeys in a cage, for other Americans to look at."

Last week both Government officials and Navahos could agree that the monkey business was just about over. The illiteracy rate among Navaho children is down from 75% ten years ago to 25%, and more little Indians than ever before are now attending school. One reason for the change: the Navahos have at last been sold on education. But perhaps more important: largely because of the work of Indian Affairs Commissioner Glenn L. Emmons, they have at last become convinced that the U.S. really intends to live up to the treaty of 1868.

THE CHANGE. A longtime friend of the Navahos ("I sorta grew up with them"), Banker Glenn Emmons of Gallup, N. Mex. was the tribal council's personal choice for commissioner, and new President Eisenhower heeded their advice. When Emmons took the job in 1953, there were 28,000 school-age Navahos, but half of these had yet to see the inside of a classroom. Though Emmons got a congressional appropriation to build scores of new schools, he decided that the shortage was too acute to wait. "The important thing," said he, "is to get every child into school as fast as possible. We can build the nice buildings later." The Bureau of Indian Affairs began to refurbish old classrooms. It added new wings to buildings already standing, put up Quonset huts, sent out trailers, arranged for some children to attend nearby public schools off the reservation. By 1954, Navaho enrollment was up 8,000.

Meanwhile, the Navaho Tribal Council was hard at work. Its biggest problem: to persuade all parents that their children must go to school.

THE REALITY. During World War II, when so many of their young men were rejected by the Army as illiterates, many Navahos learned what it means to have too little education. But there were still some who distrusted the white man's ways, and there were others who liked to have their children help out at home. To keep their children away from school, such parents often used the excuse that they had nothing to wear. The council appropriated $350,000 from its new oil and uranium royalties, announced that clothes would be given to any needy child who went to school. The bureau added a further incentive by providing free hot lunches. The tribal council has also turned its attention to higher education. In 1953 it set aside $30,000 for college scholarships. This year it upped the sum to an annual $100,000.

Last week a record 23,000 Navaho children were in school. By December, enrollments are expected to be 2,500 over last year. The hopes of 1868 were at last to be fulfilled. ■

Soldier's Burial

JOHN RICE, a Winnebago whose Indian name is Walking in Blue Sky, loved his native land and was more than willing to fight for it. He enlisted in the Army shortly after Pearl Harbor, served 40 months in the Pacific. There, as a doughboy in the 32nd Infantry Division, he was wounded in battle, contracted malaria, won the Bronze Star. After the war, he went back to the reservation at Winnebago, Neb., but soon re-enlisted as a Regular Army man. Last September, serving as a rifleman with the 1st Cavalry Division above Taegu in Korea, Sergeant John Rice, 37, was killed in action.

He had always said he wanted to be buried in a military cemetery, so his widow Evelyn bought a lot in the military section of the Memorial Park Cemetery, 25 miles from Winnebago, outside Sioux City, Ia. Last week, John Rice's funeral procession rolled through the undulating corn country from Winnebago to Sioux City. At the grave an American Legion firing squad fired the traditional three volleys of the military burial service. The service ended when Evelyn Rice was given the flag that had draped her husband's coffin.

But after all the mourners had gone, a cemetery official asked a strange question: "Was that boy an Indian?" While the coffin still rested above the grave, he explained that the cemetery articles of incorporation restrict it to "members of the Caucasian race." The body was taken back to the mortuary.

The undertaker went to the weather-beaten farmhouse where Evelyn Rice lives. She had been composed at the grave, but now she could not hold back the tears. "Why?" she sobbed. With her three small children around her, John Rice's widow tried to decide what to do.

Early next morning the President of the U.S. solved her problems. Harry Truman read the news story of what had happened, ordered a wire sent off to Sioux City: "Please advise the family of Sergeant John R. Rice that arrangements for burial in Arlington Cemetery have been authorized. The President feels that the national appreciation of patriotic sacrifice should not be limited by race, color or creed."

This week a U.S. military plane will take Mrs. Rice to Washington for her husband's second funeral. Walking in Blue Sky will be buried with full military honors in Arlington National Cemetery, where the color of a soldier's skin no longer makes a difference. ∎

Proud Men

IN MAY 1943, on the eve of their embarkation for overseas duty, 1,500 members of the 45th Infantry Division, all American Indians, staged a war dance. Last week, when the 45th returned to the U.S. from its latest overseas tour, 1,000 men marched from Manhattan's Bowling Green to City Hall, where General Matthew Ridgway, Mayor Robert Wagner, and a host of brass were waiting to welcome them home. Along Broadway the traditional ticker tape slithered down on the marching men—the first to return from Korea as a unit—and a crowd of 250,000 New Yorkers cheered them on their way. After the ceremonies, the men of the Thunderbird Division dispersed, some to other units, others to civilian life, and the 45th, a National Guard outfit, was honorably retired from active duty and sent back to its home state, Oklahoma.

SICILY TO MUNICH. Between the war dance and the Broadway parade, the Thunderbirds followed a long and bloody trail of soldiering around the world. In World War II the 45th was a crack assault division. In eight campaigns, from Sicily to Munich, it made four landings (Sicily, Salerno, Anzio, the French Riviera), spent 511 days in action, suffered 20,993 casualties (second only to the 3rd Division). The Nazi army learned to respect and fear the men of the fast-stepping "Falcon" Division, who overran 1,000 square miles of Sicily in one three-week action. ("Don't you ever sleep?" asked a German P.W.) The folks at home knew the men of the 45th as the models for Willie and Joe, Thunderbird Cartoonist Bill Mauldin's ragged, wistful G.I.s and the prototypes of World War II foot soldiers everywhere.

After V-J day, the 45th returned to Oklahoma and inactive duty. At a convention in 1951, the 45th Division Association passed a resolution demanding that the division be enlarged to Marine Corps size, and that the commanding general be given equal status on the J.C.S. The Thunderbirds, said the association, participated in four major landings, and in more combat days than any Marine division, "in fact, as many as any three Marine divisions." The marines regarded this petition as in bad taste.

BALDY TO HEARTBREAK RIDGE. In 1950 the 45th was called to federal service once more, entered combat in Korea a year later. The division found itself in a new, essentially defensive role. In 429 combat days, the 45th spent most of its time in counterattacks and blackface night patrols, but it saw plenty of action, too—at Baldy, the Punchbowl, and at Heartbreak Ridge. In the battlefield judgment of James Van Fleet, the 45th, "as far as combat effectiveness is concerned, is perhaps as good as any division we have."

By the time of the Korean armistice, the 45th was a battle-weary old Thunderbird, top-heavy with honors (more than 10,000 decorations, including nine Medals of Honor), campaigns (twelve battle stars) and casualties (preliminary count: 36,231). In the spirit of the divisional motto, *Semper Anticus* (Always Forward), the 45th had never yielded an inch of territory to the enemy. A platoon sergeant on Old Baldy once explained the 45th's fighting record. It was all a matter of pride: "The ones from Oklahoma—the Guard guys—got pride because I guess they figure they represent Oklahoma over here…The others—the draftees and R.A. guys—figure they ain't gonna let somebody they figure a Saturday-night soldier out-soldier them. And anybody that knows about a war knows that the kind of pride people are willing to pay off on can take an outfit a long, long way." ∎

*L*ong bottled up, the tension of America's racial problems erupted onto the streets. History was made in an unforgettable series of events: Birmingham. Selma. The March on Washington. "I have a dream." Watts. The Civil Rights Act of 1964. The Voting Rights Act of 1965. The murders of Malcolm X and Martin Luther King Jr. The rise of Cesar Chavez and La Causa. In the middle of the turmoil, Congress passed a new immigration law that would dramatically shift the future makeup of America, rejecting the "national origins" law that discriminated against Southern Europeans and Asians and assuring entry to immigrants from nations everywhere.

THE 1960s

Freedom—Now

A symbol of segregation, Birmingham boils over

Marching for Justice   MAY 17, 1963

BIRMINGHAM NEGROES had always been a docile lot. Downtown at night, they slouched in gloomy huddles beneath street lamps, talking softly or not at all. They knew their place: they were "niggers" in a Jim Crow town, and they bore their degradation in silence.

Last week they smashed that image forever. The scenes in Birmingham were unforgettable. There was the Negro youth, sprawled on his back and spinning across the pavement, while firemen battered him with streams of water so powerful that they could strip bark off trees. There was the Negro woman, pinned to the ground by cops, one of them with his knee dug into her throat. There was the white man who watched hymn-singing Negroes burst from a sweltering church and growled: "We ought to shoot every damned one of them." And there was the little Negro girl, splendid in a newly starched dress, who marched out of a church, looked toward a massed line of pistol-packing cops, and called to a laggard friend: "Hurry up, Lucille. If you stay behind, you won't get arrested with our group."

For more than a month, Negro demonstrations in Birmingham had sputtered, bursting occasionally into flames, then flickering out. Martin Luther King, the Negroes' inspirational but sometimes inept leader, had picked this bastion of racial inequality for the crusade, "because Birmingham is the symbol of segregation." In the last six years, there have been 18 racial bombings (Negroes call it "Bombingham") and more than 50 cross-burnings. Schools are totally segregated. So are restaurants, drinking fountains, toilets. Birmingham gave up its professional baseball team rather than have it playing integrated teams in the International League. The Metropolitan Opera Company no longer visits the city, because officials refused to integrate the municipal auditorium. Parks were shut down last year, because officials would not integrate them after a court order.

Unquestionably, Birmingham was the toughest segregation town in the South, from the Negroes' viewpoint. And it was symbolized by Public Safety Commissioner Eugene ("Bull") Connor, who had cowed Negroes for 23 years with hoarse threats and club-swinging cops.

King began planning the Birmingham action before last Christmas. He went to Birmingham himself, conducted a series of workshops in nonviolent protests and recruited 200 volunteers willing to go to jail for freedom. When he left, he told no one else in Birmingham of his plans. He didn't dare. Bull Connor had a ring of spies in the Negro community. Also King was obsessed by the fear that other groups, more aligned to violence than he was, might move into Birmingham. But he got there first.

King and Connor clashed head-on. The commissioner had his cops—plus a pack of snarling police dogs and a battery of high-pressure fire hoses. The Negro minister had only the determination and courage of his people. He had mobilized schoolchildren for his freedom parades. Hundreds of kids were in jail, and, as last week began, Birmingham was at the point of explosion.

"FORGIVE THEM." On Sunday, the Negroes tried, as they had before, to worship in white churches. But segregation in Birmingham's Christian churches is nearly as rigid as in public toilets: Negroes got into four churches, were ordered away from 17 others. Late in the afternoon, King called a mass meeting at the New Pilgrim Baptist Church. Outside, Bull Connor massed 50 policemen and a fire truck with water pressure cranked up to 700 lbs. When the crowd of 1,000 poured out of the church just before dusk, they lined up and marched toward the police. A police captain demanded their parade permit. They had none. Seeing the fire hoses, they knelt in silence as a Negro minister solemnly began to pray: "Let them turn their water on. Let them use their dogs. We are not leaving. Forgive them, O Lord."

Suddenly, inexplicably, in a moment of overt mercy, Bull Connor waved the Negroes through the police line. He allowed them 15 minutes of hymns and prayer in a small park near the city jail; inside, behind bars, hundreds of other Negroes could hear the singing. Returning to the church, the demonstrators were told that Negro children would march again next day—and should carry their toothbrushes with them to use in jail.

"THOSE BLACK APES." So there was violence. It began shortly after noon the next day. Connor's cops were relaxed, eating sandwiches and sipping soft drinks. They were caught by surprise when the doors of the 16th Street church were flung open and 2,500 Negroes swarmed out. The Negroes surged across Kelly Ingram Park, burst through the police line, and descended on downtown Birmingham. Yelling and singing, they charged in and out of department stores, jostled whites on the streets, paralyzed traffic.

Recovering, the police got reinforcements. Firemen hooked up their hoses. Motorcycles and squad cars, sirens blaring, rushed into the area. Two policemen grabbed a Negro, shoved him against a storefront—and found themselves caught inside a glowering circle of 300 Negroes. A

Water fells a Negro demonstrator: "Let them turn their water on. Let them use their dogs."

voice growled menacingly: "Let's free him." But demonstration leaders quickly broke into the circle and managed to save the policemen.

The riot ebbed—and then, an hour later, exploded again. In Kelly Ingram Park, hundreds of Negroes began lobbing bricks and bottles at the lawmen. A deputy sheriff fell to the pavement, shouting "Those black apes!"

For two hours, the battle raged, but slowly, inexorably, in trucks and cars, the police closed in on the park. The Rev. Fred Shuttlesworth, one of King's top advisers, yelled helplessly at rioters from in front of the church, finally took a blast of water that slammed him violently against a wall. An ambulance took him away, and when Bull Connor heard about it later, he leered in mock despair: "I waited a week down here to see that, and then I missed it. I wish it had been a hearse."

Now it was over. The Negroes were forced back into the church, and Commissioner Connor glared at the closed doors. Said he: "If any of those guys in that church there is a preacher, then I'm a watchmaker—and I've never seen the

inside of a watch. They say they're nonviolent? I got three men hurt today. Is that nonviolence?"

That night, Alabama's ultra-segregationist Governor George Wallace sent 600 men to reinforce Bull Connor's weary cops. And Martin Luther King appeared before his followers to say: "We will turn America upside down in order that it turn right side up."

Birmingham had already been upset—and all but overturned. Downtown merchants, plagued for more than a year by a Negro boycott that was 90% effective, saw their profits plunging even more because of the demonstrations. Birmingham's racist reputation had long been bad enough to frighten away potential industry; rioting by King's forces would further scar the city's image. And, despite the headline-hogging prominence of such racists as Bull Connor and Governor Wallace, there were a significant number of moderates in Birmingham who wanted peace, simply because they believed the Negro indeed deserved better treatment than he was getting. In fact, last month Birmingham had elected Mayor Albert Boutwell, 58, a relatively cool thinker on racial affairs, over Bull Connor.

THE PALLID PEACE. Even as Negroes fought whites on Birmingham's streets peace talks were under way. A team of Justice Department lawyers, headed by Assistant Attorney General Burke Marshall, went to Birmingham, began a series of meetings with local businessmen. Of the white negotiators, Martin Luther King made four demands: 1) desegregate all public facilities in department and variety stores; 2) give Negroes equal job opportunities; 3) drop all charges against the 2,500 Negroes who had been arrested during the demonstrations; 4) set up a biracial committee to establish a time table for reopening parks and other facilities which Birmingham's city father had closed to avoid integration.

The first meetings were held in deep secrecy, for the white businessmen involved feared both economic and physical reprisals from redneck hoodlums in Birmingham. Marshall attended nearly all of them. Negroes were represented by local committee, including A. G. Gaston one of the U.S.'s few Negro millionaires. Sidney Smyer, a lawyer and real estate man, was the chief spokesman for the whites—and, at week's end, still the only negotiator from that side who had the courage to permit himself to be publicly identified.

There were meetings on Sunday and Monday—handled much like union-management negotiations, with representatives bringing results of the conference back to their leaders. King attended none of the sessions. On Tuesday about 60 white merchants agreed to some of the Negroes' demands. They did it only after Jefferson County Sheriff Melvin Bailey laid the facts on the line: either they do something positive, or martial law would clamp down on Birmingham.

To add to the pressure, the crisis spurred dozens of pleading phone calls from Washington and such

Administration officials as Bobby Kennedy, Treasury Secretary Douglas Dillon and Defense Secretary Robert McNamara. Finally the businessmen gave halfhearted agreement to King's demands—but there was no assurance that they could persuade Birmingham's segregationist politicians to go along, and it was indeed an uneasy peace that settled on the city.

OUT THE WINDOW. It was also a peace without victory after a war without heroes. Bull Connor was by no means Birmingham's only shame; the city's newspapers, for example, put the riot story on an inside page. Yet at the same time, Negro Leader King could be criticized for using children as shock troops and for inciting the protests even as a new, relatively moderate city administration was about to take over Birmingham.

President Kennedy also came in for criticism. At his press conference, Kennedy claimed that the Federal Government had done all it legally could do about Birmingham. But that, insisted other leaders, both white and Negro, was untrue. Said Harvard Law School Dean Erwin Griswold, a member of the U.S. Civil Rights Commission: "It seems clear to me that he hasn't even started to use the powers that are available to him. There are plenty of sections of the U.S. Code under which he could act—if he wanted to." Said Roy Wilkins, executive secretary of the National Association for the Advancement of Colored People, which has long argued that the Negro battle should be fought in the courts instead of the streets: "White people in Alabama make it impossible for us even to debate whether the President should act. My objectivity went out the window when I saw the picture of those cops sitting on that woman and holding her down by the throat."

That is a point of central significance about Birmingham: the law has taken U.S. Negroes about as far as it can; court decisions are a vital Negro weapon, but the Negro masses no longer believe that their war can be won in the chambers of the law. The Negro's progress through law has been glue-footed. Nine years ago this week, the U.S. Supreme Court ruled against school segregation; yet only 7.8% of all Negroes in the South are presently attending integrated public schools—and in many the integration is merely of the token sort.

Birmingham's Negroes were not worried about legalities; they were not worried about the niceties of "timing," or even about the morality of using children as troops. Instead, theirs was a raging desire to achieve equal human status—now, and by whatever means. Massachusetts Attorney General Edward Brooke, a Negro, expressed it well: "The pressure is mounting. It has been smoldering for some time—many, many years. And it is a justifiable impatience." Bob Eckhardt, a white and a member of the Texas legisla-

ture, put it another way: "The Negroes' goals are not in reach of court decisions any longer."

IT COULD HAPPEN ANYWHERE. Birmingham therefore set off a chain reaction—uncontrolled. New lunch-counter sit-ins started in Atlanta. Nashville and Raleigh. The N.A.A.C.P. called for peaceful sympathy demonstrations in 100 cities. Jackie Robinson, now a vice president of Chock Full O' Nuts, said he would go to Birmingham to join in the Negro protest. So did Floyd Patterson. Communism was having a field day. Gloated Radio Moscow: "We have the impression that American authorities both cannot and do not wish to stop outrages by racists." More friendly foreign nations simply could not understand. Snapped a Brazilian official at the United Nations: "Talk about us underdeveloped nations. I think white Birmingham must be the really underdeveloped area—or should I say subdeveloped area?"

Perhaps most baleful of all, the Black Muslim movement within the U.S. Negro community took full recruiting advantage of the Birmingham riots. The Black Muslims do not seek integration; they want total separation of the races, with Negroes not only independent but, if possible, superior. Now Malcolm X, top Eastern torchbearer for the militant movement, could only sneer at Martin Luther King's gospel of nonviolence. Said he: "The lesson of Birmingham is that the Negroes have lost their fear of the white man's reprisals and will react with violence, if provoked. This could happen anywhere in the country today."

Last week, at the crest of the crisis, a white Birmingham waitress said to a customer from the North: "Honey, I sure hope the colored don't win. They've winned so much around the South. Why, you go down and get on a bus, and a nigger's just liable to sit right down beside you. Oh, that's hurt Birmingham somethin' awful."

Neither Malcolm X nor the Birmingham waitress represents the majority of their races. But they do represent and symbolize two fixed positions: the Negro who looks with eagerness toward a militant solution, and the unyielding Southerner who hopes not to be further disturbed. There are many other positions, and there is a long gaping valley of confusion and diffusion. It is a great uncharted space where leaders follow and followers lead, for there is no certainty of plan or purpose there. Negro Author James Baldwin has illuminated this grey gulf with bolts of intellectual lightning.

Baldwin cries out in hopelessness and helplessness as he gazes across the gulf. For that gulf cannot be bridged by law alone; the law can furnish a foundation upon which Negroes can build to achieve their rights, but it cannot provide education, or cure poverty, or enforce understanding, or give body to an old-fashioned thing called humanity.   ∎

The Sunday School Bombing SEPTEMBER 27, 1963

SUNDAY MORNING, Sept. 15, was cool and overcast in Birmingham. Sunday school classes were just ending in the basement of the yellow brick 16th Street Baptist Church, the city's largest Negro church and the scene of several recent civil rights rallies. The morning's lesson was "The Love That Forgives," from the fifth chapter of Matthew. Four girls—Carole Robertson, 14, Cynthia Wesley, 14, Addie Mae Collins, 14, and Denise McNair, 11—left the classroom to go to the bathroom.

At 10:22 the bomb exploded, with the force of ten to 15 sticks of dynamite. It had been planted under the steps behind the 50-year-old building.

Great chunks of stone shot like artillery shells through parked cars. The blast shattered the windshield of a passing car, knocked the driver unconscious. A metal railing, torn from its concrete bed, lanced across the street into the window of the Social Dry Cleaning store. Next door, customers at the Silver Springs Restaurant were knocked to the floor. In nearby Kelly Ingram Park, pieces of brick nipped the leaves off trees 200 ft. from the blast.

BENEATH THE ROBE. Inside the church, a teacher screamed, "Lie on the floor! Lie on the floor!" Rafters collapsed, a skylight fell on the pulpit. Part of a stained glass window shattered, obliterating the face of Christ. A man cried: "Everybody out! Everybody out!" A stream of sobbing Negroes stumbled through the litter—past twisted metal folding chairs, past splintered wooden benches, past shredded songbooks and Bibles. A Negro woman staggered out of the Social Dry Cleaning store shrieking "Let me at 'em! I'll kill 'em!"—and fainted. White plaster dust fell gently for a block around.

Police cars poured into the block—and even as the cops plunged into the church, some enraged Negroes began throwing rocks at them. Rescue workers found a seven-foot pyramid of bricks where once the girls' bathroom stood. On top was a child's white lace choir robe. A civil defense captain lifted the hem of the robe. "Oh, my God," he cried. "Don't look!" Beneath lay the mangled body of a Negro girl.

Bare-handed, the workers dug deeper into the rubble—until four bodies had been uncovered. The head and shoulder of one child had been completely blown off. The remains were covered with shrouds and carried out to waiting ambulances. A youth rushed forward, lifted a sheet and wailed: "This is my sister! My God—she's dead!"

The church's pastor, the Rev. John Cross, hurried up and down the sidewalk, urging the milling crowd to go home. "Please go home!" he said. "The Lord is our shepherd, and we shall not want." Another Negro minister added his pleas. "Go home and pray for the men who did this evil deed," he said. "We must have love in our hearts for these men." But a Negro boy screamed, "We give love—and we get this!" And another youth yelled: "Love 'em? Love 'em? We hate 'em!" A man wept: "My grandbaby was one of those killed! Eleven years old! I helped pull the rocks off her! You know how I feel? I feel like blowing the whole town up!"

The Birmingham police department's six-wheeled riot tank thumped onto the scene and cops began firing shotguns over the heads of the crowd while Negroes pelted them with rocks. Later, Negro youths began stoning passing white cars. The police ordered them to stop. One boy, Johnny Robinson, 16, ran, and a cop killed him with a blast of buckshot. That made five dead and 17 injured in the bomb blast.

"I CAN'T." Several miles away, on the worn-out coal-field fringe of Birmingham, two young Negro brothers, James and Virgil Ware, were riding a bicycle. Virgil, 13, was sitting on the handle bars. A motor scooter with two 16-year-old white boys aboard approached from the opposite direction. James Ware, 16, told what happened then: "This boy on the front of the bike turns and says something to the boy behind him, and the other reaches in his pocket and he says *Pow! Pow!* with a gun twice. Virgil fell and I said, get up Virgil, and he said, I can't, I'm shot."

And so six died on a Sunday in Birmingham. ∎

"The Awful Roar"

A history of the Negroes' fight for rights

If there is no struggle, there is no progress. Those who profess to favor freedom, and yet deprecate agitation, are men who want crops without plowing up the ground. They want the ocean without the awful roar of its many waters.
—ABOLITIONIST NEGRO
FREDERICK DOUGLASS, 1857

IN 1963, THAT AWFUL ROAR is heard as never before.

"My basic strength is those 300,000 lower-class guys who are ready to mob, rob, steal and kill," boasts Cecil Moore, 48, head of the Philadelphia branch of the National Association for the Advancement of Colored People.

Says Mel Ladson, 26, a Miami leader in the Congress of Racial Equality: "I want to be able to go in that restaurant and eat, and it doesn't mean a damn to me if the owner's guts are boiling with resentment. I want to nonviolently beat the hell out of him."

Predicts Dr. Gardner Taylor, 45, Negro pastor of Brooklyn's Concord Baptist Church: "The streets are going to run red with blood."

Cries the Rev. James Bevel, a Mississippi official of the Southern Christian Leadership Conference: "Some punk who calls himself the President has the audacity to tell people to go slow. I'm not prepared to be humiliated by white trash the rest of my life, including Mr. Kennedy."

These are voices—some voices—of the Negro revolution. That revolution, dramatically symbolized in this week's massed march in Washington, has burst out of the South to engulf the North. It has made it impossible for almost any Negro to stay aloof, except at the cost of ostracism by other Negroes as an "Uncle Tom." It has seared the white conscience—even while, in some of its excesses, it has created white bitterness where little or none existed before. And right up to the President of the U.S., it has forced white politicians who have long cashed in on their lip service to "civil rights" to put up or shut up.

TOWARD JIM CROW. Negroes helped blaze trails in America, sometimes as slaves but often as scouts and valued aides to many of the famed explorers. They were with Columbus, Balboa, Ponce de Leon, Cortes, Pizarro, Menendez, De Soto. Free Negroes were among the first pioneers to settle in the Mississippi Valley in the 17th century. In Virginia, Negro colonists knew no inferiority of status, owned land, voted, mingled with whites. Some 5,000 Negroes fought the British as troops in George Washington's army.

Many of the first slaves in America were, in fact, Indians. In bondage, however, the Indian proved sickly, often died. Indentured white servants were used for a time but too often broke away, easily lost their slave identity among white colonists. Only after such failures did the white man begin large-scale enslavement of the Negro, who possessed two ideal qualities: he was strong, and if he fled, his face stood out in a crowd.

Contrary to the notion that his revolution is of relatively recent origin, the Negro has always fought against his servitude. Before the Civil War ended, there were at least 250 slave revolts or conspiracies in the U.S., including the slaughter of 60 Virginia whites in 1831. Between 1810 and 1860, some 100,000 slaves, valued at more than $30 million, slipped away to freedom in the North. Others protested in more subtle ways. They took to their beds with mysterious "miseries." They "accidentally" ruined plows and wagons. They "forgot" to cinch a saddle tightly—and many a master took a painful fall.

The Civil War brought the Negro his "emancipation," and Reconstruction gave him an intoxicating power in Southern state legislatures that he was totally unprepared to exercise responsibly (Negroes outnumbered whites in the South Carolina legislature in 1868). Easily led by the Northern white carpetbagger, the Negro lawmakers, like those in some young African nations today, indulged in an orgy of pork-barreling and political corruption. It was in direct reaction to such abuses that Southern whites, on regaining political control, enacted Jim Crow laws. The first, passed by the Tennessee legislature in 1881, imposed segregated seating in railroad cars. Other Southern states followed in other, more oppressive ways. By 1910, most of the laws that Negroes are fighting today were on the books.

TWO ROWS FOR A BAD ONE. It was the first decade of the 20th century that gave birth to the National Association for the Advancement of Colored People. In 1905, the brilliant but eccentric Dr. William E. B. Du Bois, one of the founders of the American Negro Academy, set up a narrowly based protest group of Negro elite known as the Niagara Movement (its first meeting was held near Niagara Falls in 1905). Declared Du Bois: "We claim for ourselves every right that belongs to a freeborn American—political, civil and social—and until we get these rights, we will never cease to protest and assail the ears of America with the story of its shameful deeds toward us." A well-to-do New York white woman, Mary White Ovington, covered that speech for the New York *Evening Post*, with other liberals conceived the idea of a national biracial conference on the Negro question. She helped persuade *Post* Publisher Oswald Garrison Villard, who later edited the *Nation* for 15 years, to write a "Call to Action" that led directly to the formation of the N.A.A.C.P. Among those who issued the call on Lincoln's Birthday 1909 were Professor John Dewey, William Lloyd Garrison, Jane Addams, Rabbi Stephen S. Wise and Lincoln Steffens.

At that time, the N.A.A.C.P.'s most massive efforts were directed against lynchings—and it is difficult for Americans today to realize just what terror that word held for Negroes. For the 30 years ending in 1918, the N.A.A.C.P. lists 3,224 cases in which people were hanged, burned or otherwise murdered by white mobs. No Negro could feel really safe— for reasons perhaps best described in the well-authenticated report of one famed lynching: "A mob near Valdosta, Ga., frustrated at not finding the man they sought for murdering a plantation owner, lynched three innocent Negroes instead; the pregnant wife of one wailed at her husband's death so loudly that the mob seized her and burned her alive, too." Says Roy Wilkins of the priority given by the N.A.A.C.P. to its antilynch efforts: "We had to stop lynching because they were killing us. We had to provide physical security."

Wilkins himself suffered his first (and one of his few) arrests as a picket in Washington in 1934 after Franklin Roosevelt's Attorney General Homer Cummings failed to include lynching on the agenda of a national conference on crime. But as the N.A.A.C.P. had already discovered, and as Wilkins soon learned, the overt physical demonstration is not necessarily the most effective way to achieve Negro aims.

In the antilynch battle, the most powerful weapon of the N.A.A.C.P. was publicity. Wilkins' boss, Walter White, was a superb propagandist. Actually one sixty-fourth Negro in family-tree terms, White insisted upon classifying himself as a Negro. He was blond and blue-eyed, and one of his favorite tactics was to go out to investigate a lynching, pass himself off as a white newsman, win the confidence of local law officials—and return to write a brutally detailed report.

The N.A.A.C.P. never did achieve its main aim, that of a federal antilynch law. But it did impress itself enough on the white conscience to end lynching. Slowly, tortuously, the lynch rate fell from 64 in 1921 to 28 in 1933 to five in 1940 to, for the first time, none in 1952. To be sure, white hoodlums still love to lob bombs at the homes of Negro leaders, but the last real lynch killing that the U.S. has known was that of Mississippi Negro Mack Charles Parker in 1959. Says the N.A.A.C.P.'s Wilkins: "We have completely changed the thinking of the country on lynching. At one time it was defended in the Senate, and even in the pulpit. There is no comparison now with the fear we once knew."

"PAPER DECREES." Once the struggle against lynch law was won, the N.A.A.C.P. could give top priority to another drive—against segregated education. By deliberate deci-

sion, the organization made that assault not so much in the press, or on the streets, or in the lobbies of Congress, but in the courts. N.A.A.C.P. Special Counsel Thurgood Marshall pleaded the cause of school integration before the Supreme Court, was upheld in the historic decision of 1954—and in the minds of many Negroes at the time, that decision opened the way to real racial equality in the U.S.

This expectation fell far, and tragically, short of fulfillment. In both South and North, public officials found all sorts of ways to delay, avoid or simply ignore implementation of the Supreme Court's order. Dashed to the ground, Negro hopes arose once more in 1957, when President Eisenhower ordered Federal troops into Little Rock to enforce token high school integration.

But even after Little Rock, progress seemed agonizingly slow. In this epochal era of Negro frustration, new leaders and new organizations began bursting out all over. Perhaps the most successful has been the Rev. Martin Luther King's Southern Christian Leadership Conference. In 1955-56, Baptist King, an exponent of the Gandhian technique of massive but passive protest, successfully led a boycott to end bus segregation in Montgomery, Ala. The post-Little Rock disappointments gave King's movement even greater impetus. King himself has explained: "We were confronted with blasted hopes, and the dark shadow of a deep disappointment settled upon us. So we had no alternative except that of preparing for direct action, whereby we would present our very bodies as a means of laying our case before the conscience of the local and national community."

THE FANGS. Last April, King sent out marchers, including troops of Negro schoolchildren, to protest discrimination in hiring and at lunch counters, rest rooms and other public facilities in Birmingham. Many civil rights leaders, both Negro and white, thought the effort was singularly ill-timed—after all, a new, perhaps more moderate, city administration was about to take over Birmingham. But the way it turned out, King's demonstrations may reasonably be considered the sparking point for the Negro revolution of 1963.

King's accomplishment came only with the inadvertent help of Birmingham whites, particularly that of Public Safety Commissioner Eugene ("Bull") Connor, who during the Birmingham crisis became an international symbol of blind, cruel Southern racism. When King sent out his marchers, Connor had them mowed down by streams from fire hoses. Shocking news photos splashed across the pages of the world's press—of a young Negro sent sprawling by a jet of water, of a Negro woman pinioned to the sidewalk with a cop's knee at her throat, of police dogs lunging at fleeing Negroes.

With that, millions of people—North and South, black and white—felt the fangs of segregation and, at least in spirit, joined the protest movement. The revolution was on—in earnest. Places little known for anything else became bywords for racial conflict—Anniston, Ala., Albany, Ga.,

Prince Edward County, Va., Cambridge, Md., Englewood, N.J., Greenwood and Greenville, Miss., Goldsboro and Greensboro, N.C.

Baltimore Postman William Moore, a white man murdered as he walked along an Alabama highway wearing an integration sign, and Mississippi N.A.A.C.P. Leader Medgar Evers, shot in the back outside his home, became martyrs to the cause. Direct-action protests proliferated. There were more "freedom walks" and "freedom marches"—and then came the "freedom calls," in which Negroes harass white city officials by calling them on the telephone, murmuring "Freedom" and hanging up.

There are boycotts—Negro leaders prefer to call them "selective patronage movements"—against business firms that discriminate against Negroes in their personnel practices. There are rent strikes against slumlords who refuse to repair Negro tenements. There is the "sit-in" technique and its myriad variations: the "swim-in" to integrate pools, the "wade-in" at beaches, the "pray-in" at churches, the "wait-in" at housing developments. Demonstrators jam restaurant parking lots in "park-ins," line up at theater ticket booths in "stand-ins," prostrate themselves before bulldozers at construction-site "lie-ins." Demonstrators have harassed New York's Mayor Robert Wagner by a "chain-in," in which they tried to lock themselves to a city hall pillar. They even dumped tenement trash in City Hall Plaza to protest slum conditions.

A VARIETY OF WEAPONS. The National Association for the Advancement of Colored People as headed by Roy Wilkins (he succeeded White in 1955) has also suffered under the pressures of the Negro revolution. But it has survived them and maintained its leadership. One reason is that Wilkins himself is a firm believer in the idea that the Negro should use every possible means to achieve his rights. Says Wilkins:

"It's really thrilling and exciting to be a Negro in the '60s," he says. "The whole gamut of Negro life is an adventure if you can roll with the punches and not let it get you into the valley of bitterness. This urgency? This new push? Well, it's cumulative. It's the emergence of Africa. It's being hungry. It's military desegregation. It's the G.I. Bill. It's major-league baseball with Negroes. It's the 8,000 to 10,000 Negroes graduating from college each year, 100,000 since the war. It's the mechanization of farms—the move from farms to Southern cities and then to Western cities. It's the consumer demand television builds. It's kids being impatient. That's why we have it now.

"The back of segregation is broken. A whole new era is before us. This will be a period when the Negro will have to make readjustments. We must counsel our Negro population on induction into an integrated society, teach them that you can't blame all disabilities on race, because this is self-defeating. A great number of Negroes are ready for all their rights now. A great number are not fully aware of the competition and responsibility which await them in an unsegregated world.

"There's going to be beer, and doubleheaders with the Yankees, and ice cream and mortgages and taxes, and all the things that whites have in their world, and tedium too. It's not going to be heaven." ∎

The March's Meaning

One man had a dream that millions shared

THE MARCH ON WASHINGTON was a triumph. But after everybody agreed on that, the question was: Why? Civil rights leaders themselves had a hard time putting it into words. "We subpoenaed the conscience of the nation," said Martin Luther King Jr. "We have developed a new unity among the leadership of the civil rights movement," declared A. Philip Randolph. "It is the first step in the building of a coalition of conscience," said Walter Reuther.

"It did something for Negroes to see white people there with them, and not in any condescending relation," said the N.A.A.C.P.'s Roy Wilkins.

THE CHANCE THEY TOOK. In fact, none of those explanations really described the meaning of the march. It was informal, often formless—yet it somehow had great dignity. It had little of the sustained suspense of an astronaut shoot or a national political convention—but it built, despite

The March on Washington: many whites joined the blacks under a common banner

moments of boredom and restlessness—to an emotion-draining climax. It probably changed few minds that had already been made up; the chances were that integrationists would remain integrationists and segregationists would remain segregationists.

It was in the probable effects on the conscience of millions of previously indifferent Americans that the march might find its true meaning. The possibility of riot and bloodshed had always been there; and in the U.S.'s "open society" they would have been plainly visible for the whole world to see. But the marchers took that chance, and the U.S. took it with them. No one who saw the proceedings could come to any other conclusion than that those scores of thousands of marching Negroes were able to accept the responsibilities of first-class citizenship.

BEGINNING OF A DREAM. Many Negroes had looked to the march as an end in itself, a massive demonstration that would somehow solve all their problems. It was not that.

Many other Americans, both white and Negro, had looked to the march with dread. It would, they feared, be an occasion for riot and bloodshed. But it was not that either.

As against the excesses of expectation on both sides, the

day began in anticlimax. Overnight, special trains and buses began moving into Washington from all parts of the U.S. Some of the early arrivals went off to picket Bobby Kennedy's Justice Department. But most of those getting off the trains in Washington's Union Station seemed weary, bewildered and subdued.

Only when a "Freedom Special" roared in from Deep Dixie did things get lively. The train, originating in Jacksonville, Fla., carried 785 marchers—many of them youngsters in their teens or early 20s who, as a result of their participation in Negro demonstrations, had spent time in Southern jails or carried on their bodies the scars inflicted by Southern cops. They piled off the train singing the battle hymn of the Negro's 1963 revolution, *We Shall Overcome*. Their spirit perked up hundreds of other Negroes still wandering aimlessly around the depot.

OVERALLS & IVY. Even so, as of 7:30 on the morning of the great day, there were probably more cops than marchers on the assembly grounds around the Washington Monument. The District of Columbia's police chief, Robert V. Murray, had assembled a force of 5,900 men—including 350 club-carrying firemen, 1,700 National Guardsmen and 300 newly sworn-in police reserves. At nearby bases, 4,000 soldiers and marines were ready to cross the Potomac in helicopters if they were needed for riot duty.

Organizers of the march had publicly predicted a throng of 100,000, although they privately felt confident that many more than that would show up. Now, peeking out of the green-and-white circus tent that served as their headquarters on the Monument grounds, the leaders began to worry that the crowd might fall short of their minimal hopes.

But even then, the railroad tracks and highways leading to Washington were clogged. Throughout the day, the marchers poured into the nation's capital—building to a grand total of well over 200,000. Of these, somewhere between 10% and 15% were white. There were, of course, the guitar-toting, goatee-growing beatniks; but for every one of these, there were probably two or three clergymen. There were Negroes in faded blue overalls; there were even more in stylish Ivy League suits. They swirled around the Monument's assembly ground, ate peanut butter and jelly sandwiches, passed around canteens filled with water (Washington had prohibited the sale of liquor for the day), tried to keep track of their children with no conspicuous success.

If violence were to occur, it would probably have been set off by a scruffy-looking bunch of about 50 white men who stood across 15th Street from the Monument grounds, staring balefully at the assembling civil rights marchers. These were members of the nitwit American Nazi Party, led by George Lincoln Rockwell. Prohibited by cops from crossing over to the Monument grounds, Rockwell could only rage helplessly: "I can't stand niggers. I can't stand to hear *We Shall Overcome*." Even before the march started, he led his ridiculous group away from the vicinity in an agony of frustration.

The march from the Washington Monument to the Lincoln Memorial, a distance of about eight-tenths of a mile, had been scheduled to start at 11:30 A.M. But at least 20 minutes before then, a group of Negroes started strolling away from the Monument grounds on the way to the Memorial. Hundreds, then thousands and tens of thousands, followed. Constitution and Independence Avenues were transformed into oceans of bobbing placards. Some marchers wept as they walked; the faces of many more gleamed with happiness. There were no brass bands. There was little shouting or singing. Instead, for over an hour and a half, there was the sound of thousands of feet shuffling toward the temple erected in the name of Abraham Lincoln.

SALT & PEPPER. At the Memorial, the first order of business was a program of professional entertainment. Folk Singers Joan Baez, Josh White, Odetta, Bob Dylan, Peter-Paul-and-Mary rendered hymns and civil rights songs. Actor Marlon Brando brandished an electric cattle prod of the sort sometimes used by cops against civil rights demonstrations. Author James Baldwin, Actors Paul Newman, Burt Lancaster, Charlton Heston made appearances. And onetime Folies-Bergére Star Josephine Baker looked out at the biracial crowd and snapped satisfiedly: "Salt and pepper—just what it should be."

But entertainment was not what the crowd had gathered for around the great brooding statue of Lincoln. Finally, the formal program began. Speaker followed speaker to the platform. Each was supposed to talk for four minutes. Each spoke longer than that. The crowd, most of it standing and packed shoulder to shoulder, began getting restless. People began to mill around, many even started to leave. But their attention was captured by a slender, low-toned speaker wearing a blue legionnaire-type cap. He was Roy Wilkins, executive secretary of the National Association for the Advancement of Colored People, who was introduced as the "acknowledged leader" of the civil rights movement. Wilkins talked quietly of the necessity for passage of President Kennedy's bill. "The President's proposals," he said, "represent so moderate an approach that if any part is weakened or eliminated, the remainder will be little more than sugar water. Indeed, the package needs strengthening. The President should join us in fighting for something more than pap." Then Wilkins praised Republicans and Democrats who had gone on record for the bill, and snapped wryly: "In fact, we even salute those from the South who want to vote for it but don't dare to do so. And we say to those people, 'Just give us a little time, and one of these days we'll emancipate you.'" After Wilkins, everything was upbeat.

LONELY ISLAND. Now to the platform came Singer Mahalia Jackson. First she sang a slow, sorrowful Gospel song titled *I've Been Buked and I've Been Scorned*. Her voice was marvelous, but her impact was more in her manner. Near tears, she moved her huge audience to tears. But in the very next breath, she would break into an expression of expectant happiness. When that happened, people who had been sobbing a second before began laughing, sharing in her expectancy.

Mahalia was hard to follow—and there probably was only one person in the civil rights world who could have done it quite so successfully. His introduction was drowned out by the roaring cheers of those who saw him heading toward the speakers' platform. He was Atlanta's Rev. Martin Luther King Jr., the civil rights leader who holds the heart of most American Negroes in his hand.

"The Negro," he said, "lives on a lonely island of poverty in the midst of a vast ocean of material prosperity and finds himself an exile in his own land." King continued stolidly: "It would be fatal for the nation to overlook the urgency of the moment and to underestimate the determination of the Negro. This sweltering summer of the Negro's legitimate discontent will not pass until there is an invigorating autumn of freedom and equality."

TABLE OF BROTHERHOOD. Already, King's particular magic had enslaved his audience, which roared "Yes, yes!" to almost everything he said. But then, King came to the end of his prepared text—and he swept right on in an exhibition of impromptu oratory that was catching, dramatic, inspirational. "I have a dream," King cried. The crowd began cheering, but King, never pausing, brought silence as he continued. "I have a dream that one day on the red hills of Georgia the sons of former slaves and the sons of former slaveowners will be able to sit down together at the table of brotherhood.

"I have a dream," he went on, relentlessly shouting down the thunderous swell of applause, "that even the state of Mississippi, a state sweltering with people's injustices, sweltering with the heat of oppression, will be transformed into an oasis of freedom and justice." Cheers. Cheers. Cheers. "I have a dream," cried King again, "that my four little children will one day live in a nation where they will not be judged by the color of their skin but by the content of their character."

Even after King finished, there were some final ceremonies. But to all effective intents and purposes, the day was over. Obeying their leaders' injunctions to leave town as soon as the official ceremonies had ended, the demonstrators made their way back toward their trains, buses, planes and cars. It was a quiet night in Washington—after a day that would never be forgotten. ∎

Never Again Where He Was

Martin Luther King Jr. is TIME's *Man of the Year 1963*

THE JETLINER LEFT ATLANTA and raced through the night toward Los Angeles. From his window seat, the black man gazed down at the shadowed outlines of the Appalachians, then leaned back against a white pillow. In the dimmed cabin light, his dark, impassive face seemed enlivened only by his big, shiny, compelling eyes. Suddenly, the plane shuddered in a pocket of severe turbulence. The Rev. Martin Luther King Jr. turned a wisp of a smile to his companion and said: "I guess that's Birmingham down below."

It was, and the reminder of Vulcan's city set King to talking quietly of the events of 1963. "In 1963," he said, "there arose a great Negro disappointment and disillusionment and discontent. It was the year of Birmingham, when the civil rights issue was impressed on the nation in a way that nothing else before had been able to do. It was the most decisive year in the Negro's fight for equality. Never before had there been such a coalition of conscience on this issue."

SYMBOL OF REVOLUTION. In 1963, the centennial of the Emancipation Proclamation, that coalition of conscience ineradicably changed the course of U.S. life. Nineteen million Negro citizens forced the nation to take stock of itself— in the Congress as in the corporation, in factory and field and pulpit and playground, in kitchen and classroom. The U.S. Negro, shedding the thousand fears that have encumbered his generations, made 1963 the year of his outcry for equality, of massive demonstrations, of sit-ins and speeches and street fighting, of soul searching in the suburbs and psalm singing in the jail cells.

And there was Birmingham with its bombs and snarling dogs; its shots in the night and death in the streets and in the churches; its lashing fire hoses that washed human beings along slippery avenues without washing away their dignity; its men and women pinned to the ground by officers of the law.

All this was the Negro revolution. Birmingham was its main battleground, and Martin Luther King Jr., the leader of the Negroes in Birmingham, became to millions, black and white, in South and North, the symbol of that revolution—and the Man of the Year.

King is in many ways the unlikely leader of an unlikely organization—the Southern Christian Leadership Conference, a loose alliance of 100 or so church-oriented groups. King has neither the quiet brilliance nor the sharp administrative capabilities of the N.A.A.C.P.'s Roy Wilkins. He has none of the sophistication of the National Urban League's Whitney Young Jr., lacks Young's experience in dealing with high echelons of the U.S. business community. He has neither the inventiveness of CORE's James Farmer nor the raw militancy of SNICK's John Lewis nor the bristling wit of Author James Baldwin. He did not make his mark in the entertainment field, where talented Negroes have long been prominent, or in the sciences and professions where Negroes have, almost unnoticed, been coming into their own. He earns no more money than some plumbers ($10,000 a year), and possesses little in the way of material things.

He presents an unimposing figure: he is 5 ft. 7 in., weighs a heavy-chested 173 lbs., dresses with funereal conservatism (five of six suits are black, as are most of his neckties). He has very little sense of humor. He never heard of Y. A. Tittle or George Shearing, but he can discourse by the hour about Thoreau, Hegel, Kant and Gandhi.

King preaches endlessly about nonviolence, but his protest movements often lead to violence. He himself has been stabbed in the chest, and physically attacked three more times; his home has been bombed three times, and he has been pitched into jail 14 times. His mail brings him a daily dosage of opinion in which he is by turn vilified and glorified. One letter says: "This isn't a threat but a promise— your head will be blown off as sure as Christ made green apples." But another ecstatically calls him a "Moses, sent to lead his people to the Promised Land of first-class citizenship."

CADENCE. Some cynics call King "De Lawd." He does have an upper-air way about him, and, for a man who has earned fame with speeches, his metaphors can be downright embarrassing. For Negroes, he says, "the word 'wait' has been a tranquilizing Thalidomide," giving "birth to an ill-formed infant of frustration." Only by "following the cause of tender-heartedness" can man "matriculate into the university of eternal life." Segregation is "the adultery of an illicit intercourse between injustice and immorality," and it "cannot be cured by the Vaseline of gradualism."

Yet when he mounts the platform or pulpit, the actual words seem unimportant. And King, by some quality of that limpid voice or by some secret of cadence, exercises control as can few others over his audiences, black or white. He has proved this ability on countless occasions, ranging from the Negroes' huge summer March on Washington to a little meeting one recent Friday night in Gadsden, Ala. There, the exchange went like this:

King: I hear they are beating you!

Response: Yes, yes.

King: I hear they are cursing you!

Response: Yes, yes.

King: I hear they are going into your homes and doing nasty things and beating you!

Response: Yes, yes.

King: Some of you have knives, and I ask you to put them up. Some of you may have arms, and I ask you to put them up. Get the weapon of nonviolence, the breastplate of righteousness, the armor of truth, and just keep marching.

Few can explain the extraordinary King mystique. Yet he has an indescribable capacity for empathy that is the touchstone of leadership. By deed and by preachment, he has stirred in his people a Christian forbearance that nourishes hope and smothers injustice. Says Atlanta's Negro Minister Ralph D. Abernathy, whom King calls "my dearest friend and cellmate": "The people make Dr. King great. He articulates the longings, the hopes, the aspirations of his people in a most earnest and profound manner. He is a humble man, down to earth, honest. He has proved his commitment to Judaeo-Christian ideals. He seeks to save the nation and its soul, not just the Negro."

ANGRY MEMORIES. Whatever his greatness, it was thrust upon him. He was born on Jan. 15 nearly 35 years ago, at a time when the myth of the subhuman Negro flourished, and when as cultivated an observer as H. L. Mencken could write that "the educated Negro of today is a failure, not because he meets insuperable difficulties in life, but because he is a Negro. His brain is not fitted for the higher forms of mental effort; his ideals, no matter how laboriously he is trained and sheltered, remain those of a clown."

Mencken had never met the King family of Atlanta. King's maternal grandfather, the Rev. A. D. Williams, was one of Georgia's first N.A.A.C.P. leaders, helped organize a boycott against an Atlanta newspaper that had disparaged Negro voters. His preacher father was in the forefront of civil rights battles aimed at securing equal salaries for Negro teachers and the abolition of Jim Crow elevators in the Atlanta courthouse.

As a boy, Martin Luther King Jr. suffered those cumulative experiences in discrimination that demoralize and outrage human dignity. He still recalls the curtains that were used on the dining cars of trains to separate white from black. "I was very young when I had my first experience in sitting behind the curtain," he says. "I felt just as if a curtain had come down across my whole life. The insult of it I will never forget." On another occasion, he and his schoolteacher were riding a bus from Macon to Atlanta when the driver ordered them to give up their seats to white passengers. "When we didn't move right away, the driver started cursing us out and calling us black sons of bitches. I decided not to move at all, but my teacher pointed out that we

must obey the law. So we got up and stood in the aisle the whole 90 miles to Atlanta. It was a night I'll never forget. I don't think I have ever been so deeply angry in my life."

IDEALS & TECHNIQUE. Raised in the warmth of a tightly knit family, King developed from his earliest years a raw-nerved sensitivity that bordered on self-destruction. Twice, before he was 13, he tried to commit suicide. Once his brother, "A.D.," accidentally knocked his grandmother unconscious when he slid down a banister. Martin thought she was dead, and in despair ran to a second-floor window and jumped out—only to land unhurt. He did the same thing, with the same result, on the day his grandmother died.

A bright student, he skipped through high school and at 15 entered Atlanta's Negro Morehouse College. His father wanted him to study for the ministry. King himself thought he wanted medicine or the law. "I had doubts that religion was intellectually respectable. I revolted against the emotionalism of Negro religion, the shouting and the stamping. I didn't understand it and it embarrassed me." At Morehouse, King searched for "some intellectual basis for a social philosophy." He read and reread Thoreau's essay, *Civil Disobedience*, concluded that the ministry was the only framework in which he could properly position his growing ideas on social protest.

At Crozer Theological Seminary in Chester, Pa., King built the underpinnings of his philosophy. Hegel and Kant impressed him, but a lecture on Gandhi transported him, sent him foraging insatiably into Gandhi's books. "From my background," he says, "I gained my regulating Christian ideals. From Gandhi I learned my operational technique."

MONTGOMERY. The first big test of King's philosophy—or of his operating technique—came in 1955, after he had married a talented young soprano named Coretta Scott and accepted the pastorate of the Dexter Avenue Baptist Church in Montgomery, Ala.

On Dec. 1 of that year, a seamstress named Rosa Parks boarded a Montgomery bus and took a seat. As the bus continued along its route, picking up more passengers, the Negroes aboard rose on the driver's orders to give their seats to white people. When the driver told Mrs. Parks to get up, she refused. "I don't really know why I wouldn't move," she said later. "There was no plot or plan at all. I was just tired from shopping. My feet hurt." She was arrested and fined $10.

For some reason, that small incident triggered the frustrations of Montgomery's Negroes, who for years had bent subserviently beneath the prejudices of the white community. Within hours, the Negroes were embarked upon a bus boycott that was more than 99% effective, almost ruined Montgomery's bus line. The boycott committee soon became the Montgomery Improvement Association, with Martin Luther King Jr. as president. His leadership was more inspirational than administrative; he is, as an observer says, "more at home with a conception than he is with the details of its application." King's home was bombed, and when his enraged people seemed ready to take to the streets in a riot of protest, he controlled them with his calm preaching of nonviolence. King became world-famous, and in less than a year the Supreme Court upheld an earlier order forbidding Jim Crow seating in Alabama buses.

ALBANY. Montgomery was one of the first great battles won by the Negro in the South, and for a while after it was won everything seemed anticlimactic to King. When the sit-ins and freedom-ride movements gained momentum, King's S.C.L.C. help organize and support them. But King somehow did not seem very efficient, and his apparent lack of imagination was to bring him to his lowest ebb in the Negro movement. In December 1961, King joined a mass protest demonstration in Albany, Ga., was arrested, and dramatically declared that he would stay in jail until Albany consented to desegregate its public facilities. But just two days after his arrest, King came out on bail. The Albany movement collapsed, and King was bitterly criticized for helping to kill it. Today he admits mistakes in Albany.

"Looking back over it," he says, "I'm sorry I was bailed out. I didn't understand at the time what was happening. We thought that the victory had been won. When we got out, we discovered it was all a hoax. We had lost a real opportunity to redo Albany, and we lost an initiative that we never regained."

But King also learned a lesson in Albany. "We attacked the political power structure instead of the economic power structure," he says. "You don't win against a political power structure where you don't have the votes. But you can win against an economic power structure when you have the economic power to make the difference between a merchant's profit and loss."

BIRMINGHAM. It was while he was in his post-Albany eclipse that King began planning for his most massive assault on the barricades of segregation. The target: Birmingham, citadel of blind, diehard segregation. King's lieutenant, Wyatt Tee Walker, has explained the theory that governs King's planning: "We've got to have a crisis to bargain with. To take a moderate approach, hoping to get white help, doesn't work. They nail you to the cross, and it saps the enthusiasm of the followers. You've got to have a crisis."

The Negroes made their crisis, but it was no spur-of-the-moment matter. King himself went to Birmingham to conduct workshops in nonviolent techniques. He recruited 200 people who were willing to go to jail for the cause, carefully planned his strategy in ten meetings with local Negro leaders. Then, declaring that Birmingham is the "most thoroughly segregated big city in the U.S.," he announced early in 1963 that he would lead demonstrations there until "Pharaoh lets God's people go."

Awaiting King in Birmingham was Public Safety Commissioner Theophilus Eugene ("Bull") Connor, a man who was to become a symbol of police brutality yet who, in fact, merely reflected the seething hatreds in a city where

acts of violence were as common as chitlins and ham hocks. As it happened, Bull Connor was running for mayor against a relative moderate, Albert Boutwell. To avoid giving campaign fuel to Connor, King waited until after the April 2 election. Between Jan. 16 and March 29, he launched himself into a whirlwind speaking tour, made 28 speeches in 16 cities across the nation.

Moving into Birmingham in the first week of April, King and his group began putting their plans to work. Bull Connor, who had lost the election but refused to relinquish power, sent his spies into the Negro community to seek information. Fearing that their phones were tapped, King and his friends worked up a code. He became "J.F.K.," Ralph Abernathy "Dean Rusk," Birmingham Preacher Fred Shuttlesworth "Bull," and Negro Businessman John Drew "Pope John." Demonstrators were called "baptismal candidates," and the whole operation was labeled "Project C"— for "Confrontation."

The protest began. Day after day, Negro men, women and children in their Sunday best paraded cheerfully downtown to be hauled off to jail for demonstrating. The sight and sound of so many people filling his jail so triumphantly made Bull Connor nearly apoplectic. He arrested them at lunch counters and in the streets, wherever they gathered. Still they came, rank on rank. At length, on Tuesday, May 7, 2,500 Negroes poured out of church, surged through the police lines and swarmed downtown. Connor furiously ordered the fire hoses turned on. Armed with clubs, cops beat their way into the crowds. An armored car menacingly bulldozed the milling throngs. Fire hoses swept them down the streets. In all, the Birmingham demonstrations resulted in the jailing of more than 3,300 Negroes, including King himself.

THE RESPONSE. The Negroes had created their crisis— and Connor had made it a success. "The civil rights movement," said President Kennedy in a meeting later with King, "owes Bull Connor as much as it owes Abraham Lincoln." That was at best an oversimplification; nevertheless, because of Connor, the riots seared the front pages of the world press, outraged millions of people. Everywhere, King's presence, in the pulpit or at rallies, was demanded. But while he preached nonviolence, violence spread. "Freedom Walker" William Moore was shot and killed in Alabama. Mississippi's N.A.A.C.P. Leader Medgar Evers was assassinated outside his home. There was violence in Jackson, Miss., in Cambridge, Md., in Danville, Va. In Birmingham, later in the year, a church bombing killed four Negro Sunday school children, while two other youngsters were shot and killed the same day.

Those events awakened long-slumbering Negro resentments, from which a fresh Negro urgency drew strength. For the first time, a unanimity of purpose slammed into the Negro consciousness with the force of a fire hose. Class lines began to shatter. Middle-class Negroes, who were aspiring for acceptance by the white community, suddenly

King: Arrested in Birmingham with Rev. Ralph Abernathy, he went to prison to fight for freedom

found a point of identity with Negroes at the bottom of the economic heap. Many wealthy Negroes, once reluctant to join the fight, pitched in.

Now sit-in campaigns and demonstrations erupted like machine-gun fire in every major city in the North, as well as in hundreds of new places in the South. Negroes demanded better job opportunities, and end to the *de facto* school segregation that ghetto life had forced upon them.

"FREE AT LAST." Many whites also began to participate, particularly the white clergy, which cast off its lethargy as ministers, priests and rabbis tucked the Scriptures under their arms and marched to jails with Negroes whom they had never seen before. The Rev. Dr. Eugene Carson Blake, executive head of the United Presbyterian Church in the U.S.A., declared: "Some time or other, we are all going to have to stand and be on the receiving end of a fire hose." Blake thereupon joined two dozen other clergymen in a protest march—and was arrested.

In the months following Birmingham, Negroes paraded, demonstrated, sat in, stormed and fought through civil rights sorties in 800 cities and towns in the land. The revolt's basic and startling new assumption—that the black man can read and understand the Constitution, and can demand his equal rights without fear—was not lost on Washington. President Kennedy, who had been in no great hurry to produce a civil rights bill, now moved swiftly. The

Justice Department drew up a tight and tough bill, aimed particularly at voting rights, employment, and the end of segregation in public facilities.

To cap the summer's great storm of protest, the Negro leaders sponsored the now famous March on Washington. It was a remarkable spectacle, one of disorganized order, with a stateliness that no amount of planning could have produced. Some 200,000 strong, whites and blacks of all ages walked from the Washington Monument to the Lincoln Memorial. There, the Negro leaders spoke— Wilkins, A. Philip Randolph, Young and SNICK's Lewis.

But it was King who most dramatically articulated the Negro's grievances, and it was he whom those present, as well as millions who watched on television, would remember longest. "When we let freedom ring," he cried, "when we let it ring from every village and every hamlet, from every state and every city, we will be able to speed up that day when all of God's children, black men and white men, Jews and Gentiles, Protestants and Catholics, will be able to join hands and sing, in the words of the old Negro spiritual,

"*Free at last,*
Free at last.
Thank God Almighty,
We are free at last."

EVEN THE UNIONS. The march made irreversible all that had gone before in the year of the Negro revolution. In that

BRIDGES AND BORDERS

year, the Negroes made more gains than they had achieved in any year since the end of the Civil War. A speed-up in school integration in the South brought to 1,141 the number of desegregated school districts. In the North, city after city re-examined *de facto* school segregation and set up plans to redress the balance. In 300 cities in the South, public facilities—from swimming pools to restaurants—were integrated, and in scores of cities across the nation, leaders established biracial committees as a start toward resolving local inequities.

New job opportunities opened nearly everywhere, as the nation's businesses sent out calls for qualified Negro help—and, finding a shortage, began training programs for unskilled Negroes. Banks, supermarkets, hotels and department stores upgraded Negro employees. In Philadelphia, Cleveland and New York, pressure on the A.F.L.-C.I.O. construction unions—the most notorious Jim Crow organizations in the North—produced progress toward training of Negro apprentices. San Francisco's tile setters, Memphis' rubber workers and St. Louis' bricklayers opened their union rolls to willing beginners. Television and Madison Avenue blossomed with Negro actors and ad models in "non-Negro" roles. In Denver, Sears, Roebuck & Co., which hitherto had had one Negro employee (dusting shelves), hired 19 more Negroes for a variety of jobs. To varying degrees it was the same way in Houston, at Grant's five and ten, and in San Francisco, where Tidewater Oil took on a Negro for executive training. Even in the South, the job situation improved. Negroes began moving into professional positions in North Carolina's state government. Three Nashville banks agreed to hire Negroes in clerical positions, and some white-collar jobs opened in South Carolina.

Still, for every tortuous inch gained, there are miles of progress left to be covered. There remain 1,888 Southern school districts where segregation is the rule—and scores of other districts where desegregation sits uneasily in token form. Though Montgomery buses are technically integrated, the city's other public facilities still are not. Team sports are still carefully segregated in a large number of Southern institutions; the NBC television network recently canceled coverage of the annual Blue-Gray football game because Negroes are not eligible to participate. Only 22 states have enforceable fair-employment laws on the books. And not counting Mississippi, where there is a total absence of integrated public facilities, those in other Southern states are so spotty and inconsistent (a downtown lunch counter, yes; the city swimming pool, no) that it is hard for a Negro nowadays to know where he may go and where he may not.

RE-EXAMINATION. What the Negroes expect, and what they are getting to a degree that would have been astonishing at the start of 1963, is a change of attitude. "A lot of people," says Chicago's Negro Baptist Minister Arthur Brazier, "are re-examining their motives. Even if this means that a lot of hidden prejudices have been uncovered in Northerners, good will be gained from the fact that Americans have been forced to act on days other than Brotherhood Days and Weeks."

Often the changes in attitudes are tiny in scope but broad in meaning. No longer do the starters at Miami's municipal golf courses ask a trio of white men if they will accept a Negro fourth; they merely assign the Negro, and the foursome heads onto the course. A New York adoption agency is asking white families to take Negro children. Louise Morgan, a former Chicago advertising executive, says: "I had conned myself into thinking I was a liberal. The rude awakening occurred less than a year ago, when a Negro writer and his family sought an apartment in my building and were turned down. I had met him. He was bright and a gentleman. Yet I didn't lift a finger to help him. That's all changed now." In California, Real Estate Dealer Richard S. Hallmark quit his job in protest over the commonly accepted methods of restricting Negro house buying. "I had never sold to a Negro family in my life, but it grated on my conscience," he says. "I'm tired of people telling me they don't give a goddam about the law and that they're just not going to sell or rent to 'niggers.' I'm not a martyr or a crusader, but this made me ashamed. The colored people are here to stay, so we might as well get used to it."

In addition to marching in demonstrations, clergymen are welcoming Negroes to their all-white congregations in many places, and are mounting mail campaigns to Congress in support of the civil rights bill. Several Roman Catholic archdioceses now require a specific number of sermons on race relations. The National Council of Churches has budgeted $300,000 to support civil rights activities.

A DIFFERENT IMAGE. The most striking aspect of the revolt, however, is the change in Negroes themselves. The Invisible Man has now become plainly visible—in bars, restaurants, boards of education, city commissions, civic committees, theaters and mixed social activities, as well as in jobs. Says Mississippi's N.A.A.C.P. President Aaron Henry: "There has been a re-evaluation of our slave philosophy that permitted us to be satisfied with the leftovers at the back door rather than demand a full serving at the family dinner table." With this has come a new pride in race. Explains Dr. John R. Larkins, a Negro consultant in North Carolina's Department of Public Welfare: "Negroes have a feeling of self-respect that I've never seen in all my life. They are more sophisticated now. They have begun to think, to form positive opinions of themselves. There's none of that defeatism. The American Negro has a different image of himself."

Where most Negroes once deliberately ignored their African beginnings and looked down on the blacks of that continent, many now identify strongly with Africa—though not to the point where they would repudiate their American loyalties—and take pride in the emergence of the new nations there. Some Negro women are affecting African-style hairdos; Negroes are decorating their homes with paintings and sculpture that reflect interest in African cul-

Letter From a Birmingham Jail

While Martin Luther King Jr. was in Birmingham's city jail last April, a group of white clergy-men wrote a public statement criticizing him for "unwise and untimely" demonstrations. King wrote a reply—on pieces of toilet paper, the margins of newspapers, and anything else he could get his hands on—and smuggled it out to an aide in bits and pieces. Although in the tumble of events then and since, it never got the notice it deserved, it may yet live as a classic expression of the Negro revolution of 1963. Excerpts from the letter, which was addressed to "My Dear Fellow Clergymen":

WE HAVE WAITED for more than 340 years for our constitutional and God-given rights. The nations of Asia and Africa are moving with jetlike speed toward the goal of political independence, and we still creep at horse-and-buggy pace toward the gaining of a cup of coffee at a lunch counter. I guess it is easy for those who have never felt the stinging darts of segregation to say "wait."

But when you have seen vicious mobs lynch your mothers and fathers at will and drown your sisters and brothers at whim; when you have seen hate-filled policemen curse, kick, brutalize and even kill your black brothers and sisters; when you suddenly find your tongue twisted and your speech stammering as you seek to explain to your six-year-old daughter why she can't go to the public amusement park that has just been advertised on television, and see tears welling up in her little eyes when she is told that "Funtown" is closed to colored children, and see the depressing clouds of inferiority begin to form in her little mental sky, and see her begin to distort her little personality by unconsciously developing a bitterness toward white people; when you are humiliated day in and day out by nagging signs reading "white" and "colored," when your first name becomes "nigger" and your middle name becomes "boy" (however old you are) and your last name becomes "John," and when your wife and mother are never given the respected title "Mrs."; when you are harried by day and haunted by night by the fact that you are a Negro, living constantly at tiptoe stance, never quite knowing what to expect next, and plagued with inner fears and outer resentments; when you are forever fighting a degenerating sense of "nobodyness"—then you will understand why we find it difficult to wait.

In your statement you asserted that our actions, even though peaceful, must be condemned because they precipitate violence. Isn't this like condemning the robbed man because his possession of money precipitated the evil act of robbery? Isn't this like condemning Socrates because his unswerving commitment to truth and his philosophical delvings precipitated the misguided popular mind to make him drink the hemlock? Isn't this like condemning Jesus because his unique God-consciousness and never-ceasing devotion to God's will precipitated the evil act of the Crucifixion?

The question is not whether we will be extremist but what kind of extremist will we be. Will we be extremists for hate or will we be extremists for love? Will we be extremists for the preservation of injustice—or will we be extremists for the cause of justice? In that dramatic scene on Calvary's hill, three men were crucified for the same crime—the crime of extremism. Two were extremists for immorality, and thus fell below their environment. The other, Jesus Christ, was an extremist for love, truth and goodness, and thereby rose above his environment. So, after all, maybe the South, the nation and the world are in dire need of creative extremists.

Before the Pilgrims landed at Plymouth, we were here. Before the pen of Jefferson etched across the pages of history the majestic words of the Declaration of Independence, we were here. For more than two centuries, our foreparents labored in this country without wages; they made cotton "king," and they built the homes of their masters in the midst of brutal injustice and shameful humiliation—and yet out of a bottomless vitality, they continued to thrive and develop. If the inexpressible cruelties of slavery could not stop us, the opposition we now face will surely fail. We will win our freedom because the sacred heritage of our nation and the eternal will of God are embodied in our echoing demands. ■

ture. There has been a decline in sales of "whitening" creams, hair straighteners and pomades, which for years found a big market among Negroes obsessed with ridding themselves of their racial identity.

REDEMPTION. More and more, Martin Luther King spends his time in airplanes, journeying to the far corners of the U.S. to speak and preach to huge audiences. He traveled about 275,000 miles in 1963 and made more than 350 speeches. Wherever he goes, the threat of death hovers in the form of crackpots. "I just don't worry about things like this," he says. "If I did, I just couldn't get anything done. One time I did have a gun in Montgomery. I don't know why I got it in the first place. I sat down with Coretta one night and we talked about it. I pointed out that as a leader of a nonviolent movement, I had no right to have a gun, so I got rid of it. The quality, not the longevity, of one's life is what is important. If you are cut down in a movement that is designed to save the soul of a nation, then no other death could be more redemptive."

It is with this inner strength, tenaciously rooted in Christian concepts, that King has made himself the unchallenged voice of the Negro people—and the disquieting conscience of the whites. That voice in turn has infused the Negroes themselves with the fiber that gives their revolution its true stature. In Los Angeles recently, King finished a talk by saying: "I say good night to you by quoting the words of an old Negro slave preacher, who said, 'We ain't what we ought to be and we ain't what we want to be and we ain't what we're going to be. But thank God, we ain't what we was.'"

After 1963, with the help of Martin Luther King Jr., the Negro will never again be where or what he was. ∎

Death and Transfiguration

The journey of Malcolm X

MALCOLM X HAD BEEN A PIMP, a cocaine addict and a thief. He was an unashamed demagogue. His gospel was hatred: "Your little babies will get polio!" he cried to the "white devils." His creed was violence: "If ballots won't work, bullets will."

Yet even before his bullet-ripped body went to its grave, Malcolm X was being sanctified. Negro leaders called him "brilliant," said he had recently "moderated" his views, blamed his assassination on "the white power structure" or, in the case of Martin Luther King, on a "society sick enough to express dissent with murder." Malcolm's death, they agreed, was a setback to the civil rights movement.

ALIAS JOHN DOE. In fact, Malcolm X—in life and in death—was a disaster to the civil rights movement.

Malcolm's murder, almost certainly at the hands of the Black Muslims from whom he had defected, came on a bright Sunday afternoon in full view of 400 Negroes in the Audubon Ballroom, a seedy two-story building on Manhattan's upper Broadway. Characteristically, he had kept his followers waiting for nearly an hour while he lingered over tea and a banana split at a nearby Harlem restaurant.

Entering the auditorium at last, Malcolm cried "As-salaam alaikum [Peace be unto you]." The audience replied in unison: "Wa-alaikum salaam [And unto you be peace]." Suddenly a disturbance broke out several rows back. "Get your hand off my pockets!" a man shouted. "Don't be messing with my pockets!" At the distraction, Malcolm raised his hands. "Now brothers!" he cried to the crowd, "Be cool, don't get excited ..."

As he spoke, three men rushed down the aisle toward him. Eight feet away, they opened fire. One Negro with a double-barreled sawed-off shotgun blasted Malcolm at point-blank range. "There was what sounded like an explosion," said a dazed woman. "I looked at Malcolm, and there was blood running out of his goatee." Men and women threw themselves to the floor as the gunmen squeezed off at least a score of shots. Thirteen shotgun pellets tore into Malcolm's chest and heart; several slugs from .45- and .38-cal. pistols shattered his thighs and legs. A woman screamed: "Oh, black folks, black folks, why you got to kill each other?"

The man with the shotgun was hit in the left leg by a bullet from the pistol of a Malcolm X bodyguard. Crippled, he was caught by Malcolm X's furious followers, knocked down, kicked and stomped on. Cops rescued him, took him to a hospital, and charged him with homicide. He was Thomas Hagan, alias Talmadge Hayer, a New Jersey thug with a dreary police record.

Minutes after the shooting, Malcolm's body was lifted from the stage, placed on a rolling bed that had been wheeled over from the nearby Columbia Presbyterian Medical Center, and rushed to an emergency operating room. A team of doctors laid open his chest, tried to revive him via openheart massage. But Malcolm X was dead. Because he had not yet been formally identified, he was at first entered on hospital records as John Doe.

"THAT WHITE RAPIST." The man who lived as Malcolm X and died as John Doe was born Malcolm Little, in Omaha on May 19, 1925. His father was a Baptist preacher and an enthusiast for Black Nationalist Marcus Garvey's "Back to Africa" movement. The family moved to Lansing, Mich., where, Malcolm claimed, white racists set fire to his parents' home in 1929. Two years later, when Malcolm was six, his father was run over by a streetcar, his body cut almost in half. Police called it an accident, but Malcolm insisted that his father had been bludgeoned by whites and placed across the tracks. Soon afterward his mother was committed to a mental asylum in Michigan.

In his youth, Malcolm prided himself on his reddish hair and light skin, an inheritance from his maternal grandfather, a white man. Years later he wrote in his autobiography: "I was for years insane enough to feel that it was some kind of status symbol to be light-complexioned. Now I hate every drop of that white rapist's blood that is in me."

He quit school after the eighth grade, eventually made his way to New York. Nicknamed "Big Red," he was a gangling zoot-suiter who fancied yellow-toed shoes and straightened his hair with lye in a scalp-searing process called "conking." He worked briefly as a waiter at Small's Paradise, still one of Harlem's top nightspots. But an honest dollar was not for Malcolm Little. He was caught pimping on the side and fired. He thereupon turned himself into a full-time hustler whose specialties were fixing up white men with Negro whores and Negro men with white whores. He peddled marijuana, became a cocaine addict and, to satisfy his $20-a-day craving, took to burglary. In 1946 he wound up with a ten-year prison sentence in Boston.

BLEACHED-OUT. At the gloomy state prison in Charlestown, Malcolm copied a dictionary from A to Z. He wanted to improve his vocabulary, and he did. He was to become a spell-binding speaker. More important, he learned in prison about the Black Muslims, an extremist sect founded in Detroit in 1930 by a shadowy peddler named W. D. Fard, and ruled since Fard's mysterious disappearance in 1934 by Elijah Muhammad. The Muslims offered Malcolm what Marcus Garvey had offered his father—and then some. They had caparisoned their movement with the trappings of religion, along with a mythology holding that the first human beings were Negroes. Other races—red, yellow and white—resulted only after a wicked and long-lived scientist named Yacub succeeded over many generations of genetic experiments in achieving a "bleached-out white race of people."

Paroled in 1952 after serving six years, Malcolm Little became Malcolm X, loudly acclaimed the Muslims' professed prohibitions against tobacco, alcohol and pre- or extra-marital sex. He shrugged off his sordid past on the ground that "it was all done when I was part of the white man's Christian world." In 1958, he married a Muslim Sister named Betty Shabazz before a justice of the peace in Michigan.

SAVAGE SPEAKER. Malcolm soon proved one of Elijah Muhammad's best recruiters—in an organization that, then and now, desperately needed recruits. The Black Muslims had received little public notice until the civil rights movement and its street demonstrations catapulted them into the news. Today, Black Muslims claim up to 250,000 members. A much more accurate estimate would accord the group 2,000 in New York, 500 in Chicago, 350 in Los Angeles, 230 in Detroit, 220 in Washington, 150 in both St. Louis and San Francisco, 100 in Kansas City, under 100 in each of 70 other cities, including Atlanta, New Orleans, Memphis and Jacksonville. Still, it is a nice racket for Elijah, son of a Georgia sharecropper. He socks each member for $8.30 in dues a week, requires each to sell (or pay for) as many as 200 copies of the 20¢ Muslim newspaper every two weeks, saddles everybody with an additional $125 assessment for Savior's Day, Feb. 26.

Malcolm was also a savage speaker. After the 1962 plane crash in France that killed 121 whites from Georgia, he rose before a Los Angeles audience and said: "I would like to announce a very beautiful thing that has happened. I got a wire from God today. He really answered our prayers over in France. He dropped an airplane out of the sky with over 120 white people on it because the Muslims believe in an eye for an eye and a tooth for a tooth. We will continue to pray and we hope that every day another plane falls out of the sky."

THE COMEUPPANCE. In demand as a speaker, not just among Negroes but before white civic groups and on college campuses, Malcolm gained in popularity and became a threat to Elijah Muhammad's leadership of the Black Muslims.

All Elijah wanted was a chance to give Malcolm his comeuppance—and in 1963 Malcolm offered him the opportunity. After President Kennedy's assassination, Malcolm publicly called the murder a case of "the chickens coming home to roost." Cried he: "Being an old farm boy myself, chickens coming home to roost never did make me sad; they've always made me glad."

This was outrageous enough for Elijah to suspend Malcolm from the Black Muslim movement. Malcolm quit for keeps, soon had formed his own white-hating Organization of Afro-American Unity, and urged Negroes to form rifle clubs.

Malcolm, who made a point of getting along well with the press, also began leaking stories of immorality among the Muslims. In an open letter, he accused Elijah of having fathered eight illegitimate babies by six teen-age secretaries at Black Muslim headquarters in Chicago. Other defectors—including two of Elijah's sons—began following Malcolm out of the sect. Naturally, this did not sit well with Elijah. "Only those who wish to be led to hell, or to their doom, will follow Malcolm," said his biweekly newspaper, *Muhammad Speaks.* "The die is set, and Malcolm shall not escape."

PREMONITIONS & BOMBS. From the moment he left the Black Muslims, Malcolm had premonitions of mortality. "No one can get out without trouble," he said. "This thing with me will be resolved by death and violence." For once he was right.

Malcolm Little—Malcolm X—John Doe was buried as Al Hajj Malik Shabazz, the name he earned in 1964 by making his pilgrimage to Mecca and being received as a true believer. He wore the white robe that signified his faith. In the four days before his burial, more than 20,000 persons, almost all Negroes, filed past his body as it lay on view in a glass-topped, wrought-copper casket. Following Muslim custom, when Malcolm was buried in suburban Westchester's Ferncliff Cemetery, his head was to the east, toward Mecca. ■

Democracy in the Foxhole

No time for prejudice in Vietnam, where the only color is olive drab

DEEP IN "INDIAN COUNTRY," the Viet Cong's jungled heartland, a lone U.S. helicopter flapped furiously down on an abandoned dirt roadway. Even before the Huey hit the ground, its six passengers were out and running. Their faces streaked with camouflage paint, their black and green "tiger suits" blending into the foliage, their black-stocked M-16 automatic rifles at the ready, they faded swiftly into the perennial twilight of 80-ft. trees, impenetrable bamboo thickets, and tangles of thorn and "wait a minute" vines. This was "Lurp Team Two," a long-range reconnaissance patrol (LRRP) of the 173rd Airborne Brigade, sent to seek out two Viet Cong regiments that their outfit was itching to locate, engage and destroy. Within moments, Team Two was itself in imminent danger of destruction.

It did not take long for the patrol to discover that it had landed smack in the midst of a Viet Cong concentration. As skilled as Victor Charlie in the deadly blindman's buff of jungle warfare, Team Two soon realized that the enemy was following its every move. Each time Staff Sergeant Clide Brown Jr. halted his men, they could hear a couple of footfalls close behind—and then a bristling silence. As the jungle dusk deepened into blackness, Brown set up a defense perimeter and listened more closely. Above the keening of insects, geckos and night birds, he heard the snap of two fingers and the snick of a rifle bolt not 30 yards away.

"We're getting out of here," he whispered. "They're just behind us."

Linked up head and tail like circus elephants by their "escape ropes," each humping half a hundredweight of gear, the muzzles of their rifles still taped to keep out gunk, the scouts took advantage of distant artillery salvos to mask their footfalls on the way back to a prearranged retrieval zone. Brown, in the lead, groped his way back through the blackness by memorizing the map and counting his own steps; each time his left foot hit the ground 67 times, he calculated the team had covered 100 meters. Back at the landing zone, Brown's whispered message filtered into the PRC transceiver: "Four seven, this is Papa Two. I'm in trouble. This is Papa Two.." No reply. The triple-tiered jungle canopy drowned his call to the pickup helicopter. Brown moved his men soundlessly across the clearing and set up a radial defense—each man flat on his back, head to the center of the circle, his M-16 ready—behind a tangle of fallen trees.

HANGING TOUGH. Team Two measured the passage of the night in careful inhalations, silent exhalations, and the clack of bamboo signal sticks used by the Viet Cong patrols that passed within 50 feet of its hideout. Then, at 2 A.M., a single shot blasted the night: Brown's radio man, shifting his M-16, had accidentally triggered a tracer round—almost certainly disclosing the team's position. Brown hung tough,

Sergeant Clide Brown, Jr., on left: Fighting with dignity alongside whites, shattering stereotypes

hoping that the cross-wave of jungle echoes would confuse the enemy searchers. It did, and at dawn the team moved back in to hunt out the Viet Cong base camp.

Only after Brown had spotted a concentration of black pajamas did Team Two withdraw. As enemy sniper bullets stitched around and between them, the scouts blasted back with fragmentation grenades and bursts of automatic fire that chopped the brush into jungle salad. Brown "popped smoke"—yellow signal grenades—to bring in the choppers, and while hovering Huey gun-ships laced the weeds with rockets and 50-cal. bullets, Team Two made its getaway, mission accomplished.

BRIGHT STRANDS. Sergeant Brown, 24, is a Negro from the black belt of Alabama; in 16 sorties into Indian country he has not lost anyone on his five-man team, none of whom is a Negro. The cool professionalism of Clide Brown's patrol underscores in microcosm a major lesson of Viet Nam—a hopeful and creative development in a dirty, hard-fought war. For the first time in the nation's military history, its Negro fighting men are fully integrated in combat, fruitfully employed in positions of leadership, and fiercely proud of their performance. In the unpredictable search-and-destroy missions through the Central

Highlands, in the savage set-piece battles along the DMZ, in the boot-swallowing, sniper-infested mangrove swamps of the Mekong Delta, on the carrier decks and in the gun mounts of the Seventh Fleet offshore, in the cockpits of helicopters and fighter-bombers in the skies above both Viet Nams, the American Negro is winning—indeed has won—a black badge of courage that his nation must forever honor.

That badge, interlaced with all the bright strands of personal bravery and professional skill that have marked their performance in battle, proclaims a truth that Americans had not yet learned about themselves before Viet Nam: color has no place in war; merit is the only measure of the man.

CAN DO, MUST WIN. More than anything, the performance of the Negro G.I. under fire reaffirms the success—and diversity—of the American experiment. Often inchoate and inconsistent, instinctively self-serving yet naturally altruistic, the Negro fighting man is both savage in combat and gentle in his regard for the Vietnamese. He can clean out a bunker load of Viet Cong with a knife and two hand grenades, or offer smokes to a captured V.C. and then squat beside him trying to communicate in bastard Vietnamese. He may fight to prove his manhood—perhaps as a correc-

BRIDGES AND BORDERS

tive to the matriarchal dominance of the Negro ghetto back home—or to save Viet Nam for a government in Saigon about which he himself is cynical. Mostly, though, he fights for the dignity of the Negro, to shatter the stereotypes of racial inferiority, to win the judgment of noncoms and officers of whatever color: "He's got the tickets."

Even though 70% of all Negroes are rejected by the draft because of ghetto-bred ill health or non-education, the proportion of Negro army combat troops in Viet Nam is more than double the ratio of Negroes to whites in the U.S. population at large (23% v. 11%). That, according to the Negro G.I. himself and his officers, is because those who make it into military service are the "cream of the crop"—can-do, must-win competitors who volunteer for dangerous duty both for the premium pay and the extra status it gives them. "I get my jollies jumping out of airplanes," says one Negro paratrooper of his $55-a-month extra airborne pay. Unlike Negroes in previous wars, the Viet Nam breed is well disciplined: there are proportionately no more black than white inmates of L.B.J., as the Long Binh Jail is unfondly known. Many of the best Negro warriors are former civil rights demonstrators, men who marched on lunch counters and Washington itself to win equal rights for their race. Not surprisingly, Negroes pull a considerably higher combat death rate than whites.

Black-white relations in a slit trench or a combat-bound Huey are years ahead of Denver and Darien, decades ahead of Birmingham and Biloxi. "The only color out here is olive drab," says a white sergeant. Despite the foxhole comradeship of most G.I.s in Viet Nam, the war is not all interracial amity: vicious racist graffiti from both sides mar the walls of latrines in Saigon; whites and Negroes slug it out on occasion along the night-town streets of Tu Do and in "Soulsville," the Negro's self-imposed ghetto of joy along Saigon's waterfront. Sometimes they shoot it out. Like their people back home, many Negro G.I.s are skeptical of the aims of the war. Nonetheless, of scores of Negro servicemen interviewed by TIME in Viet Nam, all but a few volunteered the information that they were there to serve their country, however badly it may have treated them. "With all the inadequacies and imperfections," says a Negro infantry officer, "the U.S. still offers more individual rights than any other country; it's still worth dying for."

Foremost among the Negro combat heroes of Viet Nam are the two who won Medals of Honor. Pfc. Milton Olive, 19, won his award posthumously by throwing himself on a grenade and saving the lives of four multicolored squadmates during a fierce fire fight near Phu Cuong in 1965. The only living Negro Medal of Honor winner in the Viet Nam war is Medic Lawrence Joel 39, now stationed at Fort Bragg, N.C.

MAKING IT BIG. Product of a broken North Carolina home, reared by foster parents from the age of eight, Joel made the Army a career because he was convinced that "you couldn't make it really big" as a Negro on the outside.

Promotion came slowly, and he was once busted for arguing with a sergeant. Then, on a fiery slope near Bien Hoa in November 1965, Joel met Victor Charlie. As his platoon was devoured by enemy crossfire, and he himself took two slugs in the legs, Joel hobbled and crept through the holocaust to patch ripped chests, plug bottles of plasma into dangling arms, give bloody mouth-to-mouth resuscitation to corpses and wounded alike, shoot Syrettes of morphine into mangled men. He allowed himself only one Syrette for his own wounds, for fear that he might dull his mind and hamper his work. At dawn, the job done, Joel recalls looking at himself: hands encrusted with blood to the wrists, legs thick with edema and dirty bandages. He lay under a tree and cried for the first time since he was a boy in Winston-Salem.

Last week, in crisp dress whites, Joel and his wife were the guests of President Johnson at the annual White House military reception. A gentle, reticent man, who once thought of giving up military life to become a beautician, Joel responded firmly when reporters pressed him about the morality of the war: "Most of the men who have been to Viet Nam feel this war is right."

PERILS & GLORY. Individual Negroes have shown valor in every war: Crispus Attucks was the first American to die under British fire in the Boston Massacre; Commodore Oliver Hazard Perry, himself perhaps part Negro, mustered many colored sailors aboard his men-of-war in 1812; a battalion of 600 Negroes turned the tide at the Battle of New Orleans by defeating British General Pakenham's seasoned Napoleonic veterans. Andrew Jackson paid them a glowing tribute: "To the Men of Color—Soldiers! I invited you to share in the perils and to divide the glory of your white countrymen. I expected much from you; for I was not uninformed of those qualities which must render you so formidable. I knew you could endure hunger and thirst; I knew that you loved the land of your nativity. But you surpass my hopes. Soldiers!"

Few such encomiums greeted the Negro regiments of the Civil War—though many units fought gallantly on both sides. Negro troops also served with valor in the Indian wars and the Spanish-American War. (One of their white officers, John Pershing of the 10th Negro Cavalry, became "Black Jack" to a later generation because of his service with Negro troops.) In World Wars I and II, some of the luster was lost with reports of the sometimes cowardly performance of the Negro 92nd and 93rd Divisions, and with the rioting by off-duty Negro soldiers that accompanied a rise in racial tensions.

RACE AS A CRUTCH. Though Harry Truman ordered the military services desegregated in 1948, the Korean War found Negroes still serving in all-black outfits, or else in behind-the-lines non-combat roles. White officers—particularly in the Navy and Marine Corps—stubbornly kept Negroes out of top command positions.

That situation is better today in Viet Nam—but not much. Though more than 10% of the Army troops in Viet

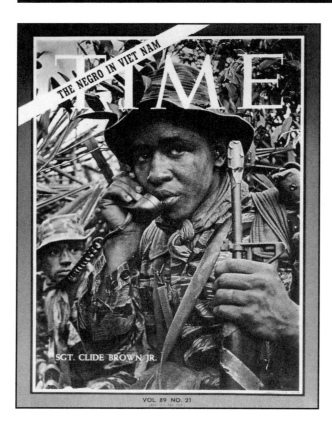

THE NEGRO IN VIET NAM

TIME

SGT. CLIDE BROWN JR.

VOL. 89 NO. 21

Nam are Negroes, only 5% of the 11,000 officers are black. Of the 380 combat-battalion commands in the war, only two are held by Negro officers. Massachusetts Senator Edward Brooke, during his Viet Nam tour in March, received many complaints that the Negro is not given the opportunity to attain command; he cites the case of a Negro colonel who, when promoted, was given a desk job that had never existed before simply to keep him from being assigned to a line command. One reason, of course, is that too many potential Negro officers lack the educational requirements for command. In fact, Captain James R. Randall, 34, a Negro psychiatrist for the 4th Infantry Division, though agreeing that many Negro officers and enlisted men complain of discrimination, says: "Many times I have found that the complaint because of race is not really that, but that race has been used by some as a crutch." To the argument that Negroes are too poor for college deferments must be added the fact that they like the military enough to re-enlist at a rate three times that of the white servicemen.

Still, many Negro soldiers prefer to pull their passes in Saigon's self-segregated Soulsville, a warren of bars and brothels along Khanh Hoi Street near the capital's waterfront. In the honky-tonks, they can dig the big beat of the Supremes singing *Come See About Me* or the kinky cool of

Ahmad Jamal's *Heat Wave*, bop about the bars in their "shades" (sunglasses) and talk "trash" (shoot the bull). The girls of Soulsville—many of them dark-skinned Cambodians or the daughters of French Senegalese soldiers—are less costly and usually less comely than their sisters on white-dominated Tu Do Street near by. The "in" spot in Soulsville is the L.& M. Guest House, a bar-restaurant and record booth run by balding, beer-bellied "Johnny" Hill, 35, a New Orleans Negro and ex-merchant sailor whose menu of "soul food" runs from No. 4 (turnip greens) through No. 8 (barbecued spareribs) to No. 9, "Kansas City Wrinkles," better known as chitlins. In Soulsville, the sustenance is psychological as well. There, no matter how close he may be to white soldiers on the line, the Negro G.I. can get away from "Chuck," the white man (the Stateside nickname "Charlie" is reserved for the Viet Cong). "Chuck's looks in those Tu Do bars!" growls one Negro pfc. "Man, they hurt more than a Claymore."

Whatever "Keep the faith, baby" might mean to Adam Clayton Powell, the phrase is used by most soldiers in Viet Nam to mean, as Negro Captain Clifford Alexander Jr. puts it: "We are fighting over here against the Viet Cong and at home against discrimination: together we can win in both places." The Negro on duty becomes a truly invisible man: "In civilian life, somebody might look at you and say 'You're a Negro,'" remarks Navy Lieut. (j.g.) Friedel C. Greene, 25, a carrier-based radar tracker from Memphis. "Over here they just look to see if you do your job." That hopeful sentiment reflects a concern with full citizenship that goes far beyond the desperate banalities of Negro dissidents in the U.S.

CONFIDENCE & SKILLS. Whatever the outcome of the war, whatever its length and its price in suffering, the result of the Viet Nam experience should pay high dividends in reshaping white Americans' attitudes toward social justice and integration: it has already given some 50,000 Negroes a sense of self-confidence and a commensurate demand for deeper participation in American society.

Melvin Stennis Jr., 24, of the 25th Division "Wolfhounds," who as a squad leader commands the life and death movements of five whites and one other Negro, has perhaps the definitive word on the future of Negro progress. Before entering the Army, Stennis watched the Watts riot from his doorstep. "I hear people are still rioting back home," he says. "It makes you feel sore, sick and guilty. Riots don't do nothing. Instead of playing the big-time part, you got to work for what you want. Don't beg, steal or burn. You got to work for it." Then he pauses. "In Viet Nam, we are working for it."

American society also has to work for him. By channeling the energies and accommodating the ambitions of the returning Negro veteran, the nation can only enrich its own life and demonstrate that democracy can work as well in the cities and fields of America as in the foxholes of Viet Nam. ∎

Historic Homage

A new bill changes the face of immigration

THEY CAME FROM every part of the globe, speaking a babble of tongues and carrying little but hope as luggage. From 1840 on, they arrived in a wave that was perpetually at flood tide, furnishing the growing U.S. with the sinew and spirit to build its railroads and create its industries. Often they faced a grinding struggle for survival in the New World's harsh slums and windwhipped prairies, but somehow the immigrants managed to take root. Out of their extraordinary exodus—which John F. Kennedy called "the largest migration of people in all recorded history"—rose an extraordinary nation.

Last week, 400 years after the Spaniards arrived in Florida to establish the first settlement in the continental U.S., the nation's Congress paid historic homage to the heterogeneous men who helped build the U.S. By a 76 to 18 vote, the Senate adopted a sweeping new immigration reform bill that strikes down the restrictive "national origins" quota system that has discriminated against Southern Europeans and Asians since 1924, when nearly 80% of white Americans traced their forebears to northern and western Europe. "After 40 years, we have returned to first principles," said Massachusetts' Senator Teddy Kennedy, the floor manager of the bill and himself the grandson of immigrants. "Immigration, more than anything else, has supplied America with the human strength that is the core of its greatness."

FIRST COME, FIRST SERVED. In accordance with the Senate bill, the national origins system will be scrapped entirely in July 1968, when all nations outside the Western Hemisphere will be allotted a total of 170,000 immigrant visas on a first-come, first-served basis. The maximum for any one nation will be 20,000—a figure exceeded last year only by Germany's 22,628 and the United Kingdom's 28,653. Until then, the unused allotments of such high-quota nations as Britain and Ireland will be transferred to such low-quota lands as Italy and India, where would-be immigrants now often have to wait a decade or more for their turn.

The Senate bill differs in one major respect from a bill that was approved by the House in a 318 to 95 vote in August. For the first time, a numerical restriction of 120,000 immigrants was imposed on the nations of the Western Hemisphere. Under Administration pressure, the House had retained the old bill's provision permitting unlimited immigration from Canada and Latin America, but the Senate rejected the provision as unfair to all the other nations of the world. When the bill goes to a Senate-House conference shortly, the restriction is expected to remain. In addition, an estimated 60,000 parents, children or spouses of U.S. citizens will be admitted each year regardless of nationality. Though the bill will increase annual immigration to 350,000 a year, some 60,000 above current levels, it inspired only halfhearted resistance; all 18 nays came from Southerners, mostly Democrats.

As early as 1782, it was already evident that the American experiment would produce something new in the history of human societies. "This is every man's country," wrote French-born Michel Guillaume St. Jean de Crévecoeur, "Here, individuals of all nations are melted into a new race of men whose labors and posterity will one day cause great changes in the world." Even as Crévecoeur wrote, the U.S. was a polyglot mix of English and Scotch, Irish and French, Dutch, German and Swedish.

Negroes began arriving in 1619, when the first Negro immigrants, a group of 20 indentured servants, landed in Virginia aboard a Dutch man-of-war. In the next two centuries hundreds of thousands more came to the U.S.—most of them shackled slaves aboard ships out of West Africa.

In the early years, the voluntary immigrants came in trickles, driven from Europe by poverty or persecution: the Puritans seeking a place to worship in New England, the bedeviled Quakers fleeing to Pennsylvania as a haven, the Huguenots escaping to South Carolina from France's intolerant Sun King. But it was not until 1840 that the tide really began to flow, and it did not ebb for nearly a century. A blight in Ireland and a pogrom in Russia, a famine in Scandinavia and civil strife in South China, starvation in Sicily and crop failures in Greece, a wave of political repression in the Austro-Hungarian Empire—all fed the tide. It crested in the decade 1905-14, when more than 10,100,000 men, women and children poured into the U.S., most of them through the grim portals of New York Harbor's Ellis Island.

MAGNATES & MUSICIANS. The newcomers inestimably enriched the U.S., making it the most incredibly diverse nation on earth. Even today, 34% of the Northeast is composed of "foreign stock," a Census Bureau classification that includes those born outside the U.S. and those who have at least one parent born outside the country. More than 20% of the population of California, New York, Illinois, Michigan and 15 other states are of foreign stock. The immigrants helped to build the great cities and shift the balance of

American life away from the farm. Half of the people in New York, Boston and Detroit, two-fifths of those in Los Angeles, one-third of those in Chicago and Cleveland are of foreign stock.

The list of immigrants and their sons who helped to mold American art and industry, politics and science is endless. There were Steel Magnate Andrew Carnegie (Scotland), Fur Trader John Jacob Astor (Germany), Inventor Alexander Graham Bell (Scotland), the Du Ponts from France and Yeast Tycoon Charles L. Fleischmann from Hungary. German-born Albert Einstein, Hungarian-born Edward Teller and Italian-born Enrico Fermi helped the U.S. to unlock the atom's secrets. There have been more immigrant musicians than one can shake a baton at, from Irving Berlin (Russia) and Victor Herbert (Ireland) to Artur Rubinstein (Poland) and Dimitri Mitropoulos (Greece).

One had to go no farther than the chamber of the U.S. Senate as the new bill was passed last week to see how variegated the U.S. is. In the presiding officer's chair sat Hubert Humphrey, son of a Norwegian mother. Much in evidence were Majority Leader Mike Mansfield, whose parents hailed from counties Kilkenny and Limerick, and Minority Leader Everett Dirksen, son of Germans. In the semicircular rows that arced to the rear of the chamber sat New York's Jack Javits, son of an Austrian and a Palestinian; Hawaii's Hiram Fong, whose parents were born in China; Connecticut's Abe Ribicoff, son of Poles; Rhode Island's John Pastore, son of Italians.

First Preference. In the future, the 350,000 immigrants who come to the U.S. each year will more often be Ph.D.s and skilled craftsmen than "the wretched refuse" to which the Statue of Liberty still beckons. Those with special talents necessarily rate first preference among a rapidly growing populace. Even so, there are certain to be many who will be "not only the opulent and respectable stranger," as George Washington put it in 1783, "but the oppressed and persecuted of all nations and religions." If the past is a guide, they, too, will add to the nation's strength. ■

The Little Strike that Grew to *La Causa*

Cesar Chavez brings hope to a "forgotten minority"

ITEM: At a dinner party in New York's Westchester County, the dessert includes grapes. The hostess notices that her fellow suburbanites fall to with gusto; the guests from Manhattan unanimously abstain.

ITEM: At St. Paul's, a fashionable New Hampshire prep school, grapes are the only part of the meal invariably left untouched.

ITEM: In San Francisco, a Safeway official observes: "We have customers who come to the store for no other reason than to buy grapes. They'll load up their car with grapes and nothing else."

ITEM: In Oakland, a conscience-ridden housewife explains apologetically to her dinner companions: "I really wanted to have this dessert, and I just decided that one little bunch of grapes wouldn't make that much difference."

ITEM: In Honolulu, the Young Americans for Freedom organizes an "emergency grape lift" by jet from the mainland, inviting "all of those starved for the sight of a California grape to come to the airport."

WHY ALL THE EXCITEMENT about this smooth, sweet and innocent fruit? The answer is that the table grape, *Vitis vinifera*, has become the symbol of the four-year-old strike of California's predominantly Mexican-American farm workers. For more than a year now, table grapes have been the object of a national boycott that has won the sympathy and support of many Americans—and the ire of many others. The strike is widely known as *la causa*, which has come to represent not only a protest against working conditions among California grape pickers but the wider aspirations of

JULY 4, 1969

TIME

THE GRAPES OF WRATH, 1969
MEXICAN-AMERICANS ON THE MARCH

CESAR
CHAVEZ

the nation's Mexican-American minority as well. *La causa*'s magnetic champion and the country's most prominent Mexican-American leader is Cesar Estrada Chavez, 42, a onetime grape picker who combines a mystical mien with peasant earthiness. *La causa* is Chavez's whole life; for it, he has impoverished himself and endangered his health by fasting. In soft, slow speech, he urges his people—nearly 5,000,000 of them in the U.S.—to rescue themselves from society's cellar. As he sees it, the first step is to win the battle of the grapes.

MAGNIFIED MOVEMENT. To enter the public consciousness, a labor conflict must ordinarily threaten the supply of essential goods and services, like steel or transportation. Politicians and the public take notice only when there is great impact on the economy, when spectacular bloodshed occurs or when well-recognized issues are at stake. The grape strike seems to meet none of these criteria. Americans could easily live without the table grape if they had to, and even that minor sacrifice has been unnecessary. The dispute has been relatively free of violence. Neither great numbers of men nor billions of dollars are involved. The welfare of agricultural workers has rarely captured U.S. attention in the past, but the grape strike—*la huelga*—and the boycott accompanying it have clearly engaged a large part of the nation.

The issue has divided husband and wife, inspired countless heated arguments at social occasions and engen-

dered public controversy from coast to coast. As if on a holy crusade, the strikers stage marches that resemble religious pilgrimages, bearing aloft their own stylized black Aztec eagle on a red field along with images of the Virgin of Guadalupe, patroness of Mexicans and particularly of those who work the soil. As the workers and their sympathizers march, supermarket chains, middle-class consumers, and even the grape growers are choosing sides. Some supermarkets are leaving the choice to the shoppers. Others sell only grapes imported from Africa or Israel, and make a point of advertising that they do not carry the California product. On Capitol Hill, diners in the House restaurants have not seen a grape for months, while the Senate refectory has been using 15 lbs. to 20 lbs. a week. When one California Congressman sent large bags of grapes to each of his colleagues, many of the recipients returned them. Within a few hours, the corridor outside the Congressman's office was asquish with trod-upon fruit.

Governor Ronald Reagan calls the strike and boycott "immoral" and "attempted blackmail." Senator George Murphy, like Reagan an old Hollywood union man-turned-conservative, terms the movement "dishonest." The Nixon Administration has seemed ambivalent, putting forward legislation that would ostensibly give farm workers organization rights but would also limit their use of strikes and boycotts. The Pentagon has substantially increased its grape orders for mess-hall tables, a move that Chavez and his followers countered last week by preparing a lawsuit to prevent such purchases on the ground that grapes are the subject of a labor dispute. Some auto-bumper stickers read: Nixon eats grapes. The growers' answering slogan: eat California grapes, the forbidden fruit.

Edward and Ethel Kennedy, following the late Robert Kennedy's example, have embraced Cesar Chavez as a brother. The so-called Beautiful People, from Peter, Paul and Mary to the Ford sisters, Anne Uzielli and Charlotte Niarchos, are helping to raise funds for the strikers. That support is one of the few issues that find Chicago Mayor Richard Daley, iconoclastic Writer Gloria Steinem, and liberal Senators Jacob Javits and George McGovern in total agreement. Ralph Abernathy lends black help to what is becoming the Brown Power movement.

The fact that it is a movement has magnified *la huelga* far beyond its economic and geographic confines. At stake are not only the interests of 384,100 agricultural workers in California but potentially those of more than 4,000,000 in the U.S. Such workers have never won collective bargaining rights, partially because they have not been highly motivated to organize and partially because their often itinerant lives have made them difficult to weld into a group that would have the clout of an industrial union. By trying to organize the grape pickers, Chavez hopes to inspire militancy among all farm laborers. Because most of the grape pickers are Mexican Americans, he also believes that he is fighting a battle on behalf of the entire Mexican-American community, which as a group constitutes the nation's second biggest deprived minority.

UNLETTERED AND UNSHOD. Like the blacks, Mexican Americans, who are known as *Chicanos*, are a varied and diverse people. Only recently have they emerged from a stereotype: the lazy, placid peasant lost in a centuries-long siesta under a sombrero. Unlike the blacks, who were brought to the U.S. involuntarily, the *Chicanos* have flocked to the U.S. over the past 30 years, legally and illegally, in an attempt to escape the poverty of their native Mexico and find a better life. Whatever their present condition may be, many obviously find it better than their former one, as evidenced by the fact that relatives have often followed families into the U.S. The *Chicanos* do not speak in one voice but many, follow no one leader or strategy. Their level of ambition and militance varies greatly from *barrio* to *barrio* between Texas and California.

No man, however, personifies the *Chicanos'* bleak past, restless present and possible future in quite the manner of Cesar Chavez. He was the unshod, unlettered child of migrant workers. He attended dozens of schools but never got to the eighth grade. He was a street-corner tough who now claims as his models Emiliano Zapata, Gandhi, Nehru and Martin Luther King. He tells his people: "We make a solemn promise: to enjoy our rightful part of the riches of this land, to throw off the yoke of being considered as agricultural implements or slaves. We are free men and we demand justice."

The dawning of Chavez's social awareness came in a seamy San Jose, Calif., *barrio* called *Sal Si Puedes*—"Get out if you can." Through Fred Ross, a tall, quiet organizer for Saul Alinsky's Community Service Organization, Cesar began to act on Alinsky's precept that concerted action is the only means through which the poor can gain political and economic power. Chavez, a Roman Catholic, has delved deeply into the papal social encyclicals. *Rerum Novarum*, published by Leo XIII in 1891, contended that the rich had in effect enslaved the poor, and that every man has a right to a decent wage and reasonable comfort. Pius XI, in *Quadragesimo Anno* (1931), criticized the economic despotism that results from "limitless free competition" and reiterated the principle of a just wage. "What Cesar wanted to reform was the way he was treated as a man," recalls his brother Richard. "We always talked about change, but how could we go about it?" Cesar Chavez went about it by working with the C.S.O. among Mexican Americans for ten years. Then, in 1962, he left to form a farm workers' union.

The conditions under which farm laborers toil have improved somewhat since the squalid Depression era so well evoked by John Steinbeck in *The Grapes of Wrath* and *In Dubious Battle*; yet field work remains one of the most unpleasant of human occupations. It demands long hours of back-breaking labor, often in choking dust amid insects and under a flaming sun. The harvest-time wage for grape pickers averages $1.65 an hour, plus a 25¢ bonus for each box

picked, while the current federal minimum wage is $1.60.

Despite this, the seasonal and sporadic nature of the work keeps total income far below the poverty level. Average family income is less than $1,600 a year. There is no job security, and fringe benefits are few. If they are migrants, the workers must frequently live in fetid shacks without light or plumbing (though housing, bad as it is, is frequently free or very cheap.) As a result, many have moved to the cities, where even unskilled labor can find work at decent wages.

Chavez was not the first to try to organize farm workers. Ineffective efforts to found agricultural unions date back to the turn of the century. But only in Hawaii, where Harry Bridges' tough longshoremen's union used its muscle to win the first farm-labor contract for sugar-cane workers in 1945, did unionization take hold. Agriculture is outside the jurisdiction of the National Labor Relations Board, which has provided federal ground rules for industrial workers' unions since 1935; on a national level, there is no similar mechanism for farm workers. In May the Nixon Administration proposed an independent Farm Labor Relations Board, but chances for passage of such a law this year are small. Without NLRB protection, and with farm labor normally transient and seasonal, the difficulties of organizing are enormous.

ROSE GRAFTS AND TABLE GRAPES. Undeterred by these obstacles, Chavez took his $1,200 in savings and started the National Farm Workers' Association seven years ago, setting up its headquarters in the San Joaquin Valley agricultural town of Delano. He clicked off 300,000 miles in a battered 1953 Mercury station wagon, crisscrossing the San Joaquin and talking to more than 50,000 workers in the first six months. His money was soon gone, but he found people who were willing to give him food. The N.F.W.A. had its first formal meeting in Fresno in September 1962; 287 people showed up. Chavez soon started a death-benefits plan for his members, a curious echo of the burial societies organized decades ago by Eastern European immigrants on their arrival in the U.S. He also set up a credit union with $35 in assets (it now has more than $50,000). By August 1964, he had 1,000 members, each paying $3.50 a month in dues—no small sum for a farm worker's family. Soon he began publishing a union newspaper called *El Malcriado* (The Misfit), whose circulation is 18,000.

At last the union felt strong enough to tackle the growers on a substantive issue. In 1964, the N.F.W.A. took one employer to court for paying less than the then minimum wage of $1.25 per hour, and after months of wrangling, won the case. The amounts of money gained were small but the point was made: a boss could be beaten. Then the association sued the Tulare County housing authority over the rents and conditions at two labor camps, built in the late 1930s and intended to be used for only a few years. The camps were a hideous collection of 9-ft. by 11-ft. tin shacks, boiling in the summer sun and lacking both indoor plumbing and heat for the chill nights. Tulare officials subsequently built modern accommodations.

In May 1965, Chavez signed up a group of rose grafters and won a strike vote for higher wages. Everyone pledged not to go to work, but just to make sure that no one did, Chavez and Dolores Huerta, his tiny, tough assistant, made the rounds early on the strike's first morning. Mrs. Huerta saw a light in one house where four of the workers lived. She reminded them of their pledge, but they had changed their minds. Mrs. Huerta moved her truck so that it blocked their driveway and put the key in her purse. The incident illustrated the charge that Chavez and his aides sometimes coerce those who would rather work than strike. After only four days of the stike, the grower agreed to give the workers a 120% wage increase.

That same spring, in the Coachella Valley east of Los Angeles, the largely Filipino grape pickers of the A.F.L.-C.I.O.'s fledgling Agricultural Workers Organizing Committee won a brief strike for pay equal to that given field hands imported from Mexico. When the workers moved north to Delano at the end of the summer, grape growers there refused to make a similar agreement, and A.W.O.C. once more went on strike. On Sept. 16, which just happened to be Mexican Independence Day, Chavez's group held a tumultuous meeting and voted unanimously to join the walkout. The hall of the Roman Catholic church on Delano's west side resounded with cries of *"Viva la huelga!" "Viva la causa! Viva la union!"* The N.F.W.A. and the A.W.O.C. merged two years later to form the United Farm Workers Organizing Committee, headed by Chavez.

Table-grape growers are particularly vulnerable to strikes because their product requires continual attention through much of the year. Since the appearance of the fruit affects its value—unlike the case of wine grapes—the bunches must be carefully picked by hand. Because of their vulnerability, Chavez picked the table-grape growers as his first target. In 1966, after a strike, he got his first contract when Schenley Industries capitulated because it had a nationally known name at stake. Later that year he won the right to represent workers at the mammoth Di Giorgio ranch in an election monitored by the American Arbitration Association. Both Di Giorgio and Schenley have since sold their table-grape holdings, however, and Chavez's only contracts now are with wine producers: Gallo, Christian Brothers, Masson, Almaden, Franzia Brothers and Novitiate.

BOYCOTT AND BREAKTHROUGH. Chavez has never been able to get large numbers of laborers to join the strike. Many of those who do follow him are fanatic in their loyalty, but a large segment of the shifting, transient work force continues to be indifferent to unionism. Wages have been rising even in the absence of contracts, and few farm workers can afford to go unpaid for long. Although federal regulations theoretically prohibit the hiring of aliens, or "greencarders," as strike breakers, the owners have nevertheless continued to use imported workers of Mexican citizenship.

Chavez decided to resort to the boycott to keep pressure on the table-grape growers. He applied it first in 1967 to the Giumarra Vineyards Corp., the largest U.S. table-grape producer. Giumarra started using the labels of other growers—in violation of Food and Drug Administration rules—to circumvent the boycott. In retaliation, the Chavez people began to appeal to stores and consumers not to buy any California table grapes at all. The boycott has been extended overseas to Britain and Scandinavia.

Chavez has now finally achieved a breakthrough: nationwide grape sales were off 12% in 1968, and prices for this year's first California grapes are down as much as 15%. Last month ten growers representing about 12% of the state's table-grape production announced that they would sit down with Chavez to write a contract. If negotiations with Chavez succeed, some other vineyards may also sing contracts, but a determined majority still barely acknowledge his existence and remain adamantly opposed to union recognition.

Chavez's claim to represent the workers is false, they say; only 3% of California's grape pickers have joined his union. Chavez has not been able to strip the fields of workers and, they argue, even if he personally preaches nonviolence, his followers do not practice it. Packing sheds have been set afire, foremen threatened, tires slashed. Chavez also has outside help. Long-haired pickets came down from Berkeley in the early days of *la huelga*, and the union gets $14,500 a month in grants from the A.F.L.-C.I.O. and Walter Reuther's United Automobile Workers. By insisting that all workers join his union, moreover, Chavez wants what amounts to a closed shop (which is illegal under the Taft-Hartley Act, but the act does not apply to agricultural workers). This means that, for now at least, Chavez's goal, however unpalatable, is a legal one. Chavez opposes placing farm workers under the National Labor Relations Board precisely because that would make the closed shop he seeks unlawful.

The growers of Delano are difficult to cast as villains. Many are self-made men, Yugoslavs and Italians who came to the valley between 1900 and 1940 with nothing and worked hard to amass enough capital to practice the grape-growing arts they learned in Europe. Most of the Delano spreads are family enterprises, and many of them have had rough going. Costs have risen sharply over the past decade, and grape prices have now begun to decline.

The California growers also pay the second highest agricultural wages in the U.S. (after Hawaii, where unionized workers average $3 an hour).

While they generally belittle the extent of his support, however, the growers have gone to some lengths to counter Chavez's moves. The anti-U.F.W.O.C. campaign even included for a time a group called Mothers Against Chavez. The growers are using the J. Walter Thompson agency to place $400,000 worth of ads extolling the benefits of table grapes. The California public relations firm of Whitaker &

Baxter has been retained to advise the growers about how to counter the boycott. Whitaker & Baxter helped to manage Richard Nixon's unsuccessful campaign for governor of California in 1962, and masterminded the American Medical Association's attempt to defeat Medicare.

ON $10 A WEEK. One reason for the lack of comprehension between Chavez and the growers is that each has different concepts of the fundamental issue. The growers see themselves as management in a classic labor dispute, while Chavez and his followers believe that the cause of all Mexican Americans is at stake.

That is what inspires Chavez's devotion to *la causa*. For years he and his wife and eight children have lived jammed into a tiny two-bedroom house in Delano, subsisting on $10 a week from the union and on food from the communal kitchen in nearby union headquarters. Chavez has grown increasingly ascetic. He has given up casual socializing as well as liquor and cigarettes; his idea of a real treat is an eclectic meal of Chinese food, matzohs and diet soda. The fight has become his life. "The days and weeks and months run together," he told TIME Correspondent Robert Anson. "I can't think back to a time when we were not on strike." Nor does he contemplate surrender to the growers. "Either the union will be destroyed," he says, "or they will sign a contract. There's no other alternative."

The use of only peaceful means has been central to his thinking since a 1953 showdown in the San Joaquin Valley between his Mexican-American C.S.O. pickets and a public official. Suddenly, he realized that if there were any violence or serious disorder it would be his responsibility. He began reading Gandhi, and he says now: "If the strike means the blood of one grower or one grower's son, or one worker or one worker's son, then it isn't worth it."

In February 1968, Chavez began a 25-day fast "as an act of penance, recalling workers to the nonviolent roots of their movement." Although he insisted that his decision was essentially a private one, the fast took on a certain circus aura and raised suspicions that its motivation was more theatrical than theological. During the fast, Chavez had to make a court appearance in Bakersfield, on charges of improper picketing, in a case that has yet to come to trial. As he did so, 2,000 farm workers knelt outside in prayer. One woman solemnly asked him if he were indeed a saint. When the fast ended, Senator Robert Kennedy knelt next to him to receive Communion. Some 8,000 others joined them in Delano's Memorial Park for a bread-breaking ceremony.

The fast, and Chavez's years of 12- to 16-hour days, took their toll. Last September he suffered a muscular breakdown in his back—he had been in pain for years before that—and found his legs nearly paralyzed. After spending more than two months in traction, he has now substantially recovered, but is still bedridden much of the time. Instead of spending long hours driving around the state, he receives a constant stream of subordinates at his bedside.

Chavez's religious conviction mingles with the exigen-cies of the movement. He opposes birth control for his people, but only partly out of conventional Catholicism; he argues that smaller families would diminish the numerical power of the poor. A priest brings him Communion daily. To Correspondent Anson he explained: "God prepares those who have to suffer and take punishment. Otherwise, how could we exist? How could the black man exist? There must be something special. I really think that He looks after us."

Cesar Chavez came to his mission from a background of poverty and prejudice that is a paradigm of that of many *Chicanos*. Like most Mexican Americans, he is of mixed Spanish and Indian blood, with liquid brown eyes, deeply bronze skin and thick, jet-black hair. He was born on an 80-acre farm in Arizona's Gila Valley near Yuma, where his parents tried to scratch a living from the arid desert earth. Chavez met racial hostility early in daily rock fights between Anglo and Chicano kids at the village school.

The farm failed in the Depression, and when Chavez was ten, the family packed everything it owned into a decrepit automobile and headed across the Colorado River into California. In Oxnard, Chavez's father found work threshing lima beans; when all the beans were harvested, the family took off, looking for other jobs and often turning up just a few days after a crop was in.

ANGLOS ON THE LEFT. That first winter back in Oxnard, with the little money earned in the fields already gone, was the family's worst time. Cesar's brother Richard remembers: "There was this nice lady there, and she had a vacant lot that she let us use. So we put up a tent. It was a very small tent—I guess about 8 by 10. That's all we had. All the family stayed there. And it rained that winter. Oh, it rained. Rain, rain, rain. We had to go to school barefoot. We had no shoes. I can't forget it."

The family lived that winter on beans, tortillas and an occasional potato. Chavez's father sometimes picked peas for 50¢ a day, half of which went to the contractor who drove the workers to the fields in the back of a flatbed truck. There was nothing else to do. By the next spring, the family had learned more of the harvest schedule, and it set off for the first of many years on the circuit familiar to every migrant worker in California. Starting in the Imperial and Coachella valleys of the south, through the state's bulging middle, the San Joaquin Valley, on up north of San Francisco and into the Napa Valley, they worked each crop in its turn: asparagus, grapes, beets, potatoes, beans, plums, apricots—anything that needed picking, hoeing, thinning, leafing, tipping, girdling, digging or pruning.

In 1941, the family moved to Delano, where Chavez met his future wife, Helen Fabela. At the movies with her one night, he had a jarring brush with discrimination. He refused to stay on the right side of the theater, which was reserved for Mexicans, and sat instead with the Anglos on the left. "The assistant manager came," Chavez recalls. "The girl who sold the popcorn came. And the girl with the tickets came. Then the manager came. They tried to pull me up, and I said, 'No, you have to break my arms before I get up.'" Chavez, then 16, was hustled off to the station house for a lecture from the chief of police, but he would not promise not to do the same thing again.

Like many other teen-age Mexican Americans, Chavez became a *pachuco*, affecting a zoot suit with pegged pants, a broad flat hat and a ducktail haircut. Some sociologists now see the *pachuco* movement as the first example of militant separatism among *Chicanos*, an assertion of a distinct identity hostile to Anglo culture. The Anglos took it that way, in any case, and reacted violently: during a series of riots in the Southwest during the summer of 1943, several thousand soldiers, sailors and Marines beat up hundreds of *Chicano* youths. Police promptly arrested some of the victims.

Because of his own experience of poverty and acquaintance with prejudice, Cesar Chavez has made *la causa* more than a labor movement. He is determined to better the lot of all Mexican Americans. There is much room for improvement. There have never been Jim Crow laws against them, like those against blacks, but overt discrimination undeniably exists.*Chicanos* still find it hard to get into the barbershops and public swimming pools of south Texas. Still, though the *Chicano* is set apart by language, assimilation is often easier for him than for the Negro. For this reason, and because most of the *Chicano* population lives in relative obscurity in the barrios or rural areas, the Mexican-American community has been slow to develop aggressive leadership.

If he is a migrant farm worker, the Mexican American has a life expectancy of about 48 years v. 70 for the average U.S. resident. The *Chicano* birth rate is double the U.S. average—but so is the rate of infant mortality. More than one-third live below the $3,000-a-year level of family income that federal statisticians define as poverty. Eighty percent of the Mexican-American population is now urban, and most live in the *barrio*.

FORBIDDEN LANGUAGE. The overwhelming majority work as unskilled or semiskilled labor in factories and packing plants, or in service jobs as maids, waitresses, yard boys and deliverymen. Particularly in Texas, Mexican Americans sometimes get less pay than others for the same work. Even the few who have some education do not escape discrimination. *Chicano* women find that jobs as public contacts at airline ticket counters are rarely open; they are welcome as switchboard operators out of the public eye. Mexican-American men who work in banks are assigned to the less fashionable branches. Promotions come slowly, responsibility hardly ever.

One major impediment to the Mexican American is his Spanish language, because it holds him back in U.S. schools. Mexican Americans average eight years of schooling, two years less than Negroes and a full four years less than whites. Often they are forced to learn English from scratch in the first grade, and the frequent result is that they become not bilingual but nearly nonlingual. In Texas, 40%

of *Chicanos* are considered functionally illiterate. In Los Angeles, only an estimated 25% can speak English fluently. *Chicano* children in some rural areas are still punished for speaking Spanish in school. Only this year, *Chicano* students at Bowie High School in El Paso—in a predominantly Mexican-American section—managed to get a rule abolished that forbade the speaking of Spanish on the school grounds.

The *Chicano* is as vulnerable to mistreatment at the hands of the law as the black. Seven Mexicans were beaten by drunken policemen at a Los Angeles police station on Christmas Eve, 1952; six of the officers were eventually given jail terms. During an 18-month period ending last April, the American Civil Liberties Union received 174 complaints of police abuses from Los Angeles Mexican Americans. Two of the recent landmark Supreme Court decisions limiting police questioning of suspects involved Mexican Americans—*Escobedo* v. *Illinois* and *Miranda* v. *Arizona*. Many Mexicans still look on the Texas Rangers and U.S. border patrols with terror.

PLURALISM V. THE MELTING POT. As with the blacks, the question for those who lead the *Chicanos* is whether progress means separatism or assimilation. Cal State Professor Rafael Guzman, who helped carry out a four-year Ford Foundation study of Mexican Americans, warns that the *barrio* is potentially as explosive as the black ghetto. He argues for a new pluralism in the U.S. that means something other than forcing minorities into the established Anglo-Saxon mold; each group should be free to develop its own culture while contributing to the whole.

Yet there is no real consensus in the *barrio*. The forces for assimilation are powerful. A young Tucson militant, Salomon Baldenegro, contends: "Our values are just like any Manhattan executive's, but we have a ceiling on our social mobility." While federal programs for bilingual instruction in Mexican-American areas are still inadequate, that kind of approach—if made readily available to all who want it—leaves the choice between separatism and assimilation ultimately to the individual *Chicano* himself. He learns in his father's tongue, but he also learns in English well enough so that language is no longer a barrier; he retains his own culture, but he also knows enough of the majority's rules and ways to compete successfully if he chooses to.

Cesar Chavez has made the *Chicano*'s cause well enough known to make that goal possible. While *la huelga* is in some respects a limited battle, it is also symbolic of the Mexican-American's quest for a full role in U.S. society. What happens to Chavez's farm workers will be an omen, for good or ill, of the Mexican-American's future. For the short term, Chavez's most tangible aspiration is to win the fight with the grape growers. If he can succeed in that difficult and uncertain battle, he will doubtless try to expand the movement beyond the vineyards into the entire Mexican-American community. ∎

Angry and proud, Native Americans took a cue from African-American demonstrators and clashed with the government in a series of highly visible showdowns. For blacks, the great civil rights struggles of the '60s gave way to a quieter period of assimilation. Changes in the South came remarkably quickly, and more and more blacks across the country achieved middle-class economic status. But the issue of integration still rankled; the forced busing of schoolchildren satisfied few, angered many. Refugees from Castro's Cuba brought another great stream of Hispanic culture to America. In Miami, in Los Angeles, in New York and in the border towns of Texas, Hispanic Americans were discovering it was their turn in the sun.

Goodbye to Tonto

Angry American Indians demand their rights

MOST AMERICANS KNOW the first Americans only by cliché. There is the 19th century image, caught in bronze and in lithograph, of the defeated warrior, head drooping forward so that his feathers nearly mingle with his pony's mane. The bow of his shoulders and the slump of his body evoke his loss of pride, of green and fertile lands, of earth's most favored continent. Then there is a recent image, often seen through air-conditioned automobile windows. Grinning shyly, the fat squaw hawks her woven baskets along the reservation highway, the dusty landscape littered with rusting cars, crumbling wickiups and bony cattle. In the bleak villages, the only signs of cheer are romping, round-faced children and the invariably dirty, crowded bar, noisy with the shouts and laughter of drunkenness.

Like most stereotypes, these caricatures possess a certain core of validity. They also help white America contain and numb the reality of past guilt and present injustice. Most important of all, they are less and less significant. After more than a century of patience and passivity, the nation's most neglected and isolated minority is astir, seeking the means and the muscle for protest and redress. Sometimes highly educated, sometimes speaking with an articulateness forged of desperation, always angry, the new American Indian is fed up with the destitution and publicly sanctioned abuse of his long-divided people. He is raising his voice and he intends to be heard. Listen:

"The next time whites try to illegally clear our land, perhaps we should get out and shoot the people in the bulldozers," contends Michael Benson, a 19-year-old Navajo and a freshman at Wesleyan University.

"It's time that Indians got off their goddam asses and stopped letting white people lead them around by their noses," says Lehman Brightman, a South Dakota Sioux now working on a Ph.D. at Berkeley. "Even the name Indian is not ours. It was given to us by some dumb honky who got lost and thought he'd landed in India."

"We weren't meant to be tourist attractions for the master race," scoffs Gerald Wilkinson, 30, a Cherokee who holds multiple degrees after attending four universities. "We don't use the language of the New Left, but that doesn't mean we're not militant."

"Some day you're going to feel like Custer, baby," shouted one unidentified Indian at Donald Dwyer, a former Minneapolis police chief recently invited to discuss city problems with a group of Minneapolis Indians.

SYMBOLIC PROTEST. That kind of rhetoric is surprising, coming from people long accustomed to equating silence with dignity. But in acts as well as speech, the newly aroused Indian is no longer content to play the obsequious Tonto to the white man's Lone Ranger. A belligerent band of 100 Indians still occupies the abandoned federal prison at Alcatraz, which the Indians propose to use as a cultural center and are willing to buy—for "$24 in glass beads and red cloth." Says one of the invaders: "Alcatraz is still better than most reservations." Angered at the whites who litter their beaches with beer cans and broken bottles, Indians in the state of Washington set up road blocks and closed 50 miles of seashore. A group of 50 Passamaquoddy Indians in Maine charged motorists fees to pass through their land on a busy highway last July. Four Indians at Dartmouth College, which was founded partly "for civilizing and christianizing Children of Pagans," protested the Indian dress of the college mascot, and officials banished it from football games.

The new Indian activism is gradually beating its way into the nation's consciousness—and into its conscience. In ways both salutary and shabby, Indians are becoming fashionable. As *The New Yorker*'s Calvin Trillin recently observed: "It is almost possible to hear the drums in the East Sixties."

The Indian is spicing his protest with a grim kind of humor. His slogans proclaim: KEMO SABE MEANS HONKY, RED POWER!, and CUSTER HAD IT COMING. More stingingly, Indian Folk Singer Buffy Sainte-Marie, a Cree with a degree in education and Oriental philosophy, confronts white audiences with pointed lyrics:

When a war between nations is lost
The loser, we know, pays the cost;
But even when Germany fell to your hands
You left them their pride and you left them their land.

The national abuse of the Indian reached Broadway last year as the subject of serious drama. Arthur Kopit's *Indians* played only twelve weeks; some critics considered it noisy, disorganized theater; some audiences seemed to find the penitential message discomforting. A pro-Indian movie, *Little Big Man*, starring Dustin Hoffman, has been filmed on Montana's Crow reservation. It portrays George Custer as a villain leading troops bent on genocide. Three books personalizing Indian alienation have won critical acclaim. A novel, *House Made of Dawn*, by N. Scott Momaday, a Kiowa who teaches English at Berkeley, won a Pulitzer prize last year. *Custer Died for Your Sins*, by Vine Deloria, a Standing Rock Sioux, wryly details the Indians' own infighting and their frustrations in dealing with white society. *Our Brother's Keeper: The Indian in White America* angrily indicts whites for keeping the Indian a stranger in his homeland—"America's prisoner of war."

THE HANDICAP OF DIGNITY. Why has it taken the Indian so long to rouse himself to turn his ire toward action? Many a white bureaucrat, ruling a reservation like a colonial army officer, has assumed that Indian acquiescence stemmed from either respect or servility. Rarely has it been either. The Indian nation was physically shattered and spiritually demoralized by the U.S. Cavalry, which systematically destroyed its leaders and the best of its manhood in the late 19th century campaigns that whites euphemistically call the pacification of the West. Long before the white man's arrival, Indian tribes had, of course, waged limited war upon one another over hunting rights, and raids for revenge were common.

Yet on a personal level, Indian culture shuns confrontation. Even the meeting of eyes and the firm handshake were long avoided. Discussions of personal problems are painful. Indians have been known to sit in Government offices for hours before deciding to air a grievance, however just. "My mother won't even get rid of a salesman," says the Navajos' Michael Benson.

For too long, Indian dissent also has been stifled by their forced dependency upon whites for land and livelihood. This has made many of them regard white authority as an almost magical thing. One veteran scholar of Arizona's Hopis, E. D. Newcomer, notes that today's young Hopis even "feel that the god of the whites must be better than their own gods, because the whites have new clothes and shiny cars."

Handicapped by their special definition of dignity and fractionalized by their allegiances to about 300 tribes, the 652,000 Indians in the U.S. have never developed a unity that would sustain massive protest. "Remember, I'm not Indian, I'm Osage," declares Charles Lohah, an Oklahoma judge who finds political intrigue both within and among tribes fascinatingly complex. "Often we have to strap our shields to our backs," he says. But Indians have also watched the nation respond to the marches, sit-ins and street tactics of restive blacks. Indians feel little affinity with blacks, and there is friction between the races in some federal antipoverty programs; still, the Indians are beginning to demand their share of the action.

That demand is not only just but long overdue. Ford Foundation President McGeorge Bundy insists flatly that "the American Indians are by any measure save cultural heritage the country's most disadvantaged minority." After studying U.S. ill-treatment of the Indian 26 years ago, Swedish Sociologist Gunnar Myrdal described it as "a morality play of profound importance" to American history. He said that it "challenges the most precious assumptions about what this country stands for—cultural pluralism, freedom of conscience and action, and the pursuit of happiness." The morality play is still a bad show today.

The indicators of Indian suffering are appalling. Their life expectancy is 44 years, compared with 71 for white Americans. The average income for each Indian family living on a reservation—and more than half do—is only $1,500. The average years of schooling is 5.5, well behind that of both the black and the Mexican American. Some officials rate 90% of reservation housing as substandard. Unemployment ranges from a low of 20% on the more affluent reservations to 80% on the poorest. The birth rate of Indians is $2\frac{1}{2}$ times that of whites—and a majority of Indians are under 20 years old. The average family has to carry water for its daily needs at least a mile. It is usually done afoot.

Indians, of course, are not statistics, and TIME Correspondent James Willwerth discovered that individual reality for Indians often consists of human deprivation in a setting of uplifting natural beauty. Visiting Arizona's White Mountain Apache reservation, he reported: "The land is like a painting—hills covered with ponderosa pine, snow-capped mountains in the distance, sprawling valleys filled with thick forests and rushing streams. In the midst of all this, there's a one-room shack with a corrugated metal roof that shows daylight from every angle. This is Judy's house. Judy is in her mid-20s, stocky but not fat, and rather pretty. But she drinks a lot, gets into fights when she does, and often ends up in jail.

"Her lovers are legion. The result of one liaison toddles toward me through broken glass and excrement. He's less than two years old. He lived with Judy's sister until recently, but Judy took him back to get some welfare money. Now they are living in this one-room place. 'It's got no windows,' she says. 'But that's nothing. I've never lived in a house with windows.'"

The grim individual vignettes are multiplied among entire tribes. In northern Arizona, twelve small villages of the deeply religious Hopis fight their uncertain struggle to avoid extinction. Reversing years of decline, the Hopis now number 6,000. Isolated for centuries, even their own villages still have no political links with one another. They live on three massive sandstone mesas in the Painted Desert, where pasture land is scarce and only their skillful dry-farming of corn provides a meager diet.

The sole tribal commerce of the Hopis is a trailer court and a few arts-and-crafts shops. Yet the hope of the Hopis lies in their determination to improve their condition. They teach their children to value schooling so highly that the average daily attendance in their elementary schools is a surprising 90%—a rarity among Indians. A score of older youngsters take a bus each day and make a 96-mile round trip to attend high school. Each day 50 adult Hopis get up at 5 A.M. to board a yellow bus and ride 65 miles to their jobs at a BVD underwear plant. Things may get better. Coal has been found on Hopi land, and a strip mine is scheduled to open this year. Ironically, the Hopi devotion to education is diluting what they value most: their own special kind of polytheistic belief that each living thing possesses a human spirit. Now, when elders hold their annual dance with rattlesnakes, many Hopi children laugh.

AGONY AND ANOMIE. To live in squalor while surrounded by beauty, to desire a better material life while clinging to tradition is, for American Indians, to know agony and anomie. Their alienation is aggravated by the fact that Indian culture is vastly different from that of whites in terms of technology, productivity and intellectual interests. From the viewpoint of what makes a modern civilization work, Indian culture appears hopelessly irrelevant. To some extent, the collision of Western and Indian cultures warped the conquerors' attitudes. When the Senecas sought assurances from President Thomas Jefferson in 1802 that their rights would be protected, no attempt was made to bridge the cultural gap. They received a patronizing note from a secretary that said: "Brothers, your father, the President, will at all times be your friend and he will protect you and all his red children from bad people." Only last fall Ted Rushton of New Mexico's Gallup Independent wrote haughtily of "the inevitable clash of a superior culture with a vastly inferior culture."

The Indian child who attends school with whites must brace himself for taunts: when it rains, he is told, "You must have done your dance." If he has a girl friend, he is asked: "How's your squaw?" Or it may be "Hey, Tonto, where's your horse?" and "What number is your teepee?" "Indian kids are shy, and can't take this," explains Gary Fife, 19, an Oklahoma Cherokee-Creek student at Northeastern State College.

Prejudice is as painful a fact to Indians as it is to blacks. Indians suffer just as harshly from biased history books. One text observes that "it is probably true that all the American Indian tribes in the course of their wandering lived for some generations on the frozen wastes of Alaska. This experience deadened their minds and killed their imagination and initiative." A white teacher in a Chippewa reservation school recently asked Indian children to write essays on "Why we are all happy the Pilgrims landed." Western movies and television, of course, still portray the Indian as the savage marauder. "How are you going to expect the Indian to feel a part of America when every television program shows him to be a brute or a stupid animal?" asks Ray Fadden, owner of a Mohawk museum in northern New York. On an Apache reservation, even an Indian girl was caught up in the TV drama. As an Indian actor crept up on an unsuspecting cowboy, the girl involuntarily shouted at the cowboy: "Get him! Get him!"

Indians smolder when the white operators of trading posts sell their Indian-crafted goods to tourists at 400% markups. They resent the white sportsmen who gun down caribou from airplanes, while their own hunting for lifesaving game is restricted by white laws. They become furious at the white shopkeepers' use of Indian religious symbols and bad portraits of Indian chiefs. Don Wilkerson, the Cherokee-Creek director of the Phoenix Indian Center, claims that a bar in Scottsdale, Ariz., has a huge picture of a great Indian chief on its roof as an advertising gimmick. "The Jewish people would not permit such treatment of one of their revered leaders," he says. "Nor would society allow Martin Luther King to be so humiliated."

ALCOHOLISM AND SUICIDE. Dispirited by poverty, rejected by a white culture in which they are often unable and unwilling to compete, many Indians choose death or drink. The suicide rate among Indian teen-agers is three times the national average; on some reservations it is ten times as high. Shattered by her parents' broken marriage, an 18-year-old Blackfoot girl not long ago killed herself on her Montana reservation with an overdose of tranquilizers, though she was an honor student. Accused of drinking during school hours, a 16-year-old youth on Idaho's Fort Hall Reservation hanged himself in the county jail. Just two days before, he had talked about conditions on the reservation with Senator Robert F. Kennedy.

Alcohol has long been a means of escape from boredom and pressures for Indians. On one Midwest reservation containing 4,600 adults, 44% of all the men and 21% of the women were arrested at least once for drunkenness in a span of three years. Many reservations have opened bars and liquor stores to keep Indians from killing themselves in auto accidents en route home from binges in the city. A much-repeated explanation quotes Bill Pensoneau, president of the National Indian Youth Council, as telling a new commissioner of Indian Affairs: "We drown ourselves in wine and smother ourselves in glue—because the only time we are free is when we're drunk."

SOMETHING OF VALUE. Indian grievances are specific, but the goals of redress so far remain diffuse. There are no Indian leaders who, with any confidence of national support from their people, can speak on precisely what should be done. Traditionalists merely tend to look at the mountains that have sheltered their tribes for centuries and at the writings of their ancestral prophets, and they say patiently: "We'll outlast you whites." There are others who seek accommodation of white and Indian cultures. Says Ronnie Lupe, tribal chairman of the White Mountain Apaches: "We know what the white man offers us. There are certain comforts in your culture—good homes, good cars, good jobs—but there is a certain way to get these and yet retain our identity, and we have yet to find it."

But even that kind of reasonableness is dismissed by the new Indian militants as the talk of "Uncle Tom-Toms" or "Uncle Tomahawks" and "Stand-Around-the-Fort Indians." What these leaders seem to want most is for the Federal Government, which now spends only $500 million a year on aid to Indians, to increase its spending for Indian schools, roads, housing and medical care—and to stop smothering Indians with restrictive regulations and unwanted advice on how to run their affairs. They want their water and land rights protected and expanded, not contracted through treaty violations. They want help in attracting job-providing industries to their reservations, but they want to determine what kinds and how they will be operated. They want federal benevolence, in short, as compensation for the loss of more than half a continent, but they want to be free to go their own way—even though they are not yet certain of their direction.

The Indians' longing to live harmoniously with nature touches recesses of nostalgia in the minds of many Americans. Indeed, at a time when the drive to protect and restore the nation's physical environment is the most popular cause of the day, whites' guilt over their spoilage of air, land and water engenders a new admiration for those who have fought for so long to protect their own plains, lakes and hunting grounds. It would be wrong to romanticize Indian culture, but there is something to be valued, or at least envied, in a society that respects the wisdom of elders, enjoys the closeness of kinship, prefers tranquility to competition, and sees little merit in 9-to-5 punctuality at a desk.

Although they now live in what one Indian calls "a schizoid world of fractured loyalties," all Indian leaders agree that the best of their ancient heritage is a priceless resource. To many white Americans, who are constantly told these days how much they have to feel guilty about, the demands of yet one more minority may seem almost more than the conscience can bear. Yet Indians can hardly be expected to keep their peace just because they have only lately joined the queue of those vociferously demanding social justice. If they continue to be rejected, many young Indians will continue to despair and will embrace the sentiments of Phil George, a young Nez Perce, who wrote:

This summer I shall
Return to our Longhouse,
Hide beneath a feathered hat,
And become an Old Man.

The new militants reject such resignation, and are determined that Indians be heard along with all of America's second-class citizens. Their aim is nothing less than to reverse the perspectives of the races. Explains one:

You will forgive me if I tell you that my people were Americans for thousands of years before your people were. The question is not how you can Americanize us but how we can Americanize you. The first thing we want to teach you is that, in the American way of life, each man has respect for his brother's vision. Because each of us respected his brother's dream, we enjoyed freedom here while your people were busy killing and enslaving one another across the water. We have a hard trail ahead of us, but we are not afraid of hard trails. ■

Rebellion on the Reservation

Militant Indians seize hallowed ground

Raid at Wounded Knee MARCH 12, 1973

THE FIRST REPORTS out of Wounded Knee, S. Dak., suggested that history had been hijacked by a band of revisionists armed with a time machine.

The tiny junction settlement (pop. 40) is the site of the infamous massacre of some 300 old men, women and children of the Sioux nation by the U.S. Cavalry in the winter of 1890. It was overrun one night last week by roughly 200 armed members of the American Indian Movement (AIM), a militant group best known for its week-long occupation of the Bureau of Indian Affairs in Washington last November. Thus a drama began to unwind at Wounded Knee, deep in an area where there is open tension between mostly impoverished Indians and whites.

DEATH. The protesters set up headquarters in a Roman Catholic church and ransacked a trading post. They took eleven hostages, all Indian residents of Wounded Knee, which lies inside the Oglala Sioux Pine Ridge Reservation, a 1 1/2 million-acre stretch of honey-colored hills. The Indians put up roadblocks around Wounded Knee in the early hours of the takeover before a contingent of U.S. marshals in turquoise jumpsuits formed a cordon about the area. Some of the people curious and foolhardy enough to wander near the stronghold were met by spurts of gunfire from the hefty Sioux arsenal. AIM Leader Russell Means, an Oglala Sioux who comes from Cleveland, announced to newsmen: "We've got the whole Wounded Knee valley, and we definitely are going to hold it until death do us part."

Two days later, while rental cars full of reporters and film crews swooshed back and forth in the dust, a helicopter arrived with Senators George McGovern and James Abourezk of South Dakota, accompanied by aides to Senators J. William Fulbright and Edward Kennedy. Shortly before their appearance, the hostages, including one man with a serious heart condition, had been told that they were free to go. All were unharmed and remained—apparently by choice—in Wounded Knee. The two Senators then met at length with AIM spokesmen to discuss grievances.

They demanded an immediate investigation of the sluggish BIA and of past Indian treaties with the U.S. Government. The protesters also made a large point of calling for the ouster of the Pine Ridge tribal council president,

AIM demonstrators celebrate in seized area

Dick Wilson. In large part, the takeover reflected civil strife—a power struggle between two competing Indian factions. Facing off at Wounded Knee were moderates, led by Wilson, and the AIM activists, mostly Indians from outside the reservation, led by Russell Means.

Late last week, there were reports that hundreds of AIM supporters were heading toward Wounded Knee from five states. Indians and lawmen traded shots for the first time since the takeover. No one was injured, but the flare-up strained a tense situation.

A group of lawyers arrived to help seek a peaceful settlement and counsel the Indians on federal charges that could be filed against them. At week's end the AIM party was still holed up and the questions remained: How much had been lost? Had anything been gained? ■

A Suspenseful Show of Red Power

FROM THE START, the confrontation at Wounded Knee, S. Dak., between militant Indians and local, state and federal authorities had all the elements of bad theater. The Indians insisted on out-moded makeup (war paint) and melodramatic lines ("Massacre us or meet our human needs"). The Federal Government brought in outrageous props, including war planes. There were too many theatrical asides aimed at the TV cameras and too many studied parallels to the Viet Nam War, including a "demilitarized zone" and "cease-fire observers." Finally there was the self-conscious symbolism of the choice of the site itself, the mass burial ground for victims of the U.S. Cavalry's most brutal massacre of the Indians.

But as the days ticked by, the drama drew an ever larger American audience under its spell. By midweek, after Justice Department officials issued an ultimatum to the Indians to abandon the trading post at Wounded Knee by 6 P.M. on Thursday, the suspense grew. In the rolling hills surrounding the Indian enclave, U.S. Army armored personnel carriers rumbled in preparation for an assault. At the roadblocks and in command posts, several of the FBI agents and marshals—there were 300 in all—restlessly broke down their M-16 rifles and adjusted the straps on their gas masks. At one point, two U.S. Air Force Phantoms streaked low overhead, reportedly on "reconnaissance" missions.

Just below the Indians' stronghold—a brilliantly whitewashed Catholic church high atop a bluff—an Indian drove a bulldozer in and out of sight as he deepened the trenches and thickened the fortifications that would shield the militants against the approaching attack. On the perimeters, patrols spied on Government operations through field glasses. An Indian guard, fingering his .30-30 under the gathering storm clouds, boasted: "They are going to see how tough we are. Anything comes down that road, we blow it apart."

TIME Correspondent Ken Huff, who spent a night inside the Indian encampment, reported what happened just before the Government deadline for evacuation:

"Seven Indian leaders stripped, some naked, others to their shorts, and entered an Indian sweat lodge—a wooden framework covered by an orange carpet and a purple blanket—to receive clarity of mind and body. The warriors, perhaps 150 of them, seemed perfectly willing to die. With the sun setting behind their backs and the chill wind whipping up puffs of dust, they formed a semicircle and watched as the tribal fathers emerged from the steaming lodge.

"A Sioux spiritual leader named Leonard Crow Dog struck up a chant in the Lakota language. As each warrior passed by, he blessed him and painted a slash or a circle of red powder under the left eye. Each warrior then stepped into a white tepee, making a holy sign over the bleached skull of a buffalo head."

WHOOPS. Fortunately, a major conflict never came to pass. The spiritual preparations were suddenly interrupted and hour before the deadline when a blue Coupe de Ville Cadillac roared up, shattering the solemnity. Dennis Banks, an Indian leader, jumped out to announce that both sides had agreed to a ceasefire proposed by the National Council of Churches of Christ. Reported Huff: "There were whoops of joy as the sun set behind a ridge spotted with the silhouettes of jagged pines." That precarious truce held despite a shootout between Indian patrol guards and federal marshals just an hour later. Two Indians were shot, one in the hand and one in the leg, and both sides argued over who had fired first.

To prevent further infractions, 34 observers from the council, clearly identified by their white armbands with the NCC logo, took up positions around Wounded Knee. At week's end the Justice Department backed down. In a sudden reversal of policy, it removed all road-blocks and withdrew all 300 U.S. marshals, FBI agents and local policemen. The Indians were free to leave—with their weapons.

AIM Leader Russell Means was jubilant. "We want to see headlines that say 'U.S. surrenders to Indians,'" he told newsmen. In fact, the Justice Department had done the only sensible thing. The wonder was not why its agents had suddenly withdrawn, but why they had not been ordered to do so earlier, to defuse a dangerous situation. At most, Justice had made a tactical retreat. It plans to convene a grand jury early this week to consider indictments, and a courtroom showdown seems inevitable. AIM leaders were not only resigned to that possibility, but almost appeared to relish it. Said Means: "Give us our day in court, and we'll take it."

The withdrawal of federal agents also did nothing to redress the underlying grievances that had brought the militants to Wounded Knee in the first place. Those remained to be thrashed out with officials from the Department of Interior, which runs the BIA. Rather than leave Wounded Knee, several AIM leaders claimed that they were planning to stay on there to meet with Interior officials this week.

Before it ended, the eleven-day siege of Wounded Knee had thoroughly disrupted the rest of the 2,400-sq.-mi. reservation. In the town of Pine Ridge, 20 miles southwest, the BIA office sent workers home and stopped distributing

Behind the Second Battle of Wounded Knee

WOUNDED KNEE has been the catalyst," says Donald White, an Oneida Indian who is a student at the University of Illinois. "We have been apathetic for too many years. The people out there are willing to die for us. Maybe it's our time to do something too." Many other Indians, particularly the young, echo his sentiments.

Although the American Indian has been the subject of insatiable curiosity and unrelieved romanticization by whites, almost 500 years of losing battles have made him nearly invisible. But recently the Indian has begun to emerge from behind the misty stereotype of smoke signals, tepees and Tonto. A chorus of angry voices has been making many demands: they call for everything from control of reservation lands and mineral rights to restoration of ancient tribal customs and the power to specify curriculums in Indian grade schools. The move to self-determination is characterized in the new cry: "Indian identification of Indian problems!"

In a sense, the basic Indian demand is to undo history. Throughout the 19th century, the westward expansion of white America, protected and assisted by the U.S. Cavalry, forced the Indian nations onto smaller and smaller reservations, usually far from their ancestral lands. The Indian population fell from about 1,150,000 at the time of Columbus to an alltime low of 250,000 by 1900. U.S. citizenship rights were withheld from the Indians until 1924. Today, the Indian population is rising fast—it is now 792,000. In the past two decades, the life expectancy of the Indian has jumped from 44 years to 63.5 years. But that is still seven years short of the national average. The rates of both alcoholism and suicide among Indians, including many teenagers, are almost twice the national norm. On the reservation, family income averages $1,500, and off it about $3,000. Nationwide, the unemployment figure hovers around 40%.

There are exceptions to this dismal catalogue. The Agua Caliente band, which owns most of the real estate in Palm Springs, Calif., is wealthy indeed. The Jicarilla Apaches in northern New Mexico, blessed with rich oil and gas deposits on their lands, have made investments in movie productions and are developing hunting and tourist facilities.

A more typical situation is that of the Osage Sioux. Less than 100 years ago, they owned all of what is now Osage County, Okla., a choice, oil-soaked region. Over the years, through legal maneuvering and corruption in the Bureau of Indian Affairs, non-Indians managed to get onto the tribal rolls and claim land rights. Today many full-blooded Osages are frozen out of oil profits and tribal affairs.

During its 149 years of existence, the BIA has been the subject of scorn from Indians and whites alike. As the protector of Indian resources and lands, the BIA wields enormous power over almost every aspect of reservation life. It runs Indian schools, from which most students drop out by the sixth grade. It is responsible for many housekeeping chores on the reservations: building and maintaining roads, overseeing construction of irrigation projects and providing welfare assistance. But the BIA does not provide services to the nearly 350,000 Indians who live off reservations. With 13,964 employees—56% of them Indians—the bureau is a lumbering monster, hopelessly inefficient. Yet it is the only constant link for Indians to federal resources and assistance.

In the surging tide of Indian militancy, the most outspoken group is the American Indian Movement, leaders of last November's occupation of the BIA building in Washington, as well as the Wounded Knee takeover. The group's tactics enrage more conservative Indians, whom AIM refers to as "apples"—red on the outside, white on the inside.

Yet AIM's tactics have produced results. "For 148 years, the tribal leaders have been going to the BIA and trying to get things done," says Owen Echohawk, a Pawnee who is a retired Sun Oil Co. executive. "They could never get in contact with the White House. By taking over that building, AIM ended up negotiating with the White House in seven days." As a result of AIM's takeover, Nixon has shuffled the top bureaucrats of the BIA. And its budget for fiscal 1974 has been increased by $50 million, to $583 million.

A nationwide convention of American Indians in 1961 adopted a statement of goals: "We, the Indian people, must be governed by principles in a democratic manner with a right to choose our way of life…What we ask of America is not charity, not paternalism…the Indians ask for assistance, technical and financial, for the time needed, however long that may be, to regain in the America of the space age some measure of the adjustment they enjoyed as the original possessors of their native land."

In 1973, as an AIM slogan phrases it: "The Red Giant is on one knee, but he's getting ready to stand up." ∎

welfare checks. Reported TIME Correspondent Richard Woodbury: "The adults are idle, since virtually all business on the mammoth reservation has come to a halt. Families wanting to take in the action have come to Pine Ridge in the dilapidated cars with crunched fenders that are the Indians' trademark. Justice Department people, a few in coats and ties but many more in flak vests, baseball caps and heavy boots, come and go in the area of the BIA building. It is a reunion for many of the federal marshals, distinctive in their flag-bedecked blue jumpsuits. Across the street, on a dried mudbank, sit a line of solemn-faced Indians taking it all in."

In Wounded Knee itself, tensions rose and fell with events. Early in the week, both sides had seemed close to resolving their differences—until Russell Means' brother Bill was wounded in a firefight. When the car transporting him to the hospital was stopped at a road-block, federal authorities discovered Molotov cocktails in the trunk and arrested the Indians. Incensed, Russell Means crammed his people into a small community hall the next morning to fire them up.

For all the rhetoric and emotion, however, the immediate issues seemed strangely vague and parochial. At the beginning of the crisis, Means had staked out vast demands: the return by the U.S. Government of territories in both Dakotas, Montana and Nebraska; the investigation of long-broken treaties and a full-scale probe by Congress of the Bureau of Indian Affairs. But then Means shifted the main focus to his demand for the ouster of Sioux Tribal Council President Dick Wilson. That issue proved to be more slippery than the larger questions over which the battle was first joined.

Means, himself a Sioux, was asking the Department of the Interior to interfere in an intratribal Sioux affair, and thus turn back the clock on the recent Indian move for self-determination. And it is far from clear whether the rest of the Sioux are as unhappy as Means with Wilson's leadership. The Interior Department maintains that disputes among the Sioux are their own problem. As for Wilson, his tribal council urged that the Justice Department clear AIM militants off the reservation.

The repercussions of Wounded Knee have already spread far beyond the Black Hills of South Dakota. Awakened by ample TV coverage of the original seizure of Wounded Knee and enraged by the Government's seeming overreaction, other groups of Indians have taken up the cry of injustice. In Chicago, 40 Indians dressed in blankets and headdresses demonstrated in the offices of Senator Adlai Stevenson III. In Lumberton, N.C., Indians in a 40-car caravan drove for three consecutive nights through the downtown district, smashing windows with rocks. Even in faraway Maine, Passamaquoddy Indians in Pleasant Point heeded the call to arms and blockaded a state highway by burning tires. Their placards read: REMEMBER WOUNDED KNEE.

They were drawing on the memory of the Sioux massacre that first made the settlement infamous. But Wounded Knee II may soon be remembered too—as a turning point for the better in the fortunes of American Indians, or the beginning of a string of disruptive red power demonstrations in many parts of the country—or both. ■

■ SCHOOLS   **SEPTEMBER 22, 1975**

The Busing Dilemma

Forced integration leads to conflicts of conscience and the law

CARRYING BOOKS and paper-bag lunches, some 200 inner-city black boys and girls walked quickly but quietly from five yellow school buses, past dozens of armed state and county troopers, and into Louisville's suburban Valley High School. Nervously they joked among themselves about the curious stares from dozens of white students pressing against the school's windows. Within minutes the same buses left, carrying a handful of apprehensive white boys and girls to the formerly all-black Shawnee High School on the city's west side. Muttered a woman driver: "I'm ashamed and worried. But this is something that we've got to make the best of."

At roughly the same time in Boston, about 500 police in riot gear and federal marshals surrounded shabby Charlestown High School, in the shadow of the Bunker Hill Monument. Armed with a high-powered rifle, a police sharpshooter carefully watched a sullen crowd of whites as three yellow buses unloaded 66 black boys and girls. They showed their student identification cards to school officials, passed through an electronic metal detector that checked for weapons, and walked into the gray stone building. Later that day, a band of 100 whites youths rampaged down Monument Street, overturning three Volkswagens, and other angry whites beat up a black student at nearby Bunker Hill College. Thus, in scenes that have become a fall ritual since the Supreme Court outlawed segregated schools in 1954, classes opened last week in the two cities that are the primary targets in this year's battle over busing. There were surprisingly few violent incidents, in part because of the massive show of strength by law authorities in both cities, which included standby contingents of National Guardsmen. Even so, this year's efforts to desegregate schools in Boston, Louisville and at least 18 other cities promise to be a searing experience for both blacks and whites chiefly because of a growing national concern about school desegregation and its much-hated stepchild, forced busing. As the ideal of integration moved from merely opening up all-white schools to blacks toward the far more difficult aim of achieving a balance in schools that does not exist in society, too much of the burden of social advance was placed on the yellow school buses.

Busing began as a well-intentioned idea to help eliminate a shameful American condition. But it ran against the deepest instincts of a clear majority of whites and quite a few blacks as well. The issue involves extremely painful conflicts of conscience and of law.

As a unanimous Supreme Court has repeatedly ruled for 21 years, the law and the Constitution require that public schools be desegregated. Because of neighborhood segregation, the only feasible way to integrate many urban schools is by busing students. Antibusing groups have tried and failed to get Congress to approve a constitutional amendment that would ban forced busing. Time and again Congress has prohibited the use of federal funds to pay for busing, but federal courts have ruled that this does not absolve the cities of the obligation to integrate schools by busing. In sum, barring an unlikely reversal of previous opinions by the Supreme Court, forced busing is here to stay for the foreseeable future and will spread to more cities.

Many black leaders regard the opposition to busing of Northern and Border-state cities like Boston and Louisville as racist and no different from the Deep South's efforts to block school desegregation in the 1950s and early 1960s. As the title of a bitter N.A.A.C.P. report put it: *It's Not the Distance, It's the Niggers.* Observes Kenneth Clark, a black psychologist and leading education theorist: "The North is trying to get away with what the South tried. If the North succeeds, and I don't think that it will, it will make a mockery of our courts and laws." But other black leaders are far less certain and wonder whether busing really moves their cause forward.

The cruel dilemma over busing has caused parents, both black and white, to raise a series of legitimate questions to which there are no easy answers: Is forced busing to balance schools racially worth all the uproar? Does it produce better schooling for disadvantaged black youngsters and no loss for the white youngsters?

Once, the answer to both was widely thought to be yes. But researchers have raised gnawing doubts about these propositions—without necessarily disproving them. Moreover, forced busing or the threat of it has accelerated the white flight to the suburbs, leaving the inner cities increasingly nonwhite. In this situation, urban desegregation may mean little more than spreading a dwindling white minority among overwhelmingly black and increasingly mediocre schools, with minimal benefit for either race. In short, does school desegregation improve or worsen race relations? Are there alternatives to busing for achieving desegregation and improving the education of black children?

Questions such as these have profoundly shaken the formerly strong national coalition of support for school integration. Besides, moral backing for busing long ago disappeared from the White House. Echoing his predecessor's doubts, President Ford recently observed: "I don't think that forced busing to achieve racial balance is the proper way to get quality education." Instead he called for "better school facilities, lower teacher-pupil ratios, the improvement of neighborhoods as such." Similarly, local politicians like Louisville Mayor Harvey I. Sloane and Boston Mayor Kevin White have misgivings about busing. Says White: "To pursue blindly a means that may not be correct is to use one wrong to correct another." Even black mayors like Coleman Young of Detroit and Maynard Jackson of Atlanta have reservations about busing, largely because they want to avoid driving out the small minority of whites who remain in their cities' public schools.

Given the supercharged atmosphere in Louisville and Boston, law-enforcement authorities feared that last week's relative calm might be only temporary. In Louisville, officials were sternly determined that the previous weekend's violent antibusing protests by whites would not be repeated. The rioting, burning of buses and looting of stores badly damaged the great political ambitions of the county's chief executive, Judge Todd Hollenbach, who delayed calling on city and state police for help until after the rampaging crowds were out of control. U.S. District Court Judge James Gordon, who had originally ordered an exchange of 22,600 students between the largely black schools in the city and the predominantly white schools of suburban Jefferson County, banned demonstrations near the 165 public schools and gatherings of more than three persons along the school bus routes.

At first, demonstrators defied Gordon's order. For four hours on Sunday night, several thousand unruly whites, blaring their cars' horns and shouting bitter epithets ("In

BRIDGES AND BORDERS

God we trust, in Gordon we don't!" and "Keep the niggers out!"), clogged four-lane Preston Highway. Gradually, however, some 400 disciplined state troopers cleared the highway, sometimes smashing windshields or subduing demonstrators with 3-ft. riot sticks.

Next morning, under the watchful eyes of 2,500 police and National Guardsmen, the 470 school buses began rolling long before dawn, each carrying an armed guard. In obedience to Gordon's order, however, there were only occasional white demonstrators along the routes or at the schools. Indeed, by week's end, a boycott of the schools by whites had become largely ineffective: on Friday, 77.3% of the merged city-county district's enrollment of 120,000 students (20% black) attended schools, up from 50% a week earlier.

Behind locked doors, teachers and students went about the business of education, uneasy yet remarkably undisturbed by the tensions in the community. Said Bart Coonce, 15, a white senior at Fairdale High School: "We're all against busing, but now we should try to make it work." Argued Joe Barnett, 17, a white senior at Shawnee High School: "The problem is parents." Added Dawn Babbage, 16, a white sophomore at Shawnee: "Mom was afraid at first and I was too, but I think that it is going to be okay." Said Reggie Foster, 16, a black sophomore at Valley High "If people don't bother me, I know that I can get a better education here."

This mood elated city and county officials. But they realized that opposition to busing had been broken only by the weekend show of force; such security will be difficult to maintain for more than another week or two. Tensions in the blue-collar neighborhoods seemed likely to remain high for some time to come, and were fanned by antibusing leaders like Bill Kellerman, automobile assembly plant foreman and president of Citizens Against Busing, which claims to have 400 followers. He vowed: "Kentucky will sit still no longer. We will make Boston look like nothing."

Meanwhile, on the day before schools opened in Boston, some 8,000 whites rallied outside city hall to protest the federal court's desegregation order, waving placards (sample slogan: "If Boston is lucky, it'll be twice as bad as Kentucky") and cheering defiant speeches. Last year 18,200 of the city's 94,000 pupils were assigned to be bused to desegregate 80 public schools; last week 26,000 students were supposed to be bused to 162 schools. City Councilwoman Louise Day Hicks, an inflammatory foe, urged the crowd to continue last year's boycott of the schools and vowed, "Whatever is going to happen in Boston is going to set the tone for the forced-busing issue elsewhere."

Despite the rhetoric, and in contrast to last year's disruptions, almost all the school openings were uneventful. But there were two trouble spots: the high schools in the blue-collar neighborhoods of Charlestown and South Boston. At both, police and federal marshals cordoned off the bused black students from the crowds of angry white protesters. The main confrontation took place in Charlestown, where about 200 white mothers, chanting Hail Marys, tried to push their way through the police lines.

Sporadic violence erupted every night, chiefly scattered skirmishes involving white youths who hurled rocks and beer bottles at police. Some whites were also irate that Senator Edward Kennedy has urged compliance with the court's busing order. The house in Brookline where John F. Kennedy was born was damaged by a Molotov cocktail. Painted on the front sidewalk was a piece of angry advice: BUS TEDDY.

By week's end attendance had risen to 68.4%, up from the 48% average during the yearlong white boycott in 1974-75, and was giving school officials some reason to hope that the boycott was crumbling. Said Lou Perullo, a school department statistician: "As parents see that it's safe, they are sending their kids." Observed Phyllis Curtis, an antibusing mother of four non-boycotting children in South Boston: "Some parents would keep their children out of school for five years to stop the busing. But the kids would have to pay the price. When they look for jobs, they won't find them because they'll have no education. That's not healthy, not for them and not for the community."

Boston and Louisville demonstrated anew that Northern cities are no happier with school desegregation than their counterparts in the South. Since the historic Supreme Court decision of 1954 that separate schools can never be equal, hundreds of communities have been forced by the courts to desegregate. Most are in the South, which had dual black and white school systems for nearly a century. More recently, the N.A.A.C.P. and other civil rights organizations have successfully challenged the legality of segregated schools in the North. They argue that such official actions as building schools in all-black or all-white neighborhoods and racial gerrymandering of district boundaries also constitute illegal segregation. To remedy such situations, the federal courts have frequently ordered cities to bus children to neighborhoods far from their homes.

To achieve integration through evolution (better incomes for blacks, better housing, in time leading to peaceful mixed neighborhoods) would obviously be excruciatingly slow. Thus busing will remain inevitable and perhaps necessary in some situations. But it is clearly not a good solution. To replace it eventually, it is necessary to: 1) make far greater use of other methods of school integration, admittedly slower and less dramatic, but perhaps more efficient in the long run; 2) upgrade the education of black youngsters in the inner city to speed the otherwise slow process of bringing them into the middle class; 3) fight for racial harmony beyond the schools and thus ease the tensions that have made school desegregation a volatile issue.

One limited approach would be to build new schools on the borders between black and white neighborhoods to make integration possible without busing. Another method would be to create more "magnet schools," which are designed to improve the education of blacks and also attract some whites. For example, Trotter High School, which was built in Boston's Roxbury ghetto in 1969, was heavily funded, staffed with some of Boston's best teachers, and given an exciting, innovative curriculum including fine arts courses. The result: before the city schools were disrupted by busing, Trotter was two-thirds black and yet had a long waiting list of whites. Just this year, previously all-black Hamilton Park Elementary School in the Dallas suburb of Richardson was turned into a model magnet school that is totally integrated. It offers an outstanding curriculum including courses in gymnastics, drama and music, and a 16-to-1 pupil-teacher ratio; 80% of the faculty hold masters' degrees. Last week 289 white students voluntarily began attending the school, balancing 265 blacks.

Such schools usually are far too expensive to be anything more than glamorous exceptions. But there are less costly approaches. In an effort to ease the antibusing sentiment among whites, Boston this year has paired nearly two-thirds of its schools with 22 colleges and universities; using $900,000 in state funds, the schools are planning new curriculums, teacher workshops and model language programs to improve the quality of instruction. The program's success cannot be measured for at least several months, but the schools averaged 6% higher enrollments than others in Boston last week.

Instead of forced busing, Columnist William Raspberry recommends that students be allowed to transfer voluntarily to any school where they would improve the racial balance. Such a policy, he notes, would "not generate the fear-spawned opposition that busing has generated." That, indeed, has been the experience in Portland. Ore., which already uses a voluntary transfer system. To date, 2,700 pupils, mostly black, have shifted to schools in white neighborhoods that have vacancies. Since whites are not forced to send their children to predominantly black schools, there has been no white flight from the city because of the transfer program.

The nation needs a greater commitment to improving the education of blacks, both those who remain in inner-city schools and those who are bused to predominantly white schools. Says a Baltimore school administrator: "These children aren't born retarded. We just haven't figured out how to teach them: so they end up functionally retarded." Tim Black, a Chicago community college teacher, has found college-level black students "who are very interested and highly motivated but cannot read above the first- or second-grade level."

Part of the solution, educators generally agree, is to concentrate on the earliest grades. Despite some contradictory evidence, many studies show that Head Start, a federal early-learning program, has improved black educational skills, particularly when the children go on to fairly sound schools. On the other hand, the gains are quickly lost if the pupils enter inferior schools. Most educators, therefore, call for spending more to upgrade the teachers at black schools and expanding Head Start.

Motivation remains a basic problem for black students. Says Phyllis Denny, a black counselor at Denver's Hamilton Junior High School: "White students feel a great deal of academic pressure. They are trying to fulfill goals set by their parents, while black kids are concerned about meeting goals set by themselves." That statement obviously does not apply to middle-class black students, who are as highly motivated as their white counterparts. But poor black students often have low self-esteem and lack pressure from their parents to do well in school. In integrated schools, there can also be a debilitating double standard for dealing with students. Complains Omar Blair, a black member of the Denver board of education: "Teachers don't discipline black students because they say that they are afraid of the consequences. Black students roam the halls and are ignored. Teachers allow black kids to talk back to them and won't do anything about it. In contrast, white kids would be sent to the principal."

Even worse, white teachers frequently push black students through the system without caring much whether they have learned anything. Says St. Louis University Instructor Ernest Calloway: "The expectation of the teacher is very low. One of the problems is raising the expectation so the child will be told, 'You can learn. You will learn.'" Good teaching indeed can motivate black students. For example, in Oakland, some 1,400 black underachievers have received remedial instruction since 1968 in math, English and science; 1,120 have gone on to college.

One approach to motivating black students would be to give new emphasis to programs that lead to technical careers, either directly from high school or after college. Kenneth Tollett notes that "Power in this society is increasingly in the hands of the technocrats. Blacks will be frozen in a sub-class if they do not increase their numbers among the technocrats."

The alternative to what Tollett and others are worrying about is the familiar vicious cycle, which may begin with segregation in housing but leads inevitably to segregation in schools and ultimately to segregation on the job and a permanent black underclass. Most experts still agree that better schooling for blacks offers the soundest hope of breaking that pattern. There are no quick or painless ways to achieve equal educational opportunity, but that is no reason to abandon it as a goal.

Court-ordered busing obviously will remain part of the effort to achieve that goal for quite a while. But given the feeling of most Americans, and its own built-in shortcomings, busing is plainly neither a long-range solution nor the best instrument to bring one about. ∎

The New South: Out of a Cocoon

Segregation Remembered

"LIKE MOST BLACK AMERICANS, my roots are in the South." So writes TIME Atlanta Correspondent Jack White, 30. Here is White's personal account of being brought up under segregation:

My father's father was born a slave somewhere near Savannah, Ga. My mother's father was the son of a white undertaker and his mulatto concubine in a small town in North Carolina.

Like many other blacks, my parents migrated North to find education and better opportunities. My father went to Howard University medical school, and my mother went to Howard's nursing school. My parents wanted to shelter their children from segregation and all its belittling aspects, so they settled in Washington, which turned out to be as segregated a city as one could find.

In the 1950s, a clerk in a department store refused to let me sip from a water fountain, despite my mother's plea that "he's just a little boy." Later, when my family got its first television set, I was entranced by the ads for Glen Echo amusement park. My mother couldn't really explain why she couldn't take me there. The reason, of course, was that Glen Echo did not admit blacks. Nor did many restaurants, movie theaters and other public facilities.

My deepest realization of what the Old South was really like came in about 1962, when my father, brother, a friend and I drove South to my grandmother's house in Stuart, Fla. On the way we were denied a room in a Holiday Inn in Savannah, and wound up sleeping in a "rooming house" (read whorehouse) that hadn't had an overnight guest in years. In Stuart, my father went into a hardware store to buy a Thermos bottle. The white clerk asked my dad, a distinguished professor of surgery at least 20 years his senior, "What you want, boy?" My father struggled to maintain his dignity as he told the clerk what he wanted. I felt in my gut, for the first time, how hard it had been for black men to preserve their self-respect under a rigid system of white supremacy.

Because of the civil rights movement, I will never have to explain to my four-year-old son that he can't go to an amusement park or swim in a public swimming pool just because he is black. He will never see me diminish in his eyes because some white man can lord it over me and make me seem like a child.

White Southerners are now taking a great deal of pride in the region's rapid adjustment to the post-civil rights era. The fact is that every change was resisted, every improvement fought, every overture turned back. Though many Southerners were made uneasy by the oppressive pattern of Southern race relations, most did little or nothing to change it. Not even Jimmy Carter resigned from his church when it voted to exclude blacks. Without unrelenting pressure from blacks and the Federal Government, white Southerners would never have changed. Southern behavior has changed, but the hearts, for the most part, are probably just the same.

White Southerners tend to have a passion for lost causes. The Washington Redskins, for example, were the South's "adopted" pro football team. They remained lily-white, and they retained their Southern constituency, even though they were consistent losers. My dad and I used to go to Redskins games just to cheer when Jim Brown, Bobby Mitchell and other black stars "integrated" the Redskins' goal line. It was great. The Redskins' ownership would rather be white than winners.

Then the team's owner, George Preston Marshall, died, and Lawyer Edward Bennett Williams took over. Williams realized that he was in a new day, and the Redskins began to get black players. Within a few years, they became winners. Now everybody loves them.

Much the same thing has happened to the South. It has become a region of winners. Blacks are playing on the team. Points are going on the scoreboard. But is the change permanent?

My own guess is that the good impulses will win out. The Southern white man, even at his most bigoted, always had some noble impulses: loyalty, independence, courage. Martin Luther King spoke of the "redemptive power" of nonviolent love, and his followers nodded amen. They believed white Southerners could be redeemed. And if they thought that, after 350 years of oppression, who am I to quarrel?

Southern newspapers routinely relegated announcements of black births, deaths and marriages to special Jim Crow pages. In 1956, the Wilmington, N.C., Star went to press with a frontpage photo of four Marines who were to testify in the court-martial of a drill instructor charged with brutality. When an editor noticed that one of the witnesses was black, he ordered an employee to chisel the Negro's image out of the press plate. The paper appeared with a ragged white space where the black face had been.

In some rural areas, remnants of the barricades remain. Voter registration is occasionally made difficult for blacks, and without it, they cannot serve as jurors. There are neighborhoods and apartment buildings that still exclude blacks. Courtrooms where blacks are not accorded the courtesy of Mr. or Mrs. still exist. Interracial couples face severe—often unbearable—harassment in small Southern towns. But because the other vestiges of a segregated Southern society have largely disappeared, there is reason to hope that those remaining will disappear as well. ∎

Things You Didn't Do, Boy

ONE BY ONE—beginning with the *Brown* v. *Board of Education* decision in 1954, which outlawed school segregation, reaching on through the Civil Rights Acts of 1957, 1964, 1965 and 1968—the barriers against blacks in the South have come tumbling down. But it is shocking to recall how high they were in 1954, and in many cases much later than that. By statute, ordinance or custom that had the force of law, blacks in most parts of the eleven states of the Confederacy, plus some Border states and Washington, D.C., did not:

Serve on juries.

Send children to white public schools.

Drink from a "whites only" water fountain.

Use a "whites only" rest room.

Rent a room in a white hotel, motel or apartment building.

Try on clothing in a store.

Sit down in a white restaurant.

Sit on the main floor of a movie theater, concert hall or other public arena.

Sit in the front of the bus.

Visit a white public park, beach or swimming pool.

Marry a white or even whistle at one. (Emmett Till, 14, from Chicago, was beaten and shot to death in Mississippi in 1955 for such a "crime," and other blacks were routinely beaten for "reckless eyeballing," i.e., looking at a white female.)

To most Southern whites, blacks were not entitled to normal courtesies. In courtrooms, black witnesses were usually called by their first names or "uncle" or "gal." In some Southern towns, blacks were obliged to step off the sidewalk into the street to make room for passing whites. In some areas they were warned to be out of town by sunset. The few black policemen could not arrest whites. ∎

A City Reborn

BIRMINGHAM! THE ALL-AMERICAN CITY!... Blacks sitting in at stores and restaurants. "Nigger lover" scrawled on shattered plate-glass windows of merchants suspected of sympathizing with them...

BIRMINGHAM! THE MAGIC CITY! ... Firemen battering black women with high-pressure hoses, snarling police dogs...

BIRMINGHAM! THE FOOTBALL CAPITAL OF THE SOUTH!... The mangled bodies of little girls in a bombed-out church. Martin Luther King Jr. and Theophilus Eugene

("Bull") Connor—the irresistible black force meeting the immovable white object—confronting each other amid the flames ...

BIRMINGHAM?

A postbellum parvenu, forged on steelmaking and railroads rather than magnolias and gentility, Birmingham dug in against the black demonstrators led by Martin Luther King Jr. Bull Connor, who really ran the city as public safety commissioner, personified entrenched white supremacy. In Birmingham's embattled spring of 1963, Connor coldly ordered his police and firemen to cut off black marches on downtown with fire hoses, police dogs and clubs. A series of bombings culminated one September morning in a blast that ripped open a black church, killing four small girls in Sunday-school class learning "the love that forgives."

Bull Connor has since died—and so has Birmingham's bitterness. It is significant in the contemporary South that Alabama's largest city (pop. 295,686) has become a model of Southern race relations. Legally, everything is integrated; blacks, who make up 40% of the population, work and shop and dine freely downtown. The only trace of the old "colored" fountains is scars on the walls where they were removed. No serious racial incident has occurred since the First Baptist Church voted six years ago not to admit two blacks as members. Even then, the pastor and many members marched away in protest and formed their own unsegregated church. Mixed housing and social mingling are advancing more slowly, but, says School Superintendent Wilmer S. Cody: "The voice of segregation is almost nonexistent in Birmingham. Not even in private conversation is it any longer acceptable to say such things."

The revolution was brought about largely because white voters became disgusted with Connor's brutish tactics and heavy political hand. In the midst of the 1963 racial outbreaks, they succeeded in scrapping the archaic and arrogant commission form of government that provided his raw power. The mayor and city council who replaced the three commissioners (including Connor) have been more responsive and progressive. Mayor David J. Vann, 48, is a hearty lawyer and Methodist Sunday-school teacher who won the job last November in a campaign without any racial issues. The nine-member city council includes three blacks.

Since the Voting Rights Act of 1965, the black vote has increased from 15% to 40% of the total. Lawyer Arthur D. Shores, whose home was twice bombed, became the first black councilman in 1968; he and two other blacks were elected or re-elected with the help of many white votes. Blacks sit on most Birmingham city boards and the metro boards that the city has set up with surrounding Jefferson County. City departments are also integrated. The police force, once the epicenter of black hatred, has 34 black officers and two black sergeants in a force of 616. The total might be higher but blacks can find higher-paying jobs in private industry.

Under a federal court order, Birmingham's school system (94 schools, 47,000 pupils) is integrating smoothly, without busing. In 1970 a rezoning brought black and white kids together in some school districts. This year, neighboring black and white schools have been paired, and alternate or "magnet" schools with special curriculums have been set up for both races on a 50%-50% enrollment basis. The main problem now is a white movement out of the city to surrounding bedroom towns—"because of affluence, not confrontation," insists Superintendent Cody—which has unbalanced school population from 50%-50% to 70%-30% black in six years.

Birmingham employers, hiring more black workers, are also finding it easier now to attract whites from other areas. Meanwhile, the outmigration of young blacks and whites has been reversed. Birmingham also shifted from blue collar to white collar, as its longtime economic base changed from heavy industry to nonmanufacturing enterprises like finance and merchandising. Steel companies closed old furnaces, built new ones that need fewer hands. The University of Alabama is now the city's principal employer, with 7,000 faculty and staff; 15,000 students are enrolled on an expanding campus that so far covers 60 blocks close to downtown. White collars demand more culture than blue: a $60 million civic center nearing completion includes a 2,900-seat symphony hall and 1,000-seat theater, as well as a coliseum and exhibition hall.

Probably the greatest catalyst in Birmingham's reformation has been a biracial Community Affairs Committee of more than 80 leaders from every segment of the community that was first organized to discuss racial problems. The group was formed in 1969 at the urging of Birmingham News Editor Vincent Townsend, now retired but still active in civic affairs at 75. Townsend, who had the ear of Birmingham's business leaders, persuaded them to meet with the city's black leaders for what he called "self-preservation." The C.A.C. still meets every Monday for breakfast, always off the record so that anyone can speak freely about any civil ill. Says one member, W. Cecil Bauer, president of South Central Bell: "The pangs and problems of deprivation—for black and white alike—are no longer merely statistics."

Birmingham, of course, has not been totally transformed. "We don't make any claim that we've licked racism," says Mayor Vann, "but we've learned to face the problem candidly and not play games." City Councilman Richard Arrington complains that much of what has been done so far in Birmingham is "still very much tokenism." Arrington protests, for instance, that blacks "still have difficulty cracking the suburbs." Mayor Vann worries about white flight from the city; black leaders complain that Birmingham may not be able to provide jobs to match new expectations, and that housing integration is limited to the poor. Adds N.A.A.C.P. Official W.C. Patton: "This is no utopia, but we're moving in the right direction." Patton likes the new Birmingham well enough to remain—for eternity. He recently bought eight plots in Elmwood Cemetery. Like everything else of value in Birmingham's bad old days, the graves there were once restricted to whites only. ∎

"It's Your Turn in the Sun"

Hispanic Americans have the melting pot bubbling again

IN WASHINGTON, D.C., leaders of 120 Spanish-speaking organizations call for a White House conference on Hispanic Americans. Among the demands they want aired: greater emphasis on bilingual education; bigger immigration quotas; more federal civil service jobs.

In Sacramento, California's Governor Jerry Brown drops in on a Mexican-American convention. "You're the leading minority in the Southwest," Brown tells the crowd. "It's your turn in the sun and I want to be part of it."

In Miami, Carlos Arboleya, president of the area's Barnett Banks (assets: $315 million), surveys the local Cuban-American community and confidently declares: "History will write Miami's future in Spanish and English."

That extraordinary vessel, the American melting pot, is bubbling once again. The source of ferment: American residents of Spanish origin, whose official numbers have increased by 14.3% in the past five years alone. Now the country's fastest growing minority, they are bidding to become an increasingly influential one.

Hispanic Americans are learning how to organize and how to win a hearing. Jimmy Carter has taken note of these stirrings; he proclaimed one week last month to be National Hispanic Heritage Week and sent tape-recorded greetings in his unpolished Spanish to Hispanic communities across the land. First Lady Rosalynn Carter underlined those *saludos* by appearing at a Washington fund raiser for Congress's five-member Hispanic Caucus.

The Hispanic presence has been a palpable one in U.S. life for centuries. But broad awareness of its scope and potential did not really dawn until the 1960s, with the unionizing struggles of Cesar Chavez's United Farm Workers and the spread of Hispanic populations. Today, migratory bands of Hispanics are picking apples in Washington and Oregon, helping with the harvest in the Midwest, tending vegetable and fruit crops in California's fertile valleys. Hispanics are also flooding virtually every important U.S. city in search of better jobs, creating latino enclaves from the crowded *barrios* of East Los Angeles and Spanish Harlem to the manicured suburbs of Dade County, Fla.

The Hispanics' very numbers guarantee that they will play an increasingly important role in shaping the nation's politics and policies. Just as black power was a reality of the 1960s, so the quest for latino power may well become a political watchword of the decade ahead. Predicts Raul Yzaguirre, director of the National Council of La Raza (The Race), an umbrella group of Hispanic-American organizations: "The 1980s will be the decade of the Hispanics."

Statistics back up Yzaguirre's contention. According to 1978 census estimates, there are 12 million Hispanic Americans in the U.S. Hispanic leaders, however, claim that their constituency was seriously undercounted in the 1970 census and all subsequent projections. The spokesmen may have a point. Until 1960, census takers counted as Hispanic only people born in Spain, Mexico, Central and South America, the West Indies, Puerto Rico and Cuba, plus any U.S. residents with Spanish surnames. In the 1970 census, the definition was broadened to include the racial origin of respondents no matter the accident of birthplace, resulting in a dramatic increase in the numbers of Hispanics. Census officials have promised to take special pains to get a more accurate count during the 1980 census, in effect acknowledging that their methods have been inadequate.

Even the most reliable census figures, however, fail to take into account the enormous numbers of Hispanics who are living and working in the U.S. illegally. At a conservative estimate, some 7.4 million "undocumented" Hispanic aliens raise the actual total to more than 19 million, and the Hispanic proportion of U.S. population to around 9%, vs. 12% for blacks. Because the rate of natural increase (births over deaths) among Hispanics is 1.8%, .6% higher than that for blacks, and because Hispanic immigration (legal and illegal) is running at the staggering rate of an estimated 1 million people a year, Hispanics may outnumber American blacks within the next decade. Already the two groups are competing fiercely for jobs and Government aid.

As blacks are united by race, Hispanic Americans are united by two powerful forces: their language and their strong adherence to Roman Catholicism. But many more factors divide them. They may be Castilian Spanish, or Caribbean island black, or Spanish-Indian mestizo. Among them are Cubans who fled to the U.S. with money and middle-class skills; impoverished Puerto Ricans or Mexican

Americans looking for a job—any job; aristocratic Spaniards, whose families settled in the Southwest before the *Mayflower* hove into Plymouth Harbor.

Of the officially recognized Hispanics, the largest single group is the chicanos, comprising some 7.2 million people of Mexican origin concentrated largely in the U.S. Southwest. An estimated 1.8 million Puerto Ricans live chiefly in the northern-central states, particularly the Northeast. Some 700,000 Cubans, mostly refugees from Fidel Castro's regime, are now in the U.S., mainly concentrated in Florida. But there are also Dominicans, Ecuadorians, Colombians and natives of other Latin American countries or of Spain itself scattered all over the U.S., totaling an additional 2.4 million Hispanics.

The groups may mix, but so far they have failed to blend. Upwardly mobile Floridian Cubans have felt little in common with lowly Mexican-American migrant citrus pickers. Even in impoverished New York ghettos, newly arrived Dominicans look down on native American Puerto Ricans who, some of the latecomers feel, have not exerted themselves to move up the economic ladder.

In their diversity, the Hispanics have brought some distinctive flavors to the American banquet: the thumping Tex-Mex music of the Southwest borderlands; the *salsa* dancers of urban discos; the splashy colors of wall murals in Latin communities across the U.S. Equally distinctive are a number of attitudes that many, if not most, latinos share.

Generally they have a strong regard for the family and maintain close kinship ties across the generations at a time when the weakening of traditional U.S. family bonds is a focus of concern. Many come from strongly patriarchal societies and find themselves in conflict with expanding social opportunities for American women. Most intangibly, latinos offer the U.S. an amalgam of buoyancy, sensuousness and flair that many northern peoples find tantalizing or mysterious—and sometimes irritating or threatening.

As has happened with almost every ethnic group in America, the Hispanics are learning that growing numbers and assertiveness often produce growing hostility. As far back as 1943, hundreds were injured in a Los Angeles race riot, an event dramatized in the current West Coast hit play, *Zoot Suit*, by Luis Valdez. But now the antipathy is becoming more intense and pervasive as the Hispanics become not only more visible but also more insistent on their rights.

As America's latest great wave of immigrants, Hispanics are learning another hard lesson: latecomers start at the bottom. Nearly 27% of Hispanic families in the U.S. earn under $7,000 a year; only 16.6% of non-Hispanic families fare as badly. For the second quarter of 1978 the Hispanic unemployment rate was 8.9%, while the national average was 5.8%. As a group, Hispanics are the most under-educated of Americans—despite their own deep belief in the maxim, *Saber es poder* (Knowledge is power). Only 40% have completed high school, vs. 46% of U.S. blacks and 67% of the whites. In urban ghetto areas, the school dropout rate

among Hispanics frequently reaches 85%. Language is an obvious handicap, but the vocal Hispanic demand for bilingual education raises particular problems.

In a society more aware of minority rights than ever, that demand is hard to brush aside. Many Hispanic spokesmen speak of "linguistic liberation" and argue that failure to provide bilingual education amounts to "cultural colonization" by the majority anglos. Others say that failure to provide bilingual instruction guarantees that most Hispanic children will fall hopelessly behind in classwork.

Critics attack bilingual programs on several grounds: that they are inadequate or inefficient; that extra efforts should not be made for Spanish-speaking children unless they are also made for French-speaking or Hebrew-speaking or Vietnamese-speaking children; and, perhaps most cogently, that Hispanic students who speak mostly Spanish at school and whose parents speak mostly Spanish at home will never really learn to compete in American society as a whole. Cultural pride notwithstanding, this could prove a fatal handicap in a specialized, highly technological nation where language skills are more important than at any other time in history. What is more, the perpetuation of a large subculture with little or no skill in English could lead to something the U.S. has so far managed to avoid: the rise of a nation-within-a-nation, the growth of the sort of linguistic or "communal" factionalism that has long haunted countries such as India, Sri Lanka, Belgium and most recently Canada.

The slow growth of Hispanic affluence and educational attainment is mirrored in politics and in Government bureaucracies. There are five Hispanics in the House of Representatives, compared with 16 blacks and 22 Jews. Hispanics hold only 3.4% of jobs in the federal bureaucracy, while blacks hold 16%, and the Hispanic proportion of federal jobholders has inched up only .7% in the past ten years. The same pattern holds true at state and local levels.

There are a number of reasons for the underrepresentation: the Hispanics' relatively late arrival as a major immigrant group; their reservations about politics, often the result of once having lived under corrupt, autocratic regimes; their traditional preoccupation with family and community affairs rather than broad political issues; outright racial and social discrimination. But the most immediate—and most easily remedied—reason is their failure to register in sufficient numbers. Of 7 million Hispanics eligible to vote, only 37.8% are registered, vs. 66.7% of the population as a whole.

Political activism is gradually—very gradually—beginning to bring Hispanics together. In Los Angeles, Latin neighborhood associations have forced city authorities to provide better services, and pressured the state government to investigate auto insurers on charges of setting unreasonable rates. In Texas, Hispanics have organized civil rights marches reminiscent of the '60s, often to protest police brutality.

More and more Hispanic Americans are settling in places like Chicago, Boston and even Greenwich, Conn. (some 10,000 in a town of 63,000). The problems, and promise, of the Hispanic-American experience in the U.S. may be best illustrated, however, by what is happening in three other cities: metropolitan Miami, whose Cuban population (430,000) is exceeded only by Havana's; metropolitan Los Angeles, whose 1.6 million Hispanic population, which is overwhelmingly chicano, makes it the world's second largest Mexican agglomeration after Mexico City; and New York, which surpasses San Juan in Puerto Rican population (1.3 million). There is a fourth community that also demands study: that furtive, elusive subculture-within-a-subculture, the illegal aliens.

MIAMI. The sharp smells of fresh pasteles (pastry) and cafe cubano waft from a hundred neighborhood coffee stands. Youngsters are everywhere, downing batidos (exotic fruit milkshakes) at open-air counters or putting away Grandes Macs at the McDonald's eatery on Flagler Street. This is Little Havana, a 5-sq.-mi. Cuban enclave in the middle of Miami.

Hispanics account for more than half of the city's population (207,000 out of 370,000), and the overwhelming majority of them are Cuban. They have given Miami, as Rum Maker Gerardo Abascal observes, "a spontaneity and boisterous flavor that it never had before."

Some 700,000 largely middle-class Cuban refugees have fled their Communist-dominated island home for the U.S. since Fidel Castro took power. Of these, 430,000 have settled in southern Florida's Dade County, where they were initially welcomed with sympathy and federal relocation grants. The Cubans have long since spread out from Little Havana. Neighboring Hialeah (pop. 133,000) is 65% Latin, and the Cubans have moved on to such well-tended suburbs as Coral Gables, Kendall and Westchester. They have prospered mightily, prompting Cuban Writer Jose Sanchez-Boudy to boast with only slight hyperbole: "We have been the most successful immigrants this country has received since it was founded."

Cuban enterprise has transformed Miami and Dade County into a dynamic commercial center. The area now boasts 230 latino restaurants, 30 furniture factories, 20 garment plants, a shoe factory that employs 3,000, and about 30 transplanted cigar factories. Hispanics are prominent in land development and make up 60% of the construction work force. They control 14 of the 67 local commercial banks. One, the Continental National; has seen its deposits swell from $2 million to $29 million in the past four years. Latinos generate an estimated $1.8 billion in annual income and have created 100,000 jobs. Every day scores of planes, from 747s to vintage C-46s, haul television sets, machinery and other U.S.-manufactured goods to the Caribbean and Latin America, returning with clothing, fresh flowers and food.

For the Cuban middle class, hatching deals over lunch at Little Havana's American Club or lounging on weekends at the Big Five Club, life in the U.S. is a dream that grew out of a nightmare. Says Frank Soler, 35, who fled to the U.S. at age 17 and is now editor of El Miami Herald, a Spanish-language edition of the Miami Herald with a daily circulation of 50,000: "Suddenly we lost everything and were confronted with potential poverty and hunger. Fear spurred us to work our tails off to regain what we once had." Result: 40% of the county's Hispanics earned more than $12,000 last year. Nearly two-thirds own their own homes.

Brief though their stay has been, the Cubans have already had considerable impact on the region's culture. They have a plethora of Spanish-language newspapers and a string of glossy magazines to choose among (including a Hispanic version of Cosmopolitan). The Cubans enjoy a Spanish-language television station and a multitude of nightclubs that have brought back Havana's brassy night life.

The youngsters of the Hispanic community make up one-third of Dade County's pupil population, and they score well above other Dade students on English and math achievement tests. They have ready access to bilingual education, and in 1976, 72% went on to college.

In 1973 Dade County declared itself to be a bilingual jurisdiction, and Spanish became the second official language for such things as election ballots, public signs and local directories. Despite this accommodating gesture, there is friction between Hispanics and non-Hispanics in Dade. Many English-speaking residents, particularly older ones, resent the pervasiveness of the new language. There are frequent complaints of Cuban clannishness (only 5% of Cubans intermarry) and of arrogance. Result: many anglos are gradually retreating from Miami.

Cubans are now taking out U.S. citizenship at the rate of 1,000 a month. They are also registering to vote at the rate of 800 a month; at present about 100,000 of the 351,000 eligible latino voters are actually registered. As a result of this increasing political involvement, two latino city commissioners were elected in Hialeah last year, and a hefty slate of Hispanic candidates is being prepared for state elections. Says Florida state Democratic Chairman Alfredo Duran: "We've been viewed as outsiders with no interest in government. This is going to change."

LOS ANGELES. On weekends, downtown Los Angeles' Broadway is a teeming mass of Hispanic shoppers. Record-store loudspeakers blare Mexican hits: *Juro que Nunca Volvere* (I Swear I'll Never Return), *Mi Fracaso* (My Downfall). The Orpheum Theater, where Al Jolson once sang in blackface, screens Spanish-language dubbings of anglo hits. An archipelago of taco and burrito carts dots the street. Stores and merchandise stands tout their wares: vestidos, tocadiscos, muebles (clothing, phonographs, furniture). Farther east, on Whittier Boulevard, young Hispanics express themselves with a unique form of Saturday night fever known as "low riding"—cruising in ornately decorated autos equipped with hydraulic pumps that lower the chassis to within inches of the roadway so as to produce showers of sparks as the car bounces along the street.

The Spanish-speaking presence in sections of downtown Los Angeles is so pervasive that other Angelenos sometimes refer to the area, with an edge in their voices, as "Baja Hollywood." Yet a strong Hispanic flavor is hardly surprising in a city that was founded in 1781 as El Pueblo de Nuestra Senora la Reina de Los Angeles de Porciuncula. At a conservative estimate, some 1.6 million of the metropolitan area's 7 million residents are Hispanics, overwhelmingly of Mexican descent. That makes Los Angeles a magnet for the estimated 7 million legally resident Hispanics scattered across the southwestern U.S.

In 1970 Hispanics replaced blacks as the largest minority in Los Angeles. They are now overhauling whites, whose share of the city population has declined from 80.9% in 1950 to a projected 44.4% in 1980. Rapid demographic swings have brought racial edginess back to Los Angeles, where the Watts ghetto riots of 1965 are still remembered with fear. Says retired Los Angeles Police Captain Rudy de Leon: "There is more outward prejudice now against Mexican people than there has ever been." Los Angeles *Times* Publisher Otis Chandler did not help when he noted in an interview that his paper did not court the city's black and Hispanic readership because "it's not their kind of newspaper. It's too big. It's too stuffy, if you will. It's too complicated."

In the militant chicano rhetoric of the '60s, middle-class Hispanics were often criticized as "Tio Tacos" or "Tio Tomases"—the equivalent of the blacks' "Uncle Toms." Today businessmen like Gilbert Vasquez, 39, head of the largest Hispanic certified public accounting firm in the U.S. (five offices, 65 employees), feel that individual successes will be "stepping-stones" to lasting change. Vasquez, who has moved out of the *barrio* to suburban Alhambra, remains involved in ghetto issues and tries to get other Hispanic professionals to take part in politics. At one chicano fundraising cocktail party, guests anted up $20,000 for Jerry Brown's re-election campaign.

NEW YORK. Most of the 1.3 million Puerto Ricans in the greater New York City area live in the grim, crumbling tenements of Manhattan's East Harlem and Lower East Side, or in Brooklyn's Williamsburg ghetto, or in the burned-out wasteland of the South Bronx. For them, life is mostly a grinding struggle for survival.

But then there are the festivals, especially Puerto Rican Day in June, when some 250,000 members of the community parade up Fifth Avenue and turn Central Park into a joyous 840-acre cookout. It is then that Puerto Rican exuberance blossoms. Hotels and nightclubs rock to the three-two rhythms of *salsa*. Hot dog vendors watch forlornly as their all-American offerings are spurned in favor of *bacalaitos* (codfish fritters), *alcapurrias* (plantain-meat

rolls) and *tostones* (fried plantains). The community comes ablaze—forgetting for a while the gritty realities of its plight.

Puerto Ricans are the largest—and most beleaguered—national group among the estimated 2.6 million Hispanics in and near New York City. They are, of course, not ordinary immigrants but U.S. citizens, as are all 3.3 million inhabitants of the Puerto Rican commonwealth. Despite that advantage, the Puerto Rican experience today is all too often one of blighted hopes. Says Carlos Garcia, 20, a school dropout and part-time carpenter on Manhattan's Lower East Side: "I expected a West Side Story, and never got it."

Puerto Ricans are even more hard pressed than New York's ghetto blacks; 48% earn less than $7,000 a year, compared with 42% among blacks. The proportion of Puerto Ricans on welfare is 34%, vs. 32% for blacks. Among Puerto Ricans over 16 years old, only 6% have completed any job training; the rate for blacks is twice as high. With 14% of New York City's population, Puerto Ricans hold only 3.1% of police department jobs and 1.3% of those in the fire department.

With Puerto Rican youngsters now making up 25% of the public school population, one of the community's highest priorities is education. But according to New York's deputy mayor for education, Herman Badillo, the city's efforts on behalf of Hispanic pupils are a "disaster in all areas." Says Badillo, a Puerto Rican: "We have plenty of jobs in the skyscrapers of mid-town Manhattan; the problem is that kids can't spell."

After heavy prompting in the form of a judicial agreement signed in 1974, New York grudgingly began providing bilingual education for Spanish-speaking youngsters. By the New York City board of education's most recent estimate, there were only 2,333 Hispanics among the city's 48,813 teachers.

Meantime, Badillo estimates the Puerto Rican school-dropout rate at 85%. Discouraged youngsters are almost natural prospects for membership in the city's underclass, quickly contributing to the ghetto plagues of violent crime, drug use and arson. Says one Lower East Side youngster: "A lot of kids want an education to get out of here. But in order to survive, they're dealing [drugs]. Kids ten and eleven make more money than their old man in the factory." Says another: "I saw some pictures of this place 20 years ago, and it had benches and trees. We took it over and we burned it up."

That could be one result of the deep ambivalence that many Puerto Ricans feel about living in the U.S. Indeed, after two decades of steadily rising immigration, the trend in recent years has been in the opposite direction—back to Puerto Rico. On any night, airliners buzz over the Statue of Liberty filled with returning or visiting Puerto Ricans who can afford the $87 fare. At Christmas, there is a two-month waiting list for night-flight seats to San Juan. Successful Puerto Ricans often prefer to export their new affluence. Says John Torres, head of the Metropolitan Spanish Merchants Association in The Bronx: "We don't vote enough nor do we get involved in the political process. I know many, many people who have two dreams: to have a house in Puerto Rico and to educate their children."

Ex-Congressman Badillo points out that only 13 years ago he was the sole Puerto Rican actively engaged in elective politics. Now the community can boast three New York City councilmen, four state representatives and two state senators. Badillo's fellow Hispanics lamented his decision to abandon Congress for his deputy mayor's job, but his successor in Washington, Robert Garcia, is applauded as a compassionate, hard-working advocate of Puerto Rican concerns. Still, activists like Dora Collazo-Levy, 42, a Democratic Party district leader, complain that political passivity is the Puerto Rican community's principal bane. Says she: "People ask us why they should vote. We give them long-range answers."

Where music and dancing and painting are concerned, though, New York City's Hispanics are anything but passive. Salsa Bandleader Eddie Palmieri, 41, has become a latino superstar who packs halls across the U.S. No fewer than 169 recognized bands regularly tour New York City's circuit of Latin clubs and dance halls. Cityarts, an artists' collective now funded by the New York State Council on the Arts,

mobilizes painters to create ghetto murals. Last March El Museo del Barrio, a Puerto Rican cultural museum begun in 1969, opened new quarters on Manhattan's Fifth Avenue. Its first show, "Resurgiemento," included Artist Domingo Garcia, whose work is in the city's Museum of Modern Art collection. Miriam Colon, whose Puerto Rican Traveling Theater gives summertime performances in ghetto streets from the back of a flatbed truck, has opened the first Hispanic off-Broadway theater in a recycled West Side firehouse and will offer plays in both English and Spanish. On the Lower East Side, the New Rican Village cultural center lures actors and dancers and poets. So whatever else the New York experience has done to Puerto Ricans, it has not stifled the creative impulse.

THE "ILLEGALS." The scene is played out in the San Jacinto Plaza of El Paso, Texas (pop. 381,500), in the dawn hours of most Mondays. Sedans cruise slowly around the square, their drivers eying clusters of young women. Every so often, one of the women is beckoned from the sidelines. Deals are struck and the cars pull away.

The object of this ritual is not prostitution and the women are not harlots. They are illegal immigrants (known euphemistically these days as "undocumented aliens") who have crossed the Rio Grande from neighboring Juárez, Mexico, looking for work as maids. Their usual rate: around $25 a week. Because of its proximity to Juárez, El Paso is the second largest crossing point for undocumented aliens in the U.S. The largest is Chula Vista, Calif., which shares part of its sewerage system with neighboring Tijuana. Aliens have been known to crawl through the common drainage pipes to reach the U.S.

Undocumented aliens are the most shadowy portion of the Hispanic community. By federal estimates, there are 8.2 million of them in the U.S. Other estimates range from as low as 3 million to as high as 12 million. As many as 90% of the total are Hispanics. A million more are suspected of joining them every year.

Whatever the exact numbers, there is little doubt that the tide of undocumented Hispanic aliens has reached flood stage. Many thousands have come from Central and South American countries like Guatemala, Colombia and Ecuador, but about 90% are Mexican. On foot, by air or in autos, they filter across the 2,000-mile-long southern U.S. border. Last year nearly 1 million illegal entrants were apprehended and deported by the Immigration and Naturalization Service. But, admits Los Angeles Police Officer Antonio Amador, "the only way we're going to stop them is to build a Berlin Wall."

Behind the mass influx are some stark economic figures: half of Mexico's 18 million-member labor force is unemployed; a devalued peso has sent prices there spiraling; the country's 3.5% population growth is one of the world's highest. Says Border Patrolman Michael S. Williams: "They're starving to death down there."

Typical of them is José B., 33, who as a tenant farmer in

an isolated area of Mexico's Jalisco state could earn no more than $500 in a good year. Now he works in a metals factory near Los Angeles and brings home $160 a week, counting overtime pay. In six years he has saved $2,000. Says José: "I love Mexico. It is very beautiful, but you can't live there. Coming to the U.S. was a question of economics."

After crossing the border three times near Yuma, Ariz., and being apprehended each time, José paid a "coyote" (smuggler) $200 to ferry him across. After a year in Los Angeles, he paid another coyote $400 to smuggle in his wife and three of their six children. Eight months later he sent for the other three, at a cost of $250. Now the family—including two children born in the U.S.—occupies a sweltering one-bedroom *barrio* apartment, in which every available piece of furniture doubles as a bed. Even such cramped quarters are an improvement over what would be available in Mexico. Pointing at his twelve-year-old daughter, José says: "If we were in Mexico, she would be working in the fields by now."

Sooner rather than later, Congress is going to have to confront the problem of halting the flow of illegals. Meanwhile, there are millions of legal Hispanics in the U.S., and it no longer matters whether they or their ancestors arrived as wet-backs splashing across the ankle-deep Rio Grande or as political refugees in fishing boats from Cuba, or in the trunks of coyote cars or the staterooms of proud galleons. What does matter is that they—and their fellow Americans—now face another problem: writing a new chapter in the perpetually unfinished story of American pluralism. Both sides will undoubtedly have ample reason to recall that in U.S. politics, representation by ethnic population is not handed out gratis, but must be fought for and won. The same goes for many of the other advantages that Hispanics are likely to demand.

"No, we haven't arrived yet," says Graciela Olivarez, director of the federal Community Services Administration and the first woman graduate of the University of Notre Dame Law School. "But never before have we had so many Hispanic assistant secretaries [in the Federal Government], or people in every Government department. We don't have someone on the Supreme Court yet, or a Cabinet Secretary, but we'll have that to look forward to in the next go-round." Olivarez's confidence is just one more proof, if another were needed, that Hispanic Americans will be pressing for many more go-rounds in the years to come. ∎

The Jews: Next Year in Which Jerusalem?

U.S. Jews search for identity

IN CINCINNATI'S PLUM STREET Temple, Reform Rabbi Albert A. Goldman marks the Sabbath of Passover Week with his civil rights-oriented "Freedom Sabbath," which is attended by representatives of the Southern Christian Leadership Conference and of the N.A.A.C.P., labor organizers and Protestant ministers. In Miami Beach, the ads for a kosher hotel promise not only an olympic-size salt-water swimming pool, but also "Passover Specials" in room rates and a cantor and choir for Seder services. In Connecticut, a self-proclaimed congregation of Jewish humanists fashions a Passover Haggadah (the Seder narrative) that manages to avoid any mention of God. In Manhattan, an ecumenical group of friends sits down to a classic Seder meal including the symbolic foods: matzoth, bitter herbs and haunch of spring lamb. After reading the Haggadah, the group invites one of the Christians present to read from the New Testament; he chooses the passage in *Luke* where Jesus celebrates his Passover meal, the Last Supper.

Thus, with their own interpretations of the ancient rituals a number of U.S. Jews marked the eight-day festival of Passover that ends this week. Most other Jews observed the feast in more traditional ways. But all told anew the old stories of Pharaoh's wrath and the Lord's good providence that took them out of Egypt, their house of bondage. Sometimes their Christian neighbors joined them, aware that their own celebration of Easter, just days away, was inextricably tied to the Jewish holiday. It was at a Seder that Jesus first offered the bread and wine as his body and blood, and in Christian liturgies he has become the archetypal Paschal Lamb.

Of course Passover and Easter carry quite different spiritual meanings. Easter is a feast of resurrection; Passover a feast of survival. Easter denotes God's sacrifice for the redemption of all men; Passover God's special compact with one people. That compact often seems "exclusive," yet according to the Old Testament, God did charge his people with a message of love and justice for the world. Thus Passover also means a kind of redemption to Jews, a redemption anticipated in the climactic affirmation that ends the Seder celebration: "Next Year in Jerusalem!" For two millenniums that cry has been the Jews' link to the homeland and each other, a confident pledge that they will one day be reunited in Israel.

For most of those two millenniums, "Next year in Jerusalem!" was only a dream, a burning reason to stay alive in the midst of the Diaspora (the Exile) and often calumny and pogrom. In recent years the real possibility of aliyah ("ascent" to the homeland) has been realized. Jerusalem is accessible, for the moment at least a precious part of Israel; yet most Jews remain in the countries they grew up in. What does the old pledge mean now, in a world where Israel and the Diaspora exist side by side? Where do Jewish loyalties lie? Who, or what, is a Jew now that Jerusalem is no longer just an evanescent goal?

The questions are part of a new and deep search for Jewish identity in Jews the world over, especially in the U.S., Israel and the Soviet Union. The search takes many forms, for Jews—as indicated by their diverse Passover observances—identify themselves with a broad assortment of labels—ethnic, religious and political. There are Ashkenazic and Sephardic Jews; Orthodox, Conservative, Reform and Reconstructionist Jews; Zionists and anti-Zionists. In the welter of causes and allegiances that vie for the Jew of the '70s, the essence of Judaism sometimes seems hard to find.

BEARING WITNESS. "I know what one must do to be Jewish," writes Author Elie Wiesel, the melancholy chronicler of the Nazi holocaust. "He must assume his Jewishness. He must assume his collective conscience. He must assume his past with its sorrows and its joys. Tell the tale. In other words, he must bear witness." Wiesel's definition, however attractive, still leaves the individual Jew with a dilemma. Bear witness to what? And how? Follow the painfully detailed 613 Precepts set down for devout Jews? Immigrate to a kibbutz in Israel? Write a check for the United Jewish Appeal? How does a modern Jew in the Americas, in Europe or even in Israel "assume his past" when it is so redolent with ancient law, so burdened with melancholy history?

In a sense, the quest for Jewish identity today is a sign that Jews are more secure than they ever have been in their history. For most of that history, the uppermost question has been one not of identity but survival. The Jews had to endure the Babylonian captivity, the leveling of Jerusalem by the Romans, and 19 centuries of exile. That exile was exacerbated by enforced conversions and by expulsions from one country after another, and capped by a crime that beggars the imagination: the Nazis' methodical murder of 6,000,000 people. Then came the painful birth of Israel. As the wandering survivors from the Old World crowded into the infant state, there seemed to be an effort, as Conservative Rabbi Marc H. Tanenbaum puts it, "to terminate the past and lock the door on it."

Many other Jews, of course, tried to lock the door on the past in a different way: assimilation. Especially in the U.S., where they made up the world's largest Jewish population (approximately 5,000,000 in 1945), Jews played a significant role in the material and intellectual life of the nation during the postwar years and won a generous slice of America's prosperity. By the mid-1960s, 80% of Jewish high school graduates went on to college, in contrast to 40% of the total population. By 1965, 57% of U.S. Jewish families had an income of $7,000 a year or more; only 35% of all U.S. families enjoyed such incomes. Jews were welcomed into most professions, sought out for government office, even invited into some hitherto exclusive white Anglo-Saxon clubs and enclaves. Jewish expressions, literature and customs began to appeal to many non-Jews for their ethnic vigor; the result was a kind of Jewish chic.

Where their parents had found new faiths in Marxism, Freudianism and a succession of liberal causes, many younger Jews followed their contemporaries into the New Left or exotic religious movements such as Krishna Consciousness, Scientology or even the Jesus Revolution. A remarkable number of young people are being won over to the "Messianic Judaism" of an evangelistic group in San Francisco called Jews for Jesus; many of them worship at synagogues and have their jackets emblazoned with Jesus slogans in Hebrew. For others, young and old, Judaism had been reduced to what one young Jew contemptuously calls a "gastronomical experience": blintzes, bagels and lox, gefilte fish.

Obviously, the spectrum of Jewish identification is a broad one. "Each man's Jewish story is different." asserts James A. Sleeper in *The New Jews*. Many Jews insist, with stubborn existentialism, that a Jew is what he chooses to be. Yet the ends of the spectrum seem discernible enough—and some of the many shades in between. At one end, a very large group stresses the peoplehood of Judaism, membership in a cultural and ethnic community that may or may not have religious significance to them. At the other end, a smaller but steadfast group regards Judaism principally as a strict and compelling faith, in which nothing less than exact adherence to Torah and Talmud will do. [The Talmud is the great body of Jewish legal and ritual commentary recorded between 300 B.C. and A.D. 500 and continuously refined by Jewish scholars ever since. Based on the Torah (the five books of Moses that make up the beginning of the Bible), it is Judaism's most authoritative source, after the Torah, and its greatest literary achievement.] In between are those who acknowledge the universal community of Judaism, but who trace that community to traditional roots in a common faith.

ETHNIC OR EXISTENTIAL JUDAISM. Jews in this group may be completely secular—even atheist—or sometimes members of a denomination like Reform Judaism. They simply do not feel that formal ritual or denominational affiliation is crucial. Though a rabbi himself, Philadelphia's Jacob Chinitz insists that "it is membership in the Jewish people that ties a Jew to Judaism, not his membership in a synagogue."

Particularly among students, this new communal Jewishness is creating a heightened interest in Hebrew, Yiddish, Jewish history and even Bible study—though for many the latter is more cultural than religious. On U.S. campuses, an impressive number of Judaic courses have been added to the curriculums, often at the students' instigation. At least 55 secular colleges and universities—more than half of them top-ranking schools—now offer courses in Jewish studies, compared with only eleven a generation ago. Where formal Jewish studies fail to meet the demand, "free Jewish universities" have sprung up for adults as well as collegians.

Samuel Pisar, who is a naturalized American living in Paris and the widely acclaimed author of *Coexistence and Commerce*, is perhaps the paradigm of the existential, communal kind of Jew. Of the 900 students in his Polish elementary school, Pisar is one of two to survive the holocaust. He calls the communal ties of Jews a "bond of suffering that comes whenever Jews are threatened." He felt the pull of that bond when he attended an international conference in Kiev last summer. After a VIP tour of the city, he became uneasy. "The [concentration camp] numbers on my arm," he recalls, "began to itch." When his turn came to speak, he threw away his prepared text and told the Soviet hosts that the tour had been incomplete: it had not included Babi Yar, where the German Occupation forces had killed hundreds of thousands of Kiev citizens, starting with 70,000 Jews. After a stunned silence the Russians gave in and bused their visitors and themselves out to Babi Yar for a mutual lesson in the bitter fruits of anti-Semitism.

Existential Judaism operates on a less cosmic scale too. What is taken for granted in the surrounding Gentile culture may make a Jew feel like an alien. "You can feel just like any other American on the Fourth of July," notes a Jew from Texas, but "you are vividly reminded that you are different" amid the ubiquitous Christmas decorations festooning American streets in December. It remains true, however, that many Jews relish the sense of unique fraternity that arises from this differentness. There is a note of pride in the old Yiddish saying *Schwer zu sein a Yid* (It is tough to be a Jew).

COMMUNITY OF FAITH JUDAISM. Partly because of such difficulties, cultural Jewishness is not enough for many Jews. A number of critics feel that it is dangerously hollow. "It makes being a Jew the religion," contends Jewish Writer Will Herberg of Drew University. "By its standards, you can be a very good Jew without faith." Herberg, once a Communist, represents the middle of the Jewish spectrum: those Jews who insist that faith must underpin any lasting sense of Jewish identity.

Theologian Abraham Joshua Heschel, professor of ethics and mysticism at the Conservatives' Jewish Theological Seminary in Manhattan, is the godfather and poet of this school of thought. He is also one of its stricter interpreters of Halakhah (*The Law*, derived from the Hebrew for *to follow*), the Jewish code of conduct and observance. For Heschel, who lost his first wife and children in the Nazi terror, Judaism is "the track of God in the wilderness of oblivion." The task, he says, is "being what we are, namely Jews; by attuning our own yearning to the lonely holiness in this world, we will aid humanity more than by any particular service we may render."

The mystical piety that animates Heschel's work is an inheritance from his forebears, a prominent Hasidic family in Poland. It is this quality of Hasidism—the 18th century revolt against the aridities of rabbinic legalism—that attracts many younger Jews. Although some are not quite willing to accept the full ritual observance that goes with Hasidism, they do seek to share the Hasidic experience of ecstatic encounter with God. Indeed, some carry it to very untraditional lengths. In Beverly Hills, Calif., on Yom Kippur, a 17-year-old high school student declined to join in the common prayers in his synagogue, explaining, "I decided I have my own concept of God as something beyond the natural world, and I don't think it is right for me to use other people's words when I could try to use my own thoughts. I can relate to God anywhere I want to."

In a recent issue of the new Jewish journal *Sh'ma*, a young woman named Joan Koehler relates a remarkable chronicle of conversion. Raised without a faith, she found Christian churches too dogmatic, was attraced by the Jewish belief that total truth "is not within man's reach." Despite the endless intricacies of Jewish law that daunt most interested outsiders—and many Jews—she concluded that "in a sense, each Jew has his own Torah, and I am working out mine." Among other observances, she keeps a kosher kitchen and a fairly strict Sabbath.

Jew and convert, a growing number of young people are joining the college-based *havurat* (fellowship) movement and similar experimental Jewish communities. Different from the culture-oriented Judaic studies programs, the *havurat* have communal houses or meeting places where Jewish students gather to study the Torah, Hebrew and other Jewish subjects and to celebrate the Sabbath and festivals together. Though they pledge no formal adherence to strict Halakhah, the students can, like Joan Koehler, be edifyingly tough on themselves. Some communities observe their own kind of kashruth (kosher laws) by vegetarianism, at least on the Sabbath. At Boston's Havurat Shalom, one of the pioneering communities in the movement, members

WHO'S WHAT IN JEWRY

To non-Jews, and indeed to many Jews, the ethnic and religious variations among the world's 14 million Jews are bewildering. Scientifically speaking, there is no Jewish "race." As Scholar Raphael Patai points out in his book, *Tents of Jacob*, Jews of one geographical area share physiological traits with their immediate non-Jewish neighbors but much less so with Jews of a distant geographical area. Still, the Jews' long history of wandering as tightly knit communities has dispersed them into a wide range of distinct ethnic groups.

By far the most numerous today are the *Ashkenazic* Jews, who became an important group in the Rhineland about the 10th century. They take their name from the medieval Hebrew name for Germany, Ashkenaz. The Ashkenazim, who spread across Europe and to North and South America, suffered most of the casualties in the Hitler years, but still account for some 84% of the world's Jews.

The remaining 16% are divided between the *Sephardic* and *Oriental* Jews. The Sephardim developed into a community in medieval Spain, where their achievements in arts, government and letters made them the most influential Jewish community of the Diaspora until their expulsion in 1492. Their language, Ladino, reflects their Spanish roots. The Oriental Jews are scattered from North Africa to Afghanistan, usually speaking Jewish varieties of Arabic or Persian, and in the case of one group, Aramaic.

Beyond these three basic groups there are several smaller Jewish communities with long histories of their own, such as the Jews of the Caucasus, the Cochin Jews of India, the black Falasha Jews of Ethiopia, and an indigenous population in Italy that dates back more than 2,000 years. Though the Italian Jews have often prospered, their numbers are now diminishing through intermarriage with Roman Catholics.

As the Jewish homeland, Israel has Jews of almost every kind, color and Judaic language, although the Sephardic pronunciation of Hebrew has been made standard for Israel. In the U.S., the oldest Jewish community is that of the Sephardim, who first arrived in 1654. They brought with them an *Orthodox* heritage, but many strayed from it in the New World. The first important wave of Ashkenazic immigration from Germany in the 1840s and '50s, on the other hand, brought with it the *Reform* movement of religious Judaism, an outgrowth of the Age of Enlightenment. Caught up in the rationalism of the age, Reform set out to modernize liturgy, rejected the binding authority of Jewish law and such key beliefs as a literal Messiah and personal immortality. But it reemphasized Jewish ethical values.

The Reform approach seemed sterile to some Jews, who in the late 19th century began to turn to a compromise between Reform and Orthodoxy known in the U.S. as *Conservative* Judaism. At the same time, waves of Eastern European Jews, some of whom clung to their Old World Orthodoxy, were emigrating to the U.S. But not until the rise of Nazism in Europe did yet another group of Orthodox Jews arrive in the U.S.—the followers of *Hasidism*, a movement of mystical enthusiasm that sprang up in Eastern Europe in the 18th century. Among them were the Satmar Hasidim, named after the Rumanian town of Satmar, and the Lubavitch Hasidim, named after the White Russian town of Lubavitch. The Satmar sect is fiercely loyal to the U.S. but anti-Zionist because only the Messiah can re-establish Israel. They remain small (about 5,000 families), but the Lubavitcher, who accept Israel and are also staunch U.S. patriots, now have perhaps 150,000 members and sympathizers.

At the other end of the spectrum is *Reconstructionism*, a sort of Jewish equivalent of Unitarianism that grew out of the naturalism and pragmatism of American thought in the 1920s and 1930s. Its adherents number some 2,300 families.

Because the question of religious affiliation has been kept out of recent U.S. censuses, the current Jewish population of the U.S. can only be estimated: about 6,000,000. Roughly half of U.S. Jewish families belong to synagogues, and the three major groups—Reform, Conservative, Orthodox—now probably share that membership in approximately equal thirds. Only a massive Jewish population survey now under way will tell Americans just how Jewish they really are. ∎

live close enough to the house that they can walk to Sabbath services—even if they might use cars for other purposes during the day.

These communal experiences reflect a new interpretation of an ancient keystone Jewish concept: membership in the *mishpochah*, a family of both blood and faith whose dining table is also an altar. It is a family on familiar terms with God—so much so that members can chastise him, as Tevye does in *Fiddler on the Roof*. One great Hasidic rabbi, Levi-Yitzhak of Berditchev, once warned God, "If you refuse to answer our prayers, I shall refuse to go on saying them." It was Levi-Yitzhak, too, who one day addressed God in exasperation: "Master of the Universe, how many years do we know each other? How many decades? So please permit me to wonder: is this any way to rule your world?" God is sometimes seen as a sort of puzzlingly eccentric grandfather. One Jewish story tells of a rich man praying for money to start a new business, and a poor man, next to him, praying for food for his starving family. God tells an astonished angel to grant the rich man's petition, explaining that he sees the poor man every week, but he has not seen the rich man in three years.

The warm circle of the *mispochah* became considerably extended as Jewish history progressed; in time it included the entire *shtetl*, the Jewish village. Now a number of Jewish thinkers would like to define that concept in a special way that embraces the Jewish people as a whole. Among the most influential is a cross-denominational group of theologians and philosophers who have become known as the "Covenant theologians."

The Covenant theologians—and many other religious Jews newly interested in Halakhic observance—generally agree that the Jews' special relationship with God demands some kind of loyalty to traditional Jewish law. "Without law the Covenant is empty and even meaningless," says Seymour Siegel. "There can be no Covenant without observance." That, of course, is an old question in Judaism, and it divides even those devoutly observant Jews whom the outside world paints with the broad brush of "Orthodoxy."

ORTHODOX JUDAISM. While more liberal Jews are willing to search for the common denominator of faith within a broader idea of Jewish peoplehood, the Orthodox are more demanding: faith must come first, peoplehood second. Indeed, for the strictest Orthodox, their rigidly sectarian faith actually separates them from other Jews. Even so, the basic Orthodox concept of Jewish identification is far healthier today than was expected just a few decades ago. Now it is burgeoning, partly because the melting pot is passé, but also partly because the Orthodox birth rate is unusually high.

Despite its monolithic aspects, Orthodoxy comprises a host of sometimes bitterly contending factions. There are arguments, for instance, about the fine points of kosher-food preparation, with the result that there are two categories of kosher food—regular kosher, acceptable to most Orthodox, and *glatt* (smooth) kosher, preferred by the more rigorous ultra-Orthodox. More serious disagreements revolve around whether a Gentile who is converted through non-Orthodox procedures is in fact a Jew, or even whether Orthodox rabbis can engage in interdenominational conversations with less observant rabbis.

At least one Orthodox group—the Lubavitch Hasidim—is dedicated to converting less observant Jews back to full observance, and the group usually goes about that task with patience, tact and good humor. One convert to Lubavitch Hasidism, Microbiologist Velvl Greene of Minneapolis, was won over simply by prayer. A young Lubavitch missionary, in the midst of a ten-minute interview with the busy Greene, suddenly looked out the window at the setting sun,

realized that it was time for prayer, and, asking Greene's pardon, abruptly stopped the conversation. Putting on a *gartel* (a cord round the waist that symbolizes the biblical "girding of the loins"), he turned to the window to pray. Greene was so impressed that he invited the young man back for further conversations and gradually became a fully observant Lubavitcher.

SABBATH COMBAT. Despite the current interest in Orthodoxy's various shades, many Jews resent its exclusiveness. Indeed, Reform Rabbi Alvin H. Reines, of Cincinnati's Hebrew Union College-Jewish Institute of Religion, turns the tables and regretfully excludes Orthodoxy from his concept of Judaism. Reines contends that there is no single entity describable as Judaism, but rather a variety of Judaisms over the ages, each fashioned to its time. Some have lingered on and now coexist, but the common denominator of most is flexibility. Reines would like to see basic unity among believing Jews under an umbrella he calls "polydoxy." Polydoxy's working principle recognizes the "radical freedom" of every human being to create his own religion for his own "finite needs." By its very nature, says Reines, this formulation excludes those, like the Orthodox, who would restrict complete human freedom with divine commandments.

Orthodoxy—especially militant Orthodoxy—does create problems within Judaism, but in the U.S. these problems are only minor ones, skirmishes of words. In Israel, Orthodox zealotry has created a national law-and-order crisis. Orthodox Jews are naturally inflamed by secular Jews who spend the sabbath sunning on the beach at Tel Aviv. Secular Jews are exasperated at the kind of Orthodox legalism that debates whether using electricity on the Sabbath violates the injunction against kindling fires on that day; or whether it is better to break the ban against working on the Sabbath by milking cows or to risk causing the animals pain—an action that is also forbidden—by not milking them.

Israelis or visitors who are unwise enough to drive their cars through the ultra-Orthodox Mea Shearim section of Jerusalem on the Sabbath often encounter a hail of stones. A teen-age girl who naively walks through the same district in a miniskirt may find herself angrily chased by Orthodox youths shouting "*Zonah! Zonah!*" ("Whore! Whore!"). Many pathologists in Israeli hospitals receive death threats from Orthodox fanatics for performing autopsies, which according to Orthodoxy are a desecration of the dead. Hospitals in Jerusalem and Tel Aviv closed down briefly in protest against police failure to curb the threats.

SHARED COURAGE. To many Jews, U.S. society represents cosmopolitanism and universalism, Israeli society a community fulfilling its tradition. U.S. society exalts conscience and individual freedom, Israeli society adherence to a communal code. Alone, either set of ideals may become narrow or destructive; exchanged, they could become more balanced and productive for both communities. Since Judaism is an inextricable mixture of religion and nationhood, a certain ambiguity about Jewish identity will always remain and may ultimately be creative. "We cannot live on borrowed courage," warns Los Angeles Rabbi Leonard Beerman, counseling U.S. Jews to define their identities out of their own roots. But shared courage could well add up to redoubled strength.

In his short story *Monte Sant' Angelo*, Arthur Miller writes of the Jewish experience: "The whole history is packing bundles and getting away." That may have been. Now the business, Jews hope, is unpacking bundles and settling where they are. They seem determined to follow

the 614th commandment as propounded by Canadian Philosopher Emil Fackenheim: Jews are forbidden to grant posthumous victories to Hitler. That includes maintaining loyalty to two Jerusalems: the earthly city and the heavenly one, the realized and the unrealized. For many Jews, the earthly Jerusalem remains an irresistible symbol of hope and triumph. For others, aliyah to the existing Jerusalem is not necessary to reach the ideal one. To them, "Next Year in Jerusalem" means a spiritual journey: contributing their special vision to help build something nearer to that heavenly city—the kingdom of God—throughout the world. ∎

St Louis: Pride on "the Hill"

In St. Louis, a renaissance of Italian pride

MANY OF THE SMALL and tightly knit ethnic communities that once dotted virtually every U.S. city have crumbled under the planner's rezoning and renewal schemes and the bulldozer's giant blade. One community that has successfully resisted the encroachment of urbanization is "the Hill," a 56-block, largely Italian area on the south side of St. Louis, where Yogi Berra and Joe Garagiola grew up. After a series of fierce, emotion-charged struggles with local, state and federal officials, Hill residents now boast a model community that has the lowest crime rate and the highest property values in the city. Time Correspondent Marguerite Michaels recently visited the Hill. Her report:

In the afternoons around 3:30, Joe ("Green") Verdi, Angelo ("Foots") Colombo, John ("Detroit") Agresti and other properly and not-so-properly nicknamed neighborhood men gather at Rose's Tavern for a glass of beer from the 7-ft. wooden cooler. Then they drift out back toward the grape arbor for a game of boccie. On Wednesdays, Amelia Garavaglia, 76, flours her plump, competent hands in the back room of Gioia's Corner Market and begins rolling out 5,000 ravioli for sale in the front room. Each evening, Ida Galli switches on the spotlight in her front yard—not to scare away burglars, but to illuminate a 3-ft.-high statue of the Blessed Virgin. It is all part of the pleasant, unhurried flavor of life today on the Hill.

ITALIAN SAUSAGE. There is a strong sense of ritual, both religious and community, on the Hill, where 90% of the population of 6,500 is Italian and 95% Catholic. There is also a bursting pride in the rows of narrow, well-scrubbed houses and in the family-run corner stores, where links of fat Italian sausage dangle in long rows. Many residents are direct descendants of the immigrants who left Lombardy at the turn of the century to work the clay mines of St. Louis under the hill that gives the section its name. Life on the Hill is as finely woven as Ann Reistino's brightly colored, crocheted afghans.

It was not always so. In the '60s, the neighborhood's youth began to drift away. Federal and state highway officials designated the path of Interstate Highway 44 through an area of the Hill. Assuming that land values would plunge with the construction of the road, many homeowners stopped maintaining their property. A local lead company began pumping slurry into the abandoned clay mines, threatening to undermine foundations. Explains Father Salvatore Polizzi, 43, associate pastor of St. Ambrose Roman Catholic Church: "The Hill was becoming a blighted cemetery."

Polizzi determined to change things. He began delivering sermons urging the residents to regain their lost sense of spirit and pride. He also made a point of cultivating leaders of the area's strong Democratic organization.

His efforts paid off in his first encounter: discouraging the sale of land to builders of a planned drive-in theater. Polizzi sent the Democratic ward committeeman into the streets with a sound truck announcing an emergency meeting in the Big Club Hall. After a session exploring the blight that the drive-in would inflict on the area, a small army of Italian dowagers volunteered to lie down in front of the bulldozers. The sellers backed down, and the Hill's alderman quickly slipped a regulation through the zoning board forbidding a building permit for any drive-in within 500 ft. of a residential area.

Buoyed by that success, Polizzi once again rallied community support and forced the lead company to stop pumping waste into the abandoned mines. But the biggest fight was yet to come. By 1971 construction was well under way on Interstate 44. It cut off a segment of the community, isolating 150 families. Yet the state planned only one vehicle overpass. In protest, some 300 citizens piled into buses and traveled to the state capital, Jefferson City; there they argued before the highway commission for an additional overpass.

The commission said no, and the residents cannily decided to turn the problem into an "Italian issue." When Secretary of Transportation John Volpe visited St. Louis on another matter, Polizzi requested a meeting and pressed for the overpass in the same, formal Italian that Volpe had learned back home in Massachusetts. Joe Garagiola began dropping hints that he might not be available any more on the Republican banquet circuit unless the Hill got its overpass. Finally Polizzi led a Hill delegation to Washington with a check for $50,000, raised by the residents themselves, to pay for the overpass. The Hill got its bridge, and the bells of St. Ambrose rang out the good news.

Polizzi has joined 1,100 of the area's 1,500 families in a nonprofit development corporation to guide the future of the area. In its four years' existence, the corporation has found 60 jobs for new—and old—residents in the neighborhood's salami and macaroni factories, tool company and glass factory. It has set up a summer youth program and hired students at $1 an hour to spruce up the area. The students redecorated the Hill's hydrants and trash cans in red, white and green (the colors of the Italian flag). More than 1,000 trees have been planted. A system of block workers set up by the corporation makes certain that leftover ravioli lands in, not outside the garbage cans. The corporation maintains a list of Italians eager to move onto the Hill. When houses become vacant, if often refurbishes and resells them at low cost to young couples.

The money for many of these projects comes from the approximately $50,000 earned at an annual summer festival, which draws 100,000 visitors. The aroma of lasagna and meat balls fills the air, and amateur Carusos croon over the loudspeakers. There are grapestomping contests and a step-by-step demonstration of how to make sfinge, an Italian confection. At the evening's end a spray of fireworks flares over the neighborhood as proud residents and guests clap and cheer, aware that they have seen the past and that on the Hill at least, it still works. ∎

■ SPORT

FEBRUARY 27, 1978

"The Greatest" Is Gone

An era ends as an aging Ali yields his crown

For God's sake, let us sit upon the ground,
And tell sad stories of the death of kings:
How some have been deposed, some slain in war,
Some haunted by the ghosts they have depos'd ...
        —SHAKESPEARE, King Richard II

"WE HAVE A SPLIT DECISION," Ring Announcer Chuck Hull proclaimed, and absolute silence fell over the plush Las Vegas boxing emporium where Muhammad Ali and Leon Spinks had struggled through 15 lashing rounds to claim sport's most special crown. "Judge Art Lurie: 143-142, Ali. Judge Lou Tabat: 145-140, Spinks. Judge Harold Buck: 144-141." A pause, a breath in that utter stillness and then: "The new Heavyweight Champion of the World, Leon Spinks!"

All but the first two words were lost in the roar of the crowd, that unmistakable, primordial voice of a fight crowd hailing a new king of the most basic sport. But the silence before the verdict had spoken too, for it anticipated the passing of a giant, a unique athlete whose skills and life had resonances far beyond the ring. As Cassius Marcellus Clay Jr., Cassius X, or Muhammad Ali, he had talked from center stage, mirror and lightning rod for a tumultuous era. Olympic gold medalist, Louisville Lip, upstart champion,

Black Muslim convert, draft resister, abomination, martyr, restored champion, road show.

In victory Ali had sought the microphones to shout that he was the prettiest, the greatest. In defeat, battered and swollen, blood splattered on his trunks from a 5th-round cut in his mouth, he did not shy from the questions: "I lost fair and square to Spinks. I did everything right, and I lost. I lost simply because Spinks was better, that's all. It's just another experience in my life, nothing to cry about."

Ali departed the next day on one of those journeys to a global constituency unique to his championship reign. This time the destination was Bangladesh, where he was to dedicate a sports stadium named in his honor. He left behind a new boxing king and a glorious—and sometimes infuriating—past.

To peer into the kaleidoscope of memories of Ali, studying the changing shapes and shifting images, is to glimpse reflections not just of a man, but of an American time. Demanding that the nation know his every thought, insisting that the public mark each of his deeds, he was bound to the events—and thus the lives—of his era.

John F. Kennedy was campaigning for the presidency when Cassius Clay Jr. returned triumphant from the Olympic Games in Rome. The blithe boy-child stepped off the plane spouting poetry and singing of his possibilities. He was bold—some said brash—with hopes and dreams, but much seemed within the reach of American aspirations in those freshening days. Cassius signed with a syndicate of wealthy Louisville businessmen, who underwrote his early training as a professional fighter against a 50% belief in purses to come. He had been boxing since the age of twelve with the heavyweight title as his unwavering goal, and he was willing to pay any price, bear any burden to fulfill his vision.

With the aid of his backers, Ali apprenticed under Trainer Angelo Dundee, a skilled groomer of fighters. Dundee recalls: "The Louisville group wanted me to train him. I told them to send him down to Miami after Christmas. Twenty minutes later, I get a call telling me Ali wasn't waiting till after Christmas, he was coming right away. They told me he said, 'I don't want to wait for Christmas. I want to fight.' That's how it all started in October 1960."

Dundee soon discovered just how good his young charge was. The strident gym voice softens, as if remembering something rare and lovely: "Oh, yes, I knew I had a winner. Of all the fighters I've ever known, only he could make the heavy bag sing when he hit it. I used to hear him make it snap like a snare drum every time I came up the stairs to the gym.

"He ran seven miles to the gym from the hotel and back every day along the causeway. He was always the first in and the last out of the gym. He is the most unspoiled kid I've ever had. He insisted on putting on his own gloves. He didn't like to be pampered."

Cassius moved up in the rankings, and with each step

Ali's journey took him from Olympic hero to outcast to national treasure

he minted new doggerel predicting the round of his opponent's defeat. The talking, talking, talking had begun in earnest now; the young, barely literate Louisville Lip displayed the stirrings of a genius more valuable in a media age: a flair for public relations, for hype and self-aggrandizement.

He superbly displayed his talents for promotion in 1964, when he was matched for the title with Champion Sonny Liston, a great, seemingly invincible giant of a man. Clay called Liston an "ugly old bear" and pranced around carrying a bear trap to the delight of the photographers. Budini Brown, Clay's corner man and cheerleader, gave his fighter the perfect line: "Float like a butterfly, sting like a bee." That is precisely what he did. Cassius attacked, disappeared on those marvelously fast feet, attacked again, disappeared again, until the bear was beaten, helpless in his corner.

Then the first shock from this narcissistic, almost coquettish new champion. He went off after the fight to eat ice cream in the company of Malcolm X, the Black Muslim leader whose unyielding words attacked the nation's racial hostilities and foretold the fire to come. The next morning, the conqueror of Liston told sportswriters he had become a Black Muslim.

It seemed at first that the conversion was just another

idiosyncrasy, some kind of gimmick. It was nothing of the kind. Clay had actually changed his religion before the Liston fight. Harold Conrad, former sportswriter, sometime promoter, and, in the years when Ali was banished from the ring, tireless seeker after the means of his return, was privy to a prefight crisis. Two weeks before the fight in Miami, Promoter Bill McDonald learned of Ali's Black Muslim associates and threatened to cancel the fight if Cassius did not denounce the Muslims. Conrad remembers: "When Ali heard that the fight was going to be nixed, he turned to Angelo and said matter of factly. 'Well, that's that.' He had absolutely no intention of renouncing his faith, not even for a crack at the world championship he'd fought and slaved so long and hard to get. It meant chucking the fight and plunging into obscurity, but he didn't hesitate."

His conversion, complete with the adoption of the new name, Muhammad Ali, raised eyebrows but not full public ire—yet. He was funny and, yes, pretty, and so what if Malcolm X was looking over the man-child's shoulder? He was still eating ice cream. How bad could it be?

Ali and the American public learned the answer to the question in 1965, when he defended his title against Floyd Patterson. A sporting event became a religious war between Catholic Patterson and Muslim Ali. It was also a terrible mismatch between a flagging ex-champ and a cruelly derisive young titleholder. By the time of the K.O. in the 12th round, even the most bloodthirsty fight fans were sickened by the gruesome giving and taking of pain. But there was more than that to the scene. White America had seen Watts burn with a deadly rage that summer. Now there stood a triumphant Black Muslim fighter, lips peeled back around his mouthpiece, sneering down at a soft-spoken, respected black who talked of moderation. Muhammad Ali had confirmed the worst fears; the rest came easy.

There was a war on. Every night, television sets in the nation's living rooms showed—in color—the horror of the fighting in Viet Nam. Ali refused to do his bit. "I ain't got no quarrel with them Viet Cong," he said, and changed his life forever. When the Army tried to draft Ali, he appealed, claiming that, as a Black Muslim, he was a conscientious objector. Ali managed to squeeze in a few fights, mostly in Europe, before the date he was supposed to take the fateful step forward to induction. Ironically, the man who read so haltingly that he was once declared below Army standards was also invited to lecture on campuses by students who were sitting out the war behind a book. Ali became the symbol of opposition to the war at a time when Lyndon Johnson still was in office and, supposedly, there was light at the end of the tunnel. He was also bitterly attacked in the press for his close association with Elijah Muhammad, the Black Muslim leader. The Chicago Tribune ran eleven anti-Ali draft stories in a single issue.

Ali and his entourage claim that the Government secretly sought to strike a deal—offering, if he would go quietly into uniform, to allow him to defend his title regularly and put on boxing exhibitions. A similar arrangement had been worked out for Joe Louis during World War II. The Pentagon last week denied that any such arrangement was ever suggested to Ali.

By April 1967, Ali had exhausted all of his appeals. At the Houston Induction Center, he refused orders to step forward to join the Army. Within minutes the New York State Athletic Commission rescinded his boxing license; it took the World Boxing Association four hours to do its patriotic duty and take away his title. The State Department confiscated his passport so that he could not travel to nations willing to sanction his fighting. For his stand, Ali was convicted of draft evasion and given a five-year prison sentence. He started the lengthy process of appeal, and discovered that he could no longer get fights in the U.S. Conrad recalls the banishment: "I canvassed 27 states trying to get him a license to fight. I even tried to set up a fight in a bullring across the border from San Diego, and they wouldn't let him leave the country. Overnight he became a 'nigger' again. He threw his life away on one toss of the dice for something he believed in. Not many folks do that."

For three and one-half years, Ali was not allowed to earn a purse at the only work he knew. The banishment cost him his fighting prime. Finally, late in 1970, he began to get some bouts: he tuned up by beating Jerry Quarry and Oscar Bonavena and then challenged Joe Frazier for the title on March 8, 1971. He lost, but three months later scored a bigger victory in another arena. On June 28, 1971, his conviction was overturned by the Supreme Court, which ruled 8 to 0 that the draft board had improperly denied Ali's claim for exemption on grounds that he was a conscientious objector. Ali returned to the frustrating trail of a contender: a broken jaw at the hands of Ken Norton, a rematch triumph over Frazier, newly dethroned by George Foreman.

No matter that his best years were gone; the fighter was back working at his craft. His championship had been a bully pulpit, and he eagerly sought it once more. The Muslims had softened their separatist hard line, and with that there was less raw, reverse-racism talk from Ali. Finally Ali reclaimed his crown in Kinshasa, Zaire. George Foreman, the hardest puncher since Sonny Liston, spent himself pounding Muhammad Ali ceaselessly—and uselessly—on the ropes one early African morning. Ali again was the underdog, but it was his galvanic personality that drew the attention of the world.

In his long odyssey, Muhammad Ali became a global celebrity on a scale known by only a handful of men. He called upon heads of state, and it is they who were thrilled by the meeting. As one of the world's most recognizable faces, he drew appreciative, knowing crowds from African village to Asian hamlet to European capital. If he walked a single block, he trailed a mob in his wake. Now an aged, dethroned champion, he can no longer light the ring with his skills. But the path he burned across his time remains. ∎

Twenty years after the U.S. abandoned the quota system that for half a century had preserved the overwhelmingly European character of the nation, TIME reported on the "changing face of America" in a special issue on the new immigrants. In 1984, the largest number of them arrived—not from Europe—but from Mexico, the Philippines and Viet Nam. The new arrivals altered not only America's racial makeup, but its cityscapes, its taste in food and clothes and music, its entire perception of itself. More Americans were eating salsa, praying to Mecca, dancing the merengue. Jesse Jackson created a new metaphor for American diversity: the melting pot gave way to a patchwork quilt of many colors.

THE 1980s

The Changing Face of America

"Just look down Broadway. That guy is Indian, next to him is a Greek, next to him is a Thai ..."

"These States are the amplest poem,
Here is not merely a nation but a teeming Nation of
*   nations."*

—WALT WHITMAN

REINA CAME FROM EL SALVADOR because of "horrible things." She says simply, "I got scared." When she finally reached Los Angeles and found a job as a housekeeper at $125 a week, her new employer pointed to the vacuum cleaner. Vacuum cleaner? Reina, 24, had never seen such a thing before. "She gave me a maid book and a dictionary," says Reina, who now writes down and looks up every new word she hears. "That's how I learn English. I don't have time to go to school, but when I don't speak English, I feel stupid, so I must learn."

Manuel Martins Simões had been a truck driver in Lisbon, but when he got to Newark in 1974, he worked on a construction gang during the week and waited on tables weekends. Eventually, he saved enough money to buy a restaurant. "The building was really broken down and dirty," Simões says, "but my wife and I rebuilt the whole thing and put in a private dining room and a barbecue in the back." After seven years, he sold the place for a $185,000 profit and returned to Lisbon to set himself and his brother up in business and live like a lord. But Simões was miserable. "All business in Portugal now is bad," he says, "and the kids are a headache, always wanting to go back to the U.S." Next week the family is emigrating all over again. "The first thing we will do," says Simões, "is become American citizens."

Lam Ton, from Viet Nam, is already a U.S. citizen, and he too did well with a restaurant, the Mekong, at the intersection of Broadway and Argyle Street in Chicago. "When I first moved in here, I swept the sidewalk after we closed," he recalls. "People thought I was strange, but now everyone does the same." Lam Ton's newest project is to build an arch over Argyle Street in honor of the immigrants who live and work there. "I will call it Freedom Gate," he says, "and it will have ocean waves with hands holding a freedom torch on top. It will represent not just the Vietnamese but all the minorities who have come here. Just look down Broadway. That guy is Indian, next to him is a Greek, next to him is a Thai, and next to him is a Mexican."

They seem to come from everywhere, for all kinds of reasons, as indeed they always have. "What Alexis de Tocqueville saw in America," John F. Kennedy once wrote, "was a society of immigrants, each of whom had begun life anew, on an equal footing. This was the secret of America: a nation of people with the fresh memory of old traditions who dared to explore new frontiers..." It was in memory of Kennedy's urging that the U.S. in 1965 abandoned the quota system that for nearly half a century had preserved the overwhelmingly European character of the nation. The new law invited the largest wave of immigration since the turn of the century, only this time the newcomers have arrived not from the Old World but from the Third World, especially Asia and Latin America. Of the 544,000 legal immigrants who came in fiscal 1984, the largest numbers were from Mexico (57,000, or more than 10%), followed by the Philippines (42,000) and Viet Nam (37,000). Britain came in ninth, with only 14,000.

This enormous migration is rapidly and permanently changing the face of America. It is altering its racial make-up, its landscapes and cityscapes, its taste in food and clothes and music, its entire perception of itself and its way of life. There have long been Chinatowns in American cities, but now there is Little Havana in Miami, Koreatown in Los Angeles, Little Saigon in Orange County, Calif., Little Odessa in Brooklyn, N.Y. Monterey Park, Calif., was the first U.S. city to have a Chinese-born woman as mayor, and the five-member city council includes two Hispanics and a Filipino American; Hialeah, Fla., has a Cuban-born mayor; Delaware, a Chinese-born Lieutenant Governor.

"It's fascinating," says New York Governor Mario Cuomo, the son of Italian immigrants. "For those of us who have been in the city for 50 years, it's wonderful to see the faces on the street now. Our diversity level has gone up." The new immigrants' contribution to America, Cuomo says, is "plus, plus, plus."

In addition to the half-million immigrants who are allowed to come to the U.S. each year, a substantial number arrive illegally. Estimates of the total vary widely. The Immigration and Naturalization Service apprehended 1.3 million illegal immigrants last year (many of them more than once) and guessed that several times that many had slipped through its net. The Census Bureau, however, estimated the total of illegal immigrants in the U.S. at between 3.5 million and 6 million in 1978. A National Academy of Sciences study issued last week denounced the INS statistics as "woefully inadequate" and put the total of illegals at no more than 2 million to 4 million. These include anyone from German students who deliberately overstay their visas to Haitian boat people who scramble ashore in South Florida, but roughly 60% of the illegals are Hispanics, and about two-thirds of these are Mexicans driven by poverty and unemployment across the highly porous 2,000-mile southern frontier.

The newest wave raises many questions: How many immigrants can the country absorb and at what rate? How much unskilled labor does a high-tech society need? Do illegals drain the economy or enrich it? Do newcomers gain their foothold at the expense of the poor and the black? Is it either possible or desirable to assimilate large numbers of immigrants from different races, languages and cultures? Will the advantages of diversity be outweighed by the dangers of separatism and conflict?

When asked about such issues, Americans sound troubled; their answers are ambiguous and sometimes contradictory. In a TIME poll taken by Yankelovich, Skelly & White Inc., only 27% agreed with the idea that "America should keep its doors open to people who wish to immigrate to the U.S. because that is what our heritage is all about." Two-thirds agreed that "this philosophy is no longer reasonable, and we should strictly limit the number." Some 56% said the number of legal immigrants was too high, and 75% wanted illegal immigrants to be tracked down. On the other hand, 66% approved of taking in people being persecuted in their homelands.

"One of the conditions of being an American," says Arthur Mann, professor of history at the University of Chicago, "is to be aware of the fact that a whole lot of people around you are different, different in their origins, their religions, their life-styles." Yet most Americans do not know exactly what to make of those differences. Of those polled by Yankelovich, 59% believe that immigrants generally end up on welfare (the best estimate is that less than 20% do), and 54% think they add to the crime problem. Yet 58% feel that immigrants are basically good, honest people, and 67% think they are productive citizens once they become established. One out of every two knows someone who came to the U.S. in the past few years; of them, a majority says this knowledge has changed their views for the better.

"Such a mess," says Roger Conner, director of the Federation for American Immigration Reform (FAIR), which advocates stronger restrictions. "We imagine ourselves as responsible for the whole world's problems, but immigration over the next 40 years will mean 50 million more people, and once they get here, they have children." "Our kids can't get jobs because the illegals take them," says Harold Ezell, Western commissioner of the INS. "If we don't control this border, we're going to lose control of this country." Says Conner: "The politicians don't want to talk about what is happening and what will happen."

But they do. "Every house needs a door, and every country needs a border," says Colorado's Democratic Governor Richard Lamm. If the U.S. fails to stop illegal immigration, he warns, "we shall leave a legacy of strife, violence and joblessness for our children." Florida's Senator Lawton Chiles is equally alarmist. "If we do not regain control of our borders...I think that within ten years, we will not recognize the United States as the United States we see today."

Much of the concern comes from people who favor continued immigration, but who fear the consequences if a slowdown in the economy were to heighten the sense that immigrants, especially illegal ones, take jobs away from Americans. "We could have a terrible backlash, a terrible period of repression," warns the Rev. Theodore Hesburgh, president of Notre Dame and chairman of the Select Commission on Immigration that was established by Congress in 1978. "People tend to forget that twice in our lifetime, this country has rounded up hundreds of thousands of Mexicans and pushed them back over the border. (About 500,000 were expelled in the early 1930s and 2.2 million from 1953 to 1955. Some were actually U.S. citizens, and some were thrown out more than once.) That was a terrible thing...but it could very well go on. Police sweeps from house to house, rounding up millions of people, pushing them back over a border, turning that border into a kind of armed camp."

Senator Alan Simpson, the Wyoming Republican who joined with Kentucky Democrat Romano Mazzoli to turn the Select Commission's findings into an immigration reform bill, estimates that Mexico would have to generate 700,000 new jobs every year (200,000 more than it is currently creating) just to keep its unemployment from getting worse. Simpson and Mazzoli have failed three times to get their bill passed, but Simpson, undaunted, presented yet another bill in May.

Xenophobia is not the force behind today's serious efforts to reform immigration. Simpson and other proponents recognize that most new immigrants, like the generations who came before them, work long and hard, and as much as possible on their own. Says Melvin Holli, professor of history at the University of Illinois, Chicago: "Their work ethic serves them well, and it serves us well. In a sense, they are refurbishing our work ethic." The new immigrants, says Lawrence H. Fuchs, chairman of American Studies at Brandeis, "have gumption, courage, ambition. They want to make it." This quality, which Fuchs has dubbed the "X-factor," is evident also among the children of immigrants. "They have a double X-factor: they are unencumbered by homesickness, alienation or the psychology of exile."

The American schoolroom has traditionally provided a hopeful glimpse of the nation's future, and some people still imagine it to be a Rockwellian scene of mostly pink-cheeked children spelling out the adventures of Dick and Jane. But come for a moment to the playground of the Franklin elementary school in Oakland, where black girls like to chant their jump-rope numbers in Chinese. "See you *mañana*," one student shouts with a Vietnamese accent. "*Ciao!*" cries another, who has never been anywhere near Italy. And let it be noted that the boy who won the National Spelling Bee in Washington last month was Balu Natarajan, 13, who was born in India, now lives in a suburb of Chicago, and speaks Tamil at home. "Milieu" was the word with which he defeated 167 other competitors. Let it also be noted that Hung Vu and Jean Nguyen in May became the first Vietnamese-born Americans to graduate from West Point.

The number of newcomers is large in itself (an amazing two-thirds of all the immigration in the world consists of people entering the U.S.), but their effect is heightened because they have converged on the main cities of half a dozen states. Nowhere is the change more evident than in California, which has become home to 64% of the country's Asians and 35% of its Hispanics. Next comes New York, followed by Texas, Florida, Illinois and New Jersey. Miami is 64% Hispanic, San Antonio 55%. Los Angeles has more Mexicans (2 million) than any other city except metropolitan Mexico City, and nearly half as many Salvadorans (300,000) as San Salvador.

These population shifts change all the bric-a-brac of life. A car in Los Angeles carries a custom license plate that says SIE SIE LI, meaning, in Chinese, "thank you." Graffiti sprayed in a nearby park send their obscure signals in Farsi. A suburban supermarket specializes in such Vietnamese delicacies as pork snouts and pickled banana buds. The Spanish-language soap opera *Tu o Nadie* gets the top ratings among independent stations every night at 8.

Such changes require adaptation not only in the schools and the marketplace but throughout society. The Los Angeles County court system now provides interpreters for 80 different languages from Albanian and Amharic to Turkish and Tongan. One judge estimates that nearly half his cases require an interpreter. Sometimes the results are freakish. A police officer testified that he had read a Chinese suspect his Miranda rights in Chinese, in the Taishan dialect. The suspect only understood Cantonese. The judge thereupon ruled out his confession.

These changes do not represent social decline or breakdown. The newcomers bring valuable skills and personal qualities: hope, energy, fresh perspectives. But the success stories should not blot out the fact that many aliens face considerable hardships with little immediate chance of advancement. Avan Wong, 20, came from Hong Kong in 1983 and hoped to go to college. She lives in the Bronx with her aged father, commutes two hours by bus to a job of up to twelve hours a day in a suburban restaurant. "I don't even read the newspapers," she says. "You don't have time. Once you go home, you go to sleep. Once you get up, you have to go to work. The only thing I'm happy about is that I can earn money and send it back to my mother. Nothing else. You feel so lonely here." College is not in sight.

José Luis Villa, who slipped across the Mexican border

last fall, has even worse prospects. He makes his home on a ragged mattress, one of about 30 lying in a row underneath the roaring traffic of Los Angeles' San Diego Freeway. Next to Villa's mattress stands a cardboard Perrier carton that contains most of his worldly possessions: a toothbrush, a tube of Colgate toothpaste, a cracked and yellowing bar of soap, a flashlight and a beginner's manual of English. Villa looks 13, but he claims to be 16. Every morning he hikes over to the "slave market" on Sawtelle Boulevard and hangs around with other youths until someone drives up and offers him $30 for a day's work shoveling gravel or moving furniture. "It's better than picking crops in Mexico," he says. "I'd rather go home than stay here forever, but I don't know when I can do that. I don't think about it, really."

Many immigrants are still the tired, the poor, the huddled masses whom the Statue of Liberty traditionally welcomed to New York Harbor. But the newcomers disembarking at Kennedy Airport or Miami or Los Angeles also include the successful. Baron Guy de Rothschild, for example, recently took refuge in New York City from the vagaries of French Socialism. Australia's publishing tycoon Rupert Murdoch, who has made a deal to buy seven television stations in the U.S., announced in May that he would become a U.S. citizen. The roster of Soviet immigrants includes not only the black-garbed babushkas huddled over their knitting in Brooklyn's Little Odessa but such artists as Alexander Solzhenitsyn and Mikhail Baryshnikov.

In greeting them with a mixture of sympathy and anxiety (lightly flavored with hypocrisy), Americans express one of their oldest national traditions. Thomas Jefferson, who proclaimed it self-evident that all men are created equal, felt considerable doubts about whether they were all equally well suited to be U.S. citizens. He complained of "the unbounded licentiousness" some of the newcomers displayed, and he warned that they would turn the nation into "a heterogeneous, incoherent, distracted mass." This at a time when the U.S. population was only 2 million, and still 80% from the British Isles.

Early in the 19th century came the great flood of Irish (2 million between 1815 and 1860) and Germans (1.5 million), some driven westward by political persecution, more by hunger and hardship. Philip Hone, mayor of New York in the 1820s, regarded both the Irish and the Germans as "filthy, intemperate, unused to the comforts of life and regardless of its proprieties." "Nativists" in Philadelphia raided Irish Catholic churches and burned Irish homes.

The next wave was more than twice as large—10 million from 1860 to 1890—but these were still mostly Northern Europeans: English, Dutch, Swedes, Norwegians. The third wave was even bigger: 16 million from 1890 to 1914, including a still unmatched record of 1.3 million in 1907 (when the total U.S. population was only 87 million). And to the dismay of the now established Irish and Germans, more than 80% of the newcomers were Eastern and Southern Europeans: Sicilians, Bulgarians, Greeks, Russian Jews fleeing the Czar's pogroms. This was the era in which Emma Lazarus wrote the Statue of Liberty's welcome to the huddled masses yearning to breathe free, but it was also the era in which the eminent Thomas Bailey Aldrich, editor of the *Atlantic Monthly*, composed a poem entitled "Unguarded Gates":

> *Wide open and unguarded stand our gates,*
> *And through them presses a wild motley throng—*
> *Men from the Volga and the Tartar steppes,*
> *Featureless figures of the Hoang-Ho*
> *Malayan, Scythian, Teuton, Kelt, and Slav...*
> *These bringing with them unknown gods and rites,*
> *Those, tiger passions, here to stretch their claws*
> *Accents of menace alien to our air,*
> *Voices that once the Tower of Babel knew!*

Even with the best intentions on all sides, the question of how to fit all these varieties of strangers into a relatively coherent American society remains difficult. Linda Wong, a Chinese-American official of the Mexican-American Legal Defense and Education Fund, sees trouble in the racial differences. "There is concern among whites that the new immigrants may be unassimilable," says Wong. "Hispanics and Asians cannot melt in as easily, and the U.S. has always had an ambivalent attitude toward newcomers. Ambivalent at best, racist at worst."

Many historians disagree. Hispanics, says Sheldon Maram, a professor of history at California State University at Fullerton, "are moving at about the same level of acculturation as the Poles and Italians earlier in the century. Once they've made it, they tend to move out of the ghetto and melt into the rest of society." Asians often have it easier because they come from urban middle-class backgrounds. "They are the most highly skilled of any immigrant group our country has ever had," says Kevin McCarthy, a demographer at the Rand Corp. in Santa Monica, Calif.

Immigrants struggling to make good in the U.S. often express dismay at what they see around them. "Many American values and customs which are very much part of the American way of life are seen [by Indians] as 'evil,'" writes Parmatma Saran, associate professor of sociology at Baruch College in Manhattan. "The American attitude toward sex... is viewed as immoral." Gaspar Ortega, a one-time Mexican prizefighter who is now a social worker in New Haven, Conn., is concerned about American treatment of the family. "I get disgusted when I see families separated. I blame the pressure of the dollar when both mother and father have to work and leave the kids in day care. In Mexico, babies are breast-fed with the milk of life. We were poor, but we were a family."

Still, the process of assimilation is inexorable. "As these students become Americanized, they want to eat hot dogs and hamburgers and pizza," says Mark Palermo, a teacher at Chicago's Senn High School. "They want designer jeans and bicycles and calculators and digital watches. We're taught maybe it's an error to be materialistic, but material things are what they want."

The genes change too. Statistically, according to one study, about 80% of European immigrants marry outside their own ethnic groups by the time they reach the third generation. Among Japanese Americans, at least in the Chicago area, the comparable figure is 15% in the second generation, 50% in the third.

How long, how complete and how painful the process of Americanization will be remains unclear. It is true that ethnic elitists have bewailed each succeeding wave of Irish or Germans or Greeks, but it is also true that the disparities among Korean merchants, Soviet Jews, Hmong tribesmen, French socialites and Haitian boat people are greater than any the U.S. or any other country has ever confronted. On the other hand, Americans are probably more tolerant of diversity than they once were. "America is much more of a pluralistic society now," says Peter Rose, professor of sociology at Smith College. "You don't hear so much talk about the melting pot today. The old ideology, the concerted effort to make people the same, has been overtaken by reality."

The question is not really whether the new Americans can be assimilated—they must be—but rather how the U.S. will be changed by that process. Economically, there will inevitably be strains, but most evidence indicates that the immigrants create more wealth than they consume. Socially and culturally, the diversity can hardly help benefiting the U.S. by acting as an antidote to everything that is bland and homogenized. The sad fact, indeed, is that uniformity is exactly what the immigrants' children will probably strive for, and their grandchildren achieve.

Politically, the prospects are uncertain. A large majority of immigrants—some illegal, some ineligible, some anxious, some apathetic—do not vote at all. Hispanic registration drives are trying to change that, but even in Los Angeles only 12% of the voters (vs. nearly 33% of the population) are Hispanic. Asians appear even more wary of political activism, though some are beginning to seek clout through financial contributions. By one estimate, they provided 25% of Los Angeles Mayor Tom Bradley's last campaign fund.

The new wave of immigrants, says former California Governor Jerry Brown, is gradually changing the country's angle of vision. "The Pacific Rim is becoming the focal point for economic and political concerns," he says. "This immigration will eventually move Europe to a lower priority in the way we look at the world." It is a mistake, though, to think of immigrants as an undifferentiated clump, politically or otherwise. Not only do they differ by national origin and social class and ideology but also according to whether they plan to stay permanently or eventually return home. "What binds Americans to one another, regardless of ethnicity or religion, is an American civic culture," says Brandeis Professor Fuchs. "It is the basis for the *unum* in

E pluribus unum. It is a complex of ideals, behaviors, institutions, symbols and heroes connected by American history and its great documents, the Declaration of Independence, the Bill of Rights, the Gettysburg Address. It is backed by a civil religion giving transcendent significance to those ideals. And it is the basis for accepting ethnic diversity while protecting individual rights. An American can be as ethnic as he or she wishes in private actions, but in public actions, the rules of the civic culture are binding."

Lam Ton, the Vietnamese restaurateur who wants to build a freedom arch in Chicago, says these things differently because he is not a professor at Brandeis, but he feels very strongly about the civic culture. "This is the last stand," he says. "There is nowhere else to run. We have to stick to this country and help it do better." ∎

To America with Skills

A wave of arrivals from the Far East enriches the country's talent pool

HISTORIAN GEORGE STEWART once amused himself by imagining the course of U.S. history if America had been discovered not on its Atlantic side by Christopher Columbus but on its Pacific side by a 15th century Chinese explorer named Ko Lum Bo. As hardy immigrants from the Orient began to establish colonies in the sweeping new continent, Stewart wrote in mock retrospect, they naturally adhered as closely as possible to the customs of their native land. Accordingly, "vast areas of the country were terraced and irrigated as rice paddies. The colonists continued to use their comfortable flowing garments, and pagodas dotted the landscape."

In 1985 it sometimes seems that the descendants of Ko Lum Bo, along with many of their neighbors throughout Asia, merely waited 500 years before turning Stewart's whimsy into something approaching reality. From the Flushing neighborhood in the New York City borough of Queens to the Sunset district of San Francisco, from the boatyards of Galveston Bay to the rich Minnesota farmlands, a burgeoning wave of Asian immigrants is pouring into the U.S. Some of the newcomers do indeed continue to wear the comfortable flowing garments of their native lands. And in cities like Westminster, a Los Angeles suburb, an elaborately decorated archway stands prominently among shops that are designed to be reminiscent of Saigon.

Asians have become, just within the past couple of years, the nation's fastest-expanding ethnic minority, as measured by growth through births and legal immigration. (Hispanics are probably still ahead if undocumented entries are counted.) Though Asians still number only around 3.6 million, or 1.6% of the total U.S. population, their ranks have been swelling at an unprecedented rate since the reform of immigration laws in 1965. Last year alone, more Asian immigrants came to the U.S.—282,000—than in the three decades from 1931 to 1960. More than half settled in California, which has the nation's largest Asian population (64%). The torrent of new arrivals is not likely to diminish in the foreseeable future: about 1 million other Asians have already applied and received preliminary clearance to come to America. By the year 2010, the Asian population in the U.S. is expected to more than double.

The newcomers are drastically changing the Asian-American mix. The 1980 census showed that Japanese Americans, the largest Asian subgroup since 1910, have dropped to third place (701,000), after Chinese Americans (806,000) and Filipino Americans (775,000). Japanese Americans play almost no role in the current wave of Asian immigration. Within the next 30 years, demographers expect Filipinos to become the largest group of Asian Americans, followed in order by Chinese, Koreans, Vietnamese, Asian Indians and, in sixth place, Japanese.

While the projections are impressive, what really distinguishes the Asians is that, of all the new immigrants, they are compiling an astonishing record of achievement. Asians are represented far beyond their population share at virtually every top-ranking university: their contingent in Harvard's freshman class has risen from 3.6% to 10.9% since 1976, and it currently stands at 18.6% at Berkeley, 18.7% at Cal Tech and 8.7% at Princeton. At Columbia, enrollment in the engineering school is more than 20%

Asian. In this year's Westinghouse Science Talent Search, nine of the 40 semifinalists were Asians, as were three of the ten winners.

Partly as a result of their academic accomplishments, Asians are climbing the economic ladder with remarkable speed. The 1980 census showed that median household income for the group as a whole was $22,700, exceeding not only that of American families in general ($19,900) but also the level reported by whites ($20,800). The national median was topped by the Japanese ($27,350), the Asian Indians ($24,990), the Filipinos ($23,680), the Chinese ($22,550) and Koreans ($20,450); among major Asian groups, only the Vietnamese ($12,840) fell below it. The household statistics are somewhat misleading, to be sure, since Asian families are much more likely than whites to rely on the paychecks of two or more family members. Even so, the overall gains in Asian earning power have come far more rapidly than those for any prior surge of immigrants, who had to labor a generation or more before catching up to average living standards.

Asians are well represented in the ranks of managers and professionals. Nearly half of Asian Indians fit into those high-status job categories, almost twice the rate for whites; a survey conducted by the Chicago *Reporter*, a monthly newsletter about minorities found that 39% of all Asians in that city were managers or professionals. The Asian hegira has also spawned a new class of small entrepreneurs, many of whom work schedules that make the 40-hour week look like child's play. Asian-owned fish markets, green groceries and restaurants have breathed fresh life into fading inner-city districts.

No single factor can account for the perseverance of so diverse a group. But a psychological insight is provided by Vachirin Chea, 27, a survivor of the Cambodian death camps who has prospered in banking and real estate in Lowell, Mass. "I have to be an American now," he says. "But I get my strength from being Cambodian. If I had been raised here in America, I would not have that kind of strength. All that suffering, the anger in me, is what keeps me going."

Unlike the mass migrations of Europeans to the U.S., the Asian movement is fueled largely by the educated middle class. Except for the Indochinese, with their large refugee contingent, the new Asian arrivals are at least twice as likely as a native-born American to be college graduates. Moreover, since many others are admitted because of a desirable vocational background, the group as a whole has greatly enriched the nation's talent pool. Says Rand Corp. Demographer Kevin McCarthy: "The Asians are the most highly skilled of any immigrant group our country has ever had."

Given the rich diversity of Asian immigrants' backgrounds, it is all but impossible to generalize about their experiences in becoming Americans. For many the closest thing to a common hurdle is the daunting necessity of adjusting to a new culture, an especially difficult challenge to non-English speakers. "English is the great prohibitor," says Martha Copenhaver, the director of a Southeast Asian education program in Arlington, Va. "Without it, you can't advance even if you are otherwise qualified."

Most Asians either have some knowledge of English before coming to the U.S. or quickly acquire the rudiments of an English vocabulary, often by methods bordering on the draconian. Son Nguyen, 18, a Vietnamese-born high school graduate in Houston, recalls that his brother-in-law required him to memorize one page of an English dictionary after school each day. More conventional teaching techniques are available throughout the U.S. in federally sponsored language programs. Those fortunate enough to have studied English at home can often make the transition easily. Cal Tech Senior Hojin Ahn, 24, a native South Korean, arrived in Los Angeles three years ago able to read and write English proficiently. Last year Ahn compiled a better-than-perfect 4.1 grade average, among the highest at Cal Tech, and was awarded a partial scholarship for his senior year.

The other all but universally shared experience is finding a job. That can be a profoundly humbling experience, especially for highly educated Asians. Degrees and credentials that took years to attain suddenly count for little or nothing. Jei Hak Suh, 43, gave up a banking career in South Korea to move with his wife and two young children to Los Angeles in 1981; with his English far from polished, he realized that the banking jobs available to him would not pay enough to support his family. He is now a construction worker.

For most the climb is frustrating but ultimately successful. Antonio Cube, 49, a Filipino attorney, immigrated with his wife and two children in 1970. Accustomed to the services of three maids and a driver at home, but unqualified to practice law in the U.S., Cube found work instead as a computer encoder in a bank. "I almost went home," he says now. "But the bank sent me to technical schools and moved me up little by little. For five years my wife and I worked two full-time jobs." Today Cube is a supervisor for Seattle's Rainier Bank and owns not only his own home but three other houses in the metropolitan area. Two of them, now rented, are earmarked for his children, both university students. "We feel that life is about saving for the future," says Cube. "We live for our children."

Like previous generations of immigrants, many Asians seek to realize their personal American dream not just by finding a good job but by starting their own business, the ultimate statement of independence. These enterprises also provide a chance to maximize the productive potentials of entire families and a way to absorb newly arrived members, who often become eligible for immigration after the pioneering one attains citizenship. The entrepreneurial impulse runs strongest among Koreans. Nearly one in eight Korean Americans is self-employed, by far the highest rate for any ethnic group. Says John Kim, a Korean-born New York lawyer: "One thing about Koreans is that they don't like to be dominated by anybody."

Many Asians complain that they are frequently the victims of racial prejudice. Lucie Cheng, head of the Asian Studies Center at the University of California, Los Angeles, charges that administrators, intent on curbing the decline in white enrollment, are actually causing an unfair reduction in admissions of Asian students. It is a claim that officials stoutly deny. While Asians seeking to buy or rent homes suffer far less hostility than in the past, the tendency of many ethnic communities to settle in clusters still bothers some whites. During the rapid influx of Chinese into California's Monterey Park, for example, bumper stickers appeared reading WILL THE LAST AMERICAN TO LEAVE MONTEREY PARK PLEASE BRING THE FLAG.

Any sign of discrimination at the portals of colleges and universities would be particularly alarming to Asian immigrants, because they almost universally see their children's future in terms of higher education. In part, this blind faith in academic achievement stems from the normal yearning of all immigrants to bootstrap their families into the comforts of middle-class American life. But it also bespeaks a deeper ethic permeating many Asian societies. Says Yong-Il Yi, 55, a New York City real estate broker from Seoul: "In Asia, if you don't have a higher education, you are a second-class citizen."

An important source of solace is maintaining ties to the old culture. This is becoming considerably easier to do as more and more Asians arrive in America. Their swelling numbers create a demand for many of the goods and services available at home, from Indian spices to Chinese acupuncture to Laotian bamboo flutes. Murali Narayanan, 32, a design group supervisor at Bell Laboratories in Naperville, Ill., makes a point of driving five times a year to Chicago's North Devon Avenue, which teems with Indian grocery stores, restaurants and sari shops. Says he: "You feel comfortable just walking down the street." New technology has added to the links available to the old country: many Asian food shops now rent video-cassettes of movies and television programs produced in Hong Kong, Taiwan and Bombay.

Still, however closely new Asian Americans choose to follow their previous ways, the vast majority look to the future as Americans. Filipino Americans or Chinese Americans or Indian Americans, perhaps. But if asked to drop one part of their compound self-description, most would do away with the first. A few commemorate the transition by Anglicizing their surnames and many more by choosing American first names for their children, the real beacons of the future. Wai-wah Cheng, 57, came to Los Angeles from Hong Kong, where he ran a successful garment business. After seven years in the U.S. he still works as a chef in a Chinese restaurant, and his wife, Nyan-ying, 52, is a seamstress. Son Joe, 22, graduated this year from Cal Tech with a degree in physics and begins work this month at California Jet Propulsion Laboratory. "I think about what they sacrificed, and it was a lot," says Joe. "You have to give up to get." ■

Caught Between Two Worlds

New immigrant children find it hard to mesh old values with new beliefs

"MY PARENTS ARE LETTING GO of some of their ways," insists Joo Hee Yoo, 13, who came to Los Angeles from South Korea ten years ago. "They are beginning to understand that America is a place of freedom." Maybe so, but the rules for Joo, who now goes by the name Jennifer, and her two younger sisters would strike many U.S. youngsters as unduly restrictive. No telephone calls to or from boys. No curling irons or pierced ears until age 15. No hair spray and makeup until after high school. "When you are a student, you should look like a student," says her mother Hae Sun Yoo. "That is hard to tell children when society contradicts that here." She and her husband have the solution. "When our daughters complain, 'Why can't we do this?' we explain to them they are Korean," says Hae Sun Yoo. But Jennifer is not totally swayed. Says she: "You can have a hairstyle and still have an education."

While other 18-year-olds agonize over which pretty dress or funky pair of shoes to buy, Juniace Sene Charles worries about "what this month's electricity and water bill are going to be." The petite teenager, who came to Miami with her mother, younger brother and sister from Haiti two years ago, is the family's financial mainstay. Every day when classes end at Edison High School, she rushes to her job at Wendy's on Biscayne Boulevard. Her take-home weekly salary of about $75 is augmented occasionally by her mother's earnings from babysitting. "I'm chief of the household," she says. Juniace is fiercely loyal to her family, but determined to make her own life: "I'm going to college, and I'm going to be an agronomist. Here in America I can make it."

Dressed in light cords and deck shoes, with sunglasses dangling from his sweat-shirt, Son Nguyen, 18, seems like any other carefree high school graduate in Houston. "But if my mother saw me today, she would be shocked," confesses Son, who fled Ho Chi Minh City at age eight with a younger brother, his older sister and her husband. "I wouldn't be her boy anymore. I would be an American stranger." Still, within the two-story brick house he shares with eight other people, Son becomes a model Vietnamese youth, industrious, responsible, deferential. In that household, Vietnamese is spoken, Vietnamese food is prepared, Vietnamese customs are followed. Son's mother has not been permitted to leave Ho Chi Minh City, and after a decade of separation, he often wonders how he would greet her. With an exuberant American-style hug? Or with a formal, respectful hello? "I'm so changed now," Son says, "that if I faced her, I wouldn't know what to do."

These conflicting tugs of direction are a perplexing constant in the lives of millions of youthful American immigrants. Growing up in two cultures is at once a source of frustration and delight, shame and pride, guilt and satisfaction. It can be both a barrier to success and a goad to accomplishment, a dislocating burden or an enriching benison. First-generation Americans have an "astonishing duality," declares Harvard Psychiatrist Robert Coles, himself the son of an English immigrant. "They tend to have a more heightened awareness both of being American and also of being connected to another country."

Immigrants' children are sometimes agonizingly aware of the traits that mark them as foreign. Among these: their names. Jorge Orellana, 8, the son of immigrants from El Salvador, says classmates in a Chicago school taunted him with the words "Mexican kid." He now introduces himself as George. Son Nguyen's 16-year-old brother asks new acquaintances whether they want "my American or Vietnamese name." He is Tien to his family, Tim to others.

Parents may encourage such a switch. Says Vietnamese Refugee Le Giau, a resident of Fountain Valley, Calif.: "They should change their names because it's easier for them when they go to work." His three daughters, Hanh, Tien and Trang, are now known as Hannah, Christina and Jennifer. Food too can be a sensitive issue. "My brother wants to become American all the way," says Imelda Ortiz, 17, who left Mexico for Houston at age one. "He tells my mother to cook American food like meat loaf and potatoes. Instead we cook rice and beans and *fajitas* [skirt steak]."

Parents' speaking a foreign language can embarrass children. Riki Hayashi, 6, shocked his Japanese-born mother Kaori last year by announcing that he did not want her to speak her native tongue when his schoolmates came to visit at their Culver City, Calif., home. "All his friends are American, and in his concept of himself he is American," sighs Kaori. The parents' poor command of English can prove awkward. Children are pressed into service for their immigrant parents in all kinds of circumstances: when the electric company sends a dunning notice, the landlord needs a lease signed, a policeman needs information.

Unlike offspring of native-born Americans, many children of immigrants learn early that frivolity is a luxury they can ill afford. Frequently they begin working before they become teenagers. "They're capitalists, almost to the person," notes Psychiatrist Coles. After school and on weekends, Le Giau's four children help out at the family's pastry shop. Hannah, 18, minds the cash register and serves customers. Vinh, 17, who has kept his name because it is easy to pronounce as "Vin," works the cleanup detail. Christina, 15, washes dishes, and Jennifer, 12, aids her mother Thérèse with the baking and cake decorating. "American children don't understand," says Hannah. "They don't know why I can't go to the beach." As a consequence, many immigrants' children look upon homegrown Americans only as casual friends.

For the children of emigres, the emphasis is on education. "When they have good knowledge, they make good money," explains Vong Ly, a Hmong tribesman from Laos who now lives in Banning, Calif., with seven of his nine children, ages eight to 17. Medicine, law, engineering, business and computer science are the favored fields. Le Trinh, a Vietnamese-born Chinese who arrived in Houston five years ago, will enter Texas A & M in the fall to study engineering. "It's not my favorite subject," she admits. "I love teaching, but that pays too low."

Highly motivated, the children of immigrants frequently feel guilty and disgraced when they do not excel at their studies. Le Giau expressed pride but daughter Jennifer was ashamed when she came in second in a spelling contest. Son Nguyen, who plans to study engineering and then become a doctor, is still concerned that he has been infected by slack U.S. student habits. Reason: instead of straight A's, he pulled a few B's in his senior year in high school.

Immigrant parents, however insistent, are not always successful in excluding distracting American influences. Le Vinh's jet black hair is cut in a moderate punk style, and he sports fashionable, wide-shouldered jackets, to his father's distress. "He would have me in the preppie look," says Vinh with disdain. Retorts Le Giau: "When I went to school we wore uniforms." Imelda Ortiz finds herself in a tug-of-war with her mother over American teens' signature apparel: tight jeans. "My mom says I look like a *Solid Gold* dancer

New world, old ways: Teacher and student in an Islamic school in Illinois

and makes me take them off," complains Imelda. "She looks at the way some Anglo girls dress and says they don't have *dominio propio* [self-control]."

The big problem, though, is dating. "I keep telling my mom that it is not bad to date and that she should trust me," says Imelda, "but a boy can't even come over to my house to talk to me. Not even outside on the steps. My mother says, 'It looks bad, no respect to the house.'" Many boys also find themselves on a short tether. Asked about dating, Vinh tosses two wallet-size photos of girls onto the table. A disapproving stare from his father and Vinh promptly jams them into his pocket. "He's the one I worry about," says Le Giau. "Girls call him a lot. I have to cut off the phone. He doesn't have time for girls. He has to study."

Once the critical faculties of the children are sharpened by schooling and broader cultural exposure, however, the gap between them and their parents usually widens. That separation is the natural consequence of what Norman Podhoretz, editor of *Commentary*, calls "the brutal bargain." As Podhoretz, the son of Jews from Galicia, explains, "The more you succeed in the wider world, the more estranged you become from your parents' mores and values. The paradox is you betray your parents by obeying them."

The unusual closeness of immigrant families makes this struggle for autonomy painful to both sides. High School Junior Imelda Ortiz plans to study engineering in college. Her parents expect her to attend the University of Houston while living at home, a pattern set by her two sisters. But Imelda wants to enroll in the University of Texas at Austin. "I'm afraid to go out on my own," she admits, "but even

though it may turn out bad, at least I'll learn, right? I'll realize what is or is not for me." Le Giau and his wife Therese expect their children to live at home until they wed and hope to arrange marriages for their daughters after they finish college. But the girls are already balking. Says Jennifer: "If the decision is up to them, they'd choose a smart man in business. I want a nice, funny man who will not always worry about his work."

Despite the tendency to revolt, many children do not want to jettison their cultural heritage. Imelda Ortiz plans to raise her children in Mexican fashion. "I'll be strict, but not as strict as my mother," she says. "I feel like an American about work, education, external things. But I feel like a Mexican inside."

To be both American and Mexican or American and anything else almost always means that one is not wholly either. For some, the dual identity breeds a sense of not belonging anywhere. But an intense attempt by an individual to wipe out an entire side of his or her character can end in tragedy. In 1979, Phéde Eugene landed on a Florida beach. He was twelve and one of the maligned boat people from Haiti. Desperate to belong, he changed his name to Fred, learned to speak fluent English and became an A student at Miami's Edison High School. He sang in the school choir and worked at a local Burger King to earn money to buy a car. No one, not even his girlfriend, suspected his Haitian background.

Then one evening last fall, his mask slipped: Fred's sister dropped in at the fast-food outlet and spoke to him in Creole in front of his girlfriend. Next day Fred bought a gun. Two days later he drove his prized '73 red-and-white Mercury to a church parking lot and shot himself to death. He was 17. Says his father, Ikanes Eugene, who shuttles migrant workers in his bus to Florida's vegetable fields: "He felt the rejection of Haitians to the point he hid his own origin."

Most children of immigrants do manage to make a satisfactory amalgam of their two worlds, keeping what they like and discarding what they do not. Le Trinh is just beginning to forge her own cultural alloy. She plays records by popular Vietnamese artists but likes European classical music. She has read *Wuthering Heights* and *Jane Eyre* in Vietnamese, but now also appreciates the novels in the original English. She favors Vietnamese food, but has taken to one American custom without hesitation, gabbing on the telephone for hours on weekends. Like many immigrant children, Le Trinh insists that shunning a familial heritage is simply not an option worth considering. "I don't think you should give up your past," she declares, "but you should also find a way to fit into life here. I want to get along with Americans but keep my culture." She pauses, then gives a tiny shake of her head and asks, "Do I want too much?" ∎

For Learning or Ethnic Pride?

Parents, politicians and pedagogues battle over bilingual classes

JUDY COLLINS, A MOTHER who lives in Ventura County, Calif., is fighting mad. "They are teaching kids the Pledge of Allegiance in Spanish," she says, of bilingual classes at San Cayetano Elementary School, which her daughter attends. "It's a United States flag," she adds indignantly. "They need to learn that in English."

Collins' exasperation reflects the feelings of millions of Americans on one side of an inflammatory issue: bilingual education in America's public schools. More than 1.3 million students whose primary language is not English are enrolled in federal, state or local study programs that provide instruction in their native tongues. These programs have their roots in the federal Bilingual Education Act, passed as a noble experiment in 1968. Its original aim was to generate optional instruction that would help immigrant youngsters and native-born Hispanic-American children learn English quickly. Meanwhile, they were to move ahead in their schoolwork by using their own language as much as necessary. That at least is what Congress thought it was doing.

Proponents of bilingual learning, however, see it not only as a way to help students with limited English proficiency (LEP) make the transition into the mainstream of American classrooms but as a means for preserving the students' native language and culture. Today bilingual programs are conducted in a gallimaufry of around 80 tongues, ranging from Spanish to Lithuanian to Micronesian Yapese. Some of these courses are designed to maintain a student's original language indefinitely, bolstering the language with enrichment studies in indigenous art, music, literature and history. The annual cost is well over $350 million.

Supporters argue that instruction in children's native tongues is essential to providing them with an adequate education. "The Federal Government has a profound responsibility to these children," says James Lyons, chief lobbyist for the National Association for Bilingual Education. But critics hotly question whether such expenditures are worthwhile. They also challenge the role of the Federal Government in favoring or heavily funding any particular method of instruction, much less sponsoring cultural-maintenance studies. "The intent of bilingual education has been distorted into a vehicle for a bicultural approach to education," says Robert Sweet, a member of the White House Office of Policy Development.

Bilingual learning, no longer just an optional classroom service, has become a fundamental issue of public policy.

"It's cultural, it's social, it's political," says Robert Calfee, professor of education and psychology at Stanford University. Nationally, by some estimates, 3.6 million school-age youngsters are rated as LEPs, 80% of them Hispanic. The voting bloc represented by their parents has generated congressional support for expanding bilingualism into cultural maintenance. Even the White House is gun-shy about attacking the concept too vehemently, although the Administration considers it both inappropriate and wasteful.

Some see bilingual education as potentially worse than that. Former California Senator S.I. Hayakawa believes the result of language maintenance could be to foster divisiveness like that of the French-speaking separatist movement in Canada that peaked in the 1970s. As an intended antidote, he introduced and still lobbies for a constitutional amendment that would make English the official U.S. language for government affairs.

Backers of bilingual education embrace it as a legal right in a dozen states. Federal guidelines specify only that school districts with more than 5% minority nationals among their pupils provide LEPs with effective English instruction. Moreover, the Supreme Court, in a 1974 decision involving 1,800 Chinese students in San Francisco, confirmed that the district had to provide for the education of the English-deficient students; but the court did not say how. "Teaching English to the students of Chinese ancestry who do not speak the language is one choice" in the method of instruction, wrote Justice William Douglas in the court's unanimous decision. "Giving instructions to this group in Chinese is another. There may be others."

Indeed there are, for if ever a law has come to mean different things to different people, it has been the Bilingual Education Act and its derivative edicts.

• To Ivan Quintanilla, 9, who just finished fourth grade in Miami, bilingual education has meant learning flawless English in the two years since he arrived from Cuba. He has also been able to keep up to grade level in his courses through a mix of his native tongue and English. "When we are in the Spanish part of our studies we all speak Spanish," says Ivan. "But when we are in the English part or in recess no one speaks Spanish." He concludes, "You must speak English if you want to have friends and be happy."

• To slim, smiling Quoc Cong Tran, 16, who arrived at a San Francisco high school from Viet Nam six months ago, language instruction means a minimum of short-term help in classroom Vietnamese, while he loads up on English in courses called English as a second language. "My future, I choose American," says Quoc.

• To Benjamin Viera, 37, a native New Yorker married to a Puerto Rican wife who speaks Spanish around the house, bilingual education used to mean trouble in communicating with his son, now going into eighth grade. Six years ago Viera switched the boy out of a bilingual program and into regular classes. "I'd talk to him in English at home, and he couldn't understand me," complains Viera. "He'd go and ask his mother what I said. His teacher was giving him Spanish all day and very little English."

• To Jackie Gutierrez, 8, of the Santa Clara pueblo in New Mexico, bilingual learning has meant sitting in a twice-a-week class listening and responding to Leon Baca, a teacher of the ancient Tewa language. During a recent session, Baca grunted, *"Nyaemangeri!"* The students replied, "Left side!" "Haa [yes]," intoned Baca; then *"Ko'ringeri!"* The children shouted, "Right side!" Asked later what the enrichment class was all about, Jackie replied, "We're learning to speak Indian."

To advocates, the learning experiences of Jackie Gutierrez and Ivan Quintanilla are what the bilingual programs are all about: easing the transition to English or holding on to one's ethnic heritage, or both. "It is very important to us that kids take pride in their own culture," says Ligaya Avenida, director of bilingual programs for the San Francisco unified school district, where some 44 languages are spoken. "In the process of acquiring English you have to develop their cognitive abilities without losing their self-image."

Others disagree vehemently. Says Cuban-born Carol Pendas Whitten, head of the Department of Education's Office of Bilingual Education: "If parents want to preserve the native language, that's fine, but I do not think it should be the role of the school." Another opponent is Bill Honig,

California's superintendent of public instruction, who insists such instruction "should be transitional...Bilingual education is not going to be used as a cultural isolation program."

Significantly, no one has proved beyond doubt that LEP youngsters learn faster or better through bilingual instruction than by any other methods, including old-fashioned "submersion," i.e., going cold turkey into regular classrooms where only English is spoken. Says Adriana de Kanter, one of the authors of a controversial 1981 study sponsored by the Department of Education: "Basically we found that sometimes [bilingualism] worked, and sometimes it didn't, and that most of the time, it made no difference at all."

Meanwhile, dedicated teachers are laboring to lead their LEPs into the mainstream, either with strict bilingual methods or with broad variations on them. In El Paso, public secondary schools are using the High Intensity Language Training program that emphasizes training in English as a second language. Until 1982, many of El Paso's Hispanic high schoolers either failed or dropped out. Today HILT students regularly appear on the honor roll; many are members of the National Honor Society and several have graduated at the top of their classes.

At Brooklyn's P.S. 189, Principal Josephine Bruno runs her school on a bilingual basis, switching back and forth so that students take one class in English and another in their native tongue. Whatever language they use, Bruno's charges are getting the message: 86% of her 1,130 students read English at grade level. Such results prompt Bruno, and thousands like her, to brush aside the furor over bilingual education. "If the kids are learning," she asks, "who cares?"

Unfortunately, this neglects the bigger question: Are they learning because of bilingual studies or in spite of them? Nearly 20 years and hundreds of millions of dollars have gone by, but the question remains. ∎

■ ESSAY   JUNE 13, 1983

Against a Confusion of Tongues

William A. Henry III

"We have room for but one language here, and that is the English language, for we intend to see that the crucible turns our people out as Americans and not as dwellers in a polyglot boarding house."

—THEODORE ROOSEVELT

IN THE STORE WINDOWS of Los Angeles, gathering place of the world's aspiring peoples, the sign today ought to read, "English spoken here." Supermarket price tags are often written in Korean, restaurant menus in Chinese, employment-office signs in Spanish. In the new city of dreams, where gold can be earned if not found on the sidewalk, there are laborers and businessmen who have lived five, ten, 20 years in America without learning to speak English. English is not the common denominator for many of these new Americans. Disturbingly, some of them insist it need not be.

America's image of itself as a melting pot, enriched by every culture yet subsuming all of them, dates back far beyond the huddled yearning masses at the Baja California border and Ellis Island, beyond the passage in steerage of victims of the potato famine and the high-minded Teutonic settlements in the nascent Midwest. Just months after the Revolution was won, in 1782, French-American Writer Michel-Guillaume-Jean de Crévecoeur said of his adopted land: "Individuals of all nations are melted into a new race of men." Americans embittered by the wars of Europe knew that fusing diversity into unity was more than a poetic ideal, it was a practical necessity. In 1820 future Congressman Edward Everett warned, "From the days of the Tower of Babel, confusion of tongues has ever been one of the most active causes of political misunderstanding."

The successive waves of immigrants did not readily embrace the new culture, even when intimidated by the xenophobia of the know-nothing era or two World Wars. Says Historian James Banks: "Each nationality group tried desperately to remake North America in the image of its native land." When the question arose of making the U.S. multiligual or multicultural in public affairs, however, Congress stood firm. In the 1790s, 1840s and 1860s, the lawmakers voted down pleas to print Government documents in German. Predominantly French-speaking Louisiana sought statehood in 1812; the state constitution that it submitted for approval specified that its official language would be English. A century later, New Mexico was welcomed into the union, but only after an influx of settlers from the North and East had made English, not Spanish, the majority tongue.

Occasional concentrations of immigrants were able to win local recognition of their language and thereby enforce an early form of affirmative action: by 1899 nearly 18,000 pupils in Cincinnati divided their school time between courses given in German and in English, thus providing employment for 186 German-speaking teachers. In 1917 San Francisco taught German in eight primary schools, Italian in six, French in four and Spanish in two. Yet when most cities consented to teach immigrant children in their native Chinese or Polish or Yiddish or Gujarati, the clearly stated goal was to transform the students as quickly as possible into speakers of English and full participants in society.

Now, however, a new bilingualism and biculturalism is being promulgated that would deliberately fragment the nation into separate, unassimilated groups. The movement seems to take much of its ideology from the black separatism of the 1960s but derives its political force from the unprecedented raw numbers—15 million or more—of a group linked to a single tongue, Spanish. The new metaphor is not the melting pot but the salad bowl, with each element distinct. The biculturalists seek to use public services, particularly schools, not to Americanize the young but to heighten their consciousness of belonging to another heritage. Contends Tomas A. Arciniega, vice president for academic affairs at California State University at Fresno: "The promotion of cultural differences has to be recognized as a valid and legitimate educational goal." Miguel Gonzalez-Pando, director of the Center for Latino Education at Florida International University in Miami, says: "I speak Spanish at home, my social relations are mostly in Spanish, and I am raising my daughter as a Cuban American. It is a question of freedom of choice." In Gonzalez-Pando's city, where Hispanics out-number whites, the anti-assimilationist theory has become accepted practice: Miami's youth can take twelve years of bilingual public schooling with no pretense made that the program is transitional toward anything. The potential for separatism is greater in Los Angeles. Philip Hawley, president of the Carter Hawley Hale retail store chain, cautions: "This is the only area in the U.S. that over the next 50 years could have a polarization into two distinct cultures, of the kind that brought about the Quebec situation in Canada." Professor Rodolfo Acuña of California State University at Northridge concurs. Says Acuña: "Talk of secession may come when there are shrinking economic resources and rising expectations among have-not Hispanics."

Already the separatists who resist accepting English have won laws and court cases mandating provision of social services, some government instructions, even election ballots in Spanish. The legitimizing effect of these decisions can be seen in the proliferation of billboards, roadside signs and other public communications posted in Spanish. Acknowledges Professor Ramon Ruiz of the University of California at San Diego: "The separatism question is with us already." The most portentous evidence is in the classrooms. Like its political cousins, equal opportunity and social justice, bilingual education is a catchall term that means what the speaker wishes it to mean.

There are at least four ways for schools to teach students who speak another language at home:

1) Total immersion in English, which relies on the proven ability of children to master new languages. Advocates of bilingual education argue that this approach disorients children and sometimes impedes their progress in other subjects, because those who have already mastered several grades' worth of material in their first language may be compelled to take English-language classes with much younger or slower students.

2) Short-term bilingual education, which may offer a full curriculum but is directed toward moving students into English-language classes as rapidly as possible. In a report last month by a Twentieth Century Fund task force, mem-

bers who were disillusioned with the performance of elaborate bilingual programs urged diversion of federal funds to the teaching of English. The panel held: "Schoolchildren will never swim in the American mainstream unless they are fluent in English."

3) Dual curriculum, which permits students to spend several years making the transition. This is the method urged by many moderate Hispanic, Chinese and other ethnic minority leaders. Says Historian Ruiz: "The direct approach destroys children's feelings of security. Bilingual education eases them from something they know to something they do not."

4) Language and cultural maintenance, which seeks to enhance students' mastery of their first language while also teaching them English. In Hispanic communities, the language training is often accompanied by courses in ethnic heritage. Argues Miami Attorney Manuel Diaz, a vice chairman of the Spanish American League Against Discrimination: "Cultural diversity makes this country strong. It is not a disease."

The rhetoric of supporters of bilingualism suggests that theirs may be a political solution to an educational problem. Indeed, some of them acknowledge that they view bilingual programs as a source of jobs for Hispanic administrators, teachers and aides. In cities with large minority enrollments, says a Chicago school principal who requested anonymity, "those of us who consider bilingual education ineffective are afraid that if we say so we will lose our jobs." Lawrence Uzzell, president of Learn Inc., a Washington-based research foundation, contends that Hispanic educational activists are cynically protecting their own careers. Says Uzzell: "The more the Hispanic child grows up isolated, the easier it is for politicians to manipulate him as part of an ethnic voting bloc."

The signal political success for bilingualism has been won at the U.S. Department of Education. After the Supreme Court ruled in 1974 that Chinese-speaking students were entitled to some instruction in a language they could understand, the DOE issued "informal" rules that now bind more than 400 school districts. Immersion in English, even rapid transition to English, does not satisfy the DOE; the rules compel school systems to offer a full curriculum to any group of 20 or more students who share a foreign language. The DOE rules have survived three presidencies, although Jesse Soriano, director of the Reagan Administration's $138 million bilingual program, concedes, "This is money that could be spent more effectively." About half of students from Spanish-speaking homes drop out before the end of high school; of the ones who remain, 30% eventually score two or more years below their age group on standardized tests. But it is hard to demonstrate the value of any bilingual approach in aiding those students. In 1982 Iris Rotberg reported in the *Harvard Education Review*: "Research findings have shown that bilingual programs are neither better nor

worse than other instructional methods." Indeed, the DOE's review found that of all methods for teaching bilingual students English and mathematics, only total immersion in English clearly worked.

One major problem in assessing the worth of bilingual programs is that they often employ teachers who are less than competent in either English or Spanish, or in the specific subjects they teach. In a 1976 test of 136 teachers and aides in bilingual programs in New Mexico, only 13 could read and write Spanish at third-grade level. Says former Boston School Superintendent Robert Wood: "Many bilingual teachers do not have a command of English, and after three years of instruction under them, children also emerge without a command of English." Another complicating factor is the inability of researchers to determine whether the problems of Hispanic students stem more from language difficulty or from their economic class. Many Hispanic children who are unable to speak English have parents with little education who hold unskilled jobs; in school performance, these students are much like poor blacks and whites. Notes Harvard's Nathan Glazer: "If these students do poorly in English, they may be doing poorly in a foreign language."

Even if the educational value of bilingual programs were beyond dispute, there would remain questions about their psychic value to children. Among the sharpest critics of bilingualism is Author Richard Rodriguez, who holds a Berkeley Ph.D. in literature and grew up in a Spanish-speaking, working-class household; in his autobiography *Hunger of Memory*, Rodriguez argues that the separation from his family that a Hispanic child feels on becoming fluent in English is necessary to develop a sense of belonging to American society. Writes Rodriguez: "Bilingualists do not seem to realize that there are two ways a person is individualized. While one suffers a diminished sense of private individuality by becoming assimilated into public society, such assimilation makes possible the achievement of public individuality." By Rodriguez's reasoning, the discomfort of giving up the language of home is far less significant than the isolation of being unable to speak the language of the larger world.

The dubious value of bilingualism to students is only part of America's valid concern about how to absorb the Hispanic minority. The U.S., despite its exceptional diversity, has been spared most of the ethnic tensions that beset even such industrialized nations as Belgium and Spain. The rise of a large group, detached from the main population by language and custom, could affect the social stability of the country. Hispanic leaders, moreover, acknowledge that their constituents have been less inclined to become assimilated than previous foreign-language communities, in part because many of them anticipated that after earning and saving, they would return to Puerto Rico, Mexico, South America or Cuba. Says Historian Doyce Nunis of the University of Southern California: "For the first time in American experience, a large immigrant group may be electing to bypass the processes of acculturation." Miami Mayor Maurice Ferré, a Puerto Rican, claims that in his city a resident can go from birth through school and working life to death without ever having to speak English. But most Hispanic intellectuals claim that their communities, like other immigrant groups before them, cling together only to combat discrimination.

The disruptive potential of bilingualism and biculturalism is still worrisome: millions of voters cut off from the main sources of information, millions of potential draftees inculcated with dual ethnic loyalties, millions of would-be employees ill at ease in the language of their workmates. Former Senator S.I. Hayakawa of California was laughed at for proposing a constitutional amendment to make English the official language of the U.S. It was a gesture of little practical consequence but great symbolic significance: many Americans mistakenly feel there is something racist, or oppressive, in expecting newcomers to share the nation's language and folkways.

Beyond practical politics and economics, separatism belittles the all-embracing culture that America has embodied for the world. Says Writer Irving Howe, a scholar of literature and the Jewish immigrant experience: "The province, the ethnic nest, remains the point from which everything begins, but it must be transcended." That transcendence does not mean disappearance. It is possible to eat a Mexican meal, dance a Polish polka, sing in a Rumanian choir, preserve one's ethnicity however one wishes, and still share fully in the English-speaking common society. Just as American language, food and popular culture reflect the past groups who landed in the U.S., so future American culture will reflect the Hispanics, Asians and many other groups who are replanting their roots. As Author Rodriguez observes after his journey into the mainstream, "Culture survives whether you want it to or not." ■

■ ESSAY   JULY 11, 1988

The Fear of Losing a Culture

Richard Rodriguez

WHAT IS CULTURE, after all? The immigrant shrugs. Latin Americans initially come to the U.S. with only the things they need in mind—not abstractions like culture. They need dollars. They need food. Maybe they need to get out of the way of bullets. Most of us who concern ourselves with Hispanic-American culture, as painters, musicians, writers—or as sons and daughters—are the children of immigrants. We have grown up on this side of the border, in the land of Elvis Presley and Thomas Edison. Our lives are prescribed by the mall, by the 7-Eleven, by the Internal Revenue Service. Our imaginations vacillate between an Edenic Latin America, which nevertheless betrayed our parents, and the repellent plate-glass doors of a real American city, which has been good to us.

Hispanic-American culture stands where the past meets the future. The cultural meeting represents not just a Hispanic milestone, not simply a celebration at the crossroads. America transforms into pleasure what it cannot avoid. Hispanic-American culture of the sort that is now in evidence (the teen movie, the rock song) may exist in an hourglass, may in fact be irrelevant. The U.S. Border Patrol works through the night to arrest the flow of illegal immigrants over the border, even as Americans stand patiently in line for *La Bamba*. While Americans vote to declare, once and for all, that English shall be the official language of the U.S., Madonna starts recording in Spanish.

Before a national TV audience, Rita Moreno tells Geraldo Rivera that her dream as an actress is to play a character rather like herself: "I speak English perfectly well …I'm not dying from poverty…I want to play that kind of Hispanic woman, which is to say, an American citizen." This is an actress talking; these are show-biz pieties. But Moreno expresses as well a general Hispanic-American predicament. Hispanics want to belong to America without betraying the past. Yet we fear losing ground in any negotiation with America. Our fear, most of all, is of losing our culture.

We come from an expansive, an intimate, culture that has long been judged second-rate by the U.S. Out of pride as much as affection, we are reluctant to give up our past. Our notoriety in the U.S. has been our resistance to assimilation. The guarded symbol of Hispanic-American culture has been the tongue of flame: Spanish. But the remarkable legacy Hispanics carry from Latin America is not language—an inflatable skin—but breath itself, capacity of soul, an inclination to live. The genius of Latin America is the habit of synthesis. We assimilate.

What Latin America knows is that people create one another when they meet. In the music of Latin America you will hear the litany of bloodlines: the African drum, the German accordion, the cry from the minaret. The U.S. stands as the opposing New World experiment. In North America the Indian and the European stood separate. Whereas Latin America was formed by a Catholic dream of one world, of meltdown conversion, the U.S. was shaped by Protestant individualism. America has believed its national strength derives from separateness, from diversity. The glamour of the U.S. is the Easter promise: you can be born again in your lifetime. You can separate yourself from your past. You can get a divorce, lose weight, touch up your roots.

Immigrants still come for that promise, but the U.S. has wavered in its faith. America is no longer sure that economic strength derives from individualism. And America is no longer sure that there is space enough, sky enough, to sustain the cabin on the prairie. Now, as we near the end of the American Century, two alternative cultures beckon the American imagination: the Asian and the Latin American. Both are highly communal cultures, in contrast to the literalness of American culture. Americans devour what they might otherwise fear to become. Sushi will make them lean, subtle corporate warriors. Combination Plate No. 3, smothered in mestizo gravy, will burn a hole in their hearts.

Latin America offers passion. Latin America has a life—big clouds, unambiguous themes, tragedy, epic—that the U.S., for all its quality of life, yearns to have. Latin America offers an undistressed leisure, a crowded kitchen table, even a full sorrow. Such is the urgency of America's need that it reaches right past a fledgling, homegrown Hispanic-American culture for the darker bottle of Mexican beer, for the denser novel of a Latin American master.

For a long time, Hispanics in the U.S. felt hostility. Perhaps because we were preoccupied by nostalgia, we withheld our Latin American gift. We denied the value of assimilation. But as our presence is judged less foreign in America, we will produce a more generous art, less timid, less parochial. Hispanic Americans do not have a pure Latin American art to offer. Expect bastard themes. Expect winking ironies, comic conclusions. For Hispanics live on this side of the border, where Kraft manufactures Mexican-style Velveeta, and where Jack in the Box serves Fajita Pita. Expect marriage. We will change America even as we will be changed. We will disappear with you into a new miscegenation.

Along and across the border there remain real conflicts, real fears. But the ancient tear separating Europe from itself—the Catholic Mediterranean from the Protestant north—may yet heal itself in the New World. For generations, Latin America has been the place, the bed, of a confluence of so many races and cultures that Protestant North America shuddered to imagine it.

The time has come to imagine it. ∎

Seeking Votes and Clout

Jesse Jackson spearheads a new black drive for political power

RUN, JESSE, RUN! *Run, Jesse, run!* The chants roll toward him, rumbling like a pent-up storm, rising to the rafters and the stained-glass portrait of the Rev. Martin Luther King Jr. With the practiced rhythms of preacher and pitchman, he launches his sermon on power. "There's a freedom train acoming," he intones. "But you got to be registered to ride." Amen! "Get on board! Get on board!" There is fire in his eyes, a pin in his starched collar, a finger in the air. "We can move from the slave ship to the championship! From the guttermost to the uppermost! From the outhouse to the courthouse! From the statehouse to the White House!" The well-dressed congregation of the First African Methodist Episcopal Church in Los Angeles erupts with the same chant that has resounded in the Delta country of Mississippi, in Chicago, in Atlanta. It is a rising cry that the self-styled country preacher seems less and less likely to resist. Run, Jesse, run! Run, Jesse, run!

Jess Louis Jackson, 41, the illegitimate son of a South Carolina high school student has for 15 years sought to don the mantle of his mentor Martin Luther King Jr. By turns he can be fascinating and frightening, inspiring and irritating, charismatic and controversial. And so too is the crusade he has been considering. On one level it would be the ultimate embodiment of the American political ideal, an affirmation that every child of the nation, yes even a black one, can some day seek the presidency. Yet on another level, it would be as far removed from conventional politics as Jackson is removed from conventional politicians.

TIME

SEEKING VOTES AND CLOUT
A New Black Drive for Political Power

Jesse Jackson

The rally in Los Angeles a week ago marked Jackson's latest tentative step toward becoming a candidate for the Democratic presidential nomination. His "exploratory committee," led by Mayor Richard Hatcher of Gary, Ind., officially became the Jesse Jackson Presidential Advisory Committee. Its purpose is to conduct a poll and sound out black leaders to see if there is sufficient support for such a race. But most of the leaders who are on the committee seem already to have made up their minds. Hatcher reminds the audience in the adobe-colored church that Americans like to tell their children that if they work hard enough they can grow up to be President. "I have one proposition to leave you with." he says. "Either we ought to stop lying to our children or we ought to start believing it and doing the things necessary to make it come true." Bishop H.H. Brookins takes the podium to ridicule the large number of black officeholders who are wary, even downright disapproving, of a Jackson candidacy. "We did not have to ask black elected officials what they thought we should do, because after all we elected them!" he preaches. "If not now, when? If not Jesse, who?"

For the past few months, Jackson has been crisscrossing the country conducting voter-registration revival meetings to bring blacks into the political process. He will cry: "We need 10,000 blacks running for office from Virginia around to Texas—county clerks, supervisors, sheriffs, judges, legislators, Governors—Just run! Run! Run!" His audience will interrupt: Run, Jesse, run! Run, Jesse, run! "When you run,

the masses register and vote. When you run, you put your program on the front burner. If you run, you might lose. If you don't run, you're guaranteed to lose." And the chant for him to run sounds again. In creating such fervor, raising such grass-roots expectations, he leaves himself little choice but to take their advice. But perhaps more important, they are taking his. Blacks are registering to vote and running for office in a groundswell of activism that promises to alter permanently the political balance on local, state and national levels.

Indeed, the significance of a potential Jackson candidacy comes not from whatever chance he would have of being a broker at a deadlocked convention (probably very little) or the possibility that he might actually win (virtually none at all). On the contrary, he could even injure the black cause, as many leaders have been quick to point out, by drawing support away from liberal candidates like Walter Mondale. His crusade also threatens to cause deep divisions within the ranks of black leadership, and it could strain the relationship between blacks and the Democratic Party.

The excitement generated by Jackson's potential campaign reflects, and contributes to, a resurgence of black political activism not seen since the 1960s. "We've spent at least ten years being mostly dormant," says Robert Starks, a professor of inner-city studies at Northeastern Illinois University. "The only people that were busy were the Jesse Helms types. Now we're going to do them one better."

There were already strong signs in 1982 of growing political involvement. Black turnout went from 37% in the off-year elections of 1978 to 43% last year, twice the percentage increase of white voters. The gap between black and white turnout fell to a historic low of 7%, and in nine states, including Illinois, blacks were reported voting in a greater proportion than whites. And the number of black state legislators increased by 35, to 355, the largest jump ever. Nevertheless, the total of 5,160 black officials nationwide represents only about 1% of all elective offices.

Although most of the nitty-gritty work is being done by the S.C.L.C., the V.E.P. and the N.A.A.C.P., the point man, catalyst and Pied Piper of the registration crusade has been Jesse Jackson. No matter that other black officials are often grudging in their praise and that they resent the publicity he attracts with his flashy appearances. "Groups do work when Jesse's not around, when the reporters and cameras aren't there," says veteran Activist and Atlanta City Councilman John Lewis. Yet most admit that the flamboyant and magnetic Jackson and the "Southern Crusade" run by his Operation PUSH (People United to Serve Humanity) have helped spark excitement among rural blacks. "After he came, enthusiasm really revived, especially among the 18-to-24-year-olds," says Thompson.

Jackson conducts his crusade with the fervor of an old-style revivalist, sometimes appearing at as many as 40 rallies a week. "All those who are not registered stand up!" he yells. Dozens of young blacks sheepishly rise. "I want you to walk right down here and get registered now!" he says, indicating the registration tables. "Isn't that wonderful! Give them a big hand!"

In Mississippi, which held state and local primaries this month, the voter-registration effort has been the largest and most successful since the passage of the 1965 Voting Rights Act. An estimated 40,000 new voters were registered since May, increasing black registration by about 11%. Aiding the effort were Georgia State Senator Julian Bond, Atlanta Mayor Andrew Young and Martin Luther King III, son of the slain civil rights leader. And, of course, Jesse Jackson, who staged a three-day barnstorming car caravan through the Delta country to spark a record black turnout in the primaries.

Jackson also persuaded William Bradford Reynolds, the patrician chief of the Justice Department's Civil Rights Division, to come to Mississippi to see for himself the need for more vigorous enforcement of federal voting-rights laws. Reynolds, who heard tale after tale of the difficulties of trying to register and vote, ended his trip by entwining arms with Jackson and other black leaders to sing *We Shall Overcome*. Within days, the Justice Department dispatched ten additional registrars to sign up voters, and later it sent 322 observers to monitor the primaries. The results: an increase of 13% in the black vote from comparable previous primaries, a black victory over a white incumbent for a seat in the legislature, and a respectable, if not overwhelming, showing by black candidates for local offices across the state.

Jackson may not be the main cause of this revival in black political participation, but he has been its most visible Tom Paine and its public symbol. He frightens some as a demagogue, annoys others as a gadfly and provokes intense hatred in a few people with his grandstanding style. Yet he has been, and clearly plans to remain, the most watched and quoted black leader since Martin Luther King Jr.

His drive to win, to be acclaimed and applauded, was forged during his childhood in Greenville, S.C., where he strove to overcome the taunts of "Jesse ain't got no daddy." Says he: "I was made aware of the odds of survival as a child. I'm still fighting those odds and defying those odds." He made the honor roll and starred in football. "My teachers did not teach me there was a ceiling on my aspirations." He was elected a student-body officer and was a member of the French club. "In church, I learned that I was God's child." He left high school with a football scholarship to the University of Illinois.

But it was when he went north to college that he felt in full force the humiliation of racial discrimination, both on the football team and in the college's fraternity life. So he transferred back south to predominantly black North Carolina Agricultural and Technical State University in Greensboro, where the student sit-ins were just beginning. Upon graduating, he entered a three-year program at Chicago Theological Seminary. But in 1965, after watching on television the brutal beatings in Selma. Ala., he left before getting his degree

Not a Melting Pot, a Rainbow Quilt

"OUR FLAG IS RED, WHITE AND BLUE, but our nation is a rainbow—red, yellow, brown, black and white—and we're all precious in God's sight. America is not like a blanket—one piece of unbroken cloth, the same color, the same texture, the same size. America is more like a quilt—many patches, many pieces, many colors, many sizes, all woven and held together by a common thread.

"The white, the Hispanic, the black, the Arab, the Jew, the woman, the native American, the small farmer, the businessperson, the environmentalist, the peace activist, the young, the old, the lesbian, the gay and the disabled make up the American quilt.

"Even in our fractured state, all of us count and all of us fit somewhere. We have proven that we can survive without each other. But we have not proven that we can win and progress without each other. We must come together." ■

—JESSE JACKSON
Addressing the Democratic National Convention,
1984

(he was later ordained a Baptist minister) and joined Martin Luther King Jr.'s staff at the S.C.L.C.

There occurs during the lives of most ambitious political figures a process of mythmaking, often self-induced. For Jackson, this began when King was shot on a motel balcony in Memphis. The 26-year-old activist appeared on the news shows the following morning in a sweatshirt he said had been smeared with the blood of the martyr. He was the last person King talked to, he said, and he had cradled the dying leader in his arms. Others who were there dispute the story. Jackson, never overburdened with humility, now takes a biblical view of the bickering, invoking his own "Peter principle." Says he: "Peter was with Jesus physically but Paul interpreted Jesus better than Peter did. Peter and them got jealous of Paul and tried to ax him out based on longevity." Those with a more earthly view of their mission feel the incident is representative of Jackson's tendency to usurp the limelight in his bid to follow King as America's pre-eminent black leader.

King's successor as head of the S.C.L.C., Ralph Abernathy, gave the ambitious young man a gritty assignment that, says Jackson, no one else wanted: mayor of Resurrection City, the tent encampment established on the Washington Mall during the 1968 Poor People's Campaign. One bleak, rainy day, a litany inviting antiphony sprang to Jackson's lips that became his slogan and made him a celebrity. He preached to the suffering campers: "Say I am somebody." I am somebody. "I may be poor but I am somebody." I am somebody! "I may be hungry but I am somebody." I am somebody!

Two years later Jackson, who had been given charge of

S.C.L.C.'s Operation Breadbasket program in Chicago, became embroiled in an internal dispute over the organization's accounting practices. Jackson quit to form his own group. That was Operation PUSH, which exhibits all the strengths and weaknesses of its founder. Its programs can be showy, bold and imaginative. But often its follow-up is slack, its results ambiguous. One initiative has been to negotiate "trade covenants" with major corporations designed to secure jobs for blacks and business for black enterprises. Another, known as PUSH-EXCEL, is a school-motivation program based on Jackson's self-help philosophy for blacks. Should Jackson run for President, the purported accomplishments of these programs are likely to come under closer public scrutiny.

At the annual convention of Operation PUSH in Atlanta earlier this month, Jackson gathered his advisers in a 70th-floor suite to put together an exploratory committee. He wants to make sure that those who have indicated support will actually come through. "I don't want 'Run, Jesse, run!' to turn into 'See Jesse run!'" But his wife Jacqueline proudly sports a button that reads DAMN STRAIGHT! IT'S TIME FOR A BLACK PRESIDENTIAL CANDIDATE, and Jackson is already acting as if he were running. At the moment, he is leaning toward a September announcement that would kick off with a three-day march through Mississippi, from the Ruleville grave of Civil Rights Crusader Fannie Lou Hamer (1917–77) to Indianola. Before then he plans to travel to the Soviet Union to meet with leaders there and to West Germany to talk to American soldiers about the racism they encounter abroad. He will also urge them to register and cast absentee ballots.

One serious qualm for Jackson is the stress that a campaign would put on Jacqueline and their three sons and two daughters, who range in age from seven to 20. Although he has a $52,000 salary from Operation PUSH and is paid up to $2,000 for some of his speeches, Jackson has no real financial security. His three-story stucco house in a black middle-class section of Chicago needs painting. He owns only three suits and two pairs of dress shoes. His car is a black Buick station wagon. Despite his showy public style, he leads a rather simple private life: his favorite recreation being a game of basketball on his backyard court. His frenetic pace on the road is occasionally slowed slightly by a mild case of sickle-cell anemia, a hereditary blood disease that affects blacks.

Jackson hopes to form a "rainbow coalition" of blacks, other minorities, women, laborers, peace activists and the white poor. Although some Hispanic leaders support his campaign, this rainbow, particularly with him as the pot of gold, is a dream that extends far beyond the visible horizon. Women are wary of Jackson's antiabortion views. He frequently tells the story of how his unwed teen-age mother, on the advice of her doctor, almost had an abortion when she was pregnant with him and was only dissuaded by her minister. Jackson has begun stressing that although he is morally opposed to abortion, he believes that the law should allow a woman free choice. Nevertheless, women have not yet rallied to his cause. Neither has labor. The AFL-CIO decided last week to make its endorsement earlier than planned, and is now set to throw its support behind Mondale at its October convention. Even a labor member of the black leadership family made it clear that he would be supporting the union's candidate rather than anyone fielded by blacks.

But while the pros are saying no, the grass roots are shouting yes. Rural farmers are inspired by Jackson's sermons on the value of the vote: teen-age urban blacks are turned on by his clenched-fist determination: the downtrodden hear in his ringing tones an authentic voice for their concerns. A hustler, perhaps, but a hustler on their behalf. "He does a lot better with the masses than with the leadership," says Holman of the National Urban Coalition. Wherever he goes he attracts enthusiastic crowds, rousing them, inspiring them and drawing them into his quest. "I feel it is important that he run," says Richard Branch, 30, an Atlanta real estate salesman. "I don't think he can win, but that's not the issue."

One promise Jackson made that greatly relieved his fellow Democrats is that he will not run as an independent in the general election. "To run as an independent," he says, "would clearly help the present Administration." Instead, he will use his following to persuade the Democratic nominee to support his positions on voting rights, affirmative action and other issues. If the nominee is agreeable, then Jackson will work to deliver votes into the Democratic column. "If the party is forthcoming, I'd put jet fuel in my butt," he promises. "If it's not, I'd sit on it."

At the heart of the country preacher's personality is a deep sense of religious calling. "I'm clearly a product of God's mission for me," he fervently says. "I'm a very ordinary person in my tastes and interests, but I have been used as an instrument in extraordinary ways." Yet he often seems beset by deep personal doubts, as if unable to erase the taunts of his youth. In private he is quiet to the point of being withdrawn. Says a friend: "People who have only seen him in public wouldn't recognize him." Despite his wide experience, he is painfully unworldly. "If you take Jesse to a fancy French restaurant," says someone who knows him, "he'll wind up with spaghetti and meatballs. He has very, very unsophisticated tastes."

Jackson becomes bitter when other black leaders, those he feels are content to serve as "trustees of the ghetto," dismiss him as opportunistic. "Part of our problem now is that some of our leaders do not seize opportunities," he says. "I was trained by Martin to be an opportunist."

King's legacy hangs over Jackson, as it does over the rest of the nation. The dream that he spoke of 20 years ago, a century after the Emancipation Proclamation, is still a dream deferred. What was then a civil rights movement has become a political movement, but the goal is still the same: an equal place for black Americans. First as a King lieutenant, now as leader in his own right, Jesse Jackson has been part of both movements. His continued presence on the public stage is a reminder that the nation's racial dilemma is far from solved. And the stark fact that he, or any other black, cannot be elected President in 1984 is, understandably to Jackson, perhaps the most compelling reason for him to run. ∎

The Amish and the Law

A farmer is trapped in a classic clash between Church and State

THERE ARE ONLY TWO KINDS OF PEOPLE in north-western Pennsylvania's Lawrence County—the "English" and the "Dutch." The first category includes nearly everybody—Wasps, Italians, Jews, Irish, blacks. The second category covers only the Amish. To say that the Amish are different is merely to state the obvious. They are followers of a sect that originated in Switzerland back in the 17th century and, in search of religious freedom, fled to England and Holland in the 18th century and moved to America in the 19th. In this day of home computers and space travel, the Amish eschew zippers as decadent, electricity as unnecessary and flush toilets as wasteful. They forgo the automobile in favor of sleek trotters and canvas-topped carriages of hickory wood. They use fine, sturdy workhorses to spread manure and plow their fields, which is what they are doing these days as spring spreads over their green country.

Ed Lee is one of 5,000 Amish in Lawrence Country. He differs from his neighbors for reasons other than the fact that he is not a Byler or a Swatzentrooper or a Hofstader or the bearer of some other traditionally Amish name. Lee is different because he has done something that the Amish rarely do. He has ended up in court. His offense: refusing to pay Social Security taxes for 30 Amish men who worked for him over an eight-year period as carpenters, building houses. The Internal Revenue Service claimed that he owed the Government $27,000. Lee challenged the IRS ruling in federal district court in Pittsburgh. To prove his good intentions, he offered his farm as security in the event he lost. As it turned out, he won, but the IRS then appealed to the Supreme Court.

Lee's refusal to pay Social Security taxes did not stem from any disrespect of the law. He personally has no quarrels with the Social Security system, and believes it is fine—for those who need it. But it is a tenet of their religious belief that Amish people should take care of their own. They do not collect unemployment or welfare benefits. They do not buy insurance of any kind. By an act of Congress in 1965, self-employed Amish men are exempt from paying Social Security taxes on religious grounds. But the act does not cover Amish men who work for Amish employers. It is this apparent inconsistency that has propelled Lee into the court.

The Supreme Court, which ruled on Lee's case in February, upheld the IRS. "A comprehensive national Social Security system providing for voluntary participation would be almost a contradiction of terms and difficult, if not impossible, to administer," wrote Chief Justice Warren Burger in the unanimous opinion.

Faced with the loss of his farm, Lee might have bowed to federal *force majeure* at this point. Instead, aided by two non-Amish friends, he is quietly carrying on his fight. Francis X. Caiazza, 46, a local lawyer who had represented Lee before the Supreme Court, was elected a judge the day after arguing the case and is now prevented by law from providing more than moral support. "Amish do not break laws; they are not seen in the courts," Caiazza says. "The Amish care about reason, law and order, and they are a God-fearing people. This wasn't just another case. It involves a sincere belief in religious freedom and religious rights. We lost the case in the Supreme Court, but I still feel the religious argument should have been the bottom line."

Lee's other friend, Robert Gardner 43, a high school teacher in New Castle, is urging another tactic. Aided by hundreds of "English" volunteers, he has collected upwards of 10,000 signatures and he hopes to get 10,000 more on petitions urging Congress to enact a law exempting all Amish from paying for Social Security. He has even written to President Reagan asking for his support. "The Amish," says Gardner, "are not a fly-by-night religion formed to avoid taxes. Legislation already exists which exempts an Amish individual from paying Social Security taxes when he is self-employed. The precedent is there, and it should be extended to cover Amish workers on the job for an Amish employer."

Amish customs, Gardner argues, constitute a "built-in form of Social Security." Forcing the Amish to pay Social Security cuts at the heart of their religion, maintains he. And it will affect others beside Ed Lee. According to Gardner, at least 30 additional Amish employers in the area could find themselves in the same predicament if the IRS decided to press them.

The predicament is something that Lee ponders as he sits by the coal stove in the kitchen of his neat, sturdy farmhouse. His feet are covered with thick blue socks; the Amish remove their shoes before entering the home. His blue eyes are gentle behind sensible, old-fashioned glasses, his beard is appropriately patriarchal, his voice surprisingly soft. "I'm a man who wakes every morning and thanks God for what is," Lee says. "I don't worry. I work. I believe that the Government of the United States is fair and just. It is not the Amish habit to be in confrontation; we avoid it. So it was with great difficulty and much prayer that I took this on."

Lee is emotionally drained from his three-year fight, and his earnings has fallen from $6,500 a year to $4,000. He says the battle has brought him closer to his "English" neighbors. "They are truly brothers," he says of Caiazza and Gardner. "I can't say enough of what's in my heart about them." His faith in his country remains steadfast, even though a bit shaken. "I still love America," he says "I won't betray her. But sometimes it is difficult for a man to know what is right and what is wrong."

Lee can survive the loss of his case. Whether he can survive the loss of his farm, which has been attached by the IRS, is another matter. A glance around his spartan home, enlivened with a touch of color from the hand-painted clay dishes displayed on a huge oaken chest, is enough to bring a catch into his voice. A look out over his 25 wooded acres, glistening with the remnants of spring rains, is enough to cause a shadow to slip across his face. His emotions are understandable. To men like Lee, their land is their life. To lose one is to lose the other. ■

Magic Shadows from a Melting Pot

For new Americans, the movies offered the ticket for assimilation

"WE ARE NOT A NATION," Herman Melville said of this country of immigrants, "so much as a world." That judgment is ringingly appropriate to an art industry that since its inception has dominated the world market and consciousness. A wistful tramp wreaks havoc in a Manhattan pawnshop, and Asians fall in love with Charlie Chaplin. Judy Garland sings about a rainbow, and Europeans know it is only a dream away from Kansas. A California child opens the eyes of his extraterrestrial friend to a toy store's worth of American brand names, and E.T. strikes a responsive chord on every continent. For most of this century the world's fantasies have been formed and reflected by the American cinema.

In the spirit of assimilation, Hollywood has thrived by embracing those immigrants who would enrich it. Today one need look no further than the awards shows, or the bottom line, to spot the crucial contributions of foreign-born filmmakers to the Hollywood movie. On Oscar night this spring, Czech-born Milos Forman walked away with a best-director statuette for his work on the laurel-laden *Amadeus*. This year's first surprise hit, *Witness*, was directed by Australian Peter Weir; this summer's runaway "Gook" buster, *Rambo: First Blood Part II*, was helmed by the Greek immigrant George Pan Cosmatos. Indeed, when America wants to cauterize its own psychology or psychopathy onscreen these days—in Birdy or *The Falcon and the Snowman*, in *The Killing Fields* or *Alamo Bay*—chances are it will call on a foreign director to perform the surgery.

It has ever been thus, for American cinema is truly an immigrant art form, made by immigrants for immigrants. From the beginning, each group of outsiders—the ones behind the scenes and the ones gazing at the screen—fed each other's good fortune. The audience made the filmmakers rich and famous; in return, movie people taught moviegoers, in the U.S. and all over the world, how to be Americans. When Film Maestro Federico Fellini was in New York City last month to receive tribute from the Film Society of Lincoln Center, he recalled the spell American movies cast over his provincial Italian boyhood in the 1920s: "I saw that there existed another way of life, a land of wide open spaces and fantastic cities that were a cross between Babylon and Mars. It was especially wonderful to know there was a country where people were free, rich and dancing on the roofs of skyscrapers, and where even a tramp could become President."

For the tens of millions of immigrants washed onto America's shores between 1880 and 1920, the infant movie industry provided more than fantastic diversion; it was a passport to the American dream. In the back rooms of penny arcades as dark and crowded as steerage on a ship chugging toward Ellis Island, they saw magic, moving shadows that served as a crash course in their adoptive country's history, behavior, values, ideals and follies. A maiden defends her honor; Jack Johnson defends a heavyweight title; firemen career through city streets toward a blazing house; bandits rob a train, and the sheriff fires his six-shooter right at the audience. True love conquers all prejudices in a land with a built-in happy ending. In the universal language of images, the movies told over and over the All-American story of assimilation and triumph—the alchemy of the melting pot.

It is not precisely a coincidence that the U.S. emerged as a world power just as its movies began girding the globe. Pushing parables of fulfillment in brash editorial rhythms, these new "moving pictures" were missionaries of American energy, traveling salesmen for life in the New World. And the sales pitch worked. How many millions, dazzled by this vision, determined right then to pack their bags and book passage for the U.S.? How many millions more stayed put, but discovered and appropriated the American style? See us and be like us. And just about everybody did. The American century began with the American cinema.

There is a stimulating irony here: America was inventing itself onscreen, but many of the fabricators were foreign born. For both producer and consumer, this was education in the dark. Though many film entrepreneurs of the first generation were native born, they were soon replaced by a bazaar of movie merchants who had arrived in the U.S. barely before the masses they hoped to enlighten. The roll call of Jewish-immigrant moguls has since become its own Hollywood legend: Adolph Zukor, the Hungarian who had worked as janitor in a Manhattan fur store (president of Paramount Pictures); Carl Laemmle, the bookkeeper from Germany (founder, Universal Pictures); Samuel Goldwyn, the glove salesman from Warsaw (founder, Goldwyn Studios); Louis B. Mayer, the scrap-metal dealer from Minsk (vice president and general manager, Metro-Goldwyn-Mayer). By the 1930s Mayer was earning $1.25 million a year and was presiding over the all-American family of Andy Hardy.

Like most of the other immigrant moguls, Mayer achieved the American dream without becoming a homogenized American. By parading their unregenerate Yiddish accents and their careful malapropisms, the studio bosses were implying that their success came from street smarts acquired on the Lower East Side and further back, in the shtetls of Eastern Europe; it took a ragman to become a Hollywood rajah. "They had grown up," wrote Film Historian Carlos Clarens, "in a trade where samples could be smelled, fingered and felt; they recognized craft when they saw it, and they respected it; rather than hoodwink the customer, they aimed to please." The moguls did not see themselves as artists, or the movies as art. Their job was to keep the assembly line rolling, in a factory called Hollywood.

Within its first decade, the movie industry had recapitulated America's century-long trek westward. In 1900, before the picturemakers arrived, Los Angeles was a sleepy city of 102,000—the population of Memphis or Omaha. But the immigrants could get drunk on the possibilities of all that air, desert, sea; ambition had elbow room there. And soon after settling in the Los Angeles suburb of Hollywood, the industry

discovered the last element it needed to achieve dominance among the popular arts: movie stars. Two of them, by turning stereotypes of Everyman and Pretty Girl into archetypes, would become the most recognizable people in the world, and among the wealthiest. The fairy tale needs one more twist: both Charlie Chaplin and Mary Pickford were immigrants.

"Not since the days of the Forty-Niners," wrote Novelist Upton Sinclair in 1933, "had there been such a way for the little fellow to get rich as in this new business." The little fellow Sinclair mentioned could have been Chaplin. Born in a London slum, the comic arrived in the U.S. in 1910. Three years later he signed his first movie contract, at $150 a week; four years after that, he was to make $1 million a year and become, for a time, the planet's most recognizable and cherished figure. Chaplin deserved no less; his poignant one-reel comedies taught the world how to love movies. Pickford, with her ringlets and coquettish ways, was hardly less popular, and no less resourceful. In 1909 the little girl from Toronto cadged an audition with Film Pioneer D.W. Griffith; by 1916 she could tell the bosses at Paramount Pictures, "No, I really cannot afford to work for only $10,000 a week" (which is precisely the fee she settled for). This sudden affluence did not short-circuit the masses' identification with the movie stars. It merely confirmed the public's image of them as extraordinary ordinary people. They were "us" on the big screen, with every wish of fame, charm, romance, wit and avarice fulfilled. They were their own movies.

As the industry's mantle spread around the world, new immigrant stars filled important character niches. The Latin lover: Rudolph Valentino (Italy); the noble warlord: Sessue Hayakawa (Japan); the tragic heroine: Pola Negri (Poland); the vamp goddess: Greta Garbo (Sweden). Nor was the flood stanched with the arrival of talking pictures in the late 1920s. Hollywood saw the Babel of exotic accents as one more earnest of its cosmopolitan reach. And so Maurice Chevalier and Charles Boyer brought their suavity from France; Marlene Dietrich (Germany), Hedy Lamarr (Austria) and Ingrid Bergman (Sweden) helped Garbo flesh out the fantasy of the European woman. From south of the border Carmen Miranda brought her fruity headdresses, Gilbert Roland his purring machismo. Half of England, it seemed, played cricket every Sunday in Griffith Park. And with bitter thanks to Adolf Hitler, Hollywood welcomed hundreds of refugees from the Third Reich. As performers, writers, directors or technicians, they would animate and dominate Hollywood for its next 30 years.

The pioneer immigrant directors—Maurice Tourneur from France, the Germans Ernst Lubitsch and F.W. Murnau—imported civilized modes of fantasy, comedy and folklore. But the new exiles had darker stories to tell, and through them Hollywood found its caustic maturity. Here were artists with an outsider's perspective and, suddenly, an insider's clout; they could celebrate the temple of American success while keeping an eye on the cracks in its facade. The industry, or at least that part of it that handed out awards, was grateful: eleven of the first 20 Oscars for best direction went to immigrants, from Frank Lloyd (*Cavalcade*) and Frank Capra (*It Happened One Night*) to William Wyler (*The Best Years of Our Lives*) and Elia Kazan (*Gentleman's Agreement*).

Other artisans found their reward in discovering, and helping to build, an artistic League of Nations in their new land. *Casablanca*, the best-loved film of the 1940s, could have served as a travel poster for this international spirit. The director, Michael Curtiz, was from Budapest; the art director, Carl Jules Weyl, from Germany; the composer, Max Steiner, from Vienna. And of the top 20 names on the cast list, only three belonged to native Americans (Humphrey Bogart, Dooley Wilson and Joy Page); the rest represented the tattered flags of Hungary, Austria, Germany, France, Britain, Canada, Italy, the Soviet Union and Sweden. For Hollywood, it was the blossoming of a beautiful friendship.

With war's end, and the onslaught of insularity in the '50s, many of the diaspora scattered again, finding refuge back home in European co-productions. Hollywood was retreating into familiar genres: into the memorial expanses of westerns like *High Noon* (directed by the Austrian Fred Zinnemann) or the paranoid apocalypse of science-fiction films like *The War of the Worlds* (produced by the Hungarian George Pal) or grandiose melodramas like *Written on the Wind* (directed by the Dane Douglas Sirk) or effervescent comedies like *Some Like It Hot* and *The Apartment* (both directed and co-written by the Austrian Billy Wilder) or the sleek thrillers of London-born Alfred Hitchcock. Audrey Hepburn, from Belgium, was crowned princess of the box office; Cary Grant, from Bristol, was still the monarch of masculinity. Everyone was so assimilated that you couldn't spot the immigrants without a security check. American films, once an obsession, were now an agree-able habit, as the rest of the world began attending to its own dreams and nightmares.

To shake things up, it took another wave of immigrants: the influx of sophisticated foreign films in the late '50s and early '60s. Soon every young Hollywood hotshot wanted to make movies just like Fellini's, or Bergman's, or Francois Truffaut's. A picture's subject could be uniquely American, but its style would be self-consciously "artistic" (read European). Two Hollywood hits of 1967 strikingly assimilated these international trends: *Bonnie and Clyde*, originally offered to Truffaut to direct, and *The Graduate*, in which Berlin-born Director Mike Nichols ransacked the mannerisms of a dozen art-house auteurs to tell a story as American as plastics.

With the triumph of the international style—episodic and oblique, offering no easy meanings or solutions—came the latest surge of immigrant directors and cinematographers. Some, like Forman, Soviet Filmmaker Slava Tsukerman (*Liquid Sky*) and the Cuban-bred camera magician Nestor Almendros, were sidestepping new tyrannies. Some, like Louis Malle (*Pretty Baby*, *Atlantic City*, *Alamo Bay*), sought a larger canvas on which to test their palettes. Many others were Australians and Englishmen attracted by the grand contradictions of a country with which they shared a language and part of a heritage. America was also, of course, where the action was. Also the power and the glory.

These artists—some immigrants, some visitors—contribute new chapters to the saga that began in the penny arcades. It is a story of gangsters and heiresses, in penthouses or on the prairie, filtered through the first industrial art form, the dream machine. The dream is America; the machine is the movies. With the help of its immigrant artists and entrepreneurs, the industry still beckons as it did to Chaplin, Goldwyn and their earliest audiences. Welcome, children of all nations, to the New World of the movies. Welcome to America. ∎

A Surging New Spirit

In film, music, theater, art, design—the Hispanic influence is exploding into the American cultural mainstream

AMERICA, THE GREAT RECEIVER. From every culture to arrive within its borders, it embraces some new ingredient. Puritan wrath. Black cool. Irish poetics. Jewish irony. One after another, America draws them down the channels of its awareness and puts them into play in new settings. They collide and cross-pollinate and mix it up, nowhere more so than in the arts and popular culture. Sparks fly at the meeting points. The Jewish novel works variations on the keynotes of Puritan gloom. The western is reseen through John Ford's Irish eyes. Sinatra meets Duke Ellington. Every offering is admitted and set dancing with new partners. It may be better to give, but it's a lot more fun to receive.

Nowadays the mainstream is receiving a rich new current. More and more, American film, theater, music, design, dance and art are taking on a Hispanic color and spirit. Look around. You can see the special lightning, the distinctive gravity, the portable wit, the personal spin. The new marquee names have a Spanish ring: Edward James Olmos, Andy Garcia, Maria Conchita Alonso. At the movies, the summer of *La Bamba* gave way last year to the autumn of Born in East L. A.; now the springtime of *Stand and Deliver* blends into the summer of *Salsa.* On the record charts the story is the same: Miami Sound Machine, Los Lobos, Lisa Lisa and Cult Jam. The rhythm is gonna get you.

An equivalent Latino surge is reaching the higher cultural circles. The art world is opening its eyes to Hispanic artists whose work, sharp and full throated, owes its strength to aesthetic intelligence, not ethnic scenery. Meanwhile, Latino playwrights are supplying off-Broadway and the regional theaters with new voices. And while the great Hispanic-American Novel is still waiting to be written, the splendid figures of Latin American literature—Gabriel Garciá Márquez, Mario Vargas Llosa, Carlos Fuentes—are being translated straight into the American literary fabric, not to mention the best-seller lists.

Then there are the developments that are harder to pin down, the Latin flavors and inflections conveyed through all the intricate paths of daily life, in the offerings at table or the bolero curve of a woman's jacket. You can't walk down the street without running into them. On the corner where the disco used to be, a Latin-beat club; kids hip hop on floors that withstood the bump. For lunch, a burrito. What's that in the salad? It's jicama. (Say *hee*-ca-ma.) Things that once seemed foreign now seem as American as…a burrito. With each fresh connection tastes are being rebuilt, new understandings concluded. The American mind is adding a new wing.

Yes, but is this really new? Was there ever a time without a Mexican spitfire in the movies, a hacienda-style suburb down the road, a Latin crooner singing *Cuando Cuando* to the stars? And in the past hasn't the U.S. joined the conga line, bought the Trini Lopez album, then moved on heedlessly to something else? It has and it did. But this time the prospects are different. Latin influences that were once just a pinch of spice for most Americans are bidding to become a vital part of the wider culture.

Demographics are the main reason. The number of Hispanics in the U.S. has increased 30% since 1980, to 19 million. They account now for about 7.9% of the nation's population. Most trace their roots back to Mexico (63%), Puerto Rico (12%) and Cuba (5%); the rest to the nations of Central and South America and the Caribbean. By the year 2000 their numbers are expected to reach 30 million, 15% of the whole. And roughly one-third of all U.S. Hispanics intermarry with non-Hispanics, promising the day when the two cultures will be as tightly entwined as a strand of DNA.

Another reason is more subtle. The creative work being done by Hispanics today is more than ever recognizable to Americans as the work of, well, Americans—Hispanic Americans. Paintings and music that spring from Latin sources are being filtered through a north-of-the-border sensibility. As in *La Bamba*: its story of Chicano life is told through myths of immigrant struggle and showbiz martyrdom that were born in the U.S.A. Increasingly, too, Hispanic artists and entertainers are courting the mass audience in English. Many of the nation's Latino theaters perform in English only. "I don't want to be a good Hispanic theater," says Max Ferra, Artistic Director of Manhattan's predominantly English INTAR Hispanic American Arts Center. "I want to be a very good American theater." After writing two books in Spanish, Novelist Roberto Fernández has just published his first in English, *Raining Backwards,* a comic account of Cuban life in Miami. "I did it for the same reason that Miami Sound Machine sings in English," he explains. "I wanted to reach a wider audience."

The greater visibility of Hispanics in the cultural landscape is a reminder that the roots of Spanish culture go deep into American life, especially in that spawning ground of the national self-image, the West. Much of the territory of the Western states, from Texas to California, was held first by Spain, then Mexico. The Spanish names of many Western cities—Los Angeles, San Francisco, Santa Fe—bear witness to the settlements of the early Franciscan friars. The first play on American soil was performed by Spanish colonists in New Mexico in 1598. Yet in the hills of New Mexico and the old mission towns of the Pacific Coast, the descendants of Spanish settlers who greeted the Anglo pioneers are amused (and sometimes not amused) to find themselves perennially arriving in the national consciousness. As Luis Valdez, writer and director of *La Bamba*, once put it, "We did not, in fact, come to the United States at all. The United States came to us."

Even so, for years most Americans were content to imagine the Latin world as a tropical paradise or a giant border town, a torrid zone just across the line of sexual decorum, that most heavily policed boundary in the American psyche. Though that image is being discarded, it is not going without a fight. In a Miami department store not long ago, the Cuban-born fashion designer Adolfo, a favorite of Nancy Reagan's, was pained to overhear two women express surprise that he was the creator of a collection that was elegant and simple. "Obviously," he laments, "they just assumed that anything a Cuban designed would be full of neon, sequins and ruffles."

Which is not to say that Hispanic culture is dowdy. (Try telling yourself that after a night at a salsa club.) What it is, however, is diverse and complex, embedded with traditions inherited from baroque Spain, from the Aztecs and Mayans, from the descendants of black slaves who peopled the Antilles, from the mountainous country of Central America. Each winds its way differently into the American imagination, where it gets put to new uses.

There are the things that come from tropical sea-bordered places like Puerto Rico, Cuba, the Dominican Republic. African influences are the legacy of the region's old status as a center of the slave trade. They can be heard in the Afro-Caribbean rhythm that the Talking Heads deploy in their new song *Mr. Jones* to pay mock homage to a straitlaced character. No other rhythm would quite do, would say quite the same thing. Why? Because the point is not just to make a danceable cut, but to set up a dialogue between David Byrne's high-strung ironies and the irresistible counterarguments of the beat. That thrumming rhythm says forget the nerdy options of the industrial world, where the commands of the dollar sign squash the spirit. Why not a world where the brain and the hips are both engaged?

The civilization of Mexico, meanwhile, is undergirded by a powerful Indian legacy. It can be felt in the somber and ceremonial notes of Mexican Catholicism. And it can be felt in the work of a Mexican-American painter like Carlos Almaraz, whose series of car-crash paintings double as jokes about the encounter between Hispanic and Anglo in America. But the paintings are also built on a notion of duality—strangeness and beauty, violence and peace—that has roots in Aztec cosmology, which saw in pairings a sign of balance in the universe.

For all the diversity of Latin cultures, there are also some shared characteristics that bring new inflections to American life. The U.S. is a nation that puts no great premium on the past. Sometimes it seems that the prevailing notion of history is a Top 40 playlist from the 1960s. But Hispanic culture is consumed with the past, on both the personal and historical levels, and drawn to the memory play, the history painting, the musical tradition to accomplish the tasks of recollection. It was only fitting that the actor Edward James Olmos should star in *The Ballad of Gregorio Cortez*, the story of a 1901 confrontation between a Mexican farmer and the Texas Rangers that has lived on ever since as a *corrido*, a story song.

Hispanic life also puts a different stress on the claims of individualism. The arts in America are absorbed by personal experience, the melodrama of the interior life, the spectacle of "me." Hispanic culture offers a counterweight in the claims of community and the shared impulse. You can see those asserting themselves in mainstream life through such means as the outdoor murals—acts of public declamation in the tradition of the great Mexican muralists—that are an essential part of the Los Angeles cityscape. Add to that sentiment the claims of family, the primal unit of Hispanic life. The Mexican poet Octavio Paz recently described it. "In the North American ethic" he wrote, "the center is the individual; in Hispanic morals the true protagonist is the family." It shows in the work of a photographer like Tony Mendoza. He sees in his extended Cuban family what it is that sometimes makes them comic, but he also knows that their fate is his, their picture is his own I.D.

So these ingredients of Hispanic feeling are absorbed, along with the Hispanic works that carry them, into the American repertory. In show business they sometimes call this process crossover, the chartmaker's term for the record or film that reaches beyond its expected audience. For many Hispanics, the whole notion is ringed all around with skepticism and mixed feelings. (Who wants to cross over anyway? You come here.) Not everyone is crazy about the term Hispanic, which came into vogue in the 1970s and was seized by marketers; it seems to smudge a dozen separate nationalities into an ethnic blur. And a phenomenon made up so heavily of pop charts and box-office receipts is not much help in the struggles against such things as low wages and poor education, the things that count most for Hispanics still in the barrios. There are misgivings too about the kind of treatment Hispanic life will get from big art galleries and entertainment conglomerates that can grind whole cultures into merchandise. Does anyone really need a sitcom with characters named Juan and Maria mouthing standard showbiz punch lines? The trick for Hispanic talents these days is to get to the market fresh, not canned.

Always chafing against cliches too narrow to contain them, Hispanics may find their greatest luxury in not being hemmed in by any preconceptions at all. Consider the Los Angeles artist known as Gronk. He has impeccable Chicano credentials: born in 1954 in mostly Chicano East Los Angeles, he was a co-founder in his younger days of an ad hoc group of Latino artists who brought their art to the streets. But all of that was the forcing ground for a talent that resists ethnic labels. His paintings carry echoes of Mexican symbolism, but they also wear the signs of European expressionism, new-wave imagery, old-fashioned camp. And he recalls low- and high-culture influences in his adolescence that are shared by half the Anglo painters in Manhattan. "Daffy Duck on TV in the morning and Camus in my back pocket," as he once described it. Someone like Gronk does not cross over at all. In him, the cultures simply converge.

Maybe convergence is the key. This is not just a box-office phenomenon, after all, but an episode in an ongoing cultural evolution, one in which Americans of all kinds learn to see a bit of Latino within themselves. In that process a Spanish term might help. The word is *corazón*, meaning heart. Let it stand for what is necessary in all relations between the Americans who are not Hispanics and the Americans who are. Their shared history, full of frictions and resentments, marked by episodes of bigotry, exploitation and even bloodshed, might yet become a comedy of reconciliation, but that would take real heart and plenty of it. Not the valentine of pop crooning, not the thumping bag inflated for election years, but the experienced heart—tread marked, willing, unconditional. The one that listens. Because, as they cross over into the American imagination, Hispanics are sending one irresistible message: we come bearing gifts. ∎

By the time of the 1990 census, one fourth of all Americans defined themselves as Hispanic or nonwhite. Hindus, Buddhists and Jains joined Muslims to make America the world's most religiously diverse nation. With a burst of energy, artists of Asian heritage began telling their stories, while Asian-American "whiz kids" dominated school honor rolls everywhere. The increasingly diverse nation struggled with new issues like "political correctness" and old ones like bilingual education. Yet the more America changed, the more it was coming to resemble its old promise to itself: E pluribus unum—from many peoples, one nation.

THE 1990s

Beyond the Melting Pot

The 21st century will see "the browning of America"—racial and ethnic groups in the U.S. will outnumber whites for the first time.

SOMEDAY SOON, surely much sooner than most people who filled out their Census forms last week realize, white Americans will become a minority group. Long before that day arrives, the presumption that the "typical" U.S. citizen is someone who traces his or her descent in a direct line to Europe will be part of the past. Already 1 American in 4 defines himself or herself as Hispanic or nonwhite. If current trends in immigration and birth rates persist, the Hispanic population will have further increased an estimated 21%, the Asian presence about 22%, blacks almost 12% and whites a little more than 2% when the 20th century ends. By 2020, a date no further into the future than John F. Kennedy's election is in the past, the number of U.S. residents who are Hispanic or nonwhite will have more than doubled, to nearly 115 million, while the white population will not be increasing at all. By 2056, when someone born today will be 66 years old, the "average" U.S. resident, as defined by Census statistics, will trace his or her descent to Africa, Asia, the Hispanic world, the Pacific Islands, Arabia—almost anywhere but white Europe.

While there may remain towns or outposts where even a black family will be something of an oddity, where English and Irish and German surnames will predominate, where a traditional (some will wistfully say "real") America will still be seen on almost every street corner, they will be only the vestiges of an earlier nation. The former majority will learn, as a normal part of everyday life, the meaning of the Latin slogan engraved on U.S. coins—*e pluribus unum*, one formed from many.

Among the younger populations that go to school and provide new entrants to the work force, the change will happen sooner. In some places an America beyond the melting pot has already arrived. In New York State some 40% of elementary- and secondary-school children belong to an ethnic minority. Within a decade, the proportion is expected to approach 50%. In California white pupils are already a minority. Hispanics (who, regardless of their complexion, generally distinguish themselves from both blacks and whites) account for 31.4% of public school enrollment, blacks add 8.9%, and Asians and others amount to 11%—for a nonwhite total of 51.3%. This finding is not only a reflection of white flight from desegregated public schools. Whites of all ages account for just ????% of California's population. In San Jose bearers of the Vietnamese surname

Elementary school students in California: The face of America's future

Nguyen outnumber the Joneses in the telephone directory 14 columns to eight.

Nor is the change confined to the coasts. Some 12,000 Hmong refugees from Laos have settled in St. Paul. At some Atlanta low-rent apartment complexes that used to be virtually all black, social workers today need to speak Spanish. At the Sesame Hut restaurant in Houston, a Korean immigrant owner trains Hispanic immigrant workers to prepare Chinese-style food for a largely black clientele. The Detroit area has 200,000 people of Middle Eastern descent; some 1,500 small grocery and convenience stores in the vicinity are owned by a whole subculture of Chaldean Christians with roots in Iraq. "Once America was a microcosm of European nationalities," says Molefi Asante, chairman of the department of African-American studies at Temple University in Philadelphia. "Today America is a microcosm of the world."

History suggests that sustaining a truly multiracial society is difficult, or at least unusual. Only a handful of great powers of the distant past—Pharaonic Egypt and Imperial Rome, most notably—managed to maintain a distinct national identity while embracing, and being ruled by, an ethnic mélange. The most ethnically diverse contemporary power, the Soviet Union, is beset with secessionist demands and near tribal conflicts. But such comparisons are flawed, because those empires were launched by conquest and maintained through an aggressive military presence. The U.S. was created, and continues to be redefined, primarily by voluntary immigration. This process has been one of the country's great strengths, infusing it with talent and energy. The "browning of America" offers tremendous opportunity for capitalizing anew on the merits of many peoples from many lands. Yet this fundamental change in the ethnic makeup of the U.S. also poses risks. The American character is resilient and thrives on change. But past periods of rapid evolution have also, alas, brought out deeper, more fearful aspects of the national soul.

POLITICS: NEW AND SHIFTING ALLIANCES. A truly multiracial society will undoubtedly prove much harder to govern. Even seemingly race-free conflicts will be increasingly complicated by an overlay of ethnic tension. For example, the expected showdown in the early 21st century between the rising number of retirees and the dwindling number of workers who must be taxed to pay for the elders' Social Security benefits will probably be compounded by the fact that a large majority of recipients will be white, whereas a majority of workers paying for them will be nonwhite.

While prior generations of immigrants believed they had to learn English quickly to survive, many Hispanics now maintain that the Spanish language is inseparable from their ethnic and cultural identity, and seek to remain bilingual, if not primarily Spanish-speaking, for life. They see legislative drives to make English the sole official language, which have prevailed in some fashion in at least 16 states, as a political backlash. Says Arturo Vargas of the Mexican American Legal Defense and Educational Fund: "That's what English-only has been all about—a reaction to the growing population and influence of Hispanics. It's human nature to be uncomfortable with change. That's what the Census is all about, documenting changes and making sure the country keeps up."

Racial and ethnic conflict remains an ugly fact of American life everywhere, from working-class ghettos to college campuses, and those who do not raise their fists often raise their voices over affirmative action and other power sharing. When Florida Atlantic University, a state-funded institution under pressure to increase its low black enrollment, offered last month to give free tuition to every qualified black freshman who enrolled, the school was flooded with calls of complaint, some protesting that nothing was being done for "real" Americans. As the numbers of minorities increase, their demands for a share of the national bounty are bound to intensify, while whites are certain to feel ever more embattled. Businesses often feel whipsawed between immigration laws that punish them for hiring illegal aliens and antidiscrimination laws that penalize them for demanding excessive documentation from foreign-

seeming job applicants. Even companies that consistently seek to do the right thing may be overwhelmed by the problems of diversifying a primarily white managerial corps fast enough to direct a work force that will be increasingly nonwhite and, potentially, resentful.

Nor will tensions be limited to the polar simplicity of white vs. nonwhite. For all Jesse Jackson's rallying cries about shared goals, minority groups often feel keenly competitive. Chicago's Hispanic leaders have leapfrogged between white and black factions, offering support wherever there seemed to be the most to gain for their own community. Says Dan Solis of the Hispanic-oriented United Neighborhood Organization: "If you're thinking power, you don't put your eggs in one basket."

Blacks, who feel they waited longest and endured most in the fight for equal opportunity, are uneasy about being supplanted by Hispanics or, in some areas, by Asians as the numerically largest and most influential minority—and even more, about being outstripped in wealth and status by these newer groups. Because Hispanics are so numerous and Asians such a fast-growing group, they have become the "hot" minorities, and blacks feel their needs are getting lower priority. As affirmative action has broadened to include other groups—and to benefit white women perhaps most of all—blacks perceive it as having waned in value for them.

THE CLASSROOM: WHOSE HISTORY COUNTS? Political pressure has already brought about sweeping change in public school textbooks over the past couple of decades and has begun to affect the core humanities curriculum at such elite universities as Stanford. At stake at the college level is whether the traditional "canon" of Greek, Latin and West European humanities study should be expanded to reflect the cultures of Africa, Asia and other parts of the world. Many books treasured as classics by prior generations are now seen as tools of cultural imperialism. In the extreme form, this thinking rises to a value-deprived neutralism that views all cultures, regardless of the grandeur or paucity of their attainments, as essentially equal.

Even more troubling is a revisionist approach to history in which groups that have gained power in the present turn to remaking the past in the image of their desires. If 18th, 19th and earlier 20th century society should not have been so dominated by white Christian men of West European ancestry, they reason, then that past society should be reinvented as pluralist and democratic. Alternatively, the racism and sexism of the past are treated as inextricable from—and therefore irremediably tainting—traditional learning and values.

While debates over college curriculum get the most attention, professors generally can resist or subvert the most wrong-headed changes and students generally have mature enough judgment to sort out the arguments. Elementary- and secondary-school curriculums reach a far broader segment at a far more impressionable age, and political expediency more often wins over intellectual honesty. Exchanges have been vituperative in New York, where a state task force concluded that "African-Americans, Asian-Americans, Puerto Ricans and Native Americans have all been victims of an intellectual and educational oppression …Negative characterizations, or the absence of positive references, have had a terribly damaging effect on the psyche of young people." In urging a revised syllabus, the task force argued, "Children from European culture will have a less arrogant perspective of being part of a group that has 'done it all.'" Many intellectuals are outraged. Political scientist Andrew Hacker of Queens College lambastes a task-force suggestion that children be taught how "Native Americans were here to welcome new settlers from Holland, Senegal, England, Indonesia, France, the Congo, Italy, China, Iberia." Asks Hacker: "Did the Indians really welcome all those groups? Were they at Ellis Island when the Italians started to arrive? This is not history but a myth intended to bolster the self-esteem of certain children and, just possibly, a platform for advocates of various ethnic interests."

VALUES: SOMETHING IN COMMON. Economic and political issues, however much emotion they arouse, are fundamentally open to practical solution. The deeper significance of America's becoming a majority nonwhite society is what it means to the national psyche, to individuals' sense of themselves and their nation—their idea of what it is to be American. People of color have often felt that whites treated equality as a benevolence granted to minorities rather than as an inherent natural right. Surely that condescension will wither.

Rather than accepting U.S. history and its meaning as settled, citizens will feel ever more free to debate where the nation's successes sprang from and what its unalterable beliefs are. They will clash over which myths and icons to invoke in education, in popular culture, in ceremonial speechmaking from political campaigns to the State of the Union address. Which is the more admirable heroism: the courageous holdout by a few conquest-minded whites over Hispanics at the Alamo, or the anonymous expression of hope by millions who filed through Ellis Island? Was the subduing of the West a daring feat of bravery and ingenuity, or a wretched example of white imperialism? Symbols deeply meaningful to one group can be a matter of indifference to another. Says University of Wisconsin chancellor Donna Shalala: "My grandparents came from Lebanon. I don't identify with the Pilgrims on a personal level." Christopher Jencks, professor of sociology at Northwestern, asks, "Is anything more basic about turkeys and Pilgrims than about Martin Luther King and Selma? To me, it's six of one and half a dozen of the other, if children understand what it's like to be a dissident minority. Because the civil rights struggle is closer chronologically, it's likelier to be taught by someone who really cares."

Traditionalists increasingly distinguish between a "multiracial" society, which they say would be fine, and a "mul-ticultural" society, which they deplore. They argue that every society needs a universally accepted set of values and that new arrivals should therefore be pressured to conform to the mentality on which U.S. prosperity and freedom were built. Says Allan Bloom, author of the best-selling *The Closing of the American Mind*: "Obviously, the future of America can't be sustained if people keep only to their own ways and remain perpetual outsiders. The society has got to turn them into Americans. There are natural fears that today's immigrants may be too much of a cultural stretch for a nation based on Western values."

The counterargument, made by such scholars as historian Thomas Bender of New York University, is that if the center cannot hold, then one must redefine the center. It should be, he says, "the ever changing outcome of a continuing contest among social groups and ideas for the power to define public culture." Besides, he adds, many immigrants arrive committed to U.S. values; that is part of what attracted them. Says Julian Simon, professor of business administration at the University of Maryland: "The life and institutions here shape immigrants and not vice versa. This business about immigrants changing our institutions and our basic ways of life is hogwash. It's nativist scare talk."

CITIZENSHIP: FORGING A NEW IDENTITY. Historians note that Americans have felt before that their historical culture was being overwhelmed by immigrants, but conflicts between earlier-arriving English, Germans and Irish and later-arriving Italians and Jews did not have the obvious and enduring element of racial skin color. And there was never a time when the nonmainstream elements could claim, through sheer numbers, the potential to unite and exert political dominance. Says Bender: "The real question is whether or not our notion of diversity can successfully negotiate the color line."

For whites, especially those who trace their ancestry back to the early years of the Republic, the American heritage is a source of pride. For people of color, it is more likely to evoke anger and sometimes shame. The place where hope is shared is in the future. Demographer Ben Wattenberg, formerly perceived as a resister to social change, says, "There's a nice chance that the American myth in the 1990s and beyond is going to ratchet another step toward this idea that we are the universal nation. That rings the bell of manifest destiny. We're a people with a mission and a sense of purpose, and we believe we have something to offer the world."

Not every erstwhile alarmist can bring himself to such optimism. Says Norman Podhoretz, editor of *Commentary*: "A lot of people are trying to undermine the foundations of the American experience and are pushing toward a more Balkanized society. I think that would be a disaster, not only because it would destroy a precious social inheritance but also because it would lead to enormous unrest, even violence."

While know-nothingism is generally confined to the

more dismal corners of the American psyche, it seems all too predictable that during the next decades many more mainstream white Americans will begin to speak openly about the nation they feel they are losing. There are not, after all, many nonwhite faces depicted in Norman Rockwell's paintings. White Americans are accustomed to thinking of themselves as the very picture of their nation. Inspiring as it may be to the rest of the world, significant as it may be to the U.S. role in global politics, world trade and the pursuit of peace, becoming a conspicuously multiracial society is bound to be a somewhat bumpy experience for many ordinary citizens. For older Americans, raised in a world where the numbers of whites were greater and the visibility of nonwhites was carefully restrained, the new world will seem ever stranger. But the new world is here. It is now. And it is irreversibly the America to come. ■

■ IMMIGRANTS   SPECIAL ISSUE: FALL 1993

And Still They Come

Around the world, would-be Americans continue to stand in long lines, in hopes of starting new lives in a new land

IN WARSAW THE VISA ENTRANCE to the American embassy is on Ulica Piekna—Beautiful Street. And it has got prettier. In the past four years, the Americans have installed flower beds and wooden benches for the people in line for visa interviews. Perhaps the amenities are meant to soften the disappointment: now that the communists are no longer playing watchdog, it falls to embassy personnel to limit the traffic to America. And although roughly 10 times as many people will be granted visas this year as were in 1987, veterans of Ulica Piekna say half of those waiting here will be turned down.

It is a lovely, mild day, and the line is about 150 people long. There are matronly women and miniskirted girls, jeans-clad students and a mustachioed man in black suit and white socks—a peasant in his Sunday Mass outfit. Robert, from the town of Plock, is among those in line. "I came to seek a visa because in Poland, there are very limited prospects of acquiring anything by work," he says. "I expect a different existence in America. I make about $200 a month. I wonder whether anybody would work for $200 a month in the U.S."

Elsewhere, the lines and the motives for standing in them, are much the same. In Beijing another line of 150 represents a far smaller slice of the general population, in part because the regime continues to frown on emigration. Still, a young lawyer explains why he wants to go to Meiguo, the Beautiful Country, the Mandarin name for America: "My colleagues tried to discourage me from going," he says. "But I feel I have to improve myself." In a displaced-persons camp on the outskirts of Nairobi, a cheery Somali is also waiting patiently to go to America, but he is in luck: he already has a visa and a seat on an upcoming flight. "There is no tribalism in the U.S.," he explains as a motive for his move. "There is a state of peace."

Embassy visa lines delineate America's outermost border; they are where cultural diversity begins. If America is a braided rope, its strands lead back to a hundred countries, each strand a line. Sometimes the line to reach America is metaphorical; more often it is as tangible as a battered suitcase, fear sweat and molded plastic furniture.

In the middle decades of the century, there was an apparent consistency to the kinds of people who waited in line and their reasons for being there. But the massive expulsions and migrations of the 1970s and '80s, combined with the recent geopolitical switch from the cold war to the new world order, scrambled all that. These days, by the time people get permission to leave, their initial motivation might have disappeared, sometimes replaced by another. Nonetheless, the longings themselves are familiar: to escape war, to find religious freedom, to join relatives, to make an honest buck.

Here are some lives that have been deeply touched by the powerful desire to realize those longings:

• Americans, wrote Alexis de Tocqueville, "have all a lively faith in the perfectability of man...They all consider society as a body in a state of improvement, humanity as a changing scene." Tesfa-Michael Tayae keeps those buoyant words and the orientation pamphlet that contains them in a place of honor in his tent, along with pictures of his two "favorite musicians," Elvis Presley and Kenny Rogers, and the autograph of nearly every U.S. citizen he has met on his desperate odyssey from the mountains of Ethiopia to a Kenyan plateau. "Americans are ahead of us in so many ways," says the 32-year-old Ethiopian gravely, "in terms of knowledge, in terms of culture."

Tayae, along with the thousand other Ethiopians, Somalis, Zairians and southern Sudanese huddled in this fenced-in tent city in the Nairobi suburb of Langata awaiting transshipment to various destinations, has heard that America is less than perfect. But what is American poverty and racism against the famine, murderous tribalism and blood politics that drove him to leave his wife and child behind in Addis Ababa? What is a mugging compared with the regular assaults, rapes and other crimes common in the vermin-plagued shantytowns that serve as collection points for the victims of the region's natural and man-made disasters? Tayae, who has waited three years for the flight that will finally take him to Cincinnati, Ohio, in a few weeks, is sincere when he says in labored English, "I am happy and all my friends are happy to go to America."

Whether America will be happy to see him is something else again. American attitudes about the "perfectability" of immigrants may have changed since Tocqueville's day. And Tayae's life experience is much farther from the average American's than were those of the Europeans who assimilated themselves into the "changing scene" of 1835. His "training" in Ethiopia's crippled economy and in the camps, where the U.S. is seen more often as a source of free grain than as a center of free enterprise, may have weakened any natural drive and self-sufficiency like those shown by such peers as a Mexican border jumper, a Haitian boat person or a passenger on the *Golden Venture*. Asks Julie Johnston, an American who has screened refugees like Langata's who apply for immigration: "What are they going to do in the U.S.? They've done nothing but wait in line—for food, for water—for years. They'll go on welfare."

Tayae still wants his chance. He has learned the lingo of the orientation films he has been shown, and will dutifully recite a list of things he must not expect in his new land: that he will become rich; that anyone will speak his language (Amharic); that Americans will greet one another Ethiopian-style, with a hug, a kiss and an extended five-minute chat. Once in America, he says, he will try to locate his wife and children and bring them from Addis Ababa.

• Not far up the line from where Yuri Khamov waits outside the American embassy in Moscow, an expediter advertises his unwelcome street wisdom: "The Americans let in only those who have sponsors in the U.S.," he says. "Otherwise, they stamp your file with a black stamp, which means, 'Forget about America.'" Khamov, 25, an electrician who wants to settle in Orvado, Colorado, ignores him. Not that the self-appointed expert is wrong: ever since communist control ended, the U.S. embassy has been cherry-pick-

ing, allowing only a small fraction of these sweat-stained, hope-driven applicants through. But Khamov and his extended family (13 in all), who have joined the visa line straight from their 55-hour train ride from Siberia, may actually have a shot. They will be applying on a time-honored ground: freedom from religious intolerance.

"We are Baptists," Yuri explains matter-of-factly, his gaze direct and intense. "We have always been persecuted here for our religious beliefs. We always will be." Some Americans, familiar with the Jewish exodus from the Soviet Union in the 1970s and '80s, assume that religious discrimination in Russia ended along with mandated Marxist atheism. But the Khamovs, whose fellow Baptists make up less than one-half of 1% of the population, say otherwise. The motherland, they say, has simply exchanged a state credo of godlessness for an older tradition: the hegemony of the Russian Orthodox Church. Yuri smiles as he recalls that under communism, his parents were denied permission to build a house because it might be used as a religious meeting place. Under the new democracy? The same: "My wife, who taught Sunday school, couldn't rent a place for classes. My relative is a pastor in Barabinsk in Siberia. The local mayor told him to get out of town. He said, 'We don't want any religious dissent.'"

So the Khamov clan is looking to Colorado, where one of Yuri's brothers has gone. Probably people will need electricians there; Yuri has never wanted for a job. "I'm not running away because I'm in dire straits. I have a two-room apartment in Novosibirsk for my wife and kids," he says. "I have skills and a job. I can make a living." Gently, he arranges the family's bags so that his wife Victoria and their son Maxim, 2, can nap on them. "But I want no constraints on how I bring up my children. If I move to America, the degradation of this society will not affect them."

• Anyone surveying the road outside the American consulate in New Delhi in the 1980s would have espied a sea of turbans. The Sikhs were leaving, fleeing a plague of anti-Sikh terrorism in Punjab and the poisonous sentiment that had seeped into other parts of India as well. "Why not join us?" Sikhs who had made it safely to New York and Toronto were asking relatives back home. That question was certainly weighing on Satbir Kang, when at age 21 she first applied for a visa.

Her sister had been in Hayward, California, since 1981, married to an engineer. After the troubles began, they sponsored her mother's trip, then that of her father Jagdish, whose strategy was to emigrate and bring in five of his children behind him. He hired a caretaker for the family's 35-acre farm in their village of Panam. Then he bought an apartment in Chandigarh for the sole purpose of housing his son and four daughters as they wait for their visas.

The waiting is longer than anticipated. When last Satbir heard, it would be at least two years before she could leave. Overwhelmed, the embassy is still processing visa requests from 1989. The waiting has also outlasted the terrorism, now seemingly under control again. She could stay now, if she wanted.

But an entire family cannot do a U-turn in the middle of a mass migration. Satbir is enrolling in a computer course that will come in handy when she helps at the store her parents run in Hayward. Her father, back in India on a visit, testifies that America is a rich country, with many "gadgets" to make life more comfortable. "I would hate to look and behave like an American," says Satbir, even among Americans. Perhaps sometimes she will wear slacks or a skirt, instead of the traditional salwar kameez tunic. Beyond that, she knows little, but expects the best. Problems? She is sure there must be some. "But is life any better here?" she asks sharply. "One can enjoy a finer lifestyle in the U.S."

The sun never sets on the line, but it is setting now over Ulica Piekna in Warsaw. Robert from Plock has been turned away, as have half of his companions. But Andrzej Zdanowski, 22, a Warsaw office clerk who has not reached the visa office, is still prepared to try his luck. "I have heard that Americans are friendly and tolerant, and one may meet an unselfish smile there," he says. Then he adds, "There are things there that don't exist here, unique things. And a man is always attracted to something new."

He may be right or wrong about the smile. But if he should succeed today, the country he meets at the end of the line will not only be new to him but also make him new. And, if the U.S. is lucky, he will return the favor. Although it is hardly a goal he is entertaining now, his arrival and those of millions like him will serve to make their adopted country a stronger and more diverse place to live. ■

One Nation Under Gods

Not without conflict, an unprecedented variety of faiths blooms across the world's most religiously diverse nation

WHEN J. HECTOR ST. JOHN CREVECOEUR praised the "strange religious medley" he observed in late 18th century America, he could hardly have imagined the full orchestral symphony of faiths that resounds in the U.S. two centuries later. The world has never seen a nation as religiously diverse as the U.S., which becomes ever more so each year under the impact of new immigrants. In addition to the various mainstream Judeo-Christian faiths that populated the original colonies, America now encompasses 700 to 800 "nonconventional" denominations, according to J. Gordon Melton, who monitors the proliferation for his Encyclopedia of American Religions. Half of them are imported variants of standard world religions, mostly Asian; the other half a creative and chaotic mix of U.S.-born creeds—everything from Branch Davidians to New Agers. In the future, says sociologist Wade Clark Roof, "clearly the bounds of religious pluralism will push further and further out, and that's very American."

While adding exotic new creeds, the tide of immigration since the 1960s has also increased the variegation within Christianity. Millions of Hispanics have brought a florid,

A mosque near Toledo, Ohio: Islam comes to America's heartland

fervent Latin sensibility into U.S. Catholicism, challenging a church hierarchy dominated by the stolid sons and grandsons of Irish immigrants, who now are struggling to recruit Hispanic priests. The bishops also face Pentecostal or Baptist soul winners who successfully target Spanish-speaking neighborhoods. Meanwhile, Koreans have had a notable impact within Protestantism with their evangelistic zeal and religious traditionalism.

Christianity still claims nearly nine-tenths of the populace, according to a City University of New York survey of 113,000 Americans. But talk of a "Christian" nation from the likes of Pat Buchanan and Mississippi Governor Kirk Fordice is increasingly misplaced. More accurately, the country's traditional consensus faith is biblical monotheism, which comfortably includes Judaism. Now, however, there is a major new player. Islam, the third great monotheistic faith, is expanding through both immigration and the conversion of African Americans and is bidding to supplant Judaism as America's second largest faith. In 1978 the Interfaith Conference of Metropolitan Washington became the first major interfaith organization to include Muslims alongside the Catholics, Protestants and Jews. It has since admitted Mormons and Sikhs; Hindus will probably be next. Other prospects: Buddhists, Baha'is.

Mapping such widening diversity is a goal of Harvard University's Pluralism Project, run by religion professor Diana Eck. Students have located, among other things, seven Buddhist temples in Salt Lake City, two Sikh gurdwaras in Phoenix, Arizona, a Taoist temple in Denver, a Jain center in Blairstown, New Jersey, and five Oklahoma City mosques. The project estimates that nationwide there are 1,139 houses of worship for Muslims, 1,515 for Buddhists and 412 for Hindus.

Despite some doctrinal hostility and episodes of the nativist hysteria that once confronted Catholic and Jewish immigrants, America has by and large managed to retain its vaunted toleration. In contrast with Bosnia, Belfast, Beirut and Bombay, interreligious conflicts are most often fought out in courtrooms, zoning boards or school boards rather than in the streets. The process is typified by events in Georgia, in the heartland of the old Southern Protestant hegemony. There certain Baptists joined non-Christians to keep the state from erecting a statue of Jesus along a highway. Prison inmate Randy James is getting ready to sue for the right to keep wearing the dreadlocks that are required by his Rastafarian faith. While Atlanta Muslims have already won from their employer, the city housing authority, the right to attend Friday worship, Muslim women may petition to obtain a driver's license without removing their veil. And a Douglasville, Georgia, family of agnostic Native Americans got federal courts to outlaw prayers before high school football games.

The U.S. Supreme Court has also grappled with the perplexities of the emerging interreligious climate. Last June the court decided that Hialeah, Florida, could not outlaw the animal sacrifices of the Santeria religion. By contrast, in 1990 it ruled against devotees of Oregon's Native American Church, who claimed the right to ingest peyote in its rituals, and a few years earlier declared that an Orthodox Jewish rabbi could not wear the skullcap his faith required because doing so would violate Air Force dress regulations. But Congress then passed a legal head-covering exemption that benefits both Orthodox Jews and turban-wearing Sikhs (although the military still requires Sikh men to violate their faith by shaving off their beard). Further confusing matters, the Supreme Court in 1987 ruled that, unlike the Georgia case, New Jersey prison rules took precedence over the demand of two Muslims to attend Friday worship.

As newly emerging religious face conflicts with the wider society, they are subtly Americanizing their internal operations. Asians incorporate their temples and organize boards just as churches do, and lay leaders often bear more practical authority than traditional holy men imported from Asia. American holidays such as the Fourth of July and New Year's are adopted for major gatherings. Though Sunday has no significance in the Hindu calendar, it is now the busiest day for worship at the ornate Hindu Temple in New York City.

Cultural pressures are usually resisted, however, when they impinge upon important tenets. In its 1992 guidelines for public school administrators (35,000 copies in print), the Islamic Society of North America urges schools to accommodate Muslim practices for adherents of Islam. These include seating boys and girls separately, exempting Muslims from music and drama classes, allowing them to leave for afternoon prayers and letting them wear special gym clothing to meet religious dictates on modesty. Though some American Muslims might take out interest-bearing loans, which are forbidden by the faith, in their personal life they shun mortgages and try always to pay cash when building their mosques.

Other faiths are no less assertive in protecting their traditions in the larger society. Hindus have discovered that they must inculcate their faith in their young much more consciously and aggressively than in India, where it could be taken for granted. As new religions find their footing and become bolder, some analysts believe that surprises are in store. Devout adherents of Asian religions, for example, are as uncomfortable as Middle American Protestant Fundamentalists with the sort of secularization that U.S. intellectuals have fostered in education, law, politics, entertainment and the arts. Phong Nguyen, leader of a Vietnamese Buddhist congregation in Washington, sounds for all the world like a Christian Coalition activist as he complains about the lack of moral teaching in the public schools.

Although proponents of secularism and separation of church and state believe they are advancing religious toleration, believers often feel that the practical result is intolerance toward religion as a whole. That view is expressed vigorously by Stephen Carter of the Yale Law School in his book *The Culture of Disbelief.* Carter claims that the leaders of American culture increasingly treat religious faith as a somewhat embarrassing or purely private affair that should be allowed to have no impact on society—unlike all other modes of thinking. The newly arriving faiths can be expected to resist that sort of limitation as they reinvigorate America's spiritual marketplace.

That is all a far cry from the narrow spectrum of mostly Christian believers so celebrated by Crevecoeur, who foresaw "religious indifference" spreading from one end of the continent to the other. Where that would lead, he wondered, "no one can tell; perhaps it may leave a vacuum fit to receive other systems." In America's third century, that vacuum has been filled to overflowing. ∎

This Land Is Their Land

*After a century of struggle, Native Americans are retrieving their rights
and their heritage to preserve an ancient culture from extinction*

March of Memory: Hundreds of Sioux made a 220-mile ride to mark the 100th anniversary of Wounded Knee

THE TEMPERATURE WAS 21° below zero, not counting the 20-m.p.h. winds blowing across the hilltop cemetery, as mourners gathered to remember a gruesome massacre. A century ago, on Dec. 29, 1890, soldiers of the 7th Cavalry slaughtered hundreds of Sioux men, women and children who had sought refuge under a white flag at a place called Wounded Knee. To mark the anniversary, descendants of the survivors came on foot and on horseback, some from hundreds of miles across the plains. They circled the chain-link fence around the grave site, saying their prayers in silence and burning sage for purification. South Dakota Governor George Mickelson offered words of sorrow and apology, the culmination of a "Year of Reconciliation" between whites and Indians in South Dakota. The journey

to the grave site, he said, "has been a prayer and a sacrifice, a wiping away of tears."

Each week brings a new installment in the fight for the survival of an ancient culture in a modern age and for dominion over lands lost a century ago. Above all, Native Americans wish to preserve the right to practice their religion, enforce their laws and educate their children without interference. Says Scott Borg, an Albuquerque attorney who regularly represents Native Americans: "The U.S. government has no more right telling the Pueblos how to run their internal affairs than does a country like Iraq to tell Kuwait how to run its internal affairs."

The vehicle, and the obstacle, to Indian autonomy is the immense, inert Bureau of Indian Affairs. The 167-year-old agency, which is in charge of everything from tribal courts and schools to social services and law enforcement on the reservations, has a sorry record of waste, corruption and choking red tape. A recent survey of government executives ranked it the least respected of 90 federal agencies, with the Indian Health Service close behind. An effort to restructure the bureau was halted by Congress until a task force of Native Americans could be assembled for consultation. But hope for progress runs thin: "Restructuring the BIA," one tribal leader noted, "is like rotating four worn-out tires."

Most Native Americans can no longer afford to wait for the government to take action. The crusade for greater self-determination reflects the desperate poverty and social pain that marks daily life on many reservations. "Indians are the most regulated people in the world," says Dale Riesling, chairman of the 2,000-member Hoopa Valley tribe in Northern California. "Self-determination means that we are completely free to set our own direction and goals, basically our own destiny." That destiny is in dire need of reshaping: life expectancy in some tribes is 45 years, the leading cause of death is alcoholism, and Indians have the lowest per capita income of any ethnic group in the U.S. A weak school system has made it nearly impossible for Native Americans to succeed in competitive jobs off the reservations. Without the resources to address these problems, tribal leaders fear that poverty and aimlessness will destroy whatever remains of traditional Indian culture.

Back around the turn of the century, the Federal Government's "progressive" policy toward Native Americans amounted to forced assimilation. The BIA shipped Indian children off to boarding schools, gave them Anglo names and banned their Native tongues and religious rituals. Each generation moved further from tribal tradition, to the point where languages, which were entirely oral, and skills, such as basketmaking, were in danger of disappearing. After decades of drift, tribes that have begun to focus on preserving their heritage for the next generation have also reduced their rates of teen suicide, illiteracy, addiction and despair.

But protecting an ancient culture also means fighting for rights that are blithely violated by neighboring communities. In last year's most celebrated confrontation, Mohawks faced down Quebec police and army troops 18 miles west of Montreal in a battle to prevent weekend golfers from putting into their ancestral graves. At the same time, Chippewa Indians, in northern Wisconsin, fought what has become an annual battle on the shores of Lake Minocqua. Their adversaries, local fishermen armed with rocks and insults, fear that the Indians' spearfishing will deplete the supply of walleyed pike and drive away sport fishermen. Though the Chippewa have voluntarily limited the size of their annual catch, they resent the fact that their ancestral claims are begrudged as concessions rather than viewed as legal rights.

Such confrontations are the flash points of a struggle heating up in courtrooms across the country. Heeding the lessons of the civil rights movement, the country's 700 Native American lawyers are using the judicial system. "There has been more Indian litigation in the past 20 years," says John Echohawk, executive director of the Native American Rights Fund, "than in the previous 200."

Most of the conflicts, in one way or another, grow out of a commitment to the land. Despite anthropologists' evidence that they came to this country across the Bering Strait land bridge, many tribes believe their ancestors emerged from an underworld through a hole in the earth known as the sipapu. Their religion, their art and their well-being are tied to the land they have guarded and revered. Now, many generations after white settlers bribed, swindled and threatened thousands of Native Americans out of millions of acres, they are determined to seek restitution.

In the Black Hills of Wyoming, 15 tribes from Wyoming, Montana and the Dakotas are fighting off an effort by the Forest Service to turn their sacred site of Medicine Wheel into a tourist attraction. The 4,000-member Northern Cheyenne tribe of Lame Deer, Mont., is battling coal miners and railroad developers on its lands. Tribe members are afraid that development would bring tourists flooding into the middle of their religious ceremonies and disturb areas rich in medicinal plants and yellow ocher earth paint needed for those rituals. "How would you like it if I took my picnic basket, my family and dog into your church while you were praying?" asks Bill TallBull, tribal elder of the Northern Cheyenne.

Many tribes are trapped between ancient environmental principles and modern economic pressures. One Alaskan tribe in dire need of funds is reluctantly trying to decide whether to sign away logging rights around Prince William Sound, permit oil drilling in a delicate wildlife area or allow an airfield to be built in the midst of a vast habitat for Kodiak bears. Other tribes have allowed waste-management companies to use reservation land for dumps and disposal sites, then suffered from the contamination of their land and water as a result. Across the vast Arizona tracts of the Navajo Nation, high-voltage wires run like silver threads to the Pacific Ocean, carrying electricity all the way to California—but not to the 200,000 Navajo who live beneath them.

A central controversy shared by Native Americans of many tribes is the crusade to have relics and remains of Indian ancestors removed from museums and returned to the tribes for burial. Some tribes believe the soul cannot rest until the body is returned to nature, by burial or cremation. Hundreds of thousands of Indian corpses were dug from their graves and carted away for display. "Grave robbing was so widespread that virtually every tribe in the country has been victimized," says Pawnee Indian Walter Echo-Hawk, staff attorney at the Native American Rights Fund.

In a landmark accord with Indian leaders last year, the Smithsonian Institution agreed to sort through its collection of 18,500 remains and to return for burial all those that were clearly identifiable as belonging to a certain tribe. Stanford University then pledged to give back its entire collection of remains of the Ohlone tribe. Other museums and collectors followed suit, and in November President Bush signed a bill to protect Indian grave sites in the U.S. and to return remains to the tribes. In some instances, however, tribes have asked a museum to retain permanent control of the objects so they could be properly conserved.

In all areas of conflict, over land or tradition or scientific collections, years of litigation lie ahead. The Bureau of Indian Affairs will have an uphill battle persuading Native Americans that it is prepared to protect their interests rather than confound them. Given the U.S. government's track record in dealing with this continent's original owners, the task of rebuilding trust will take considerable will and faith on both sides. ∎

The Hidden Hurdle

Talented black students find that one of the most insidious obstacles to achievement comes from a surprising source: their own peers

WHEN IT COMES TO ACHIEVING in school, Za'kettha Blaylock knows that even dreaming of success can mean living a nightmare. She would, above all things, like to work hard, go to college and become a doctor. But to many other black 14-year-old girls in her corner of Oakland, these ideas are anathema. The telephone rings in her family's modest apartment, and the anonymous voice murmurs daggers. "We're gonna kill you," the caller says. Za'kettha knows the threat comes from a gang of black girls, one that specializes not in drugs or street fights but in terrorizing bright black students. "They think that just because you're smart," says the eighth-grader, "they can go around beating you up."

Of all the obstacles to success that inner-city black students face, the most surprising—and discouraging—may be those erected by their own peers. Many children must also cope with broken families, inadequate schools and crumbling communities that do not value academic achievement as essential to survival and prosperity. But the ridicule of peers cuts most deeply of all. Students like Za'kettha find themselves reviled as "uppity," as trying to "act white," because many teenagers have come to equate black identity with alienation and indifference. "I used to go home and cry," says Tachelle Ross, 18, a senior at Oberlin High in Ohio. "They called me white. I don't know why. I'd say, 'I'm just as black as you are.'"

The phrase "acting white" has often been the insult of choice used by blacks who stayed behind against those who moved forward. Once it was supposed to invoke the image of an African American who had turned his back on his people and community. But the phrase has taken an ominous turn. Today it rejects all the iconography of white middle-class life: a good job, a nice home, conservative clothes and a college degree.

In the smaller world of high school, the undesirable traits are different, but the attitude is the same. Promising black students are ridiculed for speaking standard English, showing an interest in ballet or theater, having white friends or joining activities other than sports. "They'll run up to you and grab your books and say, 'I'll tear this book up,'" says Shaquila Williams, 12, a sixth-grader at Webster Academy in East Oakland. "They'll try and stop you from doing your work." Honor students may be rebuked for even showing up for class on time.

The pattern of abuse is a distinctive variation on the nerd bashing that almost all bright, ambitious students—no matter what their color—face at some point in their young lives. The anti-achievement ethic championed by some black youngsters declares formal education useless; those who disagree and study hard face isolation, scorn and violence. While educators have recognized the existence of an anti-achievement culture for at least a decade, it has only recently emerged as a dominant theme among the troubles facing urban schools.

The label "acting white" and the dismissal of white values are bound up in questions of black identity. "If you see a black girl," explains Kareema Matthews, a street-smart 14-year-old from Harlem, "and she's black, not mixed or anything, and she wants to act like something she's not, in these days nobody considers that good. She's trying to be white. That's why nobody likes her. That's how it is now." But when asked what it is to be black, Kareema pauses. "I don't have the slightest idea."

The right attitude, according to the targets of ridicule, would be shown by skipping class, talking slang and, as Tachelle says, "being cool, not combing your hair. Carrying yourself like you don't care." Social success depends partly on academic failure; safety and acceptance lie in rejecting the traditional paths to self-improvement. "Instead of trying to come up with the smart kids, they try to bring you down to their level," says eighth-grader Rachel Blates of Oakland. "They don't realize that if you don't have an education, you won't have anything—no job, no husband, no home."

It is a sad irony that achievement should have acquired such a stigma within the black community. Hard work, scholarship and respect for family values have long been a cornerstone of black identity. In the years before the Civil War, many black slaves risked their lives learning how to read. In 1867, just four years after the Emancipation Proclamation, African Americans founded Morehouse and Howard universities. According to the Bureau of the Census, between Reconstruction and 1910, the literacy rate among Southern blacks climbed from 20% to 70%. "There has always been a strong pressure toward educational achievement," says Mae Kendall, director of elementary education for the Atlanta public schools. Kendall, who grew up in semirural Thomasville, Ga., recalls, "My mother was not a lettered woman by any means, but she said, with a good education, you could turn the world upside down.

That was a strong common linkage among all black people, and it was instilled early on."

Some education experts associate the rise of the culture of anti-achievement with the advent of public school desegregation and the flight of the black middle class to the suburbs. That left fewer role models whose success reinforced the importance of education and more children from families who found little grounds for hope in schools that were decaying.

The civil-rights movement did produce pockets of progress: the number of black managers, professionals and government officials rose 52% in the past decade. Black enrollment in colleges has climbed steeply. In 1990, 33% of all black high school graduates went on to college, in contrast to 23% in 1967. Since 1976, black Scholastic Aptitude Test scores have increased by a greater percentage than those of either whites or Asians. Still, blacks have higher truancy rates, and in spite of the gains, the test scores of African Americans remain the lowest among large ethnic groups. The high school drop-out rate among young blacks averages 7.7%, nearly twice that of their white peers, at 3.9%.

As more black teachers and administrators reach positions of power in the public school system, the anti-achievement ethic presents a special challenge to them as educators. For years, the failure of black students to succeed in white-run schools was attributed in large part to institutional racism. But some black educators are reassessing the blame. "It's absolutely ridiculous for us to be talking about what's happening to black youngsters when you've got a 90% African-American staff teaching a 95% black student body," says Franklin Smith, who is superintendent of schools in Washington and black himself. "If you can't prove what you believe here in Washington, then you might as well forget it anywhere in this country."

The effort to reverse the pattern of black failure has prompted educators like Smith to try many experiments—Afrocentric curriculums, academic-achievement fairs and efforts to establish black all-male public schools that focus on building self-esteem. The reform movements seek to revive in black students the value system that prizes education as, among other things, a way out of poverty. "We dropped the ball," laments Trinette Chase, a Montgomery County, Md., mother. "Our generation failed to pass on the value of an education."

It is a truism to say the problem most often begins at home. When parents are not able to transmit the values of achievement, the ever present peer group fills the vacuum. Moniqua Woods, 12, a student at the Webster Academy in Oakland, says it is easy to spot neglected children because they "come to school every day yawning and tired. You know they stayed out late that night." Concurs classmate Mark Martin, also 12: "Some of the kids' parents are on drugs. You go in their house, and you can smell it." Such a homelife can further strengthen the attitude that school does not matter, especially if the parents themselves are without a diploma.

Kiante Brown, 15, of Oakland, knows this all too well. His mother is a recovering crack addict who, he says, pays little attention to his comings and goings, and he hasn't seen his father in two years. Kiante used to spend his afternoons selling drugs on street corners. What little education he has came in bits and pieces; he has missed so much school he'll have to repeat the eighth grade. "I didn't really drop out, but I haven't been going to school much," he says. "For a while my mom told me to get up and go to school, but she really doesn't say nothing about it anymore."

Teachers may try to move in where parents have retreated. But with class sizes increasing and school violence growing, it is often all educators can do to maintain minimal order, much less give individual attention to any child. Some teachers admit that the insidious attitudes creep into the classroom. It becomes a self-fulfilling prophecy: when teachers have lower expectations for their black students, they give them less attention and do not push them as hard to do well. Such stereotypes have crossed racial barriers to the point where even black teachers may hold these same attitudes. "If teachers feel they cannot make any headway with a youngster," says Richard Mesa, superintendent of Oakland public schools, "they may write him off."

It is especially painful for teachers to watch their most talented students sabotage their own learning in order to fit in with peers. "Some of them feign ignorance to be accepted," says Willie Hamilton, the principal of Oakland's Webster Academy. Seneca Valley's Martine Martin observed this self-destructive pattern when she formed a program for "at risk" black females at one of her previous schools. The group originally comprised girls who were pregnant or uninterested in learning. But then, little by little, Martin noticed honor students showing up in her program because they thought it was cool.

The environment outside the classroom also leaves its mark inside. The persistence of recession has made it even more difficult to inspire black students to do well in school with the carrot of a job. "The lack of association between education and post-school employment has discouraged a lot of young people," says William Julius Wilson, professor of sociology and public policy at the University of Chicago. "They see that whether you graduate from high school or you drop out, you're still going to be hanging around on a corner or the best job you're going to find is working at a McDonald's. After a time they develop a view that you're a chump if you study hard."

There are, of course, many schools that can point to their success stories, to students who overcame all the private obstacles to graduation, often with the help of innovative programs. In Cleveland, the Scholarship-in-Escrow program was set up by local businessmen in 1987. To encourage students to work toward college, the program offers cash incentives—$40 for each A they earn,

$20 for each B—which go into an escrow account for their tuition. Since its inception, SIE has paid $469,300 in earned funds for 2,199 graduates. "It's good to know that money is being put away for you," says Faith Bryant, an 11th-grader at John Adams High School. "I had always dreamed of being successful, but now I know I have a way to do it."

The hope for these students lies in their understanding that no one group in society has a monopoly on success. "As long as you're able to term success as being black or white or red," says Oberlin's Sherman Jones, a placement specialist for the Jobs for Ohio's Graduates program "as long as we put conditions and colors on success then it'll be difficult for our kids." Destroying such misconceptions is not easy, especially when they are old and deeply rooted. But given time, perhaps "acting white" can be a phrase retired to the history books as the emblem of a misguided attitude that vanished in the light of black achievement. ■

On the Backs of Blacks

Toni Morrison

FRESH FROM ELLIS ISLAND, Stavros gets a job shining shoes at Grand Central Terminal. It is the last scene of Elia Kazan's film *America, America*, the story of a young Greek's fierce determination to immigrate to America. Quickly, but as casually as an afterthought, a young black man, also a shoe shiner, enters and tries to solicit a customer. He is run off the screen—"Get out of here! We're doing business here!"—and silently disappears.

This interloper into Stavros' workplace is crucial in the mix of signs that make up the movie's happy-ending immigrant story: a job, a straw hat, an infectious smile—and a scorned black. It is the act of racial contempt that transforms this charming Greek into an entitled white. Without it, Stavros' future as an American is not at all assured.

This is race talk, the explicit insertion into everyday life of racial signs and symbols that have no meaning other than pressing African Americans to the lowest level of the racial hierarchy. Popular culture, shaped by film, theater, advertising, the press, television and literature, is heavily engaged in race talk. It participates freely in this most enduring and efficient rite of passage into American culture: negative appraisals of the native-born black population. Only when the lesson of racial estrangement is learned is assimilation complete. Whatever the lived experience of immigrants with African Americans—pleasant, beneficial or bruising—the rhetorical experience renders blacks as noncitizens, already discredited outlaws.

All immigrants fight for jobs and space, and who is there to fight but those who have both? As in the fishing ground struggle between Texas and Vietnamese shrimpers, they displace what and whom they can. Although U.S. history is awash in labor battles, political fights and property wars among all religious and ethnic groups, their struggles are persistently framed as struggles between recent arrivals and blacks. In race talk the move into mainstream America always means buying into the notion of American blacks as the real aliens. Whatever the ethnicity or nationality of the immigrant, his nemesis is understood to be African American.

Current attention to immigration has reached levels of panic not seen since the turn of the century. To whip up this panic, modern race talk must be revised downward into obscurity and nonsense if antiblack hostility is to remain the drug of choice, giving headlines their kick. *PATTERNS OF IMMIGRATION FOLLOWED BY WHITE FLIGHT*, screams the *Star-Ledger* in Newark. The message we are meant to get is that disorderly newcomers are dangerous to stable (white) residents. Stability is white. Disorder is black. Nowhere do we learn what stable middle-class blacks think or do to cope with the "breaking waves of immigration." The overwhelming majority of African Americans, hardworking and stable, are out of the loop, disappeared except in their less than covert function of defining whites as the "true" Americans.

So addictive is this ploy that the fact of blackness has been abandoned for the theory of blackness. It doesn't matter anymore what shade the newcomer's skin is. A hostile posture toward resident blacks must be struck at the Americanizing door before it will open. The public is asked to accept American blacks as the common denominator in each conflict between an immigrant and a job or between a wannabe and status. It hardly matters what complexities, contexts and misinformation accompany these conflicts. They can all be subsumed as the equation of brand X vs. blacks.

But more than a job is at stake in this surrender to whiteness, more even than what the black intellectual W.E.B. Du Bois called the "psychological wage"—the bonus of whiteness. Racist strategies unify. Savvy politicians always include in the opening salvos of their campaigns a quick clarification of their position on race. It is a mistake to think that Bush's Willie Horton or Clinton's Sister Souljah was anything but a candidate's obligatory response to the demands of a contentious electorate unable to understand itself in any terms other than race. Warring interests, nationalities and classes can be merged with the greatest economy under that racial banner.

Race talk as bonding mechanism is powerfully on display in American literature. When Nick in F. Scott Fitzgerald's *The Great Gatsby* leaves West Egg to dine in fashionable East Egg, his host conducts a kind of class audition into wasp-dom by soliciting Nick's support for the "science" of racism. "If we don't look out the white race will be ...utterly submerged," he says. "It's all scientific stuff; it's been proved." It makes Nick uneasy, but he does not question or refute his host's convictions.

The best clue to what the country might be like without race as the nail upon which American identity is hung comes from Pap, in Mark Twain's *Huckleberry Finn*, who upon learning a Negro could vote in Ohio, "drawed out. I says I'll never vote ag'in." Without his glowing white mask he is not American; he is Faulkner's character Wash, in *Absalom, Absalom!*, who, stripped of the mask and treated like a "nigger," drives a scythe into the heart of the rich white man he has loved and served so completely.

For Pap, for Wash, the possibility that race talk might signify nothing was frightening. Which may be why the harder it is to speak race talk convincingly, the more people seem to need it. As American blacks occupy more and more groups no longer formed along racial lines, the pressure accelerates to figure out what white interests really are. The enlisted military is almost one-quarter black; police forces are blackening in large urban areas. But welfare is nearly two-thirds white; affirmative-action beneficiaries are overwhelmingly white women; dysfunctional white families jam the talk shows and court TV.

The old stereotypes fail to connote, and race talk is forced to invent new, increasingly mindless ones. There is virtually no movement up—for blacks or whites, established classes or arrivistes—that is not accompanied by race talk. Refusing, negotiating or fulfilling this demand is the real stuff, the organizing principle of becoming an American. Star spangled. Race strangled. ∎

Enforcing Correctness

In a familiar scenario, a black Muslim spews bigotry, and black leaders across the U.S. are pressured to condemn him

IN A SPEECH TO A FEW DOZEN students at Kean College in Union, New Jersey, Khalid Abdul Muhammad, a senior official with the Nation of Islam, got thousands of people mad. He called Jews "hook-nosed, bagel-eatin', lox-eatin'" imposters. He attacked Catholics: "The old no-good Pope...somebody need to raise that dress up and see what's really under there." Gays: "God does not name holy books after homosexuals." And even other blacks, including Harvard scholar Henry Louis Gates: "Who let this Negro out of the gate?"

And so it began. Muhammad, who is a top aide to Louis Farrakhan, delivered his incendiary talk on Nov. 29. Ever

since, there's been a slow burn of controversy, finally exploding into the kind of racial brush fire that's become familiar in American political discourse. Here's how it works: 1) a semi-obscure black figure says something outrageous or anti-Semitic; 2) pundits pontificate, word processors whirr; 3) one by one, black leaders are forced to condemn the offending words and the offensive speaker. It happened to Professor Griff, formerly of the politically charged rap group Public Enemy. It also happened to Farrakhan, when he called Judaism a "gutter religion." Now Muhammad's words have put him—and the Nation of Islam—in the cross hairs.

Several weeks after the speech, columnists Richard Cohen of the Washington *Post* and A.M. Rosenthal of the New York *Times* called for black leaders to repudiate Muhammad publicly. The Anti-Defamation League of B'nai B'rith took out a full-page ad in the New York *Times* with excerpts from the speech and the headline "Minister Louis Farrakhan and the Nation of Islam claim they are moving toward moderation…you decide." Feeling the heat, black leaders began the ritual of condemnation and racial correctness. Jesse Jackson called Muhammad's words reprehensible, "antipapist and inane." But Farrakhan, defiant, gave a speech in Harlem during which he embraced his controversial aide onstage.

The furor comes at a bad time for Farrakhan, who has been trying to expand his power base. He publicly performed Mendelssohn (a Jewish composer) on his violin and talked of reaching out to Jews. A Farrakhan speech in New York City this December drew 30,000 people, a crowd that would be impressive for a rocker, much less a lecturer. In September U.S. Representative Kweisi Mfume of Maryland, head of the Congressional Black Caucus, announced that he had formed a "covenant" with Farrakhan and that the caucus would work with him. But after Muhammad's diatribe, Mfume asked Farrakhan to "clarify" his position on the speech. He has yet to receive an answer, and the mainstreaming of Farrakhan is on hold.

The Muhammad incident also comes at a bad time for black-Jewish relations in general, especially in New York City, which never sleeps because it's too busy fretting about race. The Justice Department recently announced plans to look into Brooklyn's 1991 Crown Heights riots, sparked when a Jewish motorist struck and killed a black younster. In January, New York police mistakenly raided a Nation of Islam mosque after a false robbery report.

The heightened tensions are made more tragic because blacks and Jews share common interests. "Jews are the most natural white allies that blacks have," says Jonathan Kaufman, author of *Broken Alliance*, a book about black-Jewish relations. "Jews still remain the one group that's willing to vote for a black candidate." And although the press dwells on alleged black anti-Semitism, Roger Wilkins, a professor of history at George Mason University, observes, "Black people didn't create the law firms and banking firms that wouldn't hire Jews. The Wasps did that."

What rankles some blacks is that some whites feel a need to make all black leaders speak out whenever one black says something stupid. "People are deeply offended that white always seem to feel that they have to tell black people what to object to, what to condemn," says Clayton Riley, a talk-show host on WLIB, a black radio station in New York City. "There is no comparable kind of instruction to whites."

Last month Senator Ernest Hollings joked about Africans being cannibals, but no other white Senators were pressured to condemn him. Rush Limbaugh and Howard Stern make questionable racial remarks, and yet former President Bush invited Limbaugh to the White House, and Senator Alfonse D'Amato attended Stern's book party. Says Jackson: "There is a broad base of objectionable language used by a lot of people in high places. It's not just Farrakhan." Or Muhammad. To make all black leaders responsible for his words, it might be argued, is just another kind of bigotry.   ■

Pride and Prejudice

He inspires African Americans, but why does America's most controversial minister continue to poison his message with racist hatred?

LOUIS FARRAKHAN IS A PROBLEM.

He is a problem for the Rev. Benjamin Chavis of the N.A.A.C.P. and Abraham Foxman of the Jewish Anti-Defamation League of B'nai B'rith, who met last week to discuss what to do about him in a meeting so sensitive they would not even confirm he was the topic under discussion. On Saturday, the N.A.A.C.P. said it would convene a national summit of black leaders and would pointedly include Farrakhan as a gesture of support, despite expected Jewish condemnation. "We have every right to convene African-American leadership," said Chavis. "There's a deep hunger in our community."

He is a problem for the Congressional Black Caucus, whose chairman, Representative Kweisi Mfume of Maryland, has embroiled himself in controversy by pledging a "covenent" of cooperation—since disavowed—with both Farrakhan and mainstream black leaders.

He is a problem for a broad range of American blacks, who rightly fear that his anti-Semitic rhetoric erodes the moral authority of his appeals against racism and who are chagrined that his Nation of Islam, long an angry voice of the underclass, now enjoys a following among college students.

He is a problem for American Jews, who want to ensure that his brand of racism means automatic disqualification from national debate.

He is a problem for the vast majority of Islamic Americans, who already suffer from having their religion equated with hostage taking and terrorism and who mostly reject Farrakhan's racial isolationism and abuse of other faiths.

He is a problem for some of his adherents, who hear in his speeches black self-love and self-help and who see the Nation of Islam as a force against crime and drugs, bringing order and discipline to neighborhoods with almost none—yet who know that many of their associates hear only hatred in his preachments.

And Farrakhan, still impetuous at 60, is a problem for himself. In private a calm, seemingly rational man yearning for a place among trusted elders of his race, he is apt in public to get carried away on a wave of rhetoric and say things so intemperate, so easily misunderstood—and sometimes not misunderstood—that he thwarts his ambition.

Above all, he is a problem for an America that is increasingly multiracial and multicultural and is consequently in growing need of tolerance and mutual respect. His success underscores two ugly truths of American life. A great many black Americans view their white fellow citizens with anger. And a great many white Americans view their black fellow citizens with fear. Farrakhan's call for separatism and economic "reparations" and his assertion of black racial superiority win respect from millions of blacks, even among those who wish he would stop calling Jews "bloodsuckers." While most whites are apt to think his abusive rhetoric should be ignored if not silenced, many blacks think he is saying some things America ought to hear.

Love Farrakhan or hate him, the inescapable fact is that he touches a nerve among blacks as almost no one else can. A TIME/CNN poll of 504 African Americans by Yankelovich Partners last week found 73% of those surveyed were familiar with him—more than with any other black political figure except Jesse Jackson and Supreme Court Justice Clarence Thomas—and two-thirds of those familiar with Farrakhan viewed him favorably. Some 62% of those familiar with him said he was good for the black community; 63% said he speaks the truth; and 67% said he is an effective leader. More than half called him a good role model for black youth. Only a fifth thought him anti-Semitic. When asked to name "the most important black leader today," 9% of those polled volunteered his name—more than for anyone except Jackson and

three times as many as Nelson Mandela. To some extent, admittedly, these results reflect a lack of broad-based, high-profile black leaders. But that vacuum only makes Farrakhan more important, and his hateful words more potent.

Farrakhan's charismatic presence has a powerful allure. In Atlanta a lecture by Farrakhan outdrew a 1992 World Series game the same night. In Los Angeles last October he filled the 16,500-seat Sports Arena. In New York City a December speech by Farrakhan drew 25,000 to the Jacob K. Javits Convention Center. This month in Chicago, when black aldermen needed a celebrity speaker to raise funds for their legal defense in a censorship case, they did not turn to Jackson or Chavis or Mfume but to Farrakhan, the one black man they felt could fill any hall in town. Wherever he presents himself as "a voice for the voiceless," crowds throng to his orations, typically almost three hours long, for entertainment and moral uplift.

What's going on? How can so many blacks take seriously a messenger who spins bogus research into a vile theology of hatred for their fellow Americans, from Asians to Jews to whites of all variety? Plainly, black America sees a very different man from the one white America sees. This dichotomy says much about our country. And it makes trying to understand Farrakhan an urgent, if daunting, task.

Some of Farrakhan's impact is his bootstrap message of independence and self-reliance. Another major appeal is the sect's commitment to rehabilitation. The Nation of Islam runs counseling programs for prisoners, drug addicts, alcoholics and street-gang members. This is partly a recruiting tactic. But it can turn around lost lives. N.A.A.C.P. president Chavis, who played a role in bringing together Farrakhan and the Congressional Black Caucus, sees substance abuse as devastating the black community, and he credits the Nation of Islam's strict code of behavior with providing effective rescue. The issue carries personal urgency for Chavis: he has an alcoholic daughter and a son who was using crack cocaine.

Much of Farrakhan's power comes from the street effectiveness of the Nation of Islam's bow-tied young soldiers. They can be contemptuous of civil liberties—a former Washington chief of police says, "They want to operate outside the law"—but they are undeniably effective at chasing away crime and drugs in communities where nothing else works. Charles Manso has sold ice cream and sundries for 20 years from a battered white truck on a desolate corner in northeast Washington, an area without grocery stores, barbershops, even Laundromats. "There used to be shootings all the time," he says. "Drug dealers used to surround my truck. The Muslims keep them away."

The idea of returning to Islam as the ancestral religion of black Americans dates at least to the early years of this century. Many blacks rejected Christianity as a slave religion—although many, many more continue to practice it today—and were looking for ethnic heritage and pride. Although the early days of the Nation of Islam are murky, the official version is that Wallace D. Fard founded it in Detroit in 1930, allegedly upon arrival from Mecca. He disappeared a few years later and was replaced by Elijah Poole, renamed Elijah Muhammad, who reigned until 1975 over a black nationalist business and religious empire. Among its most celebrated converts was boxer Cassius Clay, later Muhammad Ali.

The sect has long been riven by factionalism. The most celebrated split was the 1964 departure of Malcolm X, who turned to orthodox Islam and was murdered by three of Elijah Muhammad's followers in 1965. While Farrakhan, who joined in 1955, seems to have played no role in the killing, he gave a speech beforehand implying that Malcolm X deserved to die.

Elijah was succeeded by his son Wallace, who shifted the movement away from antiwhite anger and toward orthodox Islam. Farrakhan was one of several Nation leaders who resisted Wallace's direction and sought to reconstitute Elijah Muhammad's faith. Eventually he became not only Elijah's ideological heir but also the tenant of his castle—Farrakhan now lives in his ornate, fortress-like home where, as in Elijah's day, Nation of Islam guards are on constant patrol outside.

That was not the career for which he seemed headed in boyhood as Louis Eugene Walcott in Boston's Roxbury neighborhood, then beginning its shift from a predominantly Jewish area to a black one. A choirboy at St. Cyprian's Episcopal Church, he ran relays in track and made his way to Winston-Salem Teachers College in North Carolina, which he attended for two years. But his real gift was for music. He played the violin obsessively, retreating to the bathroom with bow in hand for three to five hours at a stretch. He also sang and played guitar and, after leaving college, appeared on *Ted Mack's Original Amateur Hour* and in nightclubs as Calypso Gene or the Charmer. He has said that after hearing Elijah Muhammad speak in 1955, he had a dream in which he was expected to choose between show business and an unknown future—and he chose the unknown.

He did not entirely give up entertaining when he joined the Nation of Islam. During his early years, he wrote and recorded *A White Man's Heaven Is a Black Man's Hell*, a favorite black Muslim anthem. And he still plays the violin between 1 and 3 o'clock most mornings. At his 60th birthday concert in Chicago last May, soon to be available on videotape, he played Mendelssohn.

As a soldier in the Fruit of Islam, the Nation's security force and training vehicle for young men, Farrakhan proved an apt disciple. He became head of the temple in Boston and then, after Malcolm X left, temple head in New York City. By he early 1960s he was prominent in the urban black community. White Americans did not notice him until two decades later.

In the early days of the 1984 presidential campaign of Jesse Jackson, Fruit of Islam guards provided security until the Secret Service took over. Farrakhan was outraged to learn that Jewish militants were shadowing Jackson, that he had received death threats and that his family had been harassed—facts confirmed by the FBI. Until then, Farrakhan's speeches had reviled white people, not only over slavery but also over what he sees as a vast white conspiracy to conceal the glorious past of blacks as the original human race and the founders of most branches of civilization and scholarship. But he had not singled out Jews for special vilification until his Savior's Day speech that year, when he tried to intimidate Jackson's harassers: "If you harm this brother, it'll be the last one you ever harm." Heard out of context, the speech seemed to be an unprovoked threat. Once he was interpreted as anti-Semitic, Farrakhan reacted with invective that removed any doubt, labeling Judaism "a gutter religion," Israel "an outlaw state" and Hitler "a very great man" ("wickedly great," he later explained).

Since then, Farrakhan claims, he has found his path blocked by Jews in numerous and unanticipated ways. The most costly, he says, came in 1986 when Jewish distributors, angry about his slurs, effectively torpedoed his plans for Nation of Islam cosmetics and toiletries sold under the Clean & Fresh label. Major black-hair-care companies, including Johnson Products Co. in Chicago, agreed to manufacture Nation of Islam products, then backed off, Farrakhan says.

As recently as last summer, however, Farrakhan seemed to be taking a softer line. According to Representative Major Owens of Brooklyn, a Congressional Black Caucus member, "Farrakhan proposed that the caucus serve as an intermediary between himself and the Jewish community. He did not indicate what he wanted to tell them, but he did insist that he wanted peace, that he had been seeking a dialogue." Yet in November when top aide Khallid Abdul Muhammad made a venom-soaked speech at New Jersey's Kean College, a state-funded school, Farrakhan rebuked him only for his "mockery" and said he could not disavow the anti-Semitic, anti-Catholic and anti-gay "truths" his aide had spoken.

Perhaps because of the turbulent and occasionally violent history of his and other black Muslim sects, both Farrakhan and the Nation of Islam are secretive, verging on paranoid. Questions about such basics as the group's size—estimated at 30,000 to 200,000 members—and budget are routinely deflected, as are questions about the family life and background of Farrakhan and his aides.

He is so protected that it is hard to be sure, but he seems scrupulous about following dictates of conventional Islam—no pork, no alcohol—plus his sect's own rule of only one meal a day, an extension of the daytime fasting during conventional Islam's month of Ramadan. He speaks fluent Arabic, as he demonstrated by performing an Islamic prayer call in Syria while accompanying Jackson on a mission to secure the release of downed U.S. airman Robert Goodman in 1984. His mansion mingles massive concrete panels with delicate stained glass, marble floors, crystal chandeliers and a fountain between the living and dining rooms. But he shares it with several aides as well as his wife of 36 years, Khadijah (formerly Betsy), and some of their nine children.

The sect has mosques or temples in 120 cities. All ministers are appointed by Farrakhan. Male recruits earn their way up in the Fruit of Islam, where they are given military-style stripes and ranks but do not carry weapons. In contrast to Martin Luther King Jr.'s Christian invocation to turn the other cheek, however, Nation of Islam leaders favor vigorous self-defense.

In addition to "manhood training" classes to learn the history of the black man, the code of discipline of the Nation of Islam and rules about how to behave and dress (coat and bow tie at virtually all times), men must prove themselves by selling the sect's newspaper, the Final Call, on street corners. Their sales totals directly affect their standing. In some cities, recruits still sell the group's trademark bean pies.

Nation of Islam women are expected to emphasize housework and child rearing and to dress "modestly." (Whereas they must be covered even in August, pants are sometimes permitted.) When religious services are crowded, it is not unknown for women to be asked to give up seats to men and listen via loudspeaker in another room.

The pivotal question is whether the appeal of the Nation of Islam—and of Farrakhan—is separable from his invective of hate. Leaders throughout history have found it is often easier to succumb to demagoguery, to define a single scapegoat and offer a single solution to life's ills, especially when proposing self-restraint and sacrifice. Would young people choose the hard way of Islam without the zealotry of separatism and resentment? Could Farrakhan fill the seats of big-city convention centers if he stopped offering the allure of the outrageous, the unpredictable, the unspeakable spoken out loud? Perhaps the answer to both questions is yes. Perhaps even if the answer is no, the Nation of Islam would have a brighter future if it stepped away from hatred. "Farrakhan faces a choice," says Harvard's Gates. "Does he want to be remembered as a great leader, someone who underwent transformation, like Malcom X? Or does he want to be remembered as one more demagogue?"

The path of reform and reconciliation takes courage—and the more power is at stake, the more courage it takes. If his moves in recent months mean anything more than tactical maneuvering, Farrakhan has his chances this week for healing. But his courage for change has already been tested once in recent weeks. And he flinched. ∎

Pacific Overtures

In movies and music videos, in fiction and fashion, Asian chic refreshes American arts with a fresh wind from the East

THE ASIANS ARE COMING! The Asians have landed! Suddenly China is chic. So are the more familiar Asian totems of American envy and remorse, Japan and Vietnam. The U.S. may dominate pop culture around the world, but at home there is a brisk new breeze—a wind from the East. In films, fiction and fashion, from Madonna's video to Fendi's new perfume (Asja), the future looms in the rising sun.

Go, for a start, to the movies. Or stay away, as Asian-American activists urged audiences to do when *Rising Sun* hit the screens. The Sean Connery thriller, which opened to yowls of bad publicity about its caustic view of Japan's business intentions in the U.S., has been a decent-size ($55 million) hit anyway. Get thee to an art house, where *Raise the Red Lantern, Ju Dou* and other sumptuous dramas directed by Zhang Yimou and starring glorious Gong Li have helped make China a new force in world cinema. Check out *Hard Target*, as millions of teenage boys already have. The director of this martial-arts pummeler is Hong Kong's John Woo—the first director from Chinese-language cinema to make a Hollywood picture. With its deft skull-crackery and its breathless chase scenes, *Hard Target* is The *Kung-Fugitive*.

Now there are two, three, many Asian-style films. Ang Lee's *The Wedding Banquet*—an ingratiating comedy-drama about a gay Taiwanese man in New York City who gets married to please his parents—has grossed $1 million in its first month of specialized release. This week the Toronto Film Festival opens with *M. Butterfly*, David Cronenberg's film of the David Henry Hwang play about a tryst between a French diplomat (Jeremy Irons) and a Chinese man (John Lone) whom he believes to be a woman; it opens commercially Oct.

1. This Wednesday, Wayne Wang's lovely *The Joy Luck Club*, a fourfold *Terms of Endearment* based on Amy Tan's best-selling novel about a quartet of Chinese-American families, premieres in New York, Los Angeles and San Francisco. "Maybe Asian is the flavor of the month," Wang says. "That taste keeps changing, but now it has coincided with the maturity of talent." Lee has a simpler explanation for the burgeoning: "Natural law. It looks like a coincidence, but nothing is a coincidence in this world."

And the hits just keep on coming. *Farewell My Concubine*, which shared the Palme d'Or at Cannes this year, brings its gorgeous panorama of Chinese history and sexual hysterics to U.S. screens in early October. Oliver Stone has returned to Southeast Asia to film *Heaven and Earth* through a Vietnamese and feminine perspective, basing his movie on the memoirs of Le Ly Hayslip. And if you can't wait for the December opening of Heaven and Earth for a Vietnamese take on the ravages of war, scout around now for *From Hollywood to Hanoi*, a singeing documentary journey on film by Tiana Thi Tranh Nga.

The Asian accent may be profound or subtle. In pop music it may stare you in the face (like the tunes and videos of the Asian trio Shonen Knife, who bop around like '60s teens—Japanese Beatles) or caress the back of your mind. This summer the two queens of pop have imported the style. Janet Jackson's music video *If* is set in a Chinese nightclub studded with Buddha statues and paper lanterns; Madonna's *Rain*, which last week won an MTV Music Video Award for its sleek art direction, has the star posing for a Japanese film crew led by singer-composer Ryuichi Sakamoto. "I wanted Rain to have a clean, Zenned-out minimalism," says director Mark Romanek. "And I love Japanese fashion, especially Rei Kawakubo, who designs Comme des Garcons' clothes."

In *Rain* Madonna wears the Maoists' stark variation on Chanel's little black dress. She could be in the style vanguard again: last week Women's Wear Daily announced that "designers are pulling out the fine China this season." Couture connoisseurs agree. "The Orient-inspired look might be the important silhouette for the '90s," says Kal Ruttenstein, senior vice president for fashion direction at Bloomingdale's. "We expect to see it in full force in the spring collections: Oriental shapes like Mao jackets and mandarin-collared dresses in luxurious fabrics like Jacquard silks and lightweight brocades."

In bookstores the fiction shelves are bursting with works by Asians and Asian Americans. Tan, with *The Joy Luck Club* and *The Kitchen God's Wife*, has been joined by Cynthia Kadohata (*The Floating World*), Fae Myenne Ng (*Bone*), David Wong Louie (*Pangs of Love*), Gus Lee (*China Boy*) and Gish Jen (*Typical American*).

Tan sees home-and-office reasons for the popularity of these artists and fashions. "People now more than ever are likely to know a person or a co-worker who is Asian American," she says. "They've had experiences beyond eating chop suey—which isn't even a Chinese dish—and probably know the differences in Szechuan, Hunan and Cantonese food. People have an interest in Asian culture but also in their own immigrant past. We're at a time when family has become more important to people." Tan wants all this newfound interest to spread beyond exotic chinoiserie: to show, on the screen, "Asian Americans who are not emperors, not martial artists, not servants in rich houses."

Can Western views of East Asia be dragged out of the mythic and into the everyday? That is a daunting challenge, because China and Japan still represent fear and fascination to Americans. They are both our wizened ancestors, being among the oldest civilizations, and our presumed successors. If the East now has the power, it has long emitted potent metaphorical odors: the spiritual mystery, the sexual kink. In *Rising Sun* a Japanese gangster makes an American call girl dip her nipple in sake—baptism by force in the waters of the future. But one needn't go to Hollywood to find directors investigating bizarre sex. Many Japanese filmmakers do; porno is a popular genre there. One example is director Ryu Murakami's *Tokyo Decadence* (now in U.S. release), which lovingly details the sexual subjugation of Japanese prostitutes by Japanese businessmen.

The problem for Asians in Hollywood is not that they feel injured but that they are invisible. Asian Americans represent about 3% of the U.S. population and get 3% of the movie and television roles—but usually minor ones. "Since the beginning of films," says Sumi Sevilla Haru, president of the Association of Asian-Pacific American Artists, "African Americans have tried to improve their image. Now Asian Americans are trying to get a piece of the action. The only Asian in prime-time television is David Carradine playing one on the syndicated *Kung Fu*. That kind of sucks, doesn't it?"

Still, in the casting offices, there is a dawning of hope. Jason Scott Lee, the Hawaiian-born Asian who played Bruce Lee in the spring hit *Dragon* ($35 million in the U.S., plenty more abroad), could be the first major Asian hunk in Hollywood since Sessue Hayakawa 75 years ago. "In this town Jason instantly became somebody who could star in a movie," says Chris Lee, senior vice president at TriStar Pictures and one of several Asian Americans (Teddy Zee at Columbia, Bonni Lee at Geffen, Richard Sakai at Jim Brooks' Gracie Productions) inching their way up Mogul Mountain. "We've entered the system and there's more of us to come, and that's changing the face of Hollywood."

What has changed is the suspicion that Asian Americans don't know American culture. Wang, who was named after John Wayne and has been in the U.S. since 1967, recalls when he would "go up for a film job and the producer would ask me what made me think I could direct a movie about teenagers in Minnesota. So I'd say to them, 'Would you ask Ridley Scott or Tony Scott [two British directors working in America] that same question?' Because I've been here much longer than they have." And what hasn't changed is that studio owners, whether American or Japanese, are not interested in promoting any cultural agenda. "I'm going to put my foot in my mouth here," says Wang, "but the Japanese probably go out of their way to say they don't want Asian films. They have absolutely no interest in promoting Asian-American culture in this country."

If one person could symbolize Asian Americans, it might be Tiana Thi Tranh Nga. She was born in Vietnam in the '50s. Her uncle was a defense minister in the Thieu government; her father served as press minister and left for California in 1966. Teenage Tiana became an American: "In school, when kids said they hated the gooks, I did too. They were killing our guys." She became an actress and fitness teacher (Karatecize with Tiana). Then she decided to visit Vietnam. *From Hollywood to Hanoi*, a record of her trip, offers an engrossing take on the images and memories that Americans have of Asia.

In Ho Chi Minh City an aunt, living in devastating poverty, is hopeful that her relatives in America will help her. "I wanted to write letters," she says between tears, "but I couldn't afford the stamp." Tiana hears gruesome testimony from Amerasian orphans and My Lai survivors. In Hanoi she dances with Oliver Stone at the Metropole hotel and converses with Le Duc Tho, Pham Van Dong, General Giap—old warriors from an old nightmare.

By exposing this wound, Tiana means to see it heal; she has established the Indochina Film Arts Commission as a friendship bridge between Vietnam and the U.S. Her film goes beyond Asian chic to Asian soul. It joins *Joy Luck Club*. *The Wedding Banquet* and *Farewell My Concubine* in offering a lesson that applies to all families, Asian and American: Never forget, only forgive. ∎

Teach Diversity—with a Smile

Barbara Ehrenreich

SOMETHING HAD TO REPLACE the threat of communism, and at last a workable substitute is at hand. "Multiculturalism," as the new menace is known, has been denounced in the media recently as the new McCarthyism, the new fundamentalism, even the new totalitarianism—take your choice. According to its critics, who include a flock of tenured conservative scholars, multiculturalism aims to toss out what it sees as the Eurocentric bias in education and replace Plato with Ntozake Shange and traditional math with the Yoruba number system. And that's just the beginning. The Jacobins of the multiculturalist movement, who are described derisively as P.C., or politically correct, are said to have launched a campus reign of terror against those who slip and innocently say "freshman" instead of "freshperson," "Indian" instead of "Native American" or, may the Goddess forgive them, "disabled" instead of "differently abled."

So you can see what is at stake here: freedom of speech, freedom of thought, Western civilization and a great many professorial egos. But before we get carried away by the mounting backlash against multiculturalism, we ought to reflect for a moment on the system that the P.C. people aim to replace. I know all about it; in fact it's just about all I *do* know, since I—along with so many educated white people of my generation—was a victim of monoculturalism.

American history, as it was taught to us, began with Columbus' "discovery" of an apparently unnamed, unpeopled America, and moved on to the Pilgrims serving pumpkin pie to a handful of grateful red-skinned folks. College expanded our horizons with courses called Humanities or sometimes Civ, which introduced us to a line of thought that started with Homer, worked its way through Rabelais and reached a poignant climax in the pensées of Matthew Arnold. Graduate students wrote dissertations on what long-dead men had thought of Chaucer's verse or Shakespeare's dramas; foreign languages meant French or German. If there had been high technology in ancient China, kingdoms in black Africa or women anywhere, at any time, doing anything worth noticing, we did not know it, nor did anyone think to tell us.

Our families and neighborhoods reinforced the dogma of monoculturalism. In our heads, most of us '50s teenagers carried around a social map that was about as useful as the chart that guided Columbus to the "Indies." There were "Negroes," "whites" and "Orientals," the latter meaning Chinese and "Japs." Of religions, only three were known—

Protestant, Catholic and Jewish—and not much was known about the last two types. The only remaining human categories were husbands and wives, and that was all the diversity the monocultural world could handle. Gays, lesbians, Buddhists, Muslims, Malaysians, Mormons, etc. were simply off the map.

So I applaud—with one hand, anyway—the multiculturalist goal of preparing us all for a wider world. The other hand is tapping its fingers impatiently, because the critics are right about one thing: when advocates of multiculturalism adopt the haughty stance of political correctness, they quickly descend to silliness or worse. It's obnoxious, for example, to rely on university administrations to enforce P.C. standards of verbal inoffensiveness. Racist, sexist and homophobic thoughts cannot, alas, be abolished by fiat but only by the time-honored methods of persuasion, education and exposure to the other guy's—or, excuse me, woman's—point of view.

And it's silly to mistake verbal purification for genuine social reform. Even after all women are "Ms." and all people are "he or she," women will still earn only 65¢ for every dollar earned by men. Minorities by any other name, such as "people of color," will still bear a hugely disproportionate burden of poverty and discrimination. Disabilities are not just "different abilities" when there are not enough ramps for wheelchairs, signers for the deaf or special classes for the "specially" endowed. With all due respect for the new politesse, actions still speak louder than fashionable phrases.

But the worst thing about the P.C. people is that they are such poor advocates for the multicultural cause. No one was ever won over to a broader, more inclusive view of life by being bullied or relentlessly "corrected." Tell a 19-year-old white male that he can't say "girl" when he means "teen-age woman," and he will most likely snicker. This may be the reason why, despite the conservative alarms, P.C.-ness remains a relatively tiny trend. Most campuses have more serious and ancient problems: faculties still top-heavy with white males of the monocultural persuasion; fraternities that harass minorities and women; date rape; alcohol abuse, and tuition that excludes all but the upper fringe of the middle class.

So both sides would be well advised to lighten up. The conservatives ought to realize that criticisms of the great books approach to learning do not amount to totalitarianism. And the advocates of multiculturalism need to regain the sense of humor that enabled their predecessors in the struggle to coin the term P.C. years ago—not in arrogance but in self-mockery.

Beyond that, both sides should realize that the beneficiaries of multiculturalism are not only the "oppressed peoples" on the standard P.C. list (minorities, gays, etc.). The "unenlightened"—the victims of monoculturalism—are oppressed too, or at least deprived. Our educations, whether at Yale or at State U, were narrow and parochial and left us ill-equipped to navigate a society that truly is multicultural and is becoming more so every day. The culture that we studied was, in fact, one culture and, from a world perspective, all too limited and ingrown. Diversity is challenging, but those of us who have seen the alternative know it is also richer, livelier and ultimately more fun. ■

Picture Credits

Index